LIBRARY OF NEW TESTAMENT STUDIES
444

Formerly Journal for the Study of the New Testament Supplement Series

Editor
Mark Goodacre

Editorial Board
John M. G. Barclay, Craig Blomberg,
R. Alan Culpepper, James D. G. Dunn, Craig A. Evans, Stephen Fowl,
Robert Fowler, Simon J. Gathercole, John S. Kloppenborg, Michael Labahn,
Robert Wall, Steve Walton, Robert L. Webb, Catrin H. Williams

THE SPIRIT AND THE "OTHER"

Social Identity, Ethnicity and Intergroup
Reconciliation in Luke–Acts

Aaron Kuecker

t&t clark

Published by T&T Clark International
A Continuum imprint
The Tower Building, 11 York Road, London SE1 7NX
80 Maiden Lane, New York, NY 10038

www.continuumbooks.com

All rights reserved. No part of this publication may be reproduced or transmitted in any form or by any means, electronic or mechanical, including photocopying, recording or any information storage or retrieval system, without permission in writing from the publishers.

Copyright © 2011 by Aaron Kuecker

Aaron Kuecker has asserted his right under the Copyright, Designs and Patents Act, 1988, to be identified as the Author of this work.

British Library Cataloguing-in-Publication Data
A catalogue record for this book is available from the British Library

ISBN: HB: 978-0-567-23570-1

Typeset and copy-edited by Forthcoming Publications Ltd. (www.forthpub.com)
Printed and bound in Great Britain

Contents

Acknowledgments	xi
Abbreviations	xiii

Chapter 1
THE HOLY SPIRIT IN LUKE–ACTS:
TRACING THE HISTORY OF RESEARCH 1
  1.1. History of Research: Pre-1900–Present 2
    1.1.1. A Scholarly Consensus? 2
    1.1.2. Early Research on Lukan Pneumatology:
        Questions of Provenance and Function 3
    1.1.3. Contemporary Research:
        The Functions of the Lukan Spirit of Prophecy 5
    1.1.4. Contemporary Research:
        New Methodological Approaches 11
    1.1.5. John R. Levison: Filled with the Spirit 12
  1.2. Gaps in the Study of the Spirit in Luke–Acts 14
  1.3. The Thesis of this Study 18
  1.4. Outline of the Argument 20
  1.5. Assumptions Concerning Luke's Audience
      and Occasion for Writing 22

Chapter 2
SOCIAL IDENTITY AND THE "OTHER":
A METHODOLOGICAL AND HISTORICAL OVERVIEW 24
  2.1. Social Identity Theory 25
    2.1.1. The Ambiguity of Social Identity 27
    2.1.2. The Process of Social Identity Formation 28
    2.1.3. The Effect of Group Status upon Intergroup Contact
        and Conflict 30
    2.1.4. Intergroup Conflict Resolution Strategies 32
    2.1.5. Social Identity and Entitlement 33
    2.1.6. Social Identity Theory Summary 35

2.2. Ethnicity and Social Identity	35
2.2.1. Ethnicity in Antiquity	38
2.2.2. Ethnic Language in this Study	39
2.3. Ethnic Identity and Israel	40
2.3.1. *Letter of Aristeas*	41
2.3.2. Tobit	41
2.3.3. *Jubilees*	42
2.3.4. *4 Ezra*	43
2.3.5. Ezra and Nehemiah	44
2.3.6. First and Second Maccabees	45
2.3.7. Summary of Israelite Responses to the "Other"	47
2.4. Conclusion	48
2.5. Social Identity Theory Glossary	48

Chapter 3
EXPANDING THE ETHNIC HORIZON:
THE SPIRIT AND ALLOCENTRIC IDENTITY IN LUKE 1–2

	51
3.1. Zechariah and Elizabeth: Awakening Israelite Ethnic Identity	52
3.2. The Spirit, John and Jesus: The Nexus of Identity and Activity	57
3.3. The Spirit and the Birth Hymns: Expanding the Field of Ethnic Vision	59
3.3.1. Mary's Song	59
3.3.2. Zechariah's Spirit-empowered Song	61
3.3.3. Angelic Annunciation	68
3.3.4. Simeon's Spirit-empowered Speech	68
3.3.5. Anna and the Hope of a Nation	70
3.4. Conclusion	71

Chapter 4
CRITIQUING DEFECTIVE IDENTITIES:
SPIRIT-EMPOWERED FIGURES AND IN-GROUP BIAS IN LUKE 3–4

	72
4.1. The Spirit and the Baptizer: Critiquing a Distortion of Ethnic Social Identity	72
4.2. The Spirit and Jesus: Identifying the Son of God	75
4.3. Jesus' Genealogy: Incorporating Ethnic Out-groups	77
4.4. Jesus and Satan: Testing Privileged Identity	78
4.5. Jesus and His Townsfolk: Ethnic Identity, Resource Allocation and the "Other"	80
4.5.1. Jesus as Social Exegete	82
4.5.2. The Positive Reception of Jesus throughout Galilee	84
4.5.3. The Positive Reception of Jesus in Nazareth	85
4.5.4. Nazareth as Jesus' πατρίς	86

4.5.5. Jesus' Awareness of Nazareth-specific Entitlement Claims	90
4.5.6. Prophets and the Out-group	93
4.5.7. The Ramifications of Jesus' Rejection of the Social Script	94
4.5.8. Luke 4:14–30: Summary	95
4.6. Conclusion	95

Chapter 5
INITIATING A SCANDAL OF UNIVERSAL PARTICULARITY:
THE SPIRIT IN ACTS 1–2   97

5.1. The Spirit and Social Categories in Acts 1:1–11: Initiating an Allocentric Identity	98
5.1.1. In-group Bias and a Truncated Expression of Israelite Identity	99
5.1.2. The Salience of Nested Galilean Identity	100
5.1.3. Luke's Gospel and Jesus' Commission: Encountering Perilous Identity Boundaries	101
5.1.4. Identified by/Identifying with Jesus	104
5.1.5. Acts 1:1–11: Summary	107
5.2. Old Identity Paradigms Before Pentecost: Choosing One Like Us	107
5.3. Pentecost and the Scandal of Universal (Ethno-linguistic) Particularity	111
5.3.1. Subgroup Identities in the Pentecost Narrative	112
5.3.1.1. Galilean Israelite Identity	112
5.3.1.2. Diaspora Israelite Subgroup Identity	112
5.3.1.3. The Spirit and the 120	114
5.3.2. Language and Identity at Pentecost	115
5.4. Peter's Pentecost Discourse	119
5.4.1. Peter's "Modification" of Joel 3:1–5a LXX	120
5.5. Conclusion	123

Chapter 6
CONSUMMATING A NEW IDENTITY:
THE COMMUNITY SUMMARIES AND THE IDENTITY-FORMING
POWER OF A GROUP   125

6.1. Understanding the Baseline Significance of the New Community	126
6.1.1. A Community of Intense Self-ascription	129
6.1.2. Identity Forged in the Midst of Conflict	131
6.1.3. Community and the Other: The Possibility of Out-group Love	132
6.1.4. Summary	135

6.2. The Spirit and the "Other," Satan and the Self: Barnabas, Ananias and Sapphira as Exemplars of Identity	136
6.2.1. Barnabas: Exemplar of a New Identity	138
6.2.2. Ananias and Sapphira: Intragroup Threat and the Community of the Spirit	141
6.2.3. Forging an Identification Between the Spirit and the Community	145
6.2.4. Barnabas, Ananias and Sapphira: Summary	146
6.3. Conclusion	146

Chapter 7
INCORPORATING THE "OTHER": THE SPIRIT AND SUPERORDINATE IDENTITY IN ACTS 6–9

	148
7.1. Acts 6:1-7: Subgroup Salience and Community Dysfunction	148
7.1.1. The Spirit and the (Fractured) Life of the Community	151
7.2. Acts 8: Incorporating Those Who Identify Themselves With the God of Israel	153
7.2.1. Luke's Socially Unique Samaritans	154
7.2.2. Social Similarity and Intergroup Conflict Intensity	155
7.2.3. The Spirit and Social Tension in Acts 8:1-25: Dual Identity Transformation	156
7.2.4. Luke's Distinct Intergroup Focus in Acts 8:1-25	158
7.2.5. The Delay (?) of the Spirit	159
7.2.6. Isaiah 56:3a, 6-7 as a Substructure for the Samaritan Incorporation	161
7.2.7. The Retention of Ethnic Particularity in Samaria	163
7.3. Acts 8:26-40: The Ethiopian Eunuch	163
7.3.1. Spirit-orchestration of In-group Incorporation	164
7.3.2. Barrier Removal and Incorporation into the Community	167
7.3.3. Summary	168
7.4. Acts 9: Spirit-orchestration and Identification for the Incorporation of an Enemy	168
7.4.1. Social Identity and Intergroup Threat in Acts 9:1-31	169
7.4.2. Saul's Encounter with the Exalted Jesus	170
7.4.3. The Role of the Spirit in the Incorporation of Saul	171
7.4.4. Apostolic Resistance to the Incorporation of Saul	173
7.4.5. Comparative Emphasis on Incorporation	175
7.4.6. The Incorporation of the "Other": A Surprising Path to Peace	177
7.5. Conclusion	179

Chapter 8
TRANSCENDING ETHNICITY:
THE SPIRIT AND TRANS-ETHNIC IDENTITY IN ACTS 10–15   181
  8.1. Interpreting Acts 10:1–11:18   181
    8.1.1. Resources from Social Identity Theory   182
    8.1.2. Luke's Use of "Ethnic Language"   184
    8.1.3. Ethnic Language and the Awareness of Ethnic
          Boundaries   187
    8.1.4. The Spirit at the Ethnic Boundary   188
    8.1.5. The Spirit and the Orchestration of Intergroup
          Encounter   188
    8.1.6. The Spirit as the Marker of a Superordinate Identity   192
  8.2. Criticism in Jerusalem: Evidence of an Intractable
      Boundary   197
  8.3. Acts 15: The Spirit and the Intragroup Expression
      of a New Identity   199
    8.3.1. Human Action vs. Divine Action at the Group
          Boundary   200
    8.3.2. James the Prototypical Israelite:
          The Universal Particularity of Spirit-formed Identity   202
    8.3.3. The Jerusalem Decree:
          An Injunction Against the Trappings of Idolatry   207
    8.3.4. The Role of the Spirit in James' Logic   210
    8.3.5. The Transformation of Identity
          After the Jerusalem Decision   212
  8.4. Conclusion   215

Chapter 9
CONCLUSION   216
  9.1. A Summary of Luke's Portrait of the Spirit,
      Social Identity and the "Other"   216
  9.2. Social Identity Theory and a Different Way
      of Being Human in Community   224
  9.3. Possibilities for Future Comparative Work on Identity
      Within the Early Jesus Movement   224
  9.4. Possibilities for Contemporary Application   226
  9.5. Conclusion   230

Bibliography   232

Index of References   254
Index of Authors   273

Acknowledgments

This monograph is a revised version of my Ph.D. thesis, completed at St. Mary's College, University of St. Andrews under the supervision of Philip Esler, Richard Bauckham, and Ben Witherington, III. Though several circumstances kept my supervisory situation fluid, I doubt many research students have the opportunity to work closely with three scholars of such erudition, reputation and integrity. Philip Esler has read and commented on every aspect of this project, even though he served as the Chief Executive of the U.K. Arts and Humanities Research Council for the duration of my work. For his encouragement always to stay close to the text and for his contagious conviction that biblical studies should be relevant in the contemporary world, I owe a tremendous debt of gratitude. Richard Bauckham, who initially served as a stand-in for Philip Esler, went far beyond his administrative duties in reading, commenting upon and advising me on many sections of my thesis. For his willingness to become involved in my project and for his unwillingness to accept imperfect argumentation, I am thankful. Upon Professor Bauckham's retirement, Ben Witherington, III assumed the mantle of supervisor and willingly and thoroughly saw me through the final stages of the project. For his excellent historical imagination and for the gracious gift of his time and energy, I am grateful. I alone bear responsibility for any errors remaining in this text.

I am grateful to my Ph.D. examiners, Edward Adams and Kelly Iverson, who read carefully and questioned and commented perceptively in ways that have strengthened the final form of this monograph.

The postgraduate community at St. Mary's College is a unique source of camaraderie and theological discourse. I suspect I will never again be in a place where formative and challenging conversations occur with such regularity. Particular thanks to Kelly Liebengood (who read and sharpened several aspects of this thesis), Kevin Diller, Luke Tallon, Josh Moon, Daniel Driver, Seth Tarrer, Jason Goroncy, Jeremy Gabrielson, Mariam Kamell, Tim Stone and Patrick Egan, through whose friendship I have become more fit in mind, body and soul. Special thanks go to my office colleagues in the Black Room, Meg Ramey, Justin Smith, Kathleen Burris, Matt Farlow and Mark Cortez for valuable feedback, a fruitful work environment and needed moments of levity.

I would like to thank series editor Mark Goodacre, along with the rest of the editorial board for the Library of New Testament Studies monograph series for giving me the opportunity to publish my work in this series. It is an honor to be included in the LNTS series. Thanks also go to Dominic Mattos and Anna Turton at T&T Clark International for seeing me through the early stages of the publication process. I owe a great debt of gratitude to my copy-editor, Duncan Burns, for his careful editorial eye, good humor, and willingness to go far beyond the call of duty—all of which combined to ensure that I was saved from many errors.

I am grateful to my colleagues at Trinity Christian College, Palos Heights, Illinois. It is a delight to teach, research and live in environment of such mutual support and ongoing enquiry. Participation in the life of a community actively wondering about issues related to ethnic identity and intergroup reconciliation has pressed me to think deeply about the practical implications of the research contained in this monograph. Trinity Christian College generously provided me with a Semester Research Fellowship and a Summer Research Grant, both of which were of inestimable value in the completion of this project.

My deepest thanks, however, are reserved for my dear family. Our parents, siblings and their families have been an unwavering source of care, support and encouragement, both while we were abroad and as we have moved back to the U.S. Our children, Gabriel, Isabel, Josiah and Adeline, have given me great joy and never have failed to show their dad exuberant and undeserved love. They are a gift. My wife, Kerri, has borne the greatest burden in the writing of this book. She has been relentlessly encouraging over the course of the project, and it is in her life that I see most clearly the Spirit-empowered love for the "other" that is a central concern of this monograph. Her tireless love for her family and her unceasing willingness to give of herself are truly humbling. I dedicate this book to her.

ABBREVIATIONS

BDAG	Bauer, W., F. W. Danker, W. F. Arndt, and F. W. Gingrich. *Greek–English Lexicon of the New Testament and Other Early Christian Literature*. 3d ed. Chicago, 1999
CIJ	*Corpus inscriptionum judaicarum*
LSJ	Liddell, H. G., R. Scott, and H. S. Jones, *A Greek–English Lexicon*. 9th ed. with revised supplement. Oxford, 1996
LXX	Septuagint
NPNF	*Nicene and Post-Nicene Fathers*. Edited by Alexander Roberts, James Donaldson, Philip Schaff and Henry Wace. 14 vols. Peabody, Mass., 1994
SIT	Social Identity Theory
Str-B	Strack, H. L., and P. Billerbeck. *Kommentar zum Neuen Testament aus Talmud und Midrasch*. 6 vols. Munich, 1922–61
TDNT	*Theological Dictionary of the New Testament,* Edited by G. Kittel and G. Friedrich. Translated by G. W. Bromiley. 10 vols. Grand Rapids, 1964–76
TLG	*Thesaurus linguae graecae: Canon of Greek Authors and Works*. Edited by L. Berkowitz and K. A. Squitier. 3d ed. Oxford, 1990

Chapter 1

THE HOLY SPIRIT IN LUKE–ACTS:
TRACING THE HISTORY OF RESEARCH

Of the many phenomena that develop as a result of human social interaction, group identity is among the most ambiguous. Life *without* social groups would scarcely be human. Groups provide a sense of belonging, identity and often a social safety net. Yet history has shown that life *with* social groups also can be scarcely human. Groups provide a ready base from which to create stereotypes, manipulate resources and all too often to cultivate social barriers that negatively impact the "other." All group identities are open to these types of mutations, but ethnic identity has proved capable of creating some of the most vexing and intractable cleavages in human society. The ambiguous potential of groups to foster both human community and intergroup strife is not new. The New Testament itself gives ample evidence of the positive and pernicious effects of membership in social groups—perhaps especially for groups best classified as "ethnic"—and nowhere is this more evident than in Luke–Acts.

Luke–Acts is marked by a concern for the way that group identities impinge upon social interaction, and it contains some of the most blatant expressions of intergroup hatred as well as some of the most poignant expressions of intergroup reconciliation in the entire New Testament. Yet, perhaps surprisingly, scholarly interest in "Jew" and "Gentile" issues in Luke–Acts has not yet led to a detailed examination either of intergroup relationships or of the mechanics of intergroup (especially interethnic) reconciliation. The few studies that have focused upon social groups in the text have yet to examine the intersection between this aspect of Luke's vision and another central Lukan concern, the Holy Spirit. In this study I will bring together these two prominent features of Luke–Acts in order better to understand Luke's interpretation of the relationship between the Holy Spirit, group identities (especially ethnic identities) and intergroup reconciliation. In so doing I hope to come to a clearer grasp of both the role of the Spirit and the place of ethnic identity among the earliest followers of Jesus, Luke's distinctively Israelite Messiah and unambiguously cosmic Lord.

1.1. *History of Research: Pre-1900–Present*

There are many profitable avenues to explore in the history of research on Luke–Acts, but I will restrict myself to literature that deals specifically with Luke's view of the Spirit. It will become quickly apparent that the relationship between the Spirit and ethnic identity has not yet been pursued.[1] This fact is not surprising, given that we are only just beginning to come to an awareness of the complex dynamics associated with ethnic identities and their social impact.

Two primary questions have driven the past century of research on the Spirit in Luke–Acts:
1. What contexts form the background for Luke's pneumatology?
2. What does Luke think the Spirit does?

1.1.1. *A Scholarly Consensus?*
Just over a decade ago, Max Turner distilled five points of consensus for research on Lukan pneumatology. I will begin by demonstrating briefly the way in which this consensus has emerged in the history of research. I will then highlight several deficits in the study of the Spirit in Luke–Acts and situate this study in the context of the ongoing scholarly conversation. First, however, Turner's five points of consensus:[2]
1. The contextual background for Luke's view of the Spirit is the Old Testament/Second Temple period.
2. The Spirit is "the uniting motif and driving force within the Lucan salvation history, and provided the legitimation of the mission to which it leads."[3]

---

1. Works that emphasize "Jew" and "Gentile" issues have largely focused upon the relationship between "Judaism" and "Gentiles," and thus have not specifically worked from an intergroup, inter-ethnic perspective. See Esler 1987 for an early treatment of intergroup dynamics in Luke–Acts. Cf. Wilson 1973; Brawley 1987; Sanders 1987; Tyson 1988; 1992; 1999; Slee 2003; Parsons 2006 (whose treatment of physiognomy deals with the "other" but is not intergroup in nature). Hays 2003 surveys the biblical theology of "race," but this is predicated on physiognomic and not group identities.
2. Turner 1998, 328–33. I largely accept points 1, 2 and 5, but will call to question points 3 and 4.
3. Turner 1998, 329.

3. Luke's Spirit is the "Spirit of prophecy" that mainly empowers witness.[4]
4. Luke is less interested (especially compared to Paul) in the Spirit's role in the "spiritual, ethical and religious renewal of the individual."[5]
5. Luke's major innovation is the attribution of "Christocentric" functions; the Spirit is poured out by, and bears witness to, Jesus.

1.1.2. Early Research on Lukan Pneumatology: Questions of Provenance and Function

The modern era of research on Lukan pneumatology was inagurated by Hermann Gunkel's 1888 work *Die Wirkungen des Heiligen Geistes nach der populären Anschauung der apostolischen Zeit und der Lehre des Apostels Paulus*. Gunkel's form-critical and *Religionsgeschichte* examination of the "concept" πνεῦμα suggested that Luke held a more conservative Old Testament view of the Spirit, one which understood the Spirit as the source of the extraordinary (everything "mysterious and mighty in Israel") but not the source of ordinary conduct, piety or morality for the individual Israelite.[6] This conservative Old Testament view especially appreciated the Spirit's prophetic function through inspired speech and glossolalia (though Gunkel did not exclude entirely other "miraculous" effects of the Spirit in the life of the individual—even if not all Christians possessed the Spirit).[7] Because Gunkel emphasized the immediate, and not consequential, effects of the Spirit, there was no room for the *effect* of Spirit-inspired speech, only the immediate phenomenon. For this reason, Gunkel saw no evidence for the effect of the Spirit in the life or formation of the community.[8] Gunkel's reading set Luke at odds with Paul, who (he thought) innovatively understood the Spirit as the source of all Christian living.[9] Gunkel's two enduring contributions were a demonstration that Luke was reliant upon Israelite tradition for his conception of the Spirit and a differentiation between "Lukan" and "Pauline" conceptions of the

---

4. Wenk 2004 is furthest removed from this point of consensus, though he expands the concept "Spirit of prophecy" rather than abandoning it.
5. Turner 1998, 331.
6. Gunkel 1979, 19, 48.
7. Gunkel 1979, 18, 42–43.
8. "Der gerechte Wandel hat mit dem Geiste nichts zu tun" (Gunkel 1899, 10; cf. 22, 26, 30, 33).
9. Gunkel 1899, 75: "Die Gemeinde also hält für pneumatisch das Ausserordentliche im Christenleben, Paulus das Gewöhnliche; jene das einzelnen Eigentümliche, Paulus das allen Gemeinsame; jene das abrput-Auftretende, er das Stetige; jene einzelnes in Christenleben, er das Christenleben selbst."

Spirit. The first has been (nearly) universally accepted. The second has gained broad, yet not unanimous, consensus.

Gunkel's effort to locate Lukan pneumatology in a Second Temple matrix was countered by Hans Leisegang's two volumes produced in the early twentieth century (1919, 1922). Leisegang attempted to demonstrate that Philo adopted "Greek" conceptions of πνεῦμα in order to speak about the Israelite "spirit of prophecy." In his second monograph, Leisegang argued that spirit-material in the life of Jesus was of late Hellenistic mystical origin.[10] Leisegang's thesis did not gain broad consensus, though the Greco-Roman influence on Luke's pneumatology has been appreciated by Menzies and Levison.

The Second Temple provenance of Luke's pneumatology was solidified by the (nearly simultaneous) publication of monographs by Friedrich Büchsel and Hans von Baer. Büchsel's work traced the coherence between the Spirit-experiences of Jesus, the early church and Pauline churches. Büchsel suggested that the Spirit was primarily the Spirit of sonship (thus deviating from Gunkel's "Spirit of prophecy"), and that charismatic manifestations were symptoms of this filial relationship.[11] Büchsel attributed a broad spectrum of the activities of the early church to the Spirit, including tongues, prophetic speech, moral and religious effects, and the life of the community—astutely noting that the Spirit was no respecter of the common social divisions in the first-century Mediterranean.[12]

Standing as a counterpoint to Büchsel's expansive view of Lukan pneumatology was Baer's focus on the "Spirit of prophecy" and his introduction of the three-epoch scheme for Lukan *Heilsgeschichte*.[13] For Baer, the Spirit moved salvation history forward in three distinct epochs:[14]

1. *Luke 1–2*: Preceding Jesus' birth, the Spirit endowed certain individuals with the Spirit of prophecy in order to accomplish specific tasks.
2. *Jesus' baptism until the ascension*: The beginning of the new covenant, symbolized by the Noachic dove.[15]

---

10. Leisegang 1922, 23. Discussion in Turner 1996, 26–29.
11. Büchsel 1926, 262; "Jesu Geistbesitz ist Gottessohnschaft" (165; cf. 170–71, 177–78).
12. Büchsel 1926, 254–55.
13. Cf. Conzelmann's scheme: (1) the period of Israel; (2) the period of Jesus; (3) the period of the church (1960, 16–17).
14. Baer's epochal schema has been thoroughly critiqued as an imposition on the text (see Menzies 1991, 133; Bovon 2006, 14–31).
15. Baer 1926, 65ff. This scheme leaves the period between the ascension and Pentecost as a (strangely) Spirit-less inter-regnum.

3. *Pentecost to the present*: All believers have access to Jesus through the Spirit.[16]

Baer was less interested in inner or communal experiences of the Spirit than with the role of the Old Testament "Spirit of prophecy" in initiating each new epoch of *Heilsgeschichte*.[17] For Baer, the parallel between Jesus and the early church is not Spirit-generated sonship, but Spirit-empowered proclamation through the "Spirit of prophecy."

By the mid-twentieth century, a consensus existed regarding the "Jewish" provenance of Luke's pneumatology. Moreover, this early period of research tended toward answering the question "What does Luke think the Spirit *does*?" by pointing toward the "Spirit of prophecy" model—though this was not without dissenting voices. A major result of the latter point has been an assumed contrast between Lukan and Pauline pneumatologies.

1.1.3. *Contemporary Research: The Functions of the Lukan Spirit of Prophecy*

Contemporary investigation of Lukan pneumatology has honed in on the question "What did Luke think the Spirit does?"[18] While this has mostly involved an attempt more clearly to understand the functions ascribed to the Spirit of prophecy in Second Temple texts and then to read Luke–Acts in light of these data, it is necessary to begin first with the counter-voice provided by James Dunn's important study.[19]

Dunn, responding to both Pentecostal "second blessing" positions and Confirmationist positions, contended that the Spirit was essential to the process of conversion and that one could not be considered a Christian apart from the Spirit.[20] Working with Conzelmann's extension of Baer's

---

16. Baer 1926, 93.
17. Baer infrequently acknowledges "non-prophetic" pneumatological activities, such as peace with God for Jesus and the community of believers (1926, 167).
18. These works share three foci: (1) the scope of activities attributable to the "Spirit of prophecy" in Second Temple texts; (2) the role of the Spirit in the experience and sequence of salvation; and (3) the ethical role of the Spirit.
19. A number of studies on the Spirit in Luke–Acts appeared in the mid- to late portion of the twentieth century and helped solidify the "Spirit of prophecy" consensus (Lampe 1951; 1977; Schweizer 1956; Haya-Prats 1975; Stronstad 1984; Mainville 1991; Shelton 1991; H. S. Kim 1993). Because of space constraints and the presence of excellent summaries elsewhere (Turner 1996, 20–81 [most extensively]; Menzies 1991, 18–46; Wenk 2004, 13–43) I will not discuss these works.
20. Dunn 1970, 4. The doctrine of Confirmation suggests the Spirit is received *after* conversion through the sacrament or practice of Confirmation.

epochal schema, Dunn saw Jesus' experience at the Jordan as the initiation *of* the messianic age (as distinct from the age of Israel) and the initiation of Jesus *into* the messianic age.[21] Hence, the Spirit was the Spirit of sonship (cf. Büchsel). After Pentecost, the Spirit initiated the new covenant for all believers (Dunn relies here upon Ezek 36:27 and Jer 31:33).[22] Dunn navigates the tension between sonship and prophecy by noting that the Spirit always functions primarily *to initiate* new believers into the covenant, but also *to equip* them for life and service in this new age.[23] Dunn has since softened his positions, leaning more toward the "Spirit of prophecy" framework, while maintaining that the Spirit is indeed part and parcel of Christian salvation and is thus primarily the gift of sonship and initiation into God's covenant. Likewise, Dunn has held less vigorously to his epochal view, but insisted that the Spirit is intimately associated with entrance into the kingdom of God.[24]

Dunn's position was challenged by R. P. Menzies' 1991 monograph, which set the agenda regarding the clarification of the functions attributable to the "Spirit of prophecy" in Second Temple texts. Menzies saw no "soteriological" effects of the Spirit in Second Temple texts (with the exception of the Wisdom tradition and 1QH, the former of which he thinks is the grist for Paul's mill).[25] Menzies argues that Luke takes up this Second Temple view, and restricts the role of the Spirit to incorporation into the active mission of God through the empowerment of special insight and inspired speech.[26]

Menzies' reading of Acts supports this narrow conception of the "Spirit of prophecy." While surely the most developed treatment of the Spirit's inspiration of speech and mission in Luke–Acts, Menzies' view raises a number of issues. First, Menzies focuses intently on Second

---

21. Dunn 1970, 25; cf. Dunn's comment: "It is not so much that Jesus became what he was not before, but that history became what it was not before; and Jesus as the one who effects these changes of history from within history, is himself affected by them" (29). See also Conzelmann 1961.

22. Dunn has been critiqued for reliance upon texts that Luke does not cite (Bovon 2006, 14–31) as well as for importing "Pauline" conceptions into Luke, a critique that highlights the Paul–Luke dichotomy inherited from earlier scholarship.

23. Dunn 1970, 32.

24. Dunn 1993. Dunn's insistence that the Spirit is given at conversion (while correct, in my view) presses him to make some awkward arguments regarding the timing of the Spirit's manifestation (see especially his treatment of Acts 8 [1970, 55–72]).

25. Menzies 1991, 48. Menzies argues that Paul absorbed his pneumatology from the same Hellenistic milieu that produced the sapiential writings (48).

26. Menzies 1991, 48.

Temple texts, but pays scant attention to the Old Testament—which is surely the most immediate context for Luke's understanding of the events in his two volumes.[27] Second, Menzies' redaction-critical approach allows him to sidestep passages that do not fit his model.[28] Third, Menzies' reading of Second Temple texts is open to critique:[29]

1. Menzies notes LXX texts that insert πνεῦμα in connection with inspired speech (Num 23:7; Zech 1:6), while overlooking *many* instances when the Spirit clearly gives miraculous power (Judg 14:6, 19; 15:14; 1 Sam 11:6; 1 Kgs 18:12; 2 Kgs 2:16; Ezek 2:2; 3:12, 14, 24; 8:3; 11:1, 5, 24; 37:1; 43:5).
2. Menzies connects the Spirit and inspired speech in *1 En.* 49:3 and 62:2, but does not note that in 49:3 the Spirit bestows wisdom, understanding and *might* upon the anointed one, or that 62:2 is a reference to the "spirit of righteousness" that allows the anointed one to speak judgment.[30]
3. Menzies does not recognize that *t. Sotah* 13.2 ("When the latter prophets died, that is, Haggai, Zechariah, and Malachi, then the Holy Spirit came to an end in Israel. But even so, they made them hear [heavenly messages] through an echo") does not necessarily equate the Spirit only with prophecy, but perhaps sees the dearth of prophecy as the last vestige of the Spirit.[31] Menzies himself notes that other texts connect the withdrawal of the Spirit with the destruction of the Temple, and hence with Israel's corporate life and worship.[32]

---

27. See Luke 24:27, 44–49; Acts 7; 8:30–35.

28. Menzies 1991, 114–15. This is evident paradigmatically in his discussion of Luke 1:35 (pp. 123–28). Menzies does not ascribe to the Spirit the creative power associated with Jesus' conception but instead classifies the reference to the Spirit as a Lukan addition formulated to connect the Baptist and Jesus (123). However, a few pages later he says, "The connection between the promise of the Spirit's presence in v. 35 and Mary's utterance in vv. 46f can hardly be questioned" (127). Again, "The tradition reflected in 1:35 indicates that the primitive church spoke of the activity of the Spirit in broader terms than Luke… While the pneumatology of the primitive church may be designated charismatic, that of Luke is more especially prophetic" (128). This confluence of positions is puzzling.

29. For extended critique, see Turner 1996, 82–137; Wenk 2004, 54–110.

30. In a similar way, Menzies connects Torah and wisdom in Sir 39:1–6, but does not follow the passage through to 39:8 where the Spirit is connected to the new covenant (see Wenk 2004, 68).

31. Menzies 1991, 93.

32. *Lam. R.* 12; *Eccl. R.* 12.7.1; *Num. R.* 15.10.

4. Menzies makes much of the use of the actual phrase "Spirit of prophecy" in *Targum Onkelos*, yet neglects the fact that *Targum Neofiti* and *Targum Pseudo-Jonathan* Gen 6:3 both depict God as counterbalancing evil by putting his Spirit in humans.[33]

Fourth, Menzies' conviction that the Spirit is always given subsequent to repentance and baptism causes serious problems in his reading of Acts, not least in Acts 10 where the Spirit comes to Cornelius' household before any ostensible signs of belief.

Fifth, Menzies' conception of "salvation" (forgiveness of sins, conferral of a status and participation in missionary endeavors) is much narrower than Luke's (renewed relationship with God, transformed human relationships, life and even health in the present).[34] Luke's broad view is evident both in Jesus' Nazareth sermon (Luke 4:18–19) and in Peter's Pentecost sermon, which claims that salvation has concrete social ramifications in the present (Acts 2:40).

One of Menzies' Ph.D. students, Youngmo Cho, follows this narrower conceptual reading of the "Spirit of prophecy," agreeing that Paul is an innovator with regard to the Spirit, agreeing that the Spirit is given *to* faith (Jesus receives the Spirit *because of* his faithful resistance of temptation, a statement only affirmed by an awkward attempt to distance Jesus from the apparent ongoing wilderness presence of the Spirit described in Luke 4:1), and agreeing that the Spirit is primarily given to inspire speech for the sake of mission.[35] Cho's addition to Menzies' position is his treatment of the relationship between the Spirit and the kingdom of God.[36] Cho concludes that for Luke the Spirit merely "inspires the proclamation of the kingdom of God and in this way, the Spirit makes it possible for people to enter the kingdom of God."[37] Hence, the Spirit has *something* to do with salvation and the life of the community, but only from a distance. Cho's thesis suffers because of its failure to account for Old Testament conceptions of the Spirit, its failure to give a definition of the kingdom of God, and its disregard of the fact that Luke's Spirit is the agent of the reign of the exalted Jesus. Cho's insistence that the Spirit only inspires prophetic speech leads him to minimize the importance of activities that

---

33. *Targum Onkelos* Gen 41:38; Exod 31:3; 35:31; Num 11:25, 26, 29; 24:2; 27:18; cited in Menzies 1991, 101 n. 1. Turner 1996, 123 notes Menzies' disregard of the Gen 6:3 tradition.
34. See Witherington 1998, 143–47 and cf. Luke 4:16–18.
35. Cho 2005, 15, 123–25, 141–42.
36. Cho 2005, 51.
37. Cho 2005, 15.

Luke both values and connects closely to the Spirit. This is most evident in his treatment of the Spirit-empowered Seven in Acts 6:1–7.[38]

Max Turner's impressive work on Lukan pneumatology holds to the "Spirit of prophecy" model, but expands that model in a way that creates a mediating position between Menzies and Dunn.[39] Turner contends that the Spirit is

> neither the matrix of new covenant existence nor a donum superadditum. Rather the Spirit, as the Spirit of prophecy, is the means of communication between God and man: essential for Christian existence yet not identical with it.[40]

In his expansion of the concept, Turner claims that the LXX depicts the Spirit as the source of deeds that must be understood as miraculous acts of power, the likes of which Menzies attributes only to δύναμις.[41] Turner places great weight on Isa 11:1–4 and 32:15–20 and argues that the "Spirit of prophecy" in Luke–Acts is the "charismatic power of Israel's restoration."[42] Restoration is begun by the Spirit-anointed Messiah (a fusion of a Davidic ruler and a "prophet like Moses") and is carried forward by Jesus' Spirit-empowered followers.[43] Turner's entire treatment of the Spirit as the executive power of Israel's exalted Messiah is set within a New Exodus paradigm that equates forgiveness of sins with New Exodus themes such as restoration, cleansing, and so on:

---

38. Cho 2005, 132. Cho calls the "table service" of the Seven "human organization" and suggests the reference to the Spirit in their selection only prepares us for the speeches of Stephen and Philip, which he calls "Spirit-working." See Chapter 7 below for further discussion.

39. "Despite the rarity of the phrase 'the Spirit of prophecy' in what are provably pre-Lukan Jewish writings, we may be relatively assured that Jews of Luke's time did indeed think of the Spirit in this way: that is, chiefly as the source of charismatic revelation, wisdom, invasive prophetic speech and invasive charismatic praise" (Turner 1996, 104).

40. Turner 1996, 47.

41. Turner 1996, 107–8. See especially Judg 14:6; 19; 15:14 but also Judg 3:10; 6:34; 11:29; 13:25; 1 Sam 11:6; Isa 11:4. Turner also highlights 4Q521; *2 Bar.* 21:4; 23:5 [which may be too late]; *4 Ezra* 6:39–41. *2 Bar.* 75:3–4 and *4 Ezra* 14:22 are significant for Turner because they reference "the Spirit of prophecy," thus demonstrating that the prophetic and the powerful/creative are not at loggerheads in Second Temple treatments of the Spirit.

42. Turner 1998, 343.

43. Turner 1998, 343–47.

> We may thus safely claim he [Luke] thought the Spirit was the principal divine power maintaining, developing and extending Israel's salvation/transformation, and that without the gift of the charismatic Spirit of prophecy the sort of "salvation" he had in mind would simply evaporate from Israel like the departure of the cloud of God's glory and presence.[44]

There is much to savor in Turner's work, not least his exploration of the Spirit within Luke's reading of Israel's salvation history. My work will expand some of Turner's themes, suggesting that the Spirit has an even broader transformational role in helping Israel to fulfill its vocation as light to the nations. I contend, however, for reasons that I will detail below, that Turner's retention of the category "Spirit of prophecy" is misleading and results in an under-appreciation of the full scope of Luke's pneumatology.

Turner's work is extended by one of his students, Matthias Wenk, who closely follows Turner's reading of the Spirit in Luke–Acts but argues more vigorously that the Spirit has an "ethical" effect upon the community.[45] Wenk examines traditions dependent upon Isa 11:1–4 and locates Jesus and John within this tradition as people who are personally influenced by the Spirit towards the "ethical qualities he…is to restore among God's people."[46] Wenk is convinced that the early community (Israel restored via a New Exodus) is the "this-worldly dimension of salvation, which is expressed in the affirmation of a universal people of God and the 'good news to the poor'."[47] Essential to this reading is Wenk's astute observation that Joel 3:1–5a LXX is not simply about the restoration of prophecy, but is, in its context, about the renewal of the community.[48] Wenk includes an excellent discussion of the reorientation of the church's "symbolic universe" as a result of the coming of the Spirit.[49] Here Wenk examines the "reconciliation" passages in Acts (Acts 8:1–25; 10:1–41; 15:1–31) and the way in which the Spirit is essential to redefining the "self-understanding" of the church.[50] He successfully resists "individualistic" models of salvation in favor of a high view of the significance of the early community, even going so far at one point as to identify the Spirit as the "identity marker" of the community.[51]

---

44. Turner 1996, 427.
45. Wenk 2004, 54–55.
46. Wenk 2004, 309.
47. Wenk 2004, 47, 259–73.
48. Wenk 2004, 58–59.
49. Wenk 2004, 274–308.
50. Wenk 2004, 308, 315.
51. Wenk 2004, 294.

Wenk's work is commendable in many ways. His use of speech-act theory, while raising some questions, is an attempt to account for the perlocutionary effect of Spirit-inspired prophetic speech.[52] His project is by far the most sensitive to the role of the Spirit both within the early community and for group reconciliation. The present monograph will leave behind Wenk's "Spirit of prophecy" model, but will extend Wenk's intergroup and intragroup foci by discussing explicitly the place of the Spirit in relation to ethnicity and seeking to indicate what happens to one's ethnic identity after one's "symbolic universe" is reoriented.

1.1.4. Contemporary Research: New Methodological Approaches
Three narrative-critical approaches to the Spirit in Luke–Acts have appeared in the past twenty years.[53] William Shepherd accepts the Old Testament "Spirit of prophecy" paradigm and connects the Spirit to mission rather than conversion, though he remains concerned most directly with the characterization of the Spirit.[54] Shepherd limits the Spirit's role in the text to "narrative reliability" by which "The Spirit functions onstage to prove the reliability of the offstage God."[55] Ju Hur extends this approach by placing greater emphasis on the plot structure of Luke–Acts, the theological implications of the Spirit and the effect of the Spirit upon the reader. For Hur, the Spirit assures narrative reliability by providing the "divine frame of reference."[56] Important speeches are "Spirit-inspired," certain conversions are marked by the Spirit's presence and Jesus himself is legitimated by the Spirit.[57] Spirit-verification of community membership is a sub-theme in his work, though he does not account for the means by which the Spirit overcomes intergroup obstacles. Hur's close reading produces insightful observations, and he helpfully demonstrates that the Lukan Spirit exhibits both continuity and discontinuity with traditional Israelite conceptions of the Spirit.[58] Finally,

---

52. One wonders how this fits with Luke's negative conception of the impact of Israel's prophets (see Luke 6:23, 26; 11:47, 49, 50; 13:33, 34; 16:31; 24:25). Regardless, Wenk's focus on the effect of the Spirit's work is a helpful corrective to Gunkel's phenomenological approach.
53. Shepherd 1994; Hur 2004; Bonnah 2007.
54. Shepherd 1994, 2, 135.
55. Shepherd 1994, 246. Shepherd develops Darr's (1992) focus on Luke's rhetorical concern to provide "certainty" for readers (cf. Luke 1:4).
56. Hur 2001, 278.
57. Hur 2001, 100, citing Darr 1992, 52–53.
58. Hur 2001, 180. Levison 1997, 235 extends this important point, noting that "creativity and diversity characterize interpretations of the Spirit in the first century CE."

George Bonnah also positions the Spirit as a character used "to legitimate the missionary activities of the church" both by marking genuine converts and by speaking through the Scriptures.[59]

1.1.5. *John R. Levison: Filled with the Spirit*

John Levison's 2009 monograph, *Filled with the Spirit*, builds upon two earlier volumes.[60] Levison re-examines the Spirit in Israelite and Second Temple contexts, arguing in the former that "the so-called life principle and the spirit of God...were understood as one in the same."[61] Hence, the Spirit animates all living things ("both prince and puma alike"), and cannot be understood as a wholly secondary or charismatic endowment.[62] When "spirit" (always anarthrous for Levison) is withdrawn, a creature dies.[63] Levison rightly sees much greater diversity in Second Temple pneumatology. Spirit-inspired activities include:

1. purification and cleansing (for life in the community?; 1QS 3.7b–8a; 1QH 6.13–14);
2. creation (*4 Ezra* 6:39; *2 Bar.* 21:4; 23:5; Jdt 16:14, riffing on Gen 2:7 and 2:22, mediated through Ps 104:29–30);
3. inspiration of prophecy;
4. inspiration of an anointed messiah (Isa 11:1–9; 42:1; 61:1–7; *1 En.* 49:2–3; *Pss. Sol.* 17:37; *T. Levi* 18:7–12);
5. wisdom or inspired interpretation of Scripture (1QH 20.11–13; Philo, *Som.* 2.252; *4 Ezra* 14:21–22);
6. other attributes or activities: praise (*L.A.B.* 32:14); military heroism (*L.A.B.* 27:9–10; 36:2); ascent of the philosophical mind (Philo, *Plant.* 18–26; *Gig.* 19–55); rhetorical prowess and concomitant qualities of the ideal Greco-Roman ruler (Philo, *Virt.* 217–19).

Levison discerns a tension in the Second Temple period between the allure of ecstasy (and here he has a solid treatment of the role of the ecstatic in Greco-Roman literature) and the disciplined spirit. The latter is a supplemental endowment of inspiration given to the internal life spirit often as a result of the study of Torah (see Sir 39). Levison sees early Christian views of the Spirit as (1) several steps removed from older

---

59. Bonnah 2007, 402, 266.
60. Levison 1997; 1999.
61. Levison 2009, 12.
62. Levison 2009, 33, 12, respectively; see 14–33 for argument.
63. This claim raises fascinating hermeneutical and theological questions that are beyond the scope of this study.

Israelite traditions and (2) so focused on "transformation and discontinuity" that they supplanted the Second Temple view of the Spirit as a supplemental endowment given to the already-present life spirit.[64]

Levison's treatment of the Spirit in Second Temple texts helpfully shows that "prophecy" is not a broad enough category for the diversity of expressions of the Spirit. I find Levison's treatment of Luke–Acts to be somewhat less helpful for a variety of reasons. First, Levison gives no attention in his Old Testament or Second Temple enquiry to Joel 3:1–5 LXX, a critical passage for Luke's reading of the Spirit and a text that is interpreted by Luke's Peter to point to the Spirit as a gift that marks the dawn of the eschatological age. Second, Levison has no treatment of the Spirit in Luke. This allows for a reading of Acts that does not fully appreciate the Lukan view of the Spirit. Third, Levison's reading of Acts seems to me to be too indebted to his history of religions approach. Levison interprets the Pentecost account as Luke's effort to hold together the "ecstatic" (he sees references to fire as evidence of the influence Greco-Roman ecstasy rather than the more commonly noted allusions to Sinai) and the respectability of inspired interpretation. Hence, Levison argues that Luke transforms an historicized experience of pure ecstasy into speech in *other* tongues in order to "blunt the edge of the ecstasy."[65] According to Levison, "Luke provokes his readers to recognize both forms of inspiration somehow melded into neither one nor the other but into some inscrutable amalgamation of both."[66] This emphasis on Luke's desire to maintain Greco-Roman views of ecstasy is apparent in Levison's account of the Philippian slave girl in Acts 16. Levison, in a creative reading, suggests that Paul is not concerned with the pythonic spirit possession of the girl (which leads to her oppression by her owners), but is only personally "annoyed." For Levison, this is an "unvarnished glimpse of inspiration" and evidence of the ecstatic in Luke's thought world.[67]

---

64. Levison 2009, 251.
65. Levison 2009, 323.
66. Levison 2009, 344.
67. Levison 2009, 318. I find this reading to be particularly problematic for its lack of recognition of the incredibly harmful effects of this spirit upon the slave girl (Levison says the girl bears none of the ill effects of demon-possessed persons in Luke's Gospel [320–21]), its insistence that Paul knew immediately that the girl was possessed, and the suggestion that the inspiration of the girl was not illicit. Levison sees the girl's words as "irenic and supportive" (321), though I argue (1) we are not bound to read the words in that tone and (2) like the demon-possessed figures in the Gospels, this demon recognizes the truth of the gospel before other human characters.

Luke's "ecstatic" traditions are also held in tension with older Israelite views that emerge in other places. For Levison, the Seven (Acts 6:1–7)—with Stephen as the central figure—are the primary exemplars of older Israelite views. The Seven, "full of the Spirit and wisdom" (Acts 6:3), are "heirs of Bezaelel, whom God filled with spirit, wisdom, intelligence, and knowledge… Here, then, in the Jerusalem church lies an authentic vestige of the scriptural perspective that a disciplined spirit within yields a harvest of wisdom."[68]

Levison's attempt to identify Luke's handling of traditions, as though Luke were moving toward a Hegelian pneumatological synthesis, does not provide the best reading of Luke's view of the role of the Spirit in the early Jesus movement. It tends to keep Luke bound overmuch to stitched-together traditions rather than allowing for Luke's own fresh interpretation of the role of the Spirit, an expression of just the type of creativity regarding the role of the Spirit that Levison sees as operative in the first century C.E.[69] It remains to be seen what effect Levison's broader reading of the Spirit in Second Temple texts will have on supplanting the "Spirit of prophecy" model that currently dominates Lukan studies.

1.2. Gaps in the Study of the Spirit in Luke–Acts

The past century has brought many advances in our understanding of the role of the Spirit in Luke–Acts. However, several critical issues remain:
1. While Luke is undoubtedly interested in the role of the Spirit in the inspiration of both ecstatic and proclamatory speech, using "Spirit of prophecy" as a category to describe Luke's appropriation of Old Testament and Second Temple concepts of the Spirit proves ultimately too restrictive for Luke–Acts. "Spirit of prophecy" is an etic category constructed by modern exegetes to organize ancient data.[70] This in itself is not problematic, but it becomes so when one begins to imagine that first-century Israelites were thinking in

---

68. Levison 2009, 242–43.
69. Levison 1997, 235.
70. "Emic" refers to "insider or indigenous points of view"—the words and conceptualities used by groups to understand themselves and their worlds. "Etic" refers to the "systematic set of concepts used by one culture to understand others" (Esler 2003, 8)—the words and concepts used by outside observers who are removed from the social context in which they are interested. If there is not "reasonable correspondence between the etic concept and the emic data" violence will be done to the emic data. Reducing the Spirit in pre-New Testament texts to only the "Spirit of prophecy" faces the danger of imposing just such an overly rigid etic category on Old Testament and Second Temple texts.

neat categorical conceptualities with regard to the Spirit even when Turner himself admits that the phrase "Spirit of prophecy" is almost non-existent before the rabbinic period.[71] This has resulted in a tendency to sequester Wisdom literature into a discrete category with regard to its influence in order to preserve the conceptual purity of the "Spirit of prophecy." This move may reflect modern generic classifications more than ancient sensibilities.

2. Focus on "Spirit of prophecy" has led to an over-emphasis on the *act* of inspired speech and has neglected important corollaries. For example, the early prototypical prophets in the Old Testament (especially Abraham and Moses, both of whom have special importance in Luke–Acts) are identified as prophets not because of inspired speech but because of their identity marked by a special relationship to God.[72] This is an indicator that the gift of prophecy is fundamentally concerned with communion: communion between the prophet and God, communion between the people and God as urged by the Spirit through the prophet, and the proper function of the community itself. Emphasis on the act of prophecy overlooks necessary implications for the identity of prophets.

3. Focus on the "Spirit of prophecy" distorts Luke's text in two important ways. First, too quickly establishing Acts 2:17–18 as foundational for Luke's "Spirit of prophecy" neglects Luke's narrative order and the concomitant fact that Luke's hearers received the text in sequence. Hence, while Peter's Pentecost discourse is enormously important to Luke's project, we must recognize that Acts 2:17–18 builds on Spirit material earlier in the Gospel and Acts. Luke gives us a great deal of Spirit material prior to Acts 2 that must be taken cumulatively and then modified or augmented by Spirit material later in Acts.[73] In point of fact, Luke is more reliant upon Isaiah for his Spirit material than Joel.[74] Second, and highly problematic for the "Spirit of prophecy" paradigm, is the fact that the density of Spirit references in Acts *distances* references to the Spirit from "missionary proclamation." There are zero

---

71. Turner 1996, 104. Turner is hard to follow at this point. He critiques "procrustean" formulations of "Spirit of prophecy" but seems only to increase the diversity of what he includes in his foundational concept (see pp. 89–91). Levison 2009 has successfully shown that "prophecy" is too neat a category.

72. Abraham: Gen 20:7; Moses: Exod 33:11; Deut 34:10.

73. Thompson 2006, 11, 26–27 discusses the role that "amplification" and "accumulation" have for shaping meaning through narrative progression.

74. Especially Isa 49; 58:6; 61:1–2.

references to the Spirit in Paul's evangelistic speeches in Acts 13, 14, 16, 17, and 18 and there are zero references to the Spirit in Paul's legal defense speeches in Acts 22, 23, 24, 25, 26 and 27. In these sections, the Spirit gives divine guidance, miraculous power and joy, it incorporates outsiders into the community and it is credited with establishing the authority of the Ephesian elders, but it does not explicitly inspire speech in the most thoroughly mission-oriented sections of Acts.[75] Conversely, sections of the text where group and social identity are at stake contain the highest density of Spirit references in all of Acts.[76]

4. Emphasis on the Second Temple provenance of the concept "Spirit of prophecy" is prone to an avoidable methodological error present in several of the works in this field. There has been a tendency to slip into a history of religions approach to the development of the concept "Spirit" that operates with the assumption that Luke must have a view of the Spirit that is in linear continuity with Old Testament and Second Temple conceptualities. Yet Luke is not bound to an evolutionary progression of concepts with regard to common interpretations of the Spirit in his milieu.[77] Recent research in epistemology has indicated that new knowledge usually requires reconceptualization of fundamentals.[78] This has long been recognized by Gospel scholars in the way that Jesus' life and vocation recast the concept "Messiah." In the same way we must allow the Spirit in Luke–Acts radically to fill out and redefine Old Testament and Second Temple expectations concerning the Spirit.[79]

In sum, the scholarly consensus that Luke's Spirit is the "Spirit of prophecy" runs the risk of failing to allow the text to speak for itself by imposing *a priori* restrictions on what can, or cannot, be a legitimate function of the Spirit in Luke–Acts. It is not necessary to abandon all the results of those who hold to the "Spirit of prophecy" paradigm (especially the more expansive results from

---

75. Acts 13:2, 4, 9, 52; 16:6, 7; 19:2, 6, 21; 20:22, 23, 28; 21:4, 11.

76. Six references in Acts 8; eight in Acts 10–11:18.

77. Hur 2001, 180 rightly sees simultaneous continuity and discontinuity between Luke and Old Testament/Second Temple conceptions. See Levison 1997, 235 for a similar focus on the creativity that surrounded conceptions of the Spirit in the first century C.E.

78. On epistemic advances, faulty reasoning in linear evolutionary epistemologies and radical discontinuity of new knowledge, see Kuhn 1996, 85; Rae 2005, 110–22.

79. The history of religions approach is more evident in some interpreters (Gunkel, Leisegang, Menzies, Cho and Levison) than others.

Wenk and Turner), since the Spirit certainly inspires speech for missionary proclamation in Luke–Acts, but my reading of Luke–Acts will demonstrate that the concept itself is misleadingly restrictive. A new starting point in reflection on the Spirit in Luke–Acts may allow for fresh discussion and fruitful enquiry.

5. Investigation into the role of the Spirit in conversion has over-emphasized the effect of the Spirit on individuals and shown relatively less interest in the thoroughly personal yet *irreducibly corporate* focus of Luke's text and world. This approach has led to two problems. First, it has not yet grasped the full significance of community membership in completing a "conversion."[80] Second, the focus on individual conversion has sought a systematic "order of salvation" with regard to the temporal relationship between repentance, baptism and Spirit-reception. Yet Luke has written a historical narrative of God's providential creation of a new kind of community, not a systematic pneumatology. Luke's concern is less with a dogmatic "order of salvation" and more with how and why a diverse collection of persons were incorporated into the Spirit-empowered Jesus community.

6. There has yet to appear a full enquiry into the relationship between the Spirit and ethnic identity in Luke–Acts. Given that these are two of Luke's central concerns, this would appear to be a fruitful area for enquiry. As a result of this gap there has been a lack of investigation into the way that the newly formed community of faith functioned differently than other groups that Luke describes. While ancient parallels are often noted (communities of goods, friendship ideals, voluntary associations and utopian impulses), it has yet to be appreciated that the community described in Acts functions in a way that is very different than the identity processes that are observable within most social groups in our own contemporary settings as well as within other groups described in Luke–Acts. There was something powerfully different about the way identity operated in Luke's early community of believers, and this difference comes out clearly in an investigation of the interplay of Spirit, ethnicity and identity.[81]

---

80. Wenk 2004 is an exception, yet he does not present a full exegetical account of the role of the Spirit in community formation. Twelftree 2009, 45–51 distances participation in the community of faith from "salvation" or "conversion."

81. Given the recent appreciation of the social ramifications of Paul's gospel, an awareness of Luke's insistence on the close relationship between the gospel and ethnic reconciliation may hint that there are clearer resonances between Luke and Paul than is sometimes acknowledged.

1.3. The Thesis of this Study

It is the thesis of this study that, for Luke, the Holy Spirit is the central figure in the formation of a new social identity that affirms yet chastens and transcends ethnic identity. The formation of this new identity is a reflection of profound transformation (not just social recategorization), and is the mechanism through which intergroup reconciliation occurs in Luke–Acts. Because Luke is writing narratively (as opposed to systematically), Luke's identity-forming program unfolds in step with the narrative and the full force of the program is only experienced cumulatively.[82] The practical effect of this observation is that Luke does not unveil his entire program from the beginning of his work, or even from the beginning of Acts, but instead includes several key building blocks that bring his identity-forming program to a climax at Acts 15:

1. The Spirit has a transformative effect on individuals, best described as the formation of an *allocentric identity*, that results simultaneously in a turn away from pure self-interest or the interests of the in-group and a turn toward the "other."[83] Allocentric identity is evident early in Luke's Gospel and has important ramifications for the relationship between privileged identity, distribution of resources and the "other." Jesus is the primary exemplar of Spirit-formed allocentric identity, though Luke's narrative will provide other important exemplars along the way.

2. The new social group described in Acts is the corporate expression of Spirit-formed allocentric identity and functions as an incubator of a *new social identity*. The group provides a base through which people come to know themselves in a new way in their intergroup context.[84]

3. The social identity formed by participation in this group transcends ethnic identities by virtue of the Spirit's relentless effort, in

---

82. Reading Luke with respect to narrative order respects the author's use of the classical rhetorical devices of accumulation and amplification gradually to bring along the hearers (see Thompson 2006, 11, 26–27). Cf. Alexander 1999, 439, who suggests that Luke's prospective clues in the progress of the narrative are best interpreted retrospectively. Luke–Acts, like most works in this genre, was intended for re-readers (Alexander 1999, 441).

83. "Allocentric" defines an identity characterized by or denoting interest centered in persons other than oneself. In the present study, an "allocentric identity" will be used to refer to an identity that can express in-group love and out-group love simultaneously, a very difficult feat within most social groups.

84. See Chapter 2 below for a detailed description of normal social identity processes.

two ways, to incorporate all manner of "other" into the group: (1) by orchestrating intergroup encounters between the Jesus-group and various categories of "other"; (2) by functioning as the marker of the common group identity shared by those loyal to Jesus. The addition of the "other" to the group requires a "dual identity transformation" in which the former "other" receives a new social identity and in which in-group members are compelled to reconceptualize their own social identity to reflect the reconfigured constitution of their in-group. This group, and the social identity it produces, is the locus of intergroup reconciliation in Luke–Acts.

4. This new social identity *does not* require the negation of ethnic identity. Ethnic hegemonies and ethnocentrisms must be abandoned, as must all identity markers that oppose the lordship of Jesus, but ethnic identification is unhindered and ethnic particularity is robustly affirmed, defended and celebrated by the Spirit.

An emphasis on the identity-forming role of the Spirit helps to overcome the dichotomy between daughtership/sonship and empowerment for mission that has arisen in scholarship on the role of the Spirit in Luke–Acts. That dichotomy itself is based upon overly narrow conceptions of both salvation and mission. It is based upon a conception of salvation that overlooks the fact that, for Luke, salvation is a present reality that is experienced in a renewed fully human existence before God. Salvation is more than a status conferred; it is a certain kind of life properly oriented toward God and "other." The dichotomy is also based upon a reductionistic conception of "mission" that includes only preaching and verbal proclamation, rather than, as for Luke, the totality of renewed life of the community.[85] In other words, for Luke, both "salvation" and "mission" are essentially the experience and expression of other-centered life lived before God in the reconciled Spirit-empowered community of Jesus, world without end.

Finally, it should be emphasized that this investigation of the role of the Spirit in Luke–Acts takes seriously the intractable nature of interethnic conflict. The Spirit is the figure in Luke–Acts who allows for examples of intergroup reconciliation that were largely unprecedented within the ancient world. The ethnic reconciliation described by Luke, sadly, remains largely unprecedented also in the contemporary world,

---

85. Luke consistently indicates that the properly ordered life of the renewed and reconciled community is itself a powerful evangelistic factor (see Acts 2:42–47; 6:1–7; 9:1–31). Roberts Gaventa notes this important dynamic: "The church's witness also takes the form of mutual responsibility in a community of believers" (2003, 41).

both inside and outside of Christian communities. It is not too much to say that of all the deeds of power done by the Spirit in Luke–Acts, the reconciliation of diverse ethnic groups is the most astonishing miracle of all. This is borne out both by Luke's text and by the annals of history, ravaged as they are by the atrocities of inter-ethnic hatred.

1.4. Outline of the Argument

This monograph is comprised of nine chapters. The argument builds sequentially in an attempt to follow Luke's narrative logic as it unfolds throughout his two volumes. Luke's own approach invites readers on a journey of transformation in so many ways—with regard to their view of Jesus, Israel, covenant, Rome, enemies, and so on. Included along this journey is the pneumatological transformation of human identity *by* and *for* the formation of a reconciled community of "others" who live together under the lordship of Jesus Christ.

Chapter 2 will outline the methodology used in the project. In order to speak with precision about the complex concept of identity I will utilize resources from social identity theory and contemporary ethnicity theory. I will also briefly survey Old Testament and Second Temple texts that describe a wide spectrum of Israelite responses to the ethnic "other" in the face of threatened identity. This will demonstrate the diversity within Israelite traditions and will locate Luke at one point in this relatively broad spectrum.

In Chapter 3 I will discuss the function of the Spirit in the birth hymns of Luke 1–2. Luke begins by activating an Abraham and Sarah-like identity that points toward God's universal purposes for humanity and that spills over into the birth hymns. I will demonstrate the connection between the presence of the Spirit and the broadening of the "ethnic horizon" for Spirit-empowered individuals. This is initial evidence that the Spirit is constitutive of an allocentric identity that focuses not on the self to the exclusion of the "other," but simultaneously on the self and the "other."

In Chapter 4 I will demonstrate that the initial public appearances of John and Jesus—Luke's paradigmatically Spirit-empowered figures— concern proper (and improper) expressions of privileged ethnic social identity. This solidifies Luke's connection between the Spirit and allocentric identity and establishes Jesus as a Spirit-empowered exemplar of this identity.

In Chapter 5, focusing on Acts 1–2, I will briefly discuss Luke's paradigmatic concern with the extension of in-group benefits to people groups that Luke's Gospel depicts as potentially hostile. I will go on to demonstrate the old paradigms of identity that exist before Pentecost, the subversion of those paradigms through Luke's description of the language miracle at Pentecost, and the reconfiguration of group identity markers in Peter's distinct version of Joel 3:1–5a LXX. In this section we begin to encounter Luke's view of the relationship between ethnic particularity and the universal availability of the gospel. We will see the Spirit guard and celebrate ethnic particularity even as it works toward intergroup reconciliation.

In Chapter 6 I will examine the role of the early community in the formation of identity, as well as the essential connection between community incorporation and "salvation." Ananias, Sapphira and Barnabas emerge in this section as exemplars of either defective or proper identification with the community and are used by Luke further to develop the relationship between the Spirit and the allocation of resources.

Chapter 7, examining Acts 6–9, will focus on the dual function of the Spirit in both orchestrating intergroup encounters with the "threatening other" and in marking a common group identity. This will highlight Luke's clear emphasis on the "dual identity transformation" elicited by the work of the Spirit. We will see that Luke is convinced that the inclusion of the "other" into the Jesus group always necessitates the continuing transformation of the social identities of existing group members. It will become evident that Luke sees something of a transformational circle in which personal transformation leads toward participation in a reconfigured and reconciled community. In turn, participation in such a community extends personal transformation. This entire transformational circle is the domain of the Spirit.

Chapter 8 will deal with the conversion of Cornelius' household and its effects, culminating with the Jerusalem Council in Acts 15. I will show Luke's clear distinction between the way group boundaries are maintained in the Jesus group and the way typical (often ethnic) groups in Luke's context functioned. Special attention will be given to Luke's use of "ethnic language" in the description of social realities and the formation of identity. Here Luke definitively demonstrates that the Spirit marks a new identity that chastens and transcends ethnicity, while simultaneously affirming ethnic identity and particularity at a penultimate level.

Chapter 9 will conclude the study by demonstrating the affirmation of my thesis as well as by suggesting several areas of relevance for both further research and contemporary application.

1.5. Assumptions Concerning Luke's Audience and Occasion for Writing

I am operating in this study with the conviction that Luke–Acts is a unified literary work. Some scholars have argued that a lack of evidence for the unified reception of the two volumes in the early history of reception calls for a reconsideration of the "hyphen" in Luke–Acts. However, the unity of the two volumes remains (arguably) the scholarly consensus.[86] My reading of Luke–Acts assumes that Luke intended for hearers of Acts to be aware of the Gospel, and vice versa.

I assume, further, that Luke–Acts is certainly addressed to non-Israelites, but even more likely to an ethnically mixed audience.[87] Luke's emphasis on issues of intergroup reconciliation seem most appropriate for persons who are grappling with this issue in a broader social context that features relatively sharp social stratification and intergroup antipathy.

Suggestions regarding Luke's occasion for writing his two-volume text are many and diverse.[88] Luke's stated intention for his work is to give "certainty" (ἀσφάλεια) to Theophilus concerning all that he has been taught about Jesus. Broadly, then, Luke is simply attempting to set forth an account of Jesus' birth, life, death, resurrection and ascension, and all the ramifications of those realities. More particularly, Luke positions Jesus as the figure who climactically fulfills the Abrahamic covenant (Luke 1:54–55, 72–73).[89] Luke clearly understands the Abrahamic covenant to have as its goal the incorporation of "all the families of the earth" into the community of God's people.[90] The formation, by the power of the Spirit, of this trans-ethnic community created a social entity that fit awkwardly into the social norms of Imperial culture. Nowhere is this exemplified as clearly as in the response of the Thessalonians in Acts 17:6: "These who have turned the world upside down have come here also."[91] If Theophilus, and the community in which he participated, lived in a manner that looked quite different from the highly stratified Roman world, there was undoubtedly great pressure to wonder whether this new

---

86. See the survey of research on this issue in Bird 2007. The most recent challenge to the unity of Luke and Acts is from Walters 2009.
87. Here I follow the hypothesis of Esler 1987, 24–26.
88. See Maddox 1982 for a list of major theories.
89. See Chapter 3 below.
90. Luke alludes to this in many places, but it appears most clearly in Luke's recounting of Peter's speech in Acts 3:25.
91. My translation.

way of being human in community was reasonable or whether it was socially aberrant. I suggest, then, that Luke is writing with the theological conviction that God has fulfilled the promise to Abraham in the life, death, resurrection and ascension of Jesus and through the pouring out of Holy Spirit.[92] One of the ramifications of this conviction is that all nations were now being gathered to God.[93] Precisely how these nations would live together in peace, and what these strangely reconciled communities would look like, is another matter. Luke, at least in part, was responding to the social pressure caused by living in this uniquely constituted Spirit-formed trans-ethnic community in order to reassure his hearers that this peculiar vision of human life was central to the goal of the gospel and, by the transforming power of the Spirit, required a certain way of configuring and expressing identity in the midst of the Roman world.

---

92. This largely agrees with Twelftree 2009, 9, who suggests "Luke was writing to reassure his readers that what they had been taught about Jesus, as well as the Christian life, is no aberration of a message from God but the true goal towards which God's dealings with Israel were moving. Therefore, Luke emphasizes that what had taken (and was taking) place in and within the group of followers of Jesus fulfilled Old Testament hopes."

93. The inaugurated eschatology evident in Luke's use of Joel 3:1–5a LXX should not be missed. For Luke, the community is (in some way) experiencing "that Day" toward which the prophets pointed.

Chapter 2

SOCIAL IDENTITY AND THE "OTHER":
A METHODOLOGICAL AND HISTORICAL OVERVIEW

Who we are deeply influences *how* we are. Our sense of identity—who we understand ourselves to be—is intimately connected to the manner in which we live and interact in all of our relationships. In a reciprocal manner, the relationships that we cultivate are inseparable from our sense of identity. *Being* and *doing* are symbiotic in human identity. From this perspective, Luke–Acts has something to say about human identity. Of the several interrelated purposes of Luke–Acts, one of Luke's clear aims is to tell its hearers *who* they are, *whose* they are and *how* they are to be within their contexts. In so doing, the text locates its hearers in relationships that redefine their identity, subverting prominent mechanisms for the maintenance of social boundaries and arriving at the surprising conclusion that its hearers should no longer understand themselves primarily in terms of their relationships with their ancestral kinfolk—their ethnic identity—but in terms of their relationship with the person of Jesus Christ through the Holy Spirit and, by extension, in terms of their relationships with all who find themselves now related to Jesus. Luke insists that his hearers are defined by an identity that simultaneously affirms yet chastens and transcends ethnic identity.

Though "identity" is a popular concept both within the broader culture and, increasingly, within biblical studies, the lack of precision with which the concept is deployed often renders it conceptually vacuous. Any thesis concerned with "identity" must consider *how* identity works, especially within and between social groups. Toward this goal, the first section of this chapter will assimilate theoretical insights from social identity theory to describe a model capable of providing etic descriptions of Luke's Spirit-laced depictions of identity formation.[1] Special attention

---

1. There are benefits and dangers in social-scientific approaches to biblical interpretation. Social-scientific approaches offer helpful checks against tacitly proceeding under the myth of presuppositionless exegesis and its attendant anachronistic or

will be given to ethnic identity. I will follow the methodological discussion with a brief survey of Second Temple texts that describe a range of Israelite identity maintenance strategies with regard to the ethnic "other." This contextual work will guard against caricatures of Israelite identity and demonstrate that it is not Israelite identity *per se* (and, for Luke, not just Israelite identity but *any* social identity that practices extreme in-group bias), but *one specific expression* of ethnic identity that Luke critiques with verve.²

2.1. *Social Identity Theory**³

Identity is a complex phenomenon, affected by many variables and deployed in diverse expressions. Reckoning with the ways identity is formed and the ways that identity affects social interaction requires a level of theoretical precision. Apart from this precision, "identity" can too easily become a wax nose, pressed this way and that by the needs of the interpreter. Because this project will use social identity theory as a theoretical resource to describe the processes and effects of identity formation, it is necessary to note the role of the theory in this study. I will deploy social identity theory as a heuristic tool that assists readers in

---

ethnocentric interpretations (see Elliott 1993; Esler 1994; and Horrell 1999). The heuristic deployment of interpretational models also produces methodological transparency, a feature important for constructive discourse. One attendant danger in social-scientific interpretation is a tendency toward sociological determinism in which actors in the text (including divine agents) are not allowed to operate outside, or in opposition to, cultural norms. Yet it is often the *atypical* that allows biblical authors to make their point. Well-deployed social-scientific approaches elucidate the *regular* in order to observe the *irregular*.

2. Buell 2005, 24 notes the problematic tendency to contrast "universalistic" "Christianity" with "particularistic" "Judaism." Cf. Barclay 1997; Dahl 1977. I hope to provide a much more nuanced account of identity formation within Luke–Acts. I am convinced that Luke, on the issue of ethnocentrism, comes closer to Paul than is sometimes acknowledged. Dunn 2008, 32 n. 122 acknowledges the critique of some New Perspective emphases on Israelite ethnocentrism, and notes the need for nuance: "Gager (*Reinventing Paul* 49) and Kim (*Paul and the New Perspective* 61 n. 212) think that the new perspective replaces one distorted picture of Judaism (as soulless legalism) with an equally distorted caricature of Judaism as a racist, nationalist religion. But the problem that Paul encountered was precisely that a messianic sect of a nationalist religion (Judaism = the religion of the Judeans) had become a missionary sect seeking to convert into and to fully accept non-Jews within a non-nationalistic version of Israel's traditional religion."

3. A glossary of technical terms related to social identity theory (marked by an asterisk at their initial appearance) is included at the end of this chapter.

noticing the group dynamics—and their identity-forming ramifications—within Luke's two volumes. Because I read from a North American social location that is largely individualistic, it has proven immensely useful to have a theoretical grid that helps to see more clearly the social dynamics in Luke–Acts. Exegetically and hermeneutically, social identity theory has helped to imagine new questions and notice dynamics that are largely obscured by some of the social assumptions prominent in my own context. Put quite simply, social identity theory can help (post)modern, Western individualists to read more as collectivists. That said, social identity theory is only a heuristic device that helps to describe at an etic level the group realities Luke's narrative reveals. Luke, of course, is not a social psychologist and is not explicitly working with the descriptive categories I will deploy. The categories, however, usefully describe the dynamics evident within the text and help us to appreciate the power of groups, the identities they form, and the intergroup realities with which Luke grapples in his account of Jesus and the early community of Jesus-followers.

Social identity theory (hereafter SIT) is a branch of social psychology that seeks to understand the effects of group membership on human identity.[4] The modern Western obsession with identity is largely an interest in *personal identity*. Personal identity is that *part* of human identity derived from the traits that we normally think of as personality: sense of humor, compassion, short temper and so on. When we relate to another human being based upon our (and their) personal identity we relate as individuals.[5]

---

4. SIT was developed by Henri Tajfel beginning in the early 1970s. For comprehensive introductions, see Brown 2000; Hogg and Abrams 1999; J.C. Turner 1996. The genesis of Tajfel's reflection on group membership and identity occurred in a WWII German POW camp. Tajfel disguised his Polish identity—and preserved his life—by posing as a Frenchman. He observed that treatment from guards and prisoners was often based solely on the group to which he portrayed himself as belonging. The application of SIT to biblical studies was pioneered by Esler 1998; 2003; 2009. See also Duling 2005.

5. Most traits constitutive of personal identity are themselves influenced by the groups to which one belongs. Tajfel 1981, 241 notes that purely interpersonal interaction is socially "absurd" and does not occur in "real life": "It is impossible to imagine a social encounter between two people which will not be affected, at least to some minimal degree, by their mutual assignments of one another to a variety of social categories about which some general expectations concerning their characteristics and behavior exist in the minds of the interactants. This will be true, for example, even of wives and husbands."

Yet the Western obsession with the individual has obscured from plain view the importance of *social identity*, a phenomenon more salient in most of the world but with enduring impact in the Western world as well. Social identity is that *part* of an individual's identity derived from "their knowledge of their membership in a social group (or groups) together with the value and emotional significance attached to that membership."[6] Social identity is a reflection *in the individual* of the group identity possessed collectively by members of a social group. When one claims to be a supporter of the Celtic football club, an Anglican, a member of a union of electrical workers, or a Pakistani, they are speaking of their social identities. Social identities have varying affective power correlated to the importance of the identity-forming group and commensurate with a society's location on a collectivism/individualism scale. In collectivist cultures (like those of the New Testament world), social identity can be especially powerful, serving sometimes "nearly to the exclusion of personal identity" and creating a sense of identity "based solely or primarily on our group memberships."[7]

While social identity impinges upon almost all human interaction, social identity is most likely to be salient when the context is composed of distinct and non-overlapping social categories that are difficult (or impossible) to pass between.[8] These conditions are especially true of ethnic groups, which are almost always highly distinct and which usually have both internal and external pressure against defection to another ethnic group.

2.1.1. *The Ambiguity of Social Identity*

Understanding the mechanisms that form social identity can alert us to the inherent ambiguity of all social groups: groups can be incubators of positive identity based upon communal solidarity or they can be breeding grounds for intergroup conflict. The potentially pernicious effects of social identity for the "other" are located within the inherently comparative mechanisms through which positive social identity is maintained. In this section I will describe the way SIT explains the following factors that constitute, or result from, social identity:

1. The multi-stage process by which social identity is formed.
2. The effect of group status upon intergroup contact and conflict.
3. Strategies to reduce intergroup conflict.

---

6. Tajfel 1982, 2.
7. Turner 1982, 19.
8. Tajfel 1981, 245; Brown 2000, 746.

4. The ramifications of group and subgroup identity for resource allocation.

2.1.2. *The Process of Social Identity Formation*
Social identity is formed in three stages: categorization, identification and comparison.

(1) *Categorization*
Categorization is the division of the social world into assessable group entities. Categorization itself is a neutral phenomenon. But the necessary precondition for social categorization, as well as its eventual result, is depersonalization in which *personal* identity is subsumed by the characteristics of the *group* category in view. This action is essential as a "reliable guide for judgment and action" in a world of social diversity.[9] Categorization results in a perceived world composed of deindividuated groups about which large-scale generalizations can be made: "All Americans are loud," "Cretans are always liars" (Titus 1:12) or "From one [Greek] acquire knowledge of all."[10] SIT theorists know this phenomenon of deindividuation as *out-group homogeneity**.[11]

(2) *Identification*
In contexts of social diversity, humans identify with the groups to which they perceive they belong. The necessary condition for group formation is nothing more than two or more individuals who perceive themselves to be members of a common social category.[12] *The self-definitions that arise from our membership in groups are our social identities.*[13]

The reasons for group ascription can be broadly classified under two headings: (1) maintenance of positive self-esteem and (2) the reduction of subjective uncertainty.[14] Both reasons reflect wholly positive aspects of group membership. The first arises when the positive evaluation of one's group is ascribed to the self, thus providing basic needs of belonging, social support and a positive view of oneself and one's people. The second arises from the fact that groups provide utilitarian advantages in an uncertain world. For example, people are more likely, all things being equal, to join a well-resourced group than a marginalized group.

---

9. Brown 2000, 751.
10. *Aeneid* II.65.
11. Huddy and Virtanen 1995; Rothgerber 1997; Brown 2000, 751.
12. Turner 1982, 15.
13. Tajfel 1981, 246; Turner 1982, 19; Hogg and Abrams 1999, 10.
14. Hogg and Mullin 1999.

There is no limit to the number of groups a human can join, hence all humans possess multiple social identities. These "dual" or "nested" identities* become salient based upon social context and intergroup contact.[15] When a football fan has intergroup contact with a supporter of Rangers football club, that fan may be likely to act based upon his identity as a fan of Celtic. When intergroup contact is with an Englishman, that same Celtic supporter is more likely to interact based upon his Scottish social identity.[16] Nested identities such as these are no modern construct. Philo's well-known quote gives evidence for this phenomenon in antiquity:

> For no one country can contain the whole Jewish ('Ιουδαῖος) nation (ἔθνος), by reason of its populousness; on which account they frequent all the most prosperous and fertile countries of Europe and Asia, whether islands or continents, looking indeed upon the holy city as their metropolis (μητρόλιν) in which is erected the sacred temple of the most high God, but accounting those regions which have been occupied by their fathers, and grandfathers, and great grandfathers, and still more remote ancestors, in which they have been born and brought up, as their country (πατρίδος).[17]

According to Philo, both the mother-city (Jerusalem) and the fatherland (Diaspora homeland) form aspects of the social identity of Diaspora Judeans.[18]

While nested identities can create a complex nexus of identity, an individual's most basic social identity is his or her *terminal identity**.[19] This social identity orients other lower-level identities and can be conceived as the answer to the question, "*Who are my people?*"

Finally, it should be noted that one important part of identification with a group is the role of group exemplars*. An exemplar is a group member who best embodies the prototypical characteristics of the in-group.[20] The characteristics of an exemplar are extended to the group as a whole as well as to individual group members.[21] We will come to see that exemplars play an important identity-forming role in Luke–Acts.

To summarize the role of *identification* in social identity formation, individuals identify with the groups in their context to which they perceive they belong. Social identity arises when individuals begin to know

---

15. Jenkins 1997; Brewer 1999, 438. Jenkins uses the helpful example of a Russian matryoshka doll for nested identity (1997, 85).
16. Burdsey 2004. Cf. Saeed et al. 1999, 840–41.
17. *Flaccus* 45.b–46a
18. See Jones and Pearce 1998 on local Israelite identities.
19. Deaux et al. 1995, 280; Cairns 1982, 281.
20. Smith and Zarate 1992; Medin et al. 1984.
21. Bodenhausen et al. 1995, 60. Out-group exemplars embody in their person the collective characteristics of the "other."

themselves based upon these group memberships. All people have multiple social identities which are oriented by the terminal identity. Finally, the attributes of group exemplars both exemplify the group and are ascribed to individual members.

(3) *Comparison*
Positive group identity, and hence positive social identity, is maintained through a process of comparison and evaluation in which the in-group favorably differentiates itself from out-groups.[22] The positive evaluation of the in-group is known as *in-group bias**. Two things must be noted about this comparative process. First, comparative criteria are fluid. Groups can evaluate themselves on whatever criteria are comparatively advantageous.[23] Second, social identity is primarily about the ascription of *positive* characteristics to the self and not about a primal disdain for the "other"; it is primarily an expression of in-group love rather than out-group hate. However, in-group bias is infrequently benign and often forms the seed bed for social tension.[24] The inherently evaluative process of social identity formation has a pernicious tendency: "social antagonism…is the result of ordinary, adaptive, and functional psychological processes."[25] Because the "we" that always stands behind the "I" is formed by comparison with the "they," the "they" are regularly conceptualized as inferior.[26] This has numerous ramifications for intergroup relations and resource allocation. For now, it suffices to say that *the fine line between in-group love and out-group hate is the line where human community is distorted*. One of the major functions of the Spirit in Luke–Acts is the formation of an identity capable simultaneously of in-group love *and* out-group love.

2.1.3. *The Effect of Group Status upon Intergroup Contact and Conflict*
The evaluative aspect of social identity formation, while regularly fostering unfavorable views of the other, does not necessarily lead to overt

---

22. Bettencourt et al. 2001, 521.
23. Bettencourt et al. 2001, 521.
24. Brewer 1999, 438: "Many forms of discrimination and bias may develop not because out-groups are hated, but because positive emotions such as admiration, sympathy, and trust are reserved for the in-group and withheld from out-groups."
25. Turner 1999, 19.
26. Ashburn-Nardo et al. 2001, 797 note "behavioral manifestations of such implicit biases undoubtedly have negative implications for out-group members, regardless of whether the biases are rooted in in-group favoritism or out-group derogation… Favoring an in-group member in the workplace, for example, necessarily results in an undesirable outcome for out-group members."

intergroup conflict. Several factors increase the likelihood of conflict, and of these factors unequal group status is particularly potent.[27] Groups that rate unfavorably on an evaluative trait esteemed in the broader context are low-status groups.[28] Whether or not these status differences (often based upon wealth, power, honor etc.) are real is inconsequential. The *perception* of status inequality is what matters for group identities.[29] In situations of perceived status inequality, four contextual factors intensify in-group bias:[30]

1. *High status stability* limits the ability of social groups as a whole to improve their position. This is often the case where there is political domination of one group over another.
2. *Impermeable group boundaries* lead to the inability of individual members to defect from their in-group to join higher status groups. Impermeability results not only from barriers erected by high-status groups, but from social pressures within the low-status group itself. This is frequently the case for ethnic minorities, religious minorities and political or ideological movements.[31]
3. *Status illegitimacy* is the perception that high-status groups hold their position illegitimately. This is often true where there is political occupation, subjugation or unequal access to resources.
4. *External threat* is the perception that group identity is threatened. This can be the case for high-status groups convinced that low-status "others" are threatening their group's "purity" or for low-status groups who feel pressured to abandon their distinct identity through assimilation.

Each of these factors prompts increased identification with the in-group, increased in-group bias and deteriorating views of the out-group. Low-status groups in these situations have three basic options to improve their negative group status (and concomitant negative social identities). I will list them in an order of escalating intergroup confrontation:

1. *Social mobility* is the movement of individuals from a low-status group to a high-status group. As noted above, societal constraints sometimes make this impossible. Tajfel claimed, "The basic condition for the appearance of extreme forms of intergroup behaviour...is the belief that the relevant social boundaries between the

27. Dovidio et al. 1998, 109.
28. This refers to the collective status of the group. Within a low status group there is a normal distribution of relative individual status.
29. Dovidio et al. 1998, 117.
30. Bettencourt et al. 2001, 521.
31. Tajfel 1981, 315.

groups are sharply drawn and immutable, in the sense that, for whatever reasons, it is impossible or at least very difficult for individuals to move from one group to the other."[32]

2. *Social creativity* is an intragroup mechanism that constructs positive social identity by either: (1) redefining the criterion for intergroup comparison; or (2) selecting a different out-group against which to evaluate the in-group.[33] An oppressed ethnic group may not compare favorably to their oppressors regarding the trait "power," and thus may elevate the evaluative trait "piety" over "power" in order to evaluate themselves positively vis-à-vis the dominant group (which of course is perceived as "impious"). Or, the oppressed group could compare itself only to an even less powerful group, again creating positive social identity. Social creativity strengthens particular group boundary markers and often occurs in Diaspora settings where the importance of intragroup interdependence is amplified.[34]

3. *Social competition* is the direct competition for status and resources. It includes collective social action, protest and intergroup violence.

Examples of each of these strategies are evident in Luke–Acts, though the Spirit works to chart a different way for the maintenance of positive identity for the (relatively) low status Jesus-groups.

2.1.4. Intergroup Conflict Resolution Strategies

Given the potentially dangerous trajectory created by intergroup evaluation, the creation of in-group bias (and out-group derogation) and potentially confrontational identity-maintenance strategies, what options are available for the reduction of identity-based conflict? SIT theorists have studied three options—each with limited results—for conflict reduction:

1. *Cross-cutting evaluative criteria*. This strategy involves the creation of evaluative criteria that avoid contested identity boundaries. One might raise the salience of "industriousness" to include some members from both of the conflicting groups marked by the traits "rich" and "poor." This has been successful in laboratory settings, but not with "real life" identities.[35]

32. Tajfel 1981, 245.
33. Jetten et al. 2005.
34. Brewer 1999, 438; Triandis 1995.
35. Brown 2000.

2. *Superordinate identity**. Moderate success has been achieved by attempts to incorporate two sub-identities into one new identity. The recent call for a renewed sense of "Britishness" among U.K. residents is an example of this strategy.[36] The insurmountable obstacle to this strategy is the fact that freshly united subgroups tend to conflict over which attributes are prototypical for the superordinate group.[37]

3. *Superordinate identity with retention of subgroup salience.* The most promising avenue for intergroup conflict reduction has been the creation of new superordinate identities that do not invalidate, but rather affirm distinct subgroup identities.[38] This can be even more effective if the new groups possess a common collaborative goal. This strategy can be seen in South Africa, where whites and blacks retained ethnic particularity under the "Rainbow People" superordinate identity.[39] Similar efforts have achieved modest success in Northern Ireland.[40] However, Hewstone contends that construction of common identity may only be strong enough to overcome powerful ethnic categorizations on a temporary basis.[41] I will argue that this approach appears to be the phenomenon most evident within the Spirit-formed communities described in Acts.

Despite consistent efforts at conflict resolution by those committed to understanding the role of social identity in intergroup conflict, real world social identities continue to be fertile sources of intergroup conflict.[42] This is especially true of ethnic identities and is heightened all the more when ethnic particularity is mutually reinforced by religious particularity.[43]

2.1.5. Social Identity and Entitlement

The comparative aspect of identity formation can have significant ramifications not only for intergroup relations but also for the relationships

---

36. See Gordon Brown's speech to the Fabian Society, 14 January 2006: http://www.fabians.org.uk/events/speeches/the-future-of-britishness (accessed 13 December 2010).
37. Mummenday and Wenzel 1999.
38. Dovidio et al. 1998; Gaertner et al. 1999; Brown 2000; Gonzalez and Brown 2000; Van Oudenhouven et al. 1996.
39. Tutu 1996; Gibson 2006.
40. Cairns 1994.
41. Hewstone 1996, 351.
42. Mullen et al. 1992, 117.
43. Wald 2005, 10.

between identity and resource allocation. Understanding the intimate relationship between identity and entitlement* will illuminate Luke–Acts at several points.⁴⁴

The first step in determining entitlement to a group's resources is the determination of who does or does not have access to a given resource or social benefit. Wenzel makes the unremarkable claim that members of the in-group have privileged access to group resources:

> All social entities that are perceived to be potential recipients of a resource distribution belong to what is called the "primary category." The primary category specifies who might be considered as a potential recipient at all, as opposed to those who are outside the allocation situation.⁴⁵

This is not the end of the process. In-groups have a tendency to divide into subgroups based upon prototypical group characteristics.⁴⁶ Subcategories "that are closer to the positively connoted end of the prototypical dimension, or that represent best the group value of this inclusive category, are valued more positively and perceived to be more deserving."⁴⁷ In other words, subgroups that perceive themselves as "normal" assume greater entitlement to the benefits of the group.⁴⁸

Subgroup claims to entitlement anticipate an acute problem: there are no purely objective measures of group prototypicality.⁴⁹ How do groups "know" what dimensions of the primary category are most prototypical? The answer is that within a primary category prototypicality is defined by *in-group projection**, a phenomenon in which a subgroup projects its own characteristics as normative for the entire group.⁵⁰ For example, research reveals that Germans who identify strongly as "German," project "German" identity as prototypical within the primary category "European." One result of this projection is that high "German" identifiers have proved more-likely to evaluate positively the 2001 decision to exclude Turkey from EU membership.⁵¹ The less benign aspect of in-group bias is

---

44. To my knowledge, I am the first to use research on social identity and entitlement for biblical interpretation (Kuecker 2009), though some interpreters associated with the New Perspective on Paul are alert to these dynamics, even if they speak more generally about "identity."
45. Wenzel 2001, 317.
46. Wenzel 2001, 317–18.
47. Wenzel 2001, 317–18.
48. By implication, less prototypical subgroups are not norm conforming and hence are "deviant" (Weber et al. 2002, 452; Waldzus et al. 2003, 32).
49. Weber et al. 2002, 452; Wenzel 2001, 319.
50. Wenzel et al. 2003, 261.
51. Research review in Wenzel 2001.

seen in the fact that the projection of German prototypicality renders Turks aprototypical and thus "justly" excludes them from the benefits of the primary category "European." Projection of subgroup prototypicality is elusively fluid and a subgroup's perceptions of precisely which of its features are "prototypical" vary with changing contexts and changing evaluative targets.[52]

Finally, individuals who have a strong sense of dual identity within the primary category are most likely to engage in projection of relative subgroup prototypicality.[53] To take an example from Luke's world, a person who identifies strongly as "Israelite" and "Nazarene" would be likely to assume that Nazarene identity is most reflective of normative Israelite identity. Strong dual identifiers are thus most likely to make powerful entitlement claims to the resources of their in-group.[54] This phenomenon emerges clearly in Luke 4 and Acts 6, as well as in some of Luke's descriptions of the activities of the apostles.

2.1.6. Social Identity Theory Summary

SIT leaves us with an unsurprising conclusion: diverse group affiliations lead to a world of divergent social identities that are not easy to reconcile. Coleman and Collins summarize this phenomenon well:

> It is a social scientific truism that identity is constructed, at whatever level (individual, cultural, social, national, transnational), through expressions of "difference"… Identity can never be created in a vacuum—it must always be produced in and through a set of relations with real or imagined others. Identifying the "in-group" makes little sense from an analytical or lay point of view unless one also identifies the "out-group(s)"… In this sense, the allocation of identity in relation to the self is both an inevitable outcome of human interaction and—at times—a more self-consciously adopted stance in relation to others.[55]

2.2. Ethnicity and Social Identity

Of the many group boundaries described in Luke–Acts, ethnic boundaries are the most intractable. For this reason, it is important briefly to discuss the essential similarities that ethnic identities bear with all other group identities, and then to note one important difference.

---

52. Waldzus et al. 2005.
53. Waldzus et al. 2003, 33.
54. This is negatively correlated with positive attitudes toward the out-group (Waldzus et al. 2003, 33).
55. Coleman and Collins 2004, 2.

It is popularly assumed that ethnic identities *result* from cultural distinctives (differences in language, religion or biological descent). This theoretical position, primordialism, ascendant in the first half of the twentieth century, hypothesized that ethnicity arose in *social isolation* and was caused by the distinct, reified cultural objects of a group.[56] Compelled by this theory, anthropologists rushed to isolated islands to find "primitive" peoples from whom they could observe the rise of ethnic identity in its "purest" forms. Within primordialism, "common descent" was believed to be the most powerful identity-forming agent:

> The attachment [between people sharing common descent] was not merely to the other family member as a person, but as a possessor of certain especially "significant relational" qualities, which could only be described as primordial...a certain ineffable significance is attributed to the tie of blood.[57]

The primordialist "ethnicity-arises-in-isolation" model was nuanced by Geertz who suggested that, *from the perspective of its actors* (an *emic* as opposed to an *etic* perspective), the "gross actualities" of "blood, speech, custom, and so on, are seen to have an ineffable, and at times overpowering coerciveness in and of themselves."[58]

Despite the popular perception that cultural distinctives *create* ethnic identity, the primordialist paradigm has a fatal flaw. Because primordialism expected ethnicity to arise in social isolation, it also predicted that increased globalization would lead to cultural assimilation and the chastening of ethnic identities. This has not proved true. Frederik Barth, drawing on the work of Max Weber and Everett Hughes (who emphasized the significance "group-ness" and differentiation from the "other" in identity formation), developed a fundamental point of departure from primordialist schemas.[59] According to Barth, ethnicity is not created by reified "cultural stuff"; it is the ethnic *boundary* that defines the group.[60] An ethnic group is not formed because of a common language or culture; rather, an ethnic group is defined by a sense "group-ness" ("self-ascription and ascription by others") that can exist only in reference to other groups.[61] Because ethnicity is formed by a bounded sense of "group-ness,"

---

56. The intellectual genealogy of primordialism flows through Tönnies, Schmalenbach, Schils and, indirectly, Geertz.
57. Schils 1957, 140.
58. Schils 1957, 258, 259.
59. Weber 1997, 385–98; Hughes 1994, 91. Jenkins 1997, 11 summarizes Hughes: "ethnic cultural differences are a function of 'group-ness,' the existence of a group is not a reflection of cultural difference."
60. Barth 1967, 15.
61. Barth 1967, 13–14.

the cultural objects of an ethnic group (language, religion, shared history etc.) can change dramatically over time while the sense of ethnic identity is perpetuated.[62] Jewish identity is a good example of this phenomenon. Contemporary Jews rightly see themselves as sharing an identity with ancient Israelites, though the practices that mark a twenty-first-century person as Jewish and those practices that marked ancient Israelites are very different. Cultural difference does not make ethnic identity; rather, ethnic identity creates a boundary in which cultural difference can develop.[63] "Ethnic identity is constituted by the "dynamic ebb and flow of social interaction, from which boundaries are constructed between 'us' and 'them'."[64]

Wallman's distillation of Barthianism demonstrates its compatibility with SIT:

> Ethnicity is the process by which "their" difference is used to enhance the sense of "us" for purposes of organisation or identification... Because it takes two, ethnicity can only happen at the boundary of "us," in contact or confrontation by contrast with "them." And as the sense of "us" changes, so the boundary between "us" and "them" shifts. Not only does the boundary shift, but the criteria which mark it change.[65]

Ethnic identity, like all group identities, is formed based on an evaluative comparison with the out-group. Thus ethnic identity, even with its typical emphasis on myths of common descent, can be fruitfully analyzed through the lens of SIT.

One critical distinction remains: the socially constructed nature of ethnic identity is only apparent at an etic level of observation. To those embedded within social systems (an emic perspective), ethnic identity *feels* primordial. As Jenkins helpfully nuances, "ethnic identity may be imagined, but it is emphatically not imaginary; locally that imagining may be very powerful."[66] To rob socially embedded actors of their powerful sense that ethnicity is a *primordial given* is to undermine our ability to

---

62. Barth 1967, 58 claimed an identity is "ethnic" when it "classifies a person in terms of his basic, most general identity, presumptively determined by his origin and background." There are no ethnic groups with pure biological descent. People who are clearly not biologically related can often gain membership to an ethnic group in spite of myths of common ancestry that control access to the group.

63. Hutchinson and Smith 1996, 6–7 have six diagnostic factors for determining whether groups are properly classed as "ethnic": (1) common proper name; (2) myth of common ancestry; (3) shared history; (4) common culture (i.e. customs, language, religion); (5) link with a homeland; (6) group solidarity.

64. Johnson 2006, 28.

65. Wallman 1979, 3.

66. Jenkins 1997, 47. Cf. Banks 1995, 185–87.

understand the tremendous affective pressures that ethnic boundaries exert upon members of social systems.[67] Understanding the depth of ethnic commitments, their often exclusive loyalty claims, and the way ethnic boundaries create fertile ground for conflict only serves to heighten the formidable nature of the group boundaries so prominent in Luke–Acts.[68]

2.2.1. Ethnicity in Antiquity

Little needs to be said about the well-known relevance of ethnicity in the ancient world. Ancients were keenly cognizant of the "people" to which they belonged and the "peoples" that surrounded them.[69] Pliny, for example, is aware of 112 "tribes" in northern Italy, 49 *gentes* in a part of the Alps, 150 *populi* in Macedonia, and 30 "peoples" in the Crimea.[70] Josephus identifies over 30 ethnic groups in his *Contra Apionem*.[71] Ancient ethnographers demonstrated an obsession with the "other," often describing people with increasingly animalistic characteristics the further away they lived from the socio-geographic center of the ethnographer's own in-group.[72] These "ethnic" identities were regularly the source of conflict in the ancient world.[73] The Maccabean revolt is a ready example of the tension created by the impingement of one "people" upon another.[74] Luke's texts were written into a world filled with competing ethnic identities and ethnic antagonism rears its ugly head at various points in Luke–Acts.[75]

---

67. Cairns 1982, 277 cites Whyte 1978 on identity-based conflict in Northern Ireland, "Anyone who studies the Ulster conflict must be struck by the intensity of feelings. It seems to go beyond what is required by a rational defense of the divergent interests which undoubtedly exist. There is an irrational element here, a welling-up of deep unconscious forces."
68. See especially Luke 4:24–30; 9:51–56; Acts 6:1–6; 22:17–23.
69. "One of the strongest modes of identification for individuals in the Roman world, one that was prior, logically and historically, to that of the city or state, was that of belonging to a 'people'" (Shaw 2000, 380).
70. *Natural History* V.4.29–30; II.15.116; IV.10–33, 12.85, respectively.
71. Esler 2009, 73–92.
72. Tacitus (*Geography* 5.4.153–59) describes inhabitants of Ierne (Ireland) as incestuous man-eaters who are "more savage than the Britons" and adds: "I am saying this only with the understanding that I have no trustworthy witnesses for it"(!).
73. Hewstone 1996, 351 calls ethnicity the "final frontier" in the mitigation of identity-based conflict.
74. 1 Macc 1:41–2:1; Josephus, *A.J.* 12.138–44.
75. Especially Luke 4:24–30; 9:51–56; Acts 6:1–6; 11:1–18; 15:1–4; 16:19–24; 19:23–41; 22:17–23.

Regarding Luke's own social categories, it is essential to note that Luke's use of ἔθνος/ἔθνη always connotes an *ethnic* category. In Luke's context ἔθνος was part of a vocabulary of group-differentiation. First appearing in Homeric literature to designate a "group" of something (i.e. bees, birds or Lycians), it came to be used in ancient Greece to categorize "barbarians" living outside the administrative influence of the Greek citystates.[76] In the parlance, γένος was reserved for Greeks while ἔθνος was used for non-Greeks.[77] This was advanced by Rome, which produced an even greater caricature of the barbarous ἔθνη.[78] In Luke's usage, the ἔθνη comprise a social category only intelligible from an emic Israelite perspective. No one self-identified as ἔθνη (save perhaps for non-Israelites attached to the synagogue). ἔθνη constituted the "them" against which Israelite identity could be forged.[79] The fact that 36 of the 43 instances of ἔθνος in Luke–Acts occur after Acts 10 indicates that ethnicity is the salient boundary and point of differentiation when the gospel encounters non-Israelites.[80]

2.2.2. Ethnic Language in this Study

Because ethnic identity is experienced at an emic level as a powerful, primordial given, and because self-identifications are the most accurate way to discuss the identities of a given group, in this study I will refer to the ethnic group with historic attachment to Judea as "Israelites." The scholarly debate over the proper nomenclature ("Jew" vs. "Judean") for this group has served to remind us that those commonly referred to as "Jews" who practice "Judaism" were not adherents to a "religion" but considered themselves a people group with their own god (who happened to be the cosmic Creator), similar to most other people groups.[81] In Luke–Acts, this group refers to itself as "Israel"/"Israelites" whenever engaged in discourse with a fellow member of the ethnic in-group.[82]

---

76. Hutchinson and Smith 1996, 4.
77. Tonkin et al. 1989, 11–17.
78. Hutchinson and Smith 1996, 4.
79. Elliott 2007, 124 n. 13. See also Stanley 1996. Jenkins 1997, 81 clarifies: "While social groups define themselves, their name(s), their nature(s), and their boundary(ies), social categories are named, characterized and delineated by others." Israel = in-group self-definition; ἔθνη = out-group categorization.
80. Like the Synoptics, there are several instances in Acts when ἔθνος (sg., never pl.) denotes a people group that may be Israelite (Acts 24:2, 10). Paul calls the Judeans his own ἔθνος (24:17; 26:4; 28:19). Esler 2009 argues that for Josephus ἔθνος (sg.) can be used to refer to Israel but that ἔθνη (pl.) never includes Israel.
81. See especially Elliott 2007.
82. See the detailed discussion in Chapter 8.

Because this autonym carries identity-shaping ramifications I will retain it to reflect the social identity of the group in question.[83] Further, I will refer to those Luke categorizes as ἔθνη as "non-Israelites," for the ἔθνη are only a coherent category over against Israelite identity.[84] Luke is alert to the variation between particular ethnic groups who compose the ἔθνη (see his contrasting characterization of the rustic residents of Lystra and the cosmopolitan Athenians in Acts 14:8–18; 17:16–34). Yet Luke is aware enough of particularly Israelite identity concerns to understand the relevance of the category ἔθνη for the description of the undifferentiated ethnic "they" in distinction from the Israelite "we."

2.3. Ethnic Identity and Israel

There were a range of options with which first-century Israelites could answer the question, "What does being a faithful Israelite mean with respect to the ethnic 'other'?" Texts that describe Diaspora, exile, return from exile, or Israelite responses to subjugation in the land provide good test cases from which to survey the effect of threatened (thus intensified) Israelite identity on the ethnic "other." This brief survey of Second Temple texts will reveal that there was no singular Israelite response to the "other," but that responses could range from social creativity to, more infrequently, social competition. A certain ambiguity in (even apparently negative) Israelite responses to the "other" arises from the fact that the strengthening of Israelite in-group boundaries was frequently done with a conscious awareness of Israel's status as God's elect people. In this regard, Israelite in-group bias arising from increased in-group solidarity could be largely positive and did not demand (and did not always feature) out-group derogation. However, as we saw earlier, in-group bias is often closely constitutive of out-group antipathy. The variegated responses to the "other" in these Second Temple texts provide a context that will highlight Luke's sharp critique of the way *one particular expression* of Israelite identity—and a certain expression of social identity in general—can impinge upon the "other." Rather than organizing the texts chronologically, I will organize them according to their responses to the ethnic "other," from the most conciliatory to the most conflictual.[85]

---

83. Though the use of "Israel"/"Israelite" poses its own problems for other literature, for the sake of consistency I will use "Israel"/"Israelites" to refer to "Jews"/"Judeans" in other relevant primary texts examined in this survey.

84. See, rightly, Stanley 1997, 101–24.

85. Attempts to trace historical development of attitudes toward the "other" are fraught with difficulty and are beyond the scope of this survey. Widely varied responses to the "other" occur across temporal and geographical distance. Strong

2.3.1. Letter of Aristeas

Because Israelites are honored guests and translators of their own sacred texts, there is little threat to Israelite identity depicted in the *Letter of Aristeas* (ca. 100 B.C.E., plus or minus 125 years, perhaps originating from Alexandria).[86] Aristeas famously describes the Law of Moses as forming

> unbroken palisades and iron walls to prevent [Israelites]...from mixing with any of the other peoples in any matter, being thus kept pure in body and soul, preserved from false beliefs, and worshiping the only God omnipotent over all creation.[87]

Yet even this tight boundary does not preclude interaction with others. The Israelite embassy to Egypt is commendable because

> they rose above conceit and contempt of other people, and instead engaged in discourse and listening to and answering each and every one, as is meet and right.[88]

The *Letter of Aristeas* demonstrates that when Israelite identity is not threatened, strong in-group bias does not necessarily have detrimental effects on relationships with non-Israelites. It should be noted that the shared meals between Israelites and Egyptians were meals in parallel, not meals in common, and therefore hardly can be described as intimate intergroup contact.[89]

2.3.2. Tobit

Tobit (Palestinian or eastern Diaspora provenance, ca. 250–175 B.C.E.) sets up a tension between "homeland" and "exile" in its prologue.[90] For Tobit, increased identification as "Israelite" is not detrimental to the "nations," who are included in the redemptive work of Israel's God as a result of Israel's faithful witness.[91] In other words, here in-group love exists without out-group hate (though out-group love is hardly evident).

out-group antipathy occurs in Ezra–Nehemiah (ca. 400–300 B.C.E.) and 1 and 2 Maccabees (ca. 150–63 B.C.E.). More congenial attitudes toward the out-group appear in the *Letter of Aristeas* (Alexandria?) and Tobit (Palestine or eastern Diaspora). This variability underscores the plurality of responses to the "other" and supports my strategy of discussing sources based upon their posture toward the out-group.

86. Davila 2005, 125.
87. *Letter of Aristeas* 139.
88. *Letter of Aristeas* 122.
89. *Letter of Aristeas* 142. See Esler 1998, 112–16.
90. Ego 2005, 70. For background, see deSilva 2002, 69.
91. Tobit 13:34; 14:5–8. Ego 2005, 53–54 notes the transcendence of the border between Israel and the nations.

Ego notes that "the strengthening of Israelite identity attains special importance" in Tobit's Diaspora framework.[92] From the start, Tobit portrays his relatives as abstaining from idol worship and the food of the ἔθνη. Tobit's investigation of the angel Raphael's tribal ancestry suggests a worldview in which ethnic identity is a reliable predictor of ethical character.[93] Finally, Tobit counsels Tobias,

> Love your brethren, and in your heart do not disdain your brethren and the sons and daughters of your people by refusing to take a wife for yourself from among them. Remember, my son, that Noah, Abraham, Isaac, and Jacob, our fathers of old, all took wives from among their brethren.[94]

Exogamy for Tobit is an act of disloyalty to the people.[95] Pressure toward endogamy is a strategy for the preservation of group identity.[96] Yet Tobit remains an example of the possibility that in-group bias does not automatically lead to an overtly negative view of non-Israelites or to outgroup antagonism.

2.3.3. Jubilees

Jubilees (ca. mid-second century B.C.E., originally in Hebrew and likely of Palestinian provenance) provides an example of one specific form of social creativity: the legitimizing retrojection of identity markers to a primeval past.[97] In rewriting Genesis, *Jubilees* locates Israelite covenantal distinctives, ranging from circumcision to Torah obedience, as features of the primeval history in Gen 1–11.[98] Levitical laws regarding childbirth impurity, Sabbath laws, and circumcision (a mark possessed by angels) are narrated into the earliest chapters of Genesis.[99] This serves to legitimize

---

92. Ego 2005, 46. Collins 2005, 27 calls observance of the law *en toto* the key boundary marker for Tobit.
93. Tobit 5:4–9.
94. Tobit 4:13. Levine 1992, 105–17 notes "In the Diaspora, no immediately clear solid ground for self-definition exists" but that genealogy helps produce identity.
95. The connection between exogamy and πορνεία in 4:12 hints at the perceived idolatrous nature of non-Israelites, a point made by Witherington 1998, 462; 2001, 248 regarding the relationship between non-Israelites, idol worship and cultic sex. Cf. Heike 2005, 113.
96. Pitkanen 2006, 115.
97. Hellerman 2003; Cf. Halpern-Amaru 1994, 25. For a Roman example, see Jupiter's declaration to Venus, "To the Roman race I set limits neither in space nor time: Unending sway have I bestowed on them" (*Aeneid* I.278–79). For the date and provenance, see van Ruiten 2000, 2.
98. For a full treatment of "rewritten history" in *Jubilees*, see van Ruiten 2000.
99. *Jub.* 2; 3; 15:27–28. Christiansen 1995, 102 notes that for *Jubilees* circumcision is the "decisive mark of identity…a symbol of affirmation of the covenant, a mark of

Israelite boundary markers in a way that heightens a timeless *ontological* distinction between Israel and the nations. The command to Abraham in *Jub.* 22:16 is a good example, "Separate yourself from the ἔθνη, and do not eat with them...because all of their ways are contaminated, and despicable, and abominable."

Jubilees retells the covenantal history in a way that presents Sinai as a restoration of the Noachic covenant. In effect, the particularity of the Sinai covenant subsumes the universality of the Noachic covenant. This strategy of identity justification through revisionist history solidifies "national and social boundaries" in powerful ways.[100] The potentially pernicious effect of this expression of in-group bias is based upon a comparative evaluation in which non-Israelites are defined by negations. They are identified as:

> *not* holy peoples, *not* of God's possession, ruled by angels/demons (cf. Jub 10:8–11). By identifying the outside with what is negative and by defining its identity in opposition to Israel's identity...a denigration of the outside world is expressed.[101]

2.3.4. 4 Ezra

What *Jubilees* projects backward, *4 Ezra* casts in the apocalyptic future. Written in the shadow of the disorienting force of the Temple destruction (Palestinian provenance, ca. 100 C.E.), the text describes ideal identity via an eschatological return of the ten "lost" tribes who have cunningly kept themselves ready for re-gathering.[102] After being taken into Assyrian exile,

> The tribes formed this plan for themselves, that they would leave the multitude of the nations and go to a more distant region, where mankind had never lived, that there at least they might keep their statutes which they had not kept in their own land... Then they dwelt there until the last times; and now, when they are about to come again, the Most High will stop the channels of the river again, so that they may be able to pass over.[103]

For the author of *4 Ezra*, the necessary precondition for covenant faithfulness is detachment from all non-Israelite contact.[104] The return to the

---

both the internal and external boundary, of national, social and religious belonging, and of inclusion and exclusion and election."
  100. Christiansen 1995, 70. Cf. Endres 1987, 250.
  101. Christiansen 1995, 89 (emphasis original).
  102. Fuller 2006, 75–76. For the date and provenance, see Davila 2005, 138–39, cf. deSilva 2002, 323.
  103. *4 Ezra* 13:41–42, 46–47.
  104. A similar impulse in the Qumran community is described by 1QS 8.12–16.

land comes after the nations have been destroyed by the *law*, a chief marker of Israelite identity in *4 Ezra*.[105] Fourth Ezra actually moves away from full-scale ethnocentric covenantalism toward a Torah-based remnant ideology.[106] The key factor, from an intergroup perspective, remains the fact that for the northern tribes, social isolation is apocalyptically depicted as a necessary precondition for faithful Israelite identity, even if not all ethnic Israelites achieve this ideal.

2.3.5. *Ezra and Nehemiah*

We now move to texts that begin to describe both *intra*group and *inter*group ramifications of Israelite in-group bias. In Ezra and Nehemiah ethnic purity is the *sine qua non* of Israelite identity.[107] Ezrahite returnees who could not prove their ancestry or "whether they belonged to Israel" were deemed temporarily unclean, and those who could not show their priestly lineage were deemed unfit for the priesthood.[108] Renewed fidelity to the law is highlighted as central to the protection of the identity of the returned people, and threat from the outside immediately strengthens ethnic in-group bias.[109]

This intensified in-group bias had striking implications for relations with non-Israelites. Most obvious in Ezra is the rejection of exogamy and the imposition of divorce from foreign wives.[110] The restriction against intermarriage is based upon a holy/unholy distinction between Israel and the nations.[111] Notably, Ezra's ban on exogamy goes beyond the Deuteronomic legislation, which only explicitly prohibits intermarriage with women of the seven Canaanite nations.[112] This intensification of Israelite identity and fortification of intergroup boundaries must have left many women and their children in a vulnerable state.[113]

---

105. *4 Ezra* 13:38.
106. Longenecker 1991, 129.
107. Dating Ezra–Nehemiah is difficult. Williamson 1985, xxxvi suggests a general date of 400 B.C.E. for Ezra 7–Neh 13 and 300 B.C.E. for Ezra 1–6.
108. Ezra 2:59–62; Neh 7:61–65.
109. Neh 4:14.
110. Ezra 9–10; Neh 10:30. Nehemiah initiates a pledge not to take foreign wives in the future.
111. Ezra 9:2.
112. See Deut 7:1–4. Blenkinsopp 2006, 67 observes that there is no law "mandating coercive divorce." Cf. Esler 1987, 85. Richard Bauckham has suggested to me in personal conversation that Ezra's ruling is a halakhic interpretation of Deut 7:1–4 based upon the people who are now in the land.
113. Heike 2005, 103.

Even more telling with regard to conceptions of Israelite identity is the interaction with the "people of the land" in Ezra 4:1–3.[114] This group, whose identity is contested by scholars, offers to assist in the rebuilding of the Temple, claiming that "we worship your God as you do, and we have been sacrificing to him ever since the days of Esar-haddon king of Assyria who brought us here."[115] The offer is rejected immediately: "You have nothing to do with us in building a house to our God; but we alone will build to the LORD, the God of Israel."[116] The strong insider/outsider language ("you," "us," "we," "our") sends a clear message; Israelite identity is based upon ethnic identity and not simply fidelity to the God of Israel.[117] The summary of Nehemiah's success highlights the attitude toward the "other" in both Ezra and Nehemiah, "Thus I cleansed them [the returnees] from everything foreign… Remember me, O my God, for good."[118] Wright correctly observes that Nehemiah's wall was both physical and social, "repairing the physical ramparts around Jerusalem and rebuilding the ethnic boundaries around Judah."[119]

Again, we need to remind ourselves that Israel's response to the "other" is somewhat ambiguous. In-group fidelity is commanded by God, as is a certain level of separation from ethnic others. However, the call to faithfulness for Israel was always meant to serve as a witness to God *for the sake of the nations* (Gen 12:3). The failure of the intensified legal observance in Ezra–Nehemiah to include the Levitical provisions for foreigners in the land is perhaps another indicator of the way that community can be distorted and that social creativity can be used to exclude. Luke will have much to say regarding these sorts of expressions of social identity.

2.3.6. First and Second Maccabees

While social creativity (with both intergroup and intragroup ramifications) was the primary identity-maintenance strategy employed in Second Temple texts, social competition was a viable alternative. First and Second Maccabees are primary examples of this strategy in the

114. Ezra 1–6 may be a later addition to Ezra–Nehemiah (Williamson 1985, xxxiv–xxxv).
115. Ezra 4:2.
116. Ezra 4:3.
117. Nehemiah's retelling of the Abrahamic covenant (Neh 9:8) omits the blessing of the nations (Gen 12:3), perhaps betraying an ideology that has little room for the ethnic "other." Complicating the reading of this passage is the apparent assumption of syncretism made by the Judeans returning from Babylon.
118. Neh 13:30–31.
119. Wright 2004, 339.

Second Temple period. Both texts interpreted the threat from Antiochus IV as a threat to Israelite identity.[120] First Maccabees (Palestinian provenance [?], mid-second to mid-first century B.C.E.) blamed the threat almost entirely upon non-Israelite aggression, but 2 Maccabees (uncertain provenance, mid-second to mid-first century B.C.E.) ascribed significant culpability to aprototypical Israelites, especially the apostate priests Jason and Menelaus.[121] The response to identity threat in 1 Maccabees was two-fold. Most obviously, Israelites took up arms against their oppressors, couching military action in symbols of Israelite ethnic identity: law observance and prototypical piety.[122] Those who participated in the campaign against Antiochus were "zealous for the law" and "support the covenant."[123] They hoped to "avenge" and pay back the ἔθνη in full.[124] Here, in-group bias was expressed through violent resistance. The rhetoric is laced with intertextual allusions, grounding this expression of identity in the stories of Israelite history, especially those of Phinehas and David.[125] The success of the Maccabean programme is described in eschatological terms: once the yoke of the ἔθνη is removed from Israel (13:41), old men sit in the streets (14:9), and each person sits under his own vine and fig trees with no one to make them afraid (14:12).[126]

The second strategy in 1 Maccabees, extreme pressure toward in-group conformity, was manifest most blatantly in the forced circumcision of all males within the borders of Israel.[127] Immediately after the foreign threat was subdued, Jonathan turned to strengthening group boundaries by acting to "judge the people" and "destroy the godless out of Israel."[128] There is no doubt that when the author tells us that Simon "built the walls of Jerusalem higher," he—like the author of Nehemiah—was referring to physical and social walls.[129]

---

120. 1 Macc 1:41–64; 2 Macc 4:11–17.
121. Doran 1981. On 1 Maccabees' provenance: Metzger 1957, 130; date: deSilva 2002, 248. On 2 Maccabees' provenance: Judea: van Henten 1997, 50; Alexandria: Metzger 1957, 140; date: deSilva 2002, 269.
122. 1 Macc 3:44–48.
123. 1 Macc 2:27. Dunn 2008, 11–13 draws attention to the tradition of "zeal" that expresses "dedication to maintain Israel's set-apartness to God" (p. 12) and is exemplified by Simeon and Levi, Phinehas, Elijah and the Maccabees.
124. 1 Macc 2:66b–67.
125. deSilva 2002, 257.
126. Cf. 1 Kgs 4:25; Isa 36:16; Hos 2:18; Mic 4:4; Zech 3:10.
127. 1 Macc 2:45–46.
128. 1 Macc 9:73b.
129. 1 Macc 14:37.

If 1 Maccabees emphasizes the role of exemplary Israelites in the destruction of enemies and the forced correction of aprototypical in-group members, 2 Maccabees highlights divine agency in response to Israelite piety. The author demonstrates a keen awareness of the dangers of exile as it impinges upon identity.[130] deSilva argues that the goal of the text is the "promotion of continued or resumed commitment to Jewish cultural values as the path to national security and prosperity."[131] This seems correct; Israelite victories are portrayed as the result of God's action in response to faithful expressions of Israelite identity.[132] Further, the ill fate of some Israelites is attributed to their appropriation of non-Israelite customs.[133] The message of 2 Maccabees is clear: betrayal of in-group norms leads to the destruction of the in-group, and vice versa.

That identity can be marshaled in different ways in the face of threat is demonstrated in 1 and 2 Maccabees. Both texts are expressions of social competition, one crediting exemplary Israelites and one crediting divine action for the success of the Maccabean campaign. What is unambiguous, and shared by both texts, is the sense that threats to Israelite identity must be destroyed—often violently—whether they originate from within or without.[134]

2.3.7. Summary of Israelite Responses to the "Other"

This brief survey has demonstrated that a wide range of options for identity maintenance were available to Israelites experiencing perceived identity threat. Two caveats should here be noted. First, not all Israelites should be considered high ethnic identifiers. It is likely that texts were written by those with a strong sense of social identity (or at least those with interested patrons who had a strong sense of Israelite identity), and thus textual evidence may skew toward high ethnic identifiers. It is important, therefore, to resist totalizing generalizations. However, these texts (including Luke–Acts) give us license to speak, at a certain level of abstraction, in broad generalities. Indeed, Luke–Acts demonstrates clearly

---

130. 2 Macc 1:27–29; 2:1–3.
131. deSilva 2002, 266.
132. 2 Macc 7; 11:38.
133. 2 Macc 12:40.
134. Though causal connections are impossible to map, one interesting datum regarding the influence of the Maccabean histories on Israelite identity is the fact that in our period of interest six of the nine most popular male names and the three most prominent female names were names of the Hasmonean family (Bauckham 2006, 85, 89; cf. Ilan 2002). When occupied peoples name their children after revolutionary heroes it may well be that the names themselves indicate a certain posture toward the "other."

that the negotiation of Israelite identity vis-à-vis the ethnic "other" was a contested issue.¹³⁵ Second, we must not fall into the trap of imagining ethnocentrism as a particularly Israelite issue. Ethnocentrism was a pervasive feature of most every ἔθνος in the ancient Mediterranean. Rome's adaptation of the Greek construction of the "barbarian" is a fine case in point for the construction of (Roman) in-group identity in contradistinction from the foil provided by the ethnic "other" (βάρβαρος).¹³⁶ At various points the Acts text will serve as a window on extreme expressions of ethnocentrism from non-Israelite ethnic groups as well.¹³⁷

2.4. Conclusion

The preceding discussion of SIT, its ramifications for intergroup relations, and the evidence for a wide variety of identity strengthening strategies in Second Temple texts combine to prepare us well for a reading of the interplay between the Spirit and social identity (especially ethnic identity) in Luke–Acts. Luke's text provides ample data that are helpfully interpreted through the lens of SIT, much of which demonstrates "regular" intragroup and intergroup dynamics. Namely, we will see that positive social identity is usually maintained by negatively evaluating the "other"—a move that often leads to the creation of barriers for intergroup contact. However, we will also see that when Luke brings the Spirit into intergroup contexts, typical identity maintenance strategies are powerfully subverted. It is in the subversion of these "normal" intergroup processes that for Luke, precisely in the midst of the Jesus-effected fulfillment of God's ancient covenantal purposes, the Holy Spirit emerges as *the central figure in the formation of a new social identity that affirms yet chastens and transcends ethnic identity.*

2.5. Social Identity Theory Glossary

Allocentric identity: An identity characterized by interest centered in persons other than oneself. Allocentric identity entails the ability to overcome normal intergroup identity processes in which positive social

---

135. The conflict between some Jesus-following Pharisees and Paul, Barnabas, Peter and James in Acts 15 is a good example of the contested nature of this issue as it impinged upon the ethnic "other."
136. See Shaw 2000; E. Hall 1989; J. Hall 1999; Harrison 2002; Baldson 1979. For Roman attitudes toward Israelites, see Stern 1984.
137. Acts 16:19–24; 19:23–41.

identity is maintained through the negative evaluation of the "other." Allocentric identity is marked by a capability to express in-group love and out-group love simultaneously.

Entitlement: "What one should get on the basis of what one has done or who one is."[138] Entitlement creates assumptions about access to group resources.

Exemplar: A member of a group who best reflects the prototypical characteristics of the group. These characteristics are "automatically assigned, along with long-term criterial traits, to all members" of the in-group.[139]

In-group bias: "In-group bias follows from a sequence of social-categorization, social identification, and social-group comparison driven by a pressure to positively differentiate one's in-group from relevant out-groups" and is the positive evaluation of the in-group over against other social groups.[140] High in-group bias often results in negative intergroup attitudes or relations.

In-group projection: The projection of the characteristics of one's own in-group or subgroup as normative or prototypical within the broader group context.[141] The projection of relative prototypicality leads to entitlement claims from subgroups.

Nested (or dual) identity: The possession of multiple social identities based upon participation in multiple social groups.[142] These identities become salient based upon contextual factors, such as the social identity of the person with whom one is interacting.

Out-group homogeneity: The assumption by members of a group that out-group members are similar to one another and that the out-group as a whole is more homogeneous than the in-group.[143] This results from the deindividuation of the out-group.

---

138. Wenzel 2001, 315.
139. Turner 1982, 29.
140. Bettencourt et al. 2001, 521.
141. Waldzus et al. 2003, 32.
142. Esler 2003, 73.
143. Brown 2000, 750.

Superordinate identity: A new identity that transcends existing group categories and incorporates diverse groups under a common identity.[144]

Terminal identity: The most significant social identity a person possesses, which "embraces and integrates a number of lesser identities."[145] Usually the terminal identity is based upon the answer to the question, "Who are my people?"

---

144. Brown 2000, 751.
145. Cairns 1982, 281.

Chapter 3

EXPANDING THE ETHNIC HORIZON:
THE SPIRIT AND ALLOCENTRIC IDENTITY
IN LUKE 1–2

Luke's Gospel opens with an immediate and stark contrast of identities. As the polished Greek of the prologue gives way to the rougher, Septuagintal Greek of the narrative proper, images of Temple, priesthood and the deliverance of God's people move to the fore.[1] Yet these markers of Israelite identity are located within the shadow of foreign oppression: Luke describes Roman client rule in Luke 1:5a and Roman decretal power in Luke 2:1–2. These early chapters of Luke, marked by symbols of ethnic identity, are saturated by references to the Spirit.[2] This overlap between Spirit and identity is no coincidence. While Luke's correlation between the Spirit and identity builds cumulatively and shines most brightly later in Luke–Acts, the birth narratives are an essential foundation for Luke's understanding of the relationship between ethnic identity, the Spirit and the "other." Two closely related features of Luke 1–2 will be examined in this chapter. First, we will examine Luke's use of allusions to Israel's ancestral and covenantal history to demonstrate the privileged status of Israelite identity even in light of Roman domination. Second, we will examine the nascent relationship between the overt influence of the Spirit upon an individual and a certain posture toward the "other" in the "birth hymns" of Luke 1–2.[3] This is our initial

---

1. See Hutchinson and Smith 1994, 6–7 for markers of ethnic identity. On the Greek of the prologue vs. the LXX-style Greek of the narrative, see Nolland 1989, 17; Ravens 1995, 28.
2. Luke 1–4 has a greater density of Spirit references (14 references; 3.5 per chapter) than Acts (56 references; 2 per chapter). Luke 5–24 contains only four Spirit references.
3. I will use "birth hymns" to describe the words spoken by Mary, Zechariah, the angels, Simeon and (indirectly) Anna.

introduction to the Spirit's formation of an *allocentric identity* capable of maintaining positive social identity without negatively evaluating the out-group.⁴

3.1. Zechariah and Elizabeth: Awakening Israelite Ethnic Identity

As we noted earlier, perceived in-group identity threat is one of the primary factors that increases identification with the in-group and intensifies in-group bias.⁵ The introduction of Herod the Great at the head of Luke's narrative (Luke 1:5) brings just such a threat to bear upon Luke's (Israelite) hearers.⁶ Herod himself was anything but an exemplary Israelite. Pharisaic criticism of his ethnic lineage prompted Herod to commission the composition of a false genealogy.⁷ Josephus panned Herod for negatively impacting Israelite identity and practice by constructing three temples to Caesar Augustus within the boundaries of Judea, introducing the quinquennial games in Caesar's honor, promulgating image-like trophies and throwing men to wild beasts:⁸

> We became guilty of great wickedness afterward, while those religious observances which used to lead the multitude to piety were now neglected.⁹

In the background of the Herodian threat to Israelite identity stood the threatening Roman "other," a pervasive reminder of Israel's low-status ethnic position. The activation of Roman domination and its implied threat is a consistent Lukan strategy and appears again at Luke 2:1–2 and 3:1–2, each time as the backdrop against which Luke narrates an important act of Israelite deliverance. With regard to Israelite ethnic identity,

---

4. SIT demonstrates that in-group love typically has (perhaps unintended) negative consequences for out-groups. The Spirit in Luke–Acts subverts these identity-forming processes.

5. Grant 1993, 43; Verkuyten 2005, 122; Gibson 2006, 697.

6. Tannehill 1996, 40 notes the importance of narrative beginnings: "What the narrator presents first, when the reading is seeking basic orientation, will stand out and affect the reading of the rest of the story." Rowe 2006, 42–43, references Harvey 1965, 52: "Literarily speaking, it would be hard to over-stress the importance of a character's first introduction into what Harvey called 'the web of human relationships'."

7. Cohen 1999, 24.

8. Temples were built in Caesarea Maritima (Josephus, *B.J.* 1.414; *A.J.* 15.339); Sebaste (*B.J.* 1.403; *A.J.* 15.298); Banias (*B.J.* 1.404; *A.J.* 15.363–64). See McLaren 2005, 259.

9. Josephus, *A.J.* 15.267; cf. *A.J.* 15.267–76; 17.255; *B.J.* 2.44.

3. Expanding the Ethnic Horizon

this strategy can be conceptualized at an etic level as "social creativity," the selection of alternative criteria upon which to make intergroup comparisons with higher status out-groups. When Israel's covenantal status was the evaluative criteria for comparison with Rome, Israel was able to maintain positive group identity and portray its own ethnic identity as high status.

Set in counterpoint to the brief but weighted notation of Herod's client rule are Zechariah and Elizabeth, two exemplary Israelites who themselves are flanked by a multitude of faithful Israelites. Luke emphasizes the importance of this couple in several ways. First, the narrative introduction to the pair contains a degree of detail largely without parallel in his text; we learn their age, ancestral lineage, occupational status, reproductive status and ethical status:[10]

> In the days of Herod, king of Judea, there was a priest named Zechariah, of the division of Abijah; and he had a wife of the daughters of Aaron, and her name was Elizabeth. And they were both righteous before God, walking in all the commandments and ordinances of the Lord blameless. But they had no child, because Elizabeth was barren, and both were advanced in years.[11]

These identifying features highlight the chief markers of ethnic identity: common ancestry (from Abijah and Aaron), shared history (Israel's covenantal history), common culture (faithfulness to the commandments) and a sense of communal solidarity.[12] Second, Zechariah's priestly ministration establishes him as a mediating representative for "the whole multitude of the people" (Luke 1:12). Third, Zechariah and Elizabeth (and their son John) are the first in the Gospel who act under the influence of the Spirit.[13] Finally, in a powerfully allusive way Luke awakens

---

10. My emphasis on the couple's significance runs counter to Malina and Rohrbaugh 2003, 225 who claim Zechariah "is mentioned at all only because of what Luke has to say about the birth of John and Jesus."

11. Luke 1:5-6.

12. Hutchinson and Smith 1996, 5-6. This information is comparable to the core elements essential to defining the essence of a human in Greco-Roman encomium: origin, training, deeds of soul, deeds of fortune (children). See Neyrey 1994, 177-206.

13. Luke 1:41-42, 67. It is more appropriate to say Mary is "acted upon" by the Spirit since her experience with the Spirit in 1:35 is passive compared to active expressions by Elizabeth and Zechariah. Commentators generally have not recognized this distinction. Nolland 1989, 54-56 makes no comparison, but suggests Elizabeth's active role results from her "inspired interpretation of the movement of the unborn child" (66). Green 1997, 90 notes "divine agency" in Mary's case, but does not differentiate between her experience and that of Zechariah and Elizabeth. Ravens (1995, 26) observes the Spirit-influence upon all three, but nothing more.

Israelite identity styled after Abraham and Sarah, the recipients of God's covenantal promises for Israel and the nations. It is this final point that is crucially important for Luke. As noted above, Luke is aware that the promise to Abraham and Sarah extends to "all the families of the earth" (Gen 12:3; cf. Acts 3:25). For Luke, the incorporation of the ἔθνη into the people of God (accomplished in Acts but proleptically anticipated in Luke) is the fulfillment of the Abrahamic covenant (and, by extension, the promises to David [Luke 1:32–33, 69–71; Acts 15:16–18]). The activation of Abraham and Sarah-like identity, the prototypical recipients of the covenant promise whose fulfillment includes "all the families of the earth," sets Luke's two volumes off on a trajectory that will clarify how, precisely, this multi-ethnic people of God will come to be. This tension is especially pertinent in the context of serious identity threat from the ethnic other (in the form of Rome and, given Josephus' testimony, Herod) that Luke activates in this section. As we will come to see, prototypical Israelites who practice Abraham and Sarah-like covenantal faithfulness can indeed recognize that Israel's privileged covenantal status is properly deployed when it issues in an identity that regards both the in-group and the out-group. To use the language of SIT, Luke will show us that in-group love and out-group love are not mutually exclusive, but that their complementarity is possible only through the transforming power of the Holy Spirit. We now turn our attention to the way that Luke activates Abraham and Sarah-like identity at the head of his narrative.

While Zechariah and Elizabeth stand in the wider biblical tradition of barren couples, it is Sarah and Abraham who are for Luke "everywhere present and nowhere mentioned."[14] The overwhelming number of allusions to Abraham and Sarah highlight Zechariah and Elizabeth's status as exemplary Israelites. Allusive techniques are powerful tools for activating identity, serving to bring contemporary events into a "hermeneutical relationship" with older texts.[15] Perhaps this is especially true for allusions to Abraham, a key figure for Israelite identity.[16] There are no fewer

---

Danker (1988, 38, 40) appears to differentiate between the "filling" of the Spirit that leads to the actions of John and Elizabeth and the "unique demonstration of God's power" that results in the birth of Jesus.

14. Rowe 2006, 33–34. Rowe is speaking about the patriarchs in general. For barren couples, see Gen 15:2; 1 Sam 1:1–2; Judg 13:2. See Bock 1994, 78; Fitzmyer 1981, 317, 323; Nolland 1989, 25–27.

15. Fishbane 1985, 351.

16. Hendel 2005, 31: "The memory of Abraham serves in varying measures to articulate Israelite identity, to motivate the remembering agent to take appropriate actions, to give solace, and to activate social, religious or political ideals." Cf. Dahl 1980, 139–40.

than fourteen possible allusions to Abraham and Sarah in Luke's Zechariah and Elizabeth material.¹⁷

Luke's reading of Abraham and Sarah appears to center upon Gen 15–18, which Westermann has identified as a conspicuous story unit composed of promises recorded in narratives.¹⁸ Eleven of Luke's fourteen allusions are situated within this unit, which includes the only two explicit occurrences of "covenant" within the Abraham and Sarah narrative.¹⁹ If Luke is drawing our attention to Abraham and Sarah, he is drawing our attention to them because of their importance as the recipients of God's covenantal promises.²⁰ It seems significant, then, that Luke chooses ἄμεμπτος, the very word God uses to describe the covenantal faithfulness required of Abraham in Gen 17:1, to describe the faithfulness expressed by Zechariah and Elizabeth. ἄμεμπτος, which stands at the emphatic position at the end of Luke 1:6, appears only here in Luke–Acts and only one time (Gen 17:1) in the Pentateuch:²¹

ἐγώ εἰμι ὁ σου εὐρέσται ἐναντί ἐμοῦ καὶ γίνου ἄμεμπτος.

I am your God, be well-pleasing before me and be blameless.²²

---

17. For a list of many (but not all) of these parallels, see Green 1997, 53–55. I note the following: *Barrenness*: Gen 11:30, 15:1//Luke 1:7; *Annunciation to husband*: Gen 12:2; 15:1; 17:1//Luke 1:15; *Promises (remembered by God)*: Gen 12:3; 15:5, 13–14, 18–21; 17:2, 4–8//Luke 1:73; *Chronological and geopolitical markers*: Gen 14:1//Luke 1:5; *"Do not be afraid"*: Gen 15:1//Luke 1:13; *Righteousness*: Gen 15:6; 17:1; 18:19; 26:5//Luke 1:6; *Old age*: Gen 17:1//Luke 1:7, 11; *Everlasting covenant*: Gen 17:4–8, 16//Luke 1:72–73; *Divine naming of child*: Gen 17:19//Luke 1:13; *Protests regarding advanced age*: Gen 17:17; 18:11–12//Luke 1:18; *Conceived and bore a son*: Gen 21:2//Luke 1:24, 57; *Removal of the shame of barrenness*: Gen 21:6//Luke 1:58; *Circumcision of the sons*: Gen 17:23; 21:4//Luke 1:59. ἄμεμπτος *righteousness*: Gen 17:1//Luke 1:6. The underlined citations indicate references in the Gen 15–18 narrative unit.
18. Westermann 1975, 57–59.
19. Brueggemann 1982, 154. Gen 15:18; 17:2–7.
20. See Luke 1:55, 73; Acts 3:21. Cf. Dahl 1966; Bock 1994, 160. Abraham is mentioned 22 times in Luke–Acts and covenant promises are a central Lukan concern.
21. ἄμεμπτος (Luke 1:6) meets six of the seven criteria for allusion and echo in Hays 1989, 20–32: availability, volume, recurrence, thematic coherence, historical plausibility and satisfaction, but not history of interpretation. Esler 2003, 231–33 suggests ἄμεμπτος often carries a comparative sense. If this is the case in Luke it would mean that Zechariah and Elizabeth are comparatively righteous (and thus exemplary). This sense is not, however, a smooth fit for Gen 17:1 LXX.
22. Gen 17:1 LXX.

ἦσαν δὲ δίκαιοι ἀμφότεροι ἐναντίον θεοῦ, πορευόμενοι ἐν πάσαις ταῖς ἐντολαῖς καὶ δικαιώμασιν τοῦ κυρίου ἄμεμπτοι.

Both of them were righteous before God, living blamelessly according to all the commandments and regulations of the Lord.[23]

Given the density of allusions to the Gen 15–18 Abraham and Sarah material, this allusion hardly seems incidental. Zechariah and Elizabeth are not just pious, they express the covenantal faithfulness required of the patriarch of the Israelite ἔθνος.[24] When this allusion is combined with the fact that Luke depicts Zechariah in a role of priestly mediation within the Temple (a location charged with implications for Israelite identity), the identity-resonances are amplified.[25]

The exemplary identities of Zechariah and Elizabeth are augmented by Luke's depiction of a multitude who also express exemplary Israelite identity. During Zechariah's Temple service "the whole assembly of the

---

23. Luke 1:6. Both constructions imply faithfulness before (ἐναντίον) the Lord. πορεύομαι, a Lukan favorite for "walking" (Luke has 69 of the 117 New Testament occurrences), parallels εὐαρέστω ἐναντίον, a common LXX rendering of "to walk before" (הלך לפני: Gen 5:22, 24; 6:9; 24:10; Pss 55:14; 114:9).

24. Bock 1994, 78 overlooks connections with Genesis. Nolland (1989, 27) references Gen 17:1 but marks no significance. Schweizer (1984, 20) notes the use of the word to describe Paul and Job, but not Abraham. Danker (1988) sees the word as reminiscent of Old Testament piety, but overlooks Gen 17:1. Carter 1988, 241 n. 14 notes that ἄμεμπτος is a *hapax legomenon* in Luke, but nothing further. Green 1997, 54 puts italicized emphasis on *walking* rather than ἄμεμπτος. ἄμεμπτος translates תמים in Gen 17:1, which according to von Rad (1972, 198–99) connotes "wholeness" or "perfection" in the sense of one's relation to God. תמים regularly describes the perfection of a sacrificial offering, but occurs only twice in the Pentateuch in relation to humans (Gen 6:9 for Noah: LXX = δίκαιος; Deut 18:13 for the nation: LXX = τέλειος). ἄμεμπτος occurs eleven times in Job, either as God's description of Job's piety or as Job's self-description, two times in Esther, as a part of the propaganda of the Persian empire (3:12 LXX; 8:13 LXX) and three times in Wisdom (10:5 [2×]; 18:21), the first two occurrences provocatively differentiating blameless Israel/Israelites from the nations (ἔθνη). There are five New Testament occurrences: Paul's status before the Torah (Phil 3:6); wholeness/blamelessness available through Christ (Phil 2:15; 1 Thess 2:10; 3:13; 5:23).

25. Lev 4:3 reflects the representative nature of the priesthood. Sir 50 suggests a faithful priest (Simon Ben Onias) benefits Israel. Hamm 2003, 220 suggests Simon's Temple ministry embodied for Israel "the fullness of life with God." In ancient Near Eastern cosmologies Temples were the nexus between heaven and earth (Eliade 1959; Baltzer 1965, 256–67; Green 1997, 61; Brawley 1999, 119; Taylor 1999, 711; cf. Josephus, *A.J.* 3.123, 180–87; less certainly, *1 En.* 26–27 and *Jub.* 8:12). Brawley 1999, 127 argues "virtually any reader from antiquity would have recognized in the centrality of Jerusalem Luke's tacit assumption that it is the axis mundi." See Bauckham 1995, 417–27 on the centrality of Jerusalem for Acts.

people (λαός) was praying outside."[26] For Luke, prior to Acts 15 λαός (singular) always represents Israel as God's chosen people.[27] The construction πλῆθος ἦν τοῦ λαοῦ occurs frequently in the Old Testament to give a sense of all the people gathered before God.[28] The gathering of the praying people of God suits Jesus' vision for the Temple's primary purpose based on Isa 56:7.[29] This is a part of a broader Lukan tendency to associate "prayer with the movement of God's redemptive drama…and with preparation for participation in that same drama."[30] While it is impossible to know with certainty the content of the prayers of the people, Acts 26:6-7 indicates that daily Temple worship was oriented around petition for the fulfillment of God's promises to the ancestors of Israel. Surely this included the promises to Abraham.

The contrast between the introduction of Herod, who represents both a prototypical Israelite identity and the pervasive threat from Rome, and the introduction of Zechariah and Elizabeth (paired with the faithfully praying λαός) creates a potent formula for the activation of Israelite ethnic identity. Though from a political perspective Israel was a low-status ethnic group, Luke uses allusions to Israel's covenantal history and ethnic lineage to present Israelite identity as a privileged identity. Israel's privileged ethnic identity, based on the covenant with Abraham, is an essential foundation for Luke's treatment of identity, and it is in this charged setting that God hears, remembers (Zechariah's name means "the LORD has remembered") and acts.[31] How this privileged ethnic identity will impinge upon the ethnic "other," especially with regard to intergroup reconciliation and resource allocation, will become a central feature of Luke's two volumes.

3.2. The Spirit, John and Jesus: The Nexus of Identity and Activity

There is much to be said about the birth announcements to Zechariah and Mary, but two initial observations (developed in the following chapter) will suffice here. First, the announced births of John and Jesus

---

26. Luke 1:10; cf. 1:21. Luke is probably describing the second of the Tamid services, which occurred twice daily. Hamm 2003 argues the Tamid services form the cultic context for key scenes in Luke–Acts. See Luke 1:10, 17, 21, 68, 77; 2:32; 7:16; 20:1; 23:2, 13; 24:19.
27. Green 1997, 71.
28. LXX: Exod 12:6; 2 Kgs 7:13; 1 Chr 29:16; 2 Chr 31:18; 1 Esd 9:6, 38, 41, 47; 1 Macc 9:63; 3 Macc 7:13; Ezek 32:32; 39:11.
29. Luke 19:46: "My house shall be a house of prayer."
30. Bartholomew and Holt 2005, 357.
31. Fitzmyer 1981, 322; Green 1997, 73.

contain Luke's initial Spirit references.³² John will be "filled" (πίμπλημι) with the Holy Spirit "even from his mother's womb," and Jesus will be born because the Holy Spirit will "come upon" (ἐπέρχομαι) Mary.³³ For Luke's Gospel, John and (especially) Jesus are the paradigmatically Spirit-endowed figures, though for Jesus this is only made explicit at 3:22. Their missions are linked by the fact that their Spirit-empowered initial public appearances feature critiques of a certain kind of (ethnic) in-group bias.³⁴ Second, it must be noted that Elizabeth's exemplary role extends to the fact that she is the second person in the text who is filled (πίμπλημι) with the Holy Spirit. Significantly, in Luke 1:41–43 the Spirit allows Elizabeth and her fetal son John properly to *identify* the fetal Jesus:

> And when Elizabeth heard the greeting of Mary, *the babe leaped in her womb*; and *Elizabeth was filled with the Holy Spirit* and she exclaimed with a loud cry, "Blessed are you among women, and blessed is the fruit of your womb! And why is this granted me, that the mother of *my Lord* should come to me?"³⁵

For Luke, *the transformative power of the Spirit enables people properly to identify those who belong to the God of Israel.*³⁶ This material from Luke 1, which ultimately climaxes in Acts, introduces Luke's emphasis on the connection between Spirit and identity. The Spirit enables humans properly to identify those who belong to God *and* the Spirit functions as the central marker of human identity.

32. Turner 1996, 165 claims "Luke 1–2 does not attempt an analysis of human experience of the Spirit across the ages, nor does it provide the raw materials for one. It is concerned rather to celebrate the arrival of Zion's Davidic restorer... The pneumatological motifs all bend toward these ends." Yet while Luke may not be speaking of universal human experience, his first descriptions of the Spirit are foundational to the *Lukan* view of the Spirit.

33. Luke 1:15, 35. These passages are problematic for a narrow conception of "Spirit of prophecy." Does a "prophetic" Spirit function in a fetus? (Perhaps John's *in utero* leap is a form of testimony?) Further, the Spirit's effect on Mary involves creation. Separately, it should be noted that John's ministry—to "turn many of the sons of Israel to the Lord their God" (Luke 1:16)—indicates that Luke assumes that ethnic identity does not guarantee right relationship with God.

34. The missions of John and Jesus will be discussed in Chapter 4.

35. Rowe 2006, 42–49 argues that "Lord" in 1:43 should be taken in its full sense.

36. Most scholars overlook this Lukan Spirit-motif and take an approach exemplified by Bock 1994, 138, who suggests that the leap is a divine sign, but who does not connect John's leap to the promise that John will be filled with the Spirit *from his mother's womb* (cf. Nolland 1989, 66). Johnson 1991, 40 also connects the leap to John's status as a prophet, but not to the Spirit (cf. Fitzmyer 1981, 363). One exception is Green 1997, 95, who notes that the Spirit "prompts his [John's] recognition" of Jesus, but Green does not take "identification" as a fundamental role of the Spirit.

3.3. The Spirit and the Birth Hymns: Expanding the Field of Ethnic Vision

The early contrast between Herodian and/or Roman identity and privileged Israelite identity is amplified by the rhetoric of the birth announcements. Luke tells his audience that God is moving to "make ready for the Lord a people prepared" (1:17) and to restore an everlasting Davidic dynasty to Israel (1:32–33). This rhetoric of status reversal is a powerful stimulus for increased in-group identification, though it remains to wonder how this will affect the "other"—especially the threatening other.[37] As we have seen, in-group identification, especially in situations where identity is threatened, typically leads to increased in-group bias and out-group differentiation. Concomitantly, increased in-group bias typically results in the restriction of resource allocation to the in-group.[38] As we turn to the catena of birth hymns in Luke 1–2, I will trace the relationship between "in-group love," the presence of the Spirit, and the "other," especially as those relationships implicate issues of resource allocation.[39] The contrast that emerges in this section demonstrates that the presence of the Spirit creates openness to sharing the benefits of the in-group with the ethnic other. This "broadening of the ethnic horizon" is further initial evidence for the Spirit's transformative effect, which results in the formation of an allocentric identity.[40]

3.3.1. *Mary's Song*

Mary's song emphasizes the ethnic in-group in a manner not uncommon within the matrix of hopes for Israel's national salvation.[41] The hymn is frequently cited as evidence of Luke's concern for the poor, often as a centerpiece for liberationist readings of the text.[42] Though sometimes

---

37. The conversion of Saul (discussed below) provides a fascinating and moving answer to this question.

38. Wenzel 2001, 318.

39. I use "resource allocation" to refer to all the benefits of in-group membership as "resources" of the group.

40. "Spirit of prophecy" approaches rely heavily upon the birth hymns to connect the Spirit and inspired speech (Cho 2005, 137–39; Turner 1996, 143), yet advocates of this position often fail to examine the *content* and *purpose* of the revelation of the Spirit. The Spirit inspires not only the act of speaking, but surely also the content of the communication. Luke 1:35 is generally admitted as an exception to the narrow prophetic function (Cho 2005, 139). Dunn 1970 only discusses Luke 1:35.

41. Farris 1985, 125; Bock 1996, 142, 159; Turner 1996, 133–36; Wright 1996, 433–75.

42. Hamel 1979; Ruether 1980; Zorrilla 1983; O'Day 1985; Gallo 1988; Mezzacasa 1988; McVerry 2003; Williamson 2005, 167–76.

neglectful of Luke's concern for God's redemption of even the powerful and the oppressor, liberationist readings helpfully alert us to the *collective* ramifications of Mary's rhetoric of status reversal.[43] Farris has demonstrated that the structure of the song sets the "destitute" (ταπεινός) of 1:52 in *contrast* to the "proud" (1:51), the "mighty" (1:52a) and the "rich" (1:53a), and *parallel* to "those who fear God" (1:50), the "hungry" (1:53b) and "Israel" (1:54).[44] *Mary's own status reversal (1:46–49) anticipates the expected status reversal for all Israel.*[45] Mary grounds this reversal in language of ethnic identity, recognizing God's faithfulness to ethnic Israel's covenantal fathers (πατέρες), to Abraham and his seed (σπέρμα).[46]

The Magnificat's entitlement claims, which are claims to access to God's restoration through deliverance, are restricted solely to the ethnic in-group. This is not surprising given what we have already discussed regarding the close relationship between entitlement and social identity. Yet what SIT describes as normal intergroup identity-forming processes, for Luke, *can* have the potential to become deeply problematic. This essential point is not without nuance. Luke everywhere *affirms* powerful expressions of in-group love (in-group bias), and the Magnificat is one such expression. In-group love is a core value for the early community in Acts. However, Luke 3 and 4 will demonstrate that in-group love is open to mutation and that in-group bias that only exists as an end in itself is a *distortion* of privileged identity. The full force of Luke's position will come into focus as we progress, but for now it is essential to note two factors. First, Luke in no way explicitly critiques Mary's extravagant expression of in-group love for its absence of concern for non-Israelites. Mary speaks without direct Spirit-influence, and it will become increasingly clear that Luke understands certain expressions of out-group love only to be possible through the influence of the Spirit.[47] Second, the

---

43. Bailey 1979, 32: "It is clear that what happens to Mary is an illustration of the past and future history of the community." Language of collective deliverance never precludes individual concern. Luke expects that poor individuals really will be filled as a result of God's action (and he demonstrates as much in the economic ethic of the Acts community). Collectivism does not preclude individuals, only individual*ism*.

44. Farris 1985, 122.

45. This representational motif appears with regard to Israel in several Psalms, where even David describes himself as "poor" and "needy." See Pss 9:11–12, 17–20; 10:1–4, 17–18; 12:1–5; 18:25–29; 40:17; 70:5; 72:2; 86:1; 109:22; 149:4; also *Pss. Sol.* 5:8–11. See Bock 1996, 156–57 and Farris 1985, 122.

46. Luke 1:55.

47. My argument that Mary, due to the absence of the Spirit, does not grasp the full implications of God's saving action is similar to the argument I will make

Magnificat gives an initial indication of a motif that will emerge in the birth hymns: the *absence of explicit Spirit-influence* in Mary's song appears to be correlated to the restriction of the benefits of group membership to the ethnic in-group alone.[48] This is clear when contrasted with Zechariah's hymn.

3.3.2. Zechariah's Spirit-empowered Song

There are many similarities between Zechariah's song and Mary's song. Zechariah uses language of national salvation (1:68–75).[49] There are multiple references to the enemies of ethnic Israel (ἐχθρῶν; χειρὸς τῶν μισούντων ἡμᾶς; χειρὸς ἐχθρῶν).[50] Covenantal language abounds. In 1:69, Zechariah praises God for raising a horn of salvation in the οἴκῳ Δαυὶδ παιδὸς αὐτοῦ.[51] The reference to the Abrahamic covenant is couched in ethnic language: God will "perform the mercy promised to our *fathers*" (πατέρες) by fulfilling the covenant with "Abraham our *father*" (πατέρ).[52] It is clear that Zechariah speaks the rhetoric of ethnic identity.[53]

---

concerning the selection of Matthias in Acts 1, an event I take to be a description of an old paradigm of social homogeneity that is expected apart from the Spirit, but which is obsolete after Pentecost. In neither case does Luke offer explicit critique. In both cases, subsequent material in the text indicates that the paradigms in question—whether Mary's in Luke 1 or Peter's in Acts 1—are open to distortion, even if they are not themselves distortions.

48. Proponents of the "Spirit of prophecy" model argue that Mary speaks the Magnificat under the Spirit's influence based upon Luke 1:35 (Menzies 1991, 127; Shepherd 1994, 121–22; Turner 1996, 143; Cho 2005, 139). Four factors make this unlikely: (1) the Spirit's work in Mary is explicitly the work of conception; (2) the Magnificat is separated from 1:35 temporally (by a significant period of time) and textually (by the visit to Elizabeth); (3) a Latin variant reading of Luke 1:46 (a, b, l. Irenaeus, Origen) has "Elizabeth" as the speaker of the Magnificat, indicating that the most natural connection between the Spirit and the speaker (by virtue of 1:41) implicated Elizabeth; (4) Luke's later usage demonstrates that his deployment of the Spirit is explicit and precise.

49. Farris 1985, 136. Tannehill 1996, 62 mitigates the force of the enemy language: "Zechariah's interpretation of the promise to Abraham is not a narrow nationalism but a hope for religious freedom so that Israel can shape its own identity as the worshiping people of God."

50. Luke 1:71a and b; Luke 1:74.

51. Brawley 1999, 114 notes that the Davidic covenant is portrayed as "a particular way God also fulfills the Abrahamic covenant."

52. Luke 1:72a, 73.

53. John's naming indicates the pressure of the ethnic in-group toward the perpetuation of kinship identity: "None of your kindred (συγγενεία) is called by this

There is, however, one great difference between the Benedictus and the Magnificat: Zechariah explicitly is filled (πίμπλημι) with the Spirit (Luke 1:67). His speech must be read in the light of this essential fact and, as I will argue, the presence of the Spirit corresponds with a turn toward the ethnic "other." This is a surprise given the treatment of the "other" in 1:68–75 where fulfillment of the oath to Abraham (1:73) results in Israel's deliverance from enemies in order that Israel might serve God without fear (1:74), in holiness and righteousness before God (1:75). Given the anti-enemy rhetoric, the possibility of "fearless" (ἀφόβος) service of God would at this point seem only to be available via God's overthrow or destruction of Israel's threatening "other." This should not be a surprise to Luke's hearers, or to contemporary readers: in-group love often produces out-group derogation.

But a different possibility emerges in 1:76–79 that results in the tantalizing possibility that Israelites and their enemies will walk together in the *"way of peace"* (1:79). While some interpreters have suggested that the Benedictus describes national deliverance in 1:65–75 and shifts to "internal" salvation in 1:76–79, I contend that the "way of peace" (1:79) available through the work of the Messiah entails literal intergroup reconciliation with ethnic non-Israelites, a group that Luke includes among those "sitting in darkness and the shadow of death" (1:79a).[54] The logic of Luke 1:77–79 works as follows: knowledge of salvation through the forgiveness of sins is given to Israelites (ἡμῶν in 1:78a) as a result of the ἐπισκέψεται of the ἀνατολή ἐξ ὕψους to ethnic Israelites (ἡμᾶς in 1:78).[55] Two events result from the visitation of the ἀνατολή to Israel. First, the ἀνατολή will shine on τοῖς ἐν σκότει καὶ σκιᾷ θανάτου καθημένοις (Luke 1:79a). Second, the ἀνατολή will guide the feet of Israelites (the clear referent of ἡμῶν in 1:79) in the way of peace.[56] Many

---

name" (Luke 1:61). Divine naming indicates that John is set apart to God. This takes precedence over in-group concerns (see Miller 1993, 197, 199).

54. Klein 2006, 121 is characteristic of the division between national and spiritual salvation: "V.68–75 thematisiert mehr die politische Befreiung von den Feinden durch einen König, V.76–79 versteht Begfreiung eher spirituell als Heil, wobei mit 'Sündenvergebung' (V.77) ein Stickwort aus der Täuferüberlieferung aufgenommen wird."

55. ἡμεῖς (12×) always refers to Israelites in the Benedictus. ἐπισκέψεται in 1:78 suggestively parallels God's visitation (ἐπεσκέψατο) of his people in 1:68, and is a possible example of Luke's high Christology.

56. Farris 1985, 141 argues that the appearances of ἡμεῖς bracketing Luke 1:79a suggest "Those who sit in darkness are doubtless the people of Israel," yet he neglects the fact that references to God's deliverance of non-Israelites and Israelites are intermingled in just such a way in Luke 2:10–14, 30–32.

commentators assume Israelites are visited by the ἀνατολή, Israelites are sitting in darkness and the shadow of death and Israelites will be guided into the way of peace.[57] I suggest, however, that at the very least Luke thinks *both* Israelites and non-Israelites (if not non-Israelites alone) sit in darkness and the shadow of death. Hence, the day that dawns upon Israel also gives light to the ἔθνη. The result of this dawning is *peace*. As we will see, the implied presence of the ἔθνη in 1:79a is important for understanding the relationship between the Spirit, ethnic identity and the "other."

Two factors support my claim that Zechariah's speech has both Israelites and non-Israelites in view: (1) the LXX provides material that describes non-Israelites sitting in darkness or bondage and (2) Luke's own usage of light/darkness imagery *always* includes non-Israelites as part of its referent. Commentators suggest four main intertextual options as source material for Luke 1:79a: Ps 106:10; Isa 9:1; 42:7; 49:9–10.[58] I will here only demonstrate that non-Israelites feature in several of these passages. In the light of the non-consensus regarding Old Testament source texts, I will argue that Luke's own patterns of usage must be given the greatest weight.

Neither Ps 106:10 LXX nor Isa 9:2 LXX provide conceptual links between non-Israelites and those sitting in darkness and the shadow of death. Psalm 106:10 LXX refers to God's deliverance of Israelites who have "rebelled against the words of God" (106:11) and as a result need deliverance from "darkness," "gloom" and "bonds" (106:14). Likewise, Isa 9:2 LXX refers to God's deliverance of Israelites who have turned to mediums rather than Torah for guidance: ὁ λαὸς ὁ πρευόμενος ἐν χώρα καί σκιᾷ θανάτου φῶς λάμψει ἐφ' ὑμᾶς. This allusion is favored by several interpreters, likely because of its proximity to the "messianic" prophecy in Isa 9:6–7.[59]

Isaiah 49:6–10 LXX clearly includes non-Israelites. The servant of the Lord has a mission that involves regathering the tribes of Jacob *and* shining light on the ἔθνη in order to bring salvation to the ends of the

---

57. See Bock 1994, 193–94; Farris 1985, 141; Talbert 1982, 28, implicitly, Nolland 1989, 90–92; Fitzmyer 1981, 388; Johnson 1991, 47. Green 1997, 119 suggests that "many" (though he gives no references) have seen the Abrahamic imagery as well as possible Isa 42:7 allusions to imply God's "universal embrace," but he does not specifically mention non-Israelites, only those in the "arena of existence ruled by cosmic forces in opposition to God."

58. See Bock 1996, 193; Nolland 1989, 90; Danker 1988, 50–51; Lieu 1997, 13. Lieu includes Isa 60:1–3 as possible background.

59. E.g. Schneider 1977, 62: "Vielleicht steht Jes 9.2, 6f im Hintergrund (Messias also Licht und Friedensbringer)."

earth (Isa 49:6).⁶⁰ The servant is given as a covenant to the ἔθνη, "saying to the ones that are in chains 'Come out!' and to the ones that are in darkness 'Reveal yourselves'" (Isa 49:8–9). While the language in Isa 49:6–10 does not mention "the shadow of death" (cf. Luke 1:79), the light/darkness imagery depicts non-Israelites in need of light and the passage features the two-step human deliverance (to Jacob and the ἔθνη) described at various key points in Luke–Acts (e.g. Luke 2:32, Acts 3:12–26).⁶¹

In Isa 42 the servant of the Lord brings justice to the ἔθνη (Isa 42:1) who hope in the servant's name (Isa 42:4). The Lord tells the servant that he has been given as "a covenant to the people (γένους), a light to the ἔθνη, to open the eyes that are blind, to bring out the prisoners from the dungeon, from the prison those who sit in darkness" (Isa 42:6–7). γένους (42:6) is differentiated from the λαῷ of v. 5 (which refers to universal humanity) and must be read as Israel.⁶² The LXX thus reinterprets the servant's calling "into a two-fold task, in relation to the people and the nations."⁶³ Thus the "context suggests that the captives are the nations, and the worldwide concern of the talk of creation in v. 5 supports this."⁶⁴

Adding to the plausibility that Luke has Isa 42 in view is the fact that in Isa 42:9 the work of God is "dawning" or "rising up" (ἀνατέλλω), resulting in "new things" that extend covenantal benefits beyond ethnic Israel (Isa 42:10). Similarly, in Luke 1:78, the ἀνατολή (the substantized cognate of ἀνατέλλω) from on high will dawn upon both the Israelites (ἡμῶν in Luke 1:78) and those (ἔθνη) sitting in darkness and the shadow of death, resulting in the extension of benefits beyond ethnic Israel.⁶⁵

It can at this point be safely assumed that the LXX provided Luke a repertoire of light/darkness imagery that *could* describe non-Israelites

60. Luke's "end of the earth" imagery (Acts 1:8; cf. Acts 13:47) draws on Isa 49:6, making this one of the more likely sources of the allusion in Luke 1:79a.
61. Koet 2005 sees Isa 49:6 as the key text legitimating the mission to non-Israelites in Luke–Acts.
62. Goldingay and Payne 2005, 227. Isa 42:6 LXX has the variant reading γένους μου (א), which clearly marks the group as ethnic Israel.
63. Goldingay and Payne 2005, 227.
64. Goldingay and Payne 2005, 230.
65. See LSJ, 123. Nolland 1989, 90 sees a similar density of Isaianic references in Luke 1:78–79, but he locates them in Isa 9:1; 58:8, 10; 60:1–3. Collectively, these passages contain several of the elements in Luke 1:78–79. However, Isa 42:1–9 contains each of these elements (the effect of the ἀνατολή upon both those in darkness and those who are imprisoned) in one unit. Two other factors point toward the influence of Isa 42 here: (1) Luke alludes to Isa 42:1 (with Ps 2:7) in Luke 3:22 (Nolland 1989, 163), and (2) Isa 42:1 and Isa 61:1 (cf. Luke 4:18) both focus on a Spirit-anointed servant of God, whereas Isa 49 lacks reference to the Spirit.

3. Expanding the Ethnic Horizon

as those sitting in darkness and the shadow of death. Against this background of possibilities, Luke's own usage of light/darkness imagery makes it clear that he thinks non-Israelites sit in darkness:

> "I have set you to be a *light for the non-Israelites* (ἔθνη), that you may bring salvation to the uttermost parts of the earth."[66]

> ...delivering you from *the people* (λαός) *and from the non-Israelites* (ἔθνη)—*to whom I send you to open their eyes, that they may turn from darkness to light* and from the power of Satan to God, that they may receive forgiveness of sins and a place among those who are sanctified by faith in me.[67]

> ...the Christ must suffer, and that, by being the first to rise from the dead, *he would proclaim light both to the people* (λαός) *and to the non-Israelites* (ἔθνη).[68]

The first passage envisions solely non-Israelites sitting in darkness, while the other two passages depict deliverance of both Israelites and non-Israelites who sit in darkness. None of Luke's 23 deployments of variations of the noun φῶς, the adjective φωτεινός or the verb φωτίζω refer exclusively to Israelites as a *group*.[69] Likewise, ἐπιφαίνω never refers to Israelites to the exclusion of non-Israelites.[70] Whenever the light shines in Luke–Acts, it shines also on the ἔθνη.

The mounting case for the inclusion of the ἔθνη in Luke 1:79a is all but clinched by the words of Simeon in Luke 2:32. According to Simeon the salvation of God is

φῶς εἰς ἀποκάλυψιν ἐθνῶν καὶ δόξαν λαοῦ σου Ἰσραήλ.

Light for revelation to the non-Israelites and glory for your people Israel. (my translation)

Here is a two-step deliverance of Israel and non-Israelites couched (for non-Israelites) in terms of light and darkness. The proximity of this passage to Luke 1:79a makes it highly likely that Luke envisions non-Israelites at the end of Zechariah's Spirit-empowered hymn. This two-step deliverance situates nicely within Luke's awareness that the God of

---

66. Acts 13:47, quoting Isa 49:6.
67. Acts 26:16–18.
68. Acts 26:22–23.
69. Luke 2:32; 8:16; 11:33, 34, 35, 36 (3×); 12:3; 16:8; 22:56; Acts 9:3; 12:7; 13:47; 16:29; 22:6, 9, 11; 26:13, 18, 23. The exception is Saul's conversion, but there the "light" is given only to an individual and is yet very much for the sake of non-Israelites.
70. Luke 1:79; Acts 2:20; 27:20.

Israel would bless the family of Abraham and, through that family, all the families of the earth.[71]

This argument reveals a possible structural feature of the Gospel that supports my view that Zechariah's song implies light to non-Israelites. The interplay between the Spirit, Israel and the ethnic "other" in Luke 1–2 forms a chiastic structure that proceeds as follows:

    A: Mary's song (1:46–55)
        B: Zechariah's [*Spirit-empowered*] song (1:68–79)
            C: Angelic announcement (2:14)
        B_1:   Simeon's [*Spirit-empowered*] speech (2:29–32, 34–35)
    A_1:   Anna's hope (2:38)

In A/A_1, Mary and Anna—who are not explicitly inspired by the Spirit—are associated with a message of deliverance that features only ethnic Israel. In B/B_1, Zechariah and Simeon—who explicitly are inspired by the Spirit—proclaim a message of deliverance that extends to non-Israelites. At the centre of the chiasmus (Luke 2:14) is a message of *peace* (cf. Luke 1:79) to ethnically undifferentiated ἄνθρωποι.[72] This inclusive angelic vision of peace, in parallel with the "way of peace" of Luke 1:79, suggests that the Benedictus at least proleptically anticipates the blessing of non-Israelites.

Finally, the inclusion of non-Israelites in 1:79a makes clear sense in parallel with 1:79b. Given the emphasis on national salvation and deliverance from enemies in both the Magnificat and the Benedictus, we cannot understand "the way of peace" (1:79a) to be merely existential peace.[73] Of Luke's 21 references to peace, the word is always used either as a greeting/salutation (e.g. "Go in peace") or to describe the interpersonal or intergroup peace that results from reconciliation.[74] Further, the closest LXX reference to the "way of peace" (ὁδός εἰρήνη), Ps 13:3, is

---

71. See Acts 3:25.
72. Lieu 1997, 13 claims the Benedictus anticipates the angelic announcement on the basis of "peace."
73. Contra Bock 1996, 190; Schweizer 1984, 44 thinks "peace" is for those who have "lost the way." Johnson 1991, 48 calls the vision of deliverance here "religious." Many here press for a holistic vision of "shalom" (so Green 1997, 119), which is undoubtedly correct (Fitzmyer 1981, 224–25 sees both Hebrew "shalom" and the *pax Augusta* in the frame of reference). Luke has a special emphasis on intergroup reconciliation in many of his "peace" passages (see Acts 9:31; 10:36).
74. Greeting/Salutation: Luke 2:14, 29 (see LaGrand 1998 on possible reconciliation in 2:29); 7:50; 8:48; 10:5, 6 (2×—this is a difficult case); 24:36; Acts 15:33; 16:36. Peace as reconciliation/absence of conflict: Luke 1:79; 11:21; 12:51; 14:32; 19:38(?), 42; Acts 7:26; 9:31; 10:36; 12:20; 24:2.

3. Expanding the Ethnic Horizon

clearly about the absence of literal conflict.[75] Luke is talking about real peace in a real socio-political context. The obstacles to peace in Zechariah's song are the non-Israelites, the enemies of ethnic Israel (Luke 1:71, 74), who sit in darkness and the shadow of death. For peace to exist there must either be reconciliation with enemies, status reversal, or the destruction of enemies.[76] Luke does not here indicate whether destruction or reconciliation will be the means to "peace," *but he will go on to demonstrate that the enemies of God are defeated through intergroup reconciliation and the formation of common identity, not through destruction.*[77] Peace, as Luke understands it, requires a partner, and the ἔθνη will be that partner.[78]

Zechariah's hymn is the first of Luke's many connections between the presence of the Spirit and a "broadening of the ethnic horizon." This stands in relief against Mary's song, which emphasizes deliverance only for the ethnic in-group. Zechariah, inspired by the Spirit, proclaims that non-Israelites (the ethnic "other") have access to certain benefits of God.[79] From an SIT perspective, Zechariah's extension of the benefits of in-group membership to non-Israelites is a subversion of typical identity-based entitlement claims. Zechariah is able to express in-group love and out-group love simultaneously and hence to extend in-group benefits beyond the boundaries of his in-group. It will become increasingly evident that only the Holy Spirit can create this kind of openness to the "other," a posture that requires profound transformation. Conversely, Luke will show that expressions of privileged ethnic identity that take their own ethnic privilege to be an end in itself are dangerously open to distortion and are breeding grounds for out-group derogation.

---

75. Cf. Isa 59:7–8 and possibly Isa 41:3.

76. Borgman 2006 suggests that "peace" is a unifying element for the birth narratives (53) and Jesus' journey to Jerusalem (78–96). He sees peace as "a shalom-justice that is all-inclusive, of outsiders, diseased, oppressed, prisoners, and enemies" (53).

77. See especially Saul's conversion (Acts 9:1–31).

78. Ravens (2005, 45) suggests that Simeon's words are the first hint that non-Israelites are implicated in God's deliverance. If I am correct, non-Israelites are implicated by Zechariah and the angels.

79. Suggestions that Luke is here being patriarchal are forestalled by the fact that (1) Mary outperforms Zechariah when it comes to the exercise of faith in response to angelic annunciation and (2) Luke's high esteem for women is well known. In Luke's view it is not necessary to say that Zechariah inherently is more open to the "other," but that the Spirit in this instance enables Zechariah to become something he naturally is not.

3.3.3. Angelic Annunciation

It needs only to be mentioned briefly that the angelic annunciation in Luke 2, the centre of the chiasmus discussed above, extends the peace of God to ethnically undifferentiated humankind (ἄνθρωπος):[80]

> Glory to God in the highest, and on earth peace among men (ἄνθρωποι) with whom he is pleased![81]

Luke's use of ἄνθρωπος (Luke 2:14) refers to generic "humanity" and is differentiated from his use of the singular form of λαός, which prior to Acts 15 only ever refers to Israelites.[82] Luke 20:6 demonstrates this nuance clearly.

> But if we say, "From humankind [ἄνθρωποι—referring to generic humanity]," all the people [ὁ λαός—referring to Israelites gathered at the Jerusalem Temple] will stone us; for they are convinced that John was a prophet."

The peace that is for all humans is the outworking of a message of good news specific to the λαός of Israel (Luke 2:10). Note again that Luke features a two-step deliverance that moves from Israel to the nations. In the angelic announcement at the center of the birth narratives Luke uses authoritative heavenly messengers to clarify that the benefits of God—manifest in "peace"—will transcend ethnic boundaries.

3.3.4. Simeon's Spirit-empowered Speech

Luke's introduction of Simeon is remarkable. In 2:26–27 we learn that the "Holy Spirit was upon" Simeon, the Spirit revealed special knowledge to Simeon concerning God's plan to let him see the Messiah and the Spirit inspired Simeon to come into the Temple.[83] If there is any ambiguity regarding what Simeon will say or do, Luke completely erases it by

---

80. Menzies 1991; M. Turner 1996; Wenk 2004 and Cho 2005 do not treat 2:10–14.

81. Luke 2:14.

82. In Luke, ἄνθρωπος is contrasted with the angels (Luke 12:9) and describes sinful humankind (Luke 24:7) and every "nation of humans" (ἔθνος ἀνθρώπων, Acts 17:26). The only time λαός in the plural refers to Israel is Acts 4:27. This is likely because of Luke's effort to retain verbal parallelism with the plural usage from Ps 2:1 cited in Acts 4:25 (Metzger 1975, 323). Brown 1978, 120 notes Luke's careful use of singular forms of λαός to refer to Israel (cf. DuPont 1985, 321–35). Prior to Acts 15, "people" refers to Israel, while "peoples" refers to the ἔθνη. In Chapter 8 I will discuss the paradigm shift that occurs after Acts 15. My position differs from Fitzmyer 1981, 422, who assumes, without extended discussion, that 2:10–14 relates only to Israel.

83. LaGrand 1998 offers an interesting, yet hard to verify, reading of Simeon as a violent zealot turned peaceful after his encounter with Jesus (cf. Fitzmyer 1981, 422).

drawing attention to the Spirit *three times*.⁸⁴ Simeon's song makes it explicit that the salvation of God is prepared in the presence of all the λαῶν, which, according to Luke's distinctive plural usage, includes ethnically undifferentiated humanity.⁸⁵ Simeon describes God's two-step deliverance as a "light for revelation" to the ἔθνη and "glory to your people (λαός) Israel" (Luke 2:32).⁸⁶ Once again we see that for Luke the presence of the Spirit appears to have a transformative affect that broadens the ethnic horizon, turning one outward toward the "other" and allowing for the extension of in-group benefits/resources to the out-group. Simeon's speech is a fine example of the simultaneous expression of Spirit-empowered in-group love and Spirit-empowered out-group love. Where the Spirit is present, Israelite identity does not resist the inclusion of non-Israelites in the work of God.

Simeon's claim (Luke 2:34–45) that Jesus will cause varying responses among Israelites recalls Gabriel's annunciation of John's task: there are sons of Israel whose hearts need to be turned to the Lord (Luke 1:16):

> Behold, this child is set for the fall and rising of many in Israel, and for a sign that is spoken against (and a sword will pierce through your [Mary] own soul also), that thoughts out of many hearts may be revealed.

First, Simeon knows that ethnic identity does not, *de facto*, give access to God. Second, Simeon's hymn places Mary in the same boat as Israel (just as she was in the Magnificat) and a discernment process must go on in her own response to Jesus.⁸⁷ The fact that Luke uses Mary later in the text

---

84. Farris (1985, 144) cannot be correct to claim, "The hymn could be omitted without disruption of the narrative." Fitzmyer (1981, 422) notes the uniqueness of Simeon's relationship with the Spirit. Radl (1999, 299) notes Simeon's proleptic importance, but makes no connection to the Spirit: "Die Sichtwese dieses Gebets unterscheidet sich nicht nur von der Konzentration auf Israel im rest der Erzaëh-lung, sie deckt sich auch mit der weltweiten Perspektive im Korpus des Evangeliums und in der Apostelgeschichte."

85. Brown 1978, 120. Acts 4:27 is the exception.

86. Menzies 1991 and Cho 2005 make no reference to Simeon's speech beyond their connection with the "Spirit of prophecy." Turner (1996, 301) and Wenk (2004, 316) see Simeon as an important paradigm for the mission that stretches to the nations, but whereas I think the Spirit is the causal factor in Simeon's disposition, neither Turner nor Wenk make the connection between the trans-ethnic scope of Simeon's speech and the presence of the Spirit.

87. Perhaps this discernment is at issue when Mary "kept all these things in her heart" (Luke 2:51). Fitzmyer 1981, 429, argues the "sword" referred to is the Old Testament "sword of discrimination," which has connotations of judgment and decision. Reicke 1978, 105 thinks the sword is Mary's "own division over Jesus, evidenced in her sometimes resistance of him." I maintain that Luke presents uncertainty rather than "resistance," the latter of which is a feature of Mark 3:21.

to emphasize that kinship ties are less important than hearing and doing the word of God serves further to suggest that Luke understands Mary as a figure in need of the same Spirit-empowered, Jesus-centered transformation as most other Israelites.[88] Luke's composite portrait of Mary reveals that even such an honored a person as Jesus' mother, without the identity-forming work of the Spirit, cannot rightly conceive of either the scope of God's work or of the proper function of the privileged covenantal identity of ethnic Israelites.

3.3.5. *Anna and the Hope of a Nation*

The introduction of Anna, whom we provocatively learn is of the "lost" northern tribe of Asher, closes off the catena of "hymns" that I have identified as a chiasmus formed also by Mary, Zechariah, angels and Simeon. Anna does not herself speak in the passage, but the people gathered to hear her are "looking for the redemption of Jerusalem" (Luke 2:38). Here again the text suggests a hope restricted to ethnic Israel and here again there is *no mention of the Spirit*. The hope of Anna's audience is another expression of unmitigated in-group bias/love, a point emphasized if Bauckham is correct that Luke's inclusion of Anna (the Asherite) implies the regathering and reconstitution of the twelve tribes of Israel.[89] Simeon, too, expresses in-group love (he hopes for "the consolation of Israel": Luke 2:25) but the Spirit's transformative work upon Simeon has broadened his ethnic horizon with regard to the extension of the benefits of the people of God.[90] Once again, where the Spirit is present, there is a discernable turn to the "other"; where the Spirit is absent, expressions of in-group love privilege only the "us."

---

88. Luke 8:21; 11:27–28. Mary's still-incomplete knowledge of the significance of Jesus' identity is evident in Luke 2:49–51. It cannot be questioned that Mary is highly honored by Luke, but it should at least be noted that she is not the most highly exalted human in the eyes of Luke's Jesus, an honor reserved for John the Baptizer (Luke 7:28).

89. Bauckham 2001, 458.

90. Bauckham 2001, 458 suggests Simeon and Anna are complements of two different poles of Israelite salvation. I agree with Bauckham, but would extend his view to suggest that the Spirit clearly seems to be necessary in order for humans comprehensively to grasp the scope of God's redemptive activity. For Luke, deliverance of Israel is intimately connected to God's action for the nations. Zechariah sings of deliverance of the people and light to non-Israelites, the angels sing of great joy to the people (λαός) and peace to all humans (ἄνθρωπος), Simeon connects Israel's glory and light to the nations (ἔθνη). Only the Spirit, or a privileged angelic perspective, appears to cultivate this robust awareness of the inclusion of all the families of the earth in God's incorporative redemption.

3.4. Conclusion

Luke's strategy in the birth narratives is extremely subtle, and in some ways is more evident retrospectively after reading his entire narrative.[91] He begins by activating Israelite identity through the Abraham and Sarah-like figures of Zechariah and Elizabeth, who are set in contrast with Herod and references to Roman rule. This is the initial manner by which Luke brings the Abrahamic covenant to the fore, elevating the status of Israelite identity and hinting at potential implications for the ἔθνη. The focus on Israelite in-group identity continues through the birth hymns, all of which are powerful expressions of in-group love that position Israelite ethnic identity as a privileged identity on the basis of Israel's covenantal history. Delicately, however, Luke here begins to elevate the role of the Spirit in the formation of an allocentric identity that can love both the in-group and the "other." For the explicitly Spirit-inspired figures Zechariah and Simeon (and for the angels, who have a decidedly heavenly perspective), strong expressions of Israelite in-group love extend the benefits of Israelite in-group membership to non-Israelites. Two ramifications should be noted. First, the persistence with which Luke connects the Spirit and the sort of "turn to the other" that carries transformed assumptions about entitlement is characteristic of Luke–Acts and will crescendo toward a climax in Acts 15. For Luke, positive or negative views of the "other" are inherently Spirit-effected matters and it is the Spirit alone that can foster an allocentric identity within an individual. Luke's text repeatedly reveals data suggesting that the subversion of the normally agonistic and comparative processes of social identity can only happen through the power of the Spirit. Second, Luke in no way denigrates the in-group love expressed by Mary or Anna. Israelite in-group bias always has positive connotations for Luke, *so long as it is accompanied by the extension of group benefits beyond the ethnic boundary*. This will be clarified in succeeding chapters as Luke uses his paradigmatically Spirit-empowered figures John the Baptizer and (especially) Jesus to chasten mutated expressions of ethnic identity.

---

91. I am not the first to notice Luke's subtlety in narrative construction. Darr 1992, 52–53 notes the importance of overt reference to the Spirit in Luke: "Every speech that purports to represent the divinity (especially prophetic or predictive words) must bear the Spirit's stamp of approval, or else it remains subject to suspicion."

Chapter 4

CRITIQUING DEFECTIVE IDENTITIES:
SPIRIT-EMPOWERED FIGURES AND IN-GROUP BIAS
IN LUKE 3–4

In Luke 3–4, Luke gives narrative expression to his initial indication that the presence of the Spirit is essential to the formation of an allocentric identity capable of a broad ethnic horizon that extends in-group benefits to the "other." For Luke, the ability to love both the in-group and the out-group is a Spirit-created possibility. This is emphasized in Luke 3–4 by the neglected fact that the initial public appearances of John and Jesus, Luke's paradigmatically Spirit-empowered figures, both feature critiques of defective expressions of privileged social identities. I will demonstrate three points in this chapter: (1) John's preaching contrasts a defective expression of Israelite ethnic identity with an identity marked by a concern for the "other"; (2) Jesus' baptism, genealogy and temptation combine to demonstrate that apart from the Spirit Jesus' true identity can be neither accurately discerned nor adequately expressed; and (3) Jesus' encounter in Nazareth stands both as a critique of faulty assumptions about in-group identity and entitlement as well as an initial paradigm for the expression of Spirit-formed allocentric identity.

4.1. *The Spirit and the Baptizer:*
Critiquing a Distortion of Ethnic Social Identity

Against the backdrop of identity threat inherent in the Roman oppression highlighted in Luke 3:1–2, Luke's quote of Isa 40:3–5 (Luke 3:4–6) again activates Israel's privileged status as God's elect.[1] Yet John's preaching indicates that any attempt to understand privileged Israelite identity

---

1. Isa 40 was often associated with end-time salvation. See 1QS 9.19–20; 8.14–15; Bar 5:7, *T. Moses* 10.3–4, *Pesikta Rabbati* 29/30A, 29/30B, 30, 33; and *Lev. R.* 1.14 on 1.1. See Bock 1994, 291; Snodgrass 1980. Marshall 1978, 137 suggests in Luke's view πᾶσα σάρξ (Isa 40:6; Luke 3:6) implies non-Israelites (cf. Acts 28:28).

as an end in itself, void of any benefit for the "other," constitutes a mutation of that identity. It is difficult to overstate the significance of the fact that John—thus far the Spirit-empowered figure par excellence (cf. Luke 1:15)—begins his public ministry with a *critique of a particular expression of ethnic social identity*. Appreciating the fundamental position of John's critique in Luke 3:8 helps us to notice that John's answers to the triple "What shall we do?" (Luke 3:10, 12, 14) are inseparably connected to, and function as correctives against, the assumptions associated with anticipated claims to privileged ethnic identity.[2] The logic of the passage runs in this way:

1. John urges his hearers to live lives that show evidence of proper relationship to God via repentance:

    Bear fruits that befit repentance. (3:8a)

2. John warns that ethnic descent does not guarantee proper relationship to God.[3]

    Do not begin to say to yourselves, "We have Abraham as our father"; for I tell you, God is able from these stones to raise up children to Abraham. (3:8b)

3. John's answers to the "What should we do?" questions (3:10, 12, 14) exemplify proper repentance *and* properly expressed identity as a "son of Abraham." If inappropriate claims to Abrahamic descent and appropriate repentance are antitheses, it logically follows that proper repentance and properly expressed Israelite ethnic identity are two sides of the same coin. John's answers, unique to Luke's Gospel, tell us both what repentance looks like and what Israelite identity looks like in both general and specific cases:[4]

---

2. Schweizer (1984, 74–76) says Abrahamic descent is "not enough" but he does not connect this with John's commands. John's instructions are commonly interpreted as "ethical commands" detached from the ethnic identity activated in 3:8. Böhlemann (1997, 178–97) thinks the instructions are for solidarity with the "Randgruppen," but misses the fact that Luke is not only calling for solidarity with, but also a certain social posture *from*, all classes of Israelites. Sahlin 1948, 57 strangely suggests that John's commands "derartig bleibt die Grund anschauung der rabbinischen Ethik."

3. Fitzmyer 1981, 469 suggests a first-century tradition that assumed Abrahamic descent provided protection from divine wrath. See *Pss. Sol.* 18.4; Str-B 116–21; Luke 16:24; John 8:33–39; Acts 7:2; Rom 4:1.

4. Fitzmyer 1981, 470 argues tax collectors and soldiers were Israelites.

To all people: "He who has two coats, let him share with him who has none; and he who has food, let him do likewise." (Luke 3:11)

To tax collectors: "Collect no more than is appointed you." (Luke 3:13)

To soldiers: "Rob no one by violence or by false accusation, and be content with your wages." (Luke 3:14)

John's examples of lives befitting repentance, and hence of proper Israelite identity, are bound by two threads: the *refusal to abuse privileged identity* to the detriment of others (Luke 3:12–14) and the *willingness to use privilege* to bless others (Luke 3:10–11). These threads imply a broadly conceived turn beyond the self to the "other" and reflect precisely the Spirit-empowered ministry anticipated for John in Luke 1:16–17:

He [John] will *turn* many of the sons of Israel to the Lord their God... *turn* the hearts of the fathers to the children, and the disobedient to the wisdom of the just, to make ready for the Lord a people prepared.

In other words, preparation for the coming of the Lord involves what can be conceptualized as a two-step turning away from the self and toward (1) God and (2) the "other." This anticipates the Great Commandment in Luke 10:27, a fact made more significant by Luke's illustration in that passage that neighbor-love is best exemplified when it crosses social boundaries.[5] For John, Israelite identity and concern for the "other" appear to be inseparable.[6] Therefore, expressions of ethnic identity that exhaust themselves in in-group bias but have no concern for the "other" are improper. SIT is helpful here to understand that, because groups are highly constitutive of individual social identity, the turn beyond the self and the turn beyond the group are two closely related phenomena in the formation of an allocentric identity. Just as Zechariah and Simeon, filled by the Spirit, envisioned the benefits of God extending beyond the in-group, so the Spirit-filled John urges a turn beyond the self toward God and other.

Several conclusions rest upon this reading of John's preaching. First, though ethnic identity is not equated with proper relationship to God, Israelite identity has not lost its significance for Luke.[7] To the contrary,

---

5. Bovon 2002, 37 links Luke 1:16–17 and 10:25–28, but not Luke's explanatory parable in 10:29–37. Esler 2000, 325–57 discusses the social boundary issues in 10:25–37.

6. Robertson 1982, 406 connects "radical vocational fidelity and integrity" but does not appreciate the expression of ethnic identity critiqued in Luke 3:8.

7. Some have seen Luke 3:8 as a repudiation of the value of Abrahamic descent; see Kazmierski 1987, 30–31: "For the prophet, Israel's historic prerogative [as children of Abraham] now counts for nothing." Marshall 1978, 140 comments less

Israel's identity—privileged as God's elect ἔθνος—remains fundamental.[8] Second, the critique that John levels indicates that Luke is convinced that the proper expression of privileged identity is demonstrated by a refusal to take privileged identity as an end in itself. Israel's privilege is to be leveraged for the "other." The anticipation of this theme in John's preaching will become increasingly clear in Luke–Acts with regard to the expression of all manifestations of identity. Third, the scholarly tendency to refer to John's teaching as "timeless ethical instruction" or "ein anständiges Leben" marked by "Solidarität mit dem Volk" is far too weak.[9] John is not simply pressing his hearers toward a sense of moral decency, but toward a fundamentally different posture toward the "other" in fulfillment of Gabriel's announcement in Luke 1:16–17. John, *who must be interpreted as a bearer of the Spirit*, presses his hearers toward what I have categorized as an allocentric identity.

4.2. The Spirit and Jesus: Identifying the Son of God

The baptism of Jesus marks the beginning of Luke's definitive answer to John's critique of defective expressions of Israelite ethnic identity.[10] There is no doubt that the baptism of Jesus is a paradigmatic moment in Luke's Gospel. The search for the appropriate parallel between Jesus' baptismal experience and Spirit-reception and the experience of the early church has proved to be a decisive dividing point in understanding Luke's conception of the Spirit.[11] In this section I will argue that the Spirit serves

---

stringently, "Abrahamic descent does not count for anything: all are required to repent." Dennison 1982, 16 suggests the family of Abraham at this point is conceived "universally," but this races ahead of Luke's text. Luke will demonstrate that distinct identity is not problematic, but that privileged identity implies the leveraging of resources for the sake of the "other."

    8. See Acts 3:25, but note (with Bock 1994, 301) that Luke 3:8 opens the door for "surprising" children of Abraham.

    9. Bovon 2002, 123; Klein 2006, 166.

    10. There is not space to discuss John's proclamation that Jesus will baptize "with the Holy Spirit and with fire" (Luke 3:16), other than to note that we will later see that it is Jesus who pours out the Spirit on his early followers. Interpretive options are set forth in Nolland 1989, 142. Dunn 1970, 43 suggests the disappearance of "and with fire" in Acts 1:5; 11:16 is because Jesus exhausted the fiery tribulation in his own "baptism with fire" (cf. Luke 12:49–50). I suggest that Luke builds toward a definitive interpretation of Spirit-baptism in Acts 11:16 when Peter connects Spirit-baptism with the mark of a common in-group identity that crosses ethnic boundaries.

    11. I am referring to the tendency either to make Jesus' experience the paradigmatic experience of divine sonship (Büchsel 1929; Dunn 1970) or the paradigmatic experience of missionary (messianic) empowerment (Menzies 1991; Cho 2005).

a crucial identity-marking function in relation to Jesus that sets off a concentrated reflection on Jesus' *identity* as "Son of God." This is highlighted by the overtly public nature of the Spirit manifestation at Jesus' baptism.

Jesus' baptism is the first in a series of four identifications of Jesus as "Son of God":[12]

> Lukas legt durch seine Komposition von Taufe (Lk 3.21–22), Genealogie (3.23–38) und Versuchung Jesu (4.1–13) einen besonderen Akzent auf die verbindende Sohnesthematik.[13]

Because Luke's readers are already aware of Jesus' "Son of God" identity (1:35; 2:49), we must attend closely to the context of the baptismal affirmation of Jesus' sonship in order to understand how it fits into Luke's program:[14]

> Now when all the people were baptized, and when Jesus also had been baptized and was praying, the heaven was opened, and the Holy Spirit descended on him in bodily form, as a dove, and a voice came from heaven, "You are my beloved Son; with you I am well pleased."[15]

Three observations are relevant. First, Luke's Jesus is already aware of his divine sonship (Luke 2:49), so the proclamation is not for Jesus' benefit. Second, Jesus' identity as "Son of God," among other things, positions Jesus as a (the?) prototypical Israelite. The title is a distinct allusion to Ps 2:7 LXX, in which context the king of Israel is designated God's son.[16] The title itself, when understood to be a title for the king of Israel, or indeed for Israel itself (cf. Exod 4:22; Deut 14:1; Hos 11:1), stands in counterpoint to the entitlement claim John anticipates in Luke 3:8. Third, unique Lukan material in the passage demonstrates that Luke envisions this as Jesus' *public identification* by the heavenly voice and the Spirit.

Luke's intention that his hearers assume the public nature of Jesus' identification by the Spirit is evident in two ways.[17] First, Luke alone sets

---

12. Luke 3:22, 38; 4:3, 9.
13. Hasitschka 2002, 75.
14. The references to Jesus as "Son of God" in Luke 1:35 and 2:49 defeat adoptionist readings of Luke 3:22 (Miller 1986, 54).
15. Luke 3:21–22.
16. The designation of Jesus as the well-pleasing son of God is a likely allusion to Ps 2:7 and Isa 42:1 (see Nolland 1989, 163). Bock (1994, 341–43) lists other options (Ps 2:7 alone; Isa 42:1 alone; Exod 4:22–23; for "beloved," see possibly Gen 22:12; Isa 41:8 and/or 44:2). It is significant that Isa 42:1 depicts a Spirit-anointed servant extending justice (42:1) and light (42:6) to the ἔθνη.
17. Bock 1994, 340–41 contends, "Jesus had a private experience of the Spirit, but it was not an entirely private or internal vision, for John the Baptist also could testify

4. Critiquing Defective Identities

Jesus' baptism in the context of "all the people" (Luke 3:21: ἄπαντα τὸν λαόν). The explicitly public nature of the event is not emphasized in the other three Gospels.[18] Second, Mark, Matthew and John restrict the visible experience of the Spirit manifestation only to Jesus or to the Baptizer (Mark 1:10: "*he* saw [εἶδεν]...the Spirit descending"; Matt 3:16: "*he* saw [εἶδεν]...the Spirit of God descending"; John 1:32, the Baptizer speaking: "*I* saw [τεθέαμαι]...the Spirit descend). The use of the third person pronoun in Matt 3:17 ("*This* is my beloved son") may indicate that others heard the voice, though they did not see the dove-like manifestation of the Spirit. Luke, who alone sets Jesus in the midst of "all the people," does not restrict the experience to Jesus, but narrates a *publicly visible* manifestation of the Spirit and the heavenly voice:

> The heaven was opened, and the Holy Spirit descended on him in bodily form, as a dove, and a voice came from heaven.[19]

This is the first of many instances for Luke in which the Spirit, especially when manifest publicly with either visible or audible effect, is integral to *properly discerning a person's identity, especially as it regards that person's relationship to God.*[20] It is no coincidence that these public identifications regularly occur when social identity boundaries are in question.

4.3. Jesus' Genealogy: Incorporating Ethnic Out-groups

The focus on Jesus' identity is immediately drawn in another way in Jesus' genealogy in Luke 3:23–28, which, like all genealogies, functions socially to determine who has access to an in-group.[21]

> One's place in the genealogy is a sign of cultural self-definition more than it is a sign of biological descent.[22]

---

to that event." See also Nolland 1989, 161; Keck 1971. But cf. Lieu 1997, 26; Dennison 1982, 19. Fitzmyer 1981, 480 suggests the second person singular "you" implies only Jesus heard the voice but that all saw the visible manifestations. Johnson 1991, 69 emphasizes the "physical reality" of the event.

18. Parallels: Mark 1:9–11; Matt 3:13–17; John 1:29–34.
19. Luke 3:22.
20. Cf. Acts 2:1–4; 8:17 (ostensibly); 10:44–46; 19:6. Klein 2006, 171 recognizes the public significance, but does not connect Jesus' "identification" with the Spirit: "Die Himmelsstimme spricht die öffentliche Proklamation Jesu zum Gottessohn aus."
21. Hanson and Oakman 1998, 28–29. In Greco-Roman literature, see Diogenes Laertius, *Life of Plato* 3.1–2; Plutarch, *Parallel Lives* 2.1.
22. Hendel 2006, 10. See Cohen 1999, 24 on Herod's fabricated genealogy.

Luke's genealogy traces Jesus' "Son of God" lineage through *Adam* in order to situate Jesus not simply within the Israelite ἔθνος, but within universal humankind. This point is well known.[23]

> Als "sogenannter" Sohn des Joseph und als Kind der Maria ist Jesus allerdings auch noch in anderer Weise Gottessohn und damit unmittelbarer zu Gott als alle anderen Menschen.[24]

Matthew's genealogy includes some non-Israelites (Tamar, Rahab, Ruth, Uriah's wife—all women!), but, by only tracing ancestry to Abraham, creates an out-group composed of people not "related" to Jesus though Abrahamic descent.[25] Luke, while presenting Jesus as fully Israelite, allows Jesus to be situated within an in-group that, even by the most formal reasoning, has no *a priori* ethnic outsiders.[26]

The baptism and genealogy demonstrate that Jesus is "Son of God" in two ways: (1) uniquely, by virtue of his Spirit-creation and special relationship to the Father and (2) in a way analogous to all humankind by virtue of common Adamic descent.

4.4. *Jesus and Satan: Testing Privileged Identity*

Luke gives narrative description to Jesus' "Son of God" identity in Jesus' wilderness temptation (Luke 4:1–14). While commentators regularly note the focus on the faithful expression of Jesus' identity in this pericope, the passage is not usually read in light of the Baptizer's preaching in Luke 3:8.[27] But the logic of the narrative to this point, with its concentrated emphasis on Jesus as "Son of God" in his baptism, his genealogy, and now the temptation, suggests that Luke is contrasting Jesus' identity as "Son of God" (and hence, as representative of Israel) with John's anticipation of the crowd's defective claim to be sons of Abraham.[28] Luke's distinct interest in the relationship between the Spirit and identity leads

---

23. Danker 1988, 98; Johnson 1991, 72, among others.

24. Klein 2006, 174.

25. Keener 1999, 79. The inclusio formed by Matthew's genealogy and the Great Commission (Matt 28:20) appears to be Matthew's means of connecting the Abrahamic covenant with "all the families of the earth."

26. Recognition that Luke's genealogy creates no social "other" is slightly different than Green 1997, 189, who claims the genealogy marks "Jesus' solidarity with all humanity."

27. Wenk 2004, 195; Fitzmyer 1981, 509; Green 1997, 194, among others.

28. For "Son of God" as representative of Israel, see Green 1997, 193; Fitzmyer 1981, 510–11; Wright 1996, 457–63. Jesus' deployments of Deut 8:3; 6:13, 16, narratives of Israel's wilderness testing, further suggest that Luke envisions Jesus as representative of Israel.

him to magnify the role of the Spirit in relation to the Synoptic treatments of Jesus' temptation: (1) Jesus enters the wilderness "full (πλήρης) of the Spirit" (4:1); (2) the Spirit remains with Jesus during the trial (4:1: ἤγετο ἐν τῷ πνεύματι ἐν τῇ ἐρήμῳ); and (3) Jesus emerges from the wilderness "in the power of the Spirit" (4:14: ἐν τῇ δυνάμει τοῦ πνεύματος).[29]

The narrative structure creates a double frame formed by reference to the Spirit's influence upon Jesus (4:1, 14) and the "If you are the Son of God" temptations (4:3, 9). Luke's order is different than Matthew's, which places the "If you are the Son of God" temptations as the first two tests (Matt 4:3, 6). The effect for Luke is that Jesus' "Son of God" identity and the Spirit are brought into close proximity. The "If you are the Son of God" tests tempt Jesus to use his privileged identity to accrue self-benefit by (1) providing food for himself (4:3–4) or (2) taking advantage of the likelihood of God's miraculous rescue (4:9–12 in Luke's context can perhaps be seen as a temptation to gain honor through the miraculous). Luke's unique focus on the temptation to *self*-benefit is evident in his use of the singular λίθος ("stone") in 4:3 (cf. Matt 4:3: λίθοι), which indicates that the temptation was not to be a miraculous provider for his people but simply to use his privileged identity to satisfy himself.[30] Surely it is significant that Jesus never renders a miracle on his own behalf, but only for the benefit of others.[31]

Framed by the "Son of God" temptations is the devil's offer of world dominion. Green is correct to note, given Luke's use of Ps 2 LXX in Luke 3:22—a Psalm which indicates that God will give his "son" all the nations—that the temptation is "an invitation for Jesus to deny his identity as God's Son, substituting in its place an analogous relationship to the devil."[32]

Two features of this story are notable. First, the presence of the Spirit is connected to Jesus' refusal to leverage his privileged identity solely for

---

29. Neither Matthew nor Mark explicitly refers to Jesus' pre-temptation fullness of the Spirit, post-temptation Spirit-empowerment or the role of the Spirit *during* the temptation. Jesus is only "driven into" (Mark 1:12: ἐκβάλλει εἰς) or "led into" (Matt 4:1: ἀνήχθη εἰς) the wilderness by the Spirit (cf. Luke 4:1: ἤγετο ἐν). Fitzmyer 1981, 514 suggests the present participle of πειράζω in 4:2 indicates the simultaneity of the temptations and the Spirit's leading.

30. Johnson 1991, 74 does not account for the singular noun λίθος when he suggests that this is a temptation to "give 'bread in the wilderness' to the people." Fitzmyer 1981, 515 overlooks Luke's point when he suggests Luke changed "Q" in the interest of "plausibility." Bock 1994, 372; Marshall 1978, 179–81; Green 1997, 193–94 observe the personal nature of this test.

31. Cf. Johnson 1991, 76.

32. Green 1997, 194.

self-benefit. Jesus' special relationship with the Father confers many legitimate benefits, but his identity does not exhaust itself in those personal benefits alone. Jesus' Spirit-empowered expression of privileged identity is a counterpoint to the anticipated entitlement claim reflected in Luke 3:8.

The second point anticipates a key Lukan theme that emerges fully in Acts, so I will only briefly mention it here. Luke expresses a distinct contrast between the influence of the Spirit and the influence of Satan as it impinges upon relationships with the "other." For Luke, Satan turns people away from the other and inward towards themselves. Conversely, the Spirit turns people away from the self (or from a restrictive focus on the in-group) and outward toward the other.[33] Jesus refuses the devil's temptation to turn inward in pure self-interest. This anticipation of allocentric identity—the ability to love self/in-group and the "other"— will become a consistent theme in Jesus' ministry.

4.5. Jesus and His Townsfolk: Ethnic Identity, Resource Allocation and the "Other"

Jesus emerges from his temptation as a figure who has, by virtue of the Spirit, resisted the temptation to turn inward and to leverage privileged identity only for the sake of the self. Beginning particularly in Nazareth (Luke 4:16–30), Jesus will give a positive demonstration of Spirit-empowered allocentric identity that will become a central feature of Luke's identity-forming program. It is precisely this allocentric identity—with a horizon beyond the in-group—that interacts disastrously with the identity-based assumptions of Jesus' townsfolk in Nazareth. SIT is a useful heuristic tool with which to interpret Luke 4:14–30, and here I call attention to the relationship between subgroup identity, relative prototypicality and entitlement discussed in Chapter 2. There we learned that subgroups tend to project their characteristics as prototypical for their ingroup. The resulting assumption of subgroup prototypicality prompts entitlement claims that implicate group resource allocation. *I will argue that the Nazareth incident can be interpreted compellingly as Jesus' refusal to be bound by the entitlement claims of his own Nazareth subgroup.*[34] The ability to look beyond one's own group (which, in a collectivistic culture,

---

33. See, for example, Peter: Luke 22:31–32; Judas: Luke 22:3–4; Acts 1:24–25; Ananias and Sapphira: Acts 5:1–11; Simon the Samaritan: Acts 8:18–24.

34. My position has affinity with Tannehill 1972, 62: "It is not so much that Jesus goes elsewhere because he is rejected as that he is rejected because he announces that it is God's will and his mission to go elsewhere."

is highly constitutive of social identity) will become paradigmatic for Luke's treatment of identity in the Gospel.[35]

While there is little question about the programmatic nature of Luke 4:16–30 (Luke moves the passage to an extremely prominent narrative position, especially compared to its location in Mark 6:1–6), the passage itself has proved difficult.[36] If the passage is programmatic, we would expect it to reverberate throughout Luke. Thus, proper interpretation is imperative. It must be asked, what is it about the shared social script in Nazareth that prompts Jesus to reject the apparently positive response of his townsfolk? There are four main interpretive options, each of which leaves significant questions:

1. Nothing in the response of the crowd elicits a negative response from Jesus.[37] Yet it is not clear how this position cannot account for Jesus' seemingly confrontational reply to the crowd.
2. ἐμαρτύρουν and ἐθαύμαζον (4:22) have positive connotations, but the question regarding Jesus' parentage expresses the animosity clearly evident in the Matthean and Markan presentations where Jesus' rhetorical skill is appreciated but his claims are understood to overstep his humble origins.[38] It is difficult to account for the sudden change of the crowd's heart—mid-sentence, no less—in

---

35. Major pneumatological enquiries of Luke–Acts pay little attention to this full pericope. Menzies and Turner dispute Luke's redaction of the Isaiah passages in Luke 4:18–19 to determine whether Luke's Spirit does more than empower speech. So Menzies 1991, 168: "The passage as it stands undeniably emphasizes preaching as the most prominent dimension of Jesus' mission." Turner 1996, 266 thinks Luke portrays Jesus as the "Isaianic soteriological prophet," the "Mosaic prophet" and the "Davidic king" in service of Luke's "New Exodus" scheme, thus the Spirit is connected to the inauguration of the New Exodus. Neither Menzies nor Turner comment on the *effect* of the Spirit-anointed proclamation upon the crowd. Wenk 2004, 220 does not treat the entire passage, but links prophetic speech in 4:18–19 with perlocutionary effect: "The Spirit serves to authorize the prophet in proclaiming a message, guarantees the God-spoken character of it, and is the agent by which the salvation is accomplished." Cho 2005 and Dunn 1970 do not address the passage.

36. For Luke 4:16–30 as programmatic, see Fitzmyer 1981, 529; Nolland 1989, 195, and so on. Because 4:14–15 forms indispensable context for 4:16–30, I will treat 4:14–30 as a unit.

37. Fitzmyer 1981, 528–35; Schürmann 1969, 234; Kerr 2006, 139; Green 1997, 214–15. Green's alternative explanation, that Jesus is "one of us" (215–17), bears similarity to my position.

38. See Rohrbaugh 1995. Cf. Ellis 1974, 97; Malina and Rohrbaugh 2003, 243; Bock 1994, 415; Nolland 1989, 198; Turner 1996, 218 n. 14. Porter 2006, 115–16 takes this view furthest and suggests that it is Jesus' veiled reference to his own divinity that provokes the crowd.

this reading.[39] I suspect this position is colored by Matthean and Markan concerns more than Lukan concerns.[40]
3. All three verbs in 4:22 carry negative connotations.[41] This suggests the translation, "And they all testified against him and were aghast at the words of grace which proceeded from his mouth," to which Jesus simply responds in kind.[42] This solution assumes that Jesus' omission in his reading of Isa 61:2, "the day of vengeance of our God" (presumably applied to non-Israelites), prompts the crowd to be angry about the words of grace *only*. Nolland and Hill have defeated this position.[43]
4. Luke is a clumsy editor who has conflated two sources or events.[44]

4.5.1. *Jesus as Social Exegete*

The interpretive crux of the passage is the hinge between the crowd's positive reception in 4:22 and Jesus' response in 4:23:

> And all spoke well (ἐμαρτύρουν) of him, and wondered (ἐθαύμαζον) at the gracious words which proceeded out of his mouth; and they said (ἔλεγον) "Is this not Joseph's son?"
>
> And he said to them, "Doubtless (πάντως) you will quote to me the proverb, 'Physician heal thyself; what we have heard you did at Capernaum, do here also in your own hometown (πατρίδι)'."[45]

---

39. Luke's typical use of ἔλεγον (which introduces the question of patrilineage) is neutral in tone, with context determining whether the words spoken are adversarial (e.g. Luke 22:65) or appreciative (e.g. Luke 9:31). This form appears 12 times in Luke–Acts (Luke 4:22; 9:31; 22:65; 24:10; Acts 2:13; 9:21; 12:15; 17:18; 21:4; 25:20; 28:4, 6). Contextual factors in Luke 4 do not clearly call for a negative reading.

40. Hill 1971, 163.

41. Jeremias 1958, 45.

42. Jeremias 1958, 45; Marshall 1978, 185–86.

43. Hill 1971, 164–65 gives six counterarguments: (1) because the Semitic character of Luke's language is questionable, arguing that ἐμαρτύρουν is an Aramaic dative of disadvantage is problematic; (2) if Luke intended unmitigated rage to be conveyed by the audience he could have been clearer; (3) Luke does not use μαρτυρεῖν in a negative sense; (4) "Is not this Joseph's son?" does not require disbelief and criticism; (5) the final clause of 4:20—ἀτενίζω—is used often by Luke and always means a "gaze of expectant faith or trust" (See Acts 1:10; 6:15; also 3:4; 7:55; 11:6; 13:9; Luke 22:56); (6) heavily weighting the omission of "vengeance of God" is difficult given Luke's use of a composite Isaianic quotation. Cf. Nolland 1979b, 220.

44. Luce 1933, 121. For source suggestions, see Fitzmyer 1981, 526–27, who claims, "The story in its present form is obviously conflated. The sequence of sentences is not smooth" (527). Danker 1988, 108 surrenders: "Any attempt to analyze the thinking of the crowd at Nazareth is bound to fail."

45. My translation.

4. Critiquing Defective Identities

Jesus' ability to anticipate the forthcoming request to do Capernaum-like acts of power ("Doubtless you will quote to me…") is first of all indicative of Jesus' acuity as an interpreter of his own social context.[46] I suggest that Jesus' pointed response is a rejection not of Nazarene acceptance full stop, but rather of a social assumption that Jesus' townsfolk share. Jesus' townsfolk assume that their privileged status as members of Jesus' subgroup grants them special entitlement to benefits conferred by Jesus.

Before turning to the narrative itself, it is essential to map the potentially available nested identities within this pericope.[47] Luke has made it clear that the terminal identity in view to this point is Israelite ethnic identity. John's warning to those claiming Abrahamic descent in Luke 3:8 indicates that the benefits of the in-group were broadly anticipated to be available to ethnic Israelites writ large. Nested here within Israelite identity is Galilean regional identity, a fact of which Luke among all the Gospel writers seems most keenly cognizant.[48] Yet in this pericope Luke appears to be drawing our attention particularly to Nazareth as the locus of identity for Jesus and his townsfolk.[49] From an etic perspective we can conceptualize these identities as follows:

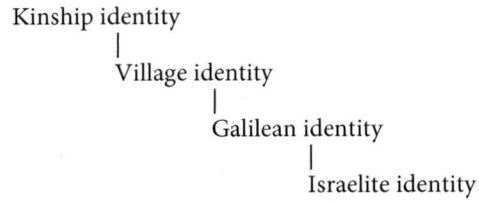

Potentially Salient Social Identities in Luke 4:14–30[50]

While Jesus is broadly interpreted by Galileans as "one of us," in Nazareth Jesus both operates with and is interpreted through the shared frame of Nazarene social identity.[51]

---

46. The issue is not Jesus' "omniscience," *pace* Green 1997, 216. See Kerr 2006, 139; Tannehill 1986, 70 for Jesus as an astute social interpreter.

47. See Chapter 2 for a discussion of nested identity. Nested identities become salient based upon intergroup contact. In inter-ethnic situations, ethnicity is salient, while in inter-regional situations, regional identity can be salient, and so on.

48. See the discussion in following section.

49. Esler 2003, 40–76 argues that one's city of residence can be the basis for the formation of a viable subgroup identity. Paul reflects this when claiming to be a citizen of "no mean city" (Tarsus) in Acts 21:39 as do the Ephesian devotees to Artemis in Acts 19:24–35. Cf. Philo, *Flaccus* 46.

50. Cf. the nested identities in Wales described in Jenkins 1997, 41.

51. Geiger 2002, 242 claims "Multiple and complex identities may have been almost the rule, rather than the exception [in ancient Galilee]."

According to SIT, we would expect that members of the Nazareth subgroup would project their village identity as prototypical Galilean (and probably even Israelite) identity, and would therefore make entitlement claims to the benefits of Jesus' ministry based upon their shared membership in Jesus' subgroup. I suggest that Jesus' response to his townsfolk indicates his awareness of this implicit claim and subverts the assumption by pressing his hearers toward an allocentric understanding of the proper deployment of privileged identity. I will demonstrate this claim in a close reading that focuses upon five features of the text and its context: (1) Jesus' overwhelmingly positive reception in Galilee; (2) Luke's emphasis on Jesus' village identity as opposed to kinship identity (especially vis-à-vis Matthew and Mark), as well as the social assumptions inherent in common village identity; (3) the intelligibility of Jesus' enigmatic response as a rejection of these entitlement assumptions; (4) the role of the Elijah and Elisha stories in reorienting social assumptions; and (5) the resulting disenfranchisement of Jesus from his own subgroup.

4.5.2. *The Positive Reception of Jesus throughout Galilee*

The Nazareth pericope is situated within an inclusio of Galilean approval framed by Luke 4:14–15, where Jesus' synagogue teaching brings him "glorification by all," and Luke 4:31–44, where Jesus' work in "Capernaum, *a city of Galilee*" causes the people to be "astonished." Luke, emphatically in comparison to the other Gospels, sees Galilean identity as essential to the initial Jesus-movement and understands Galilee to be largely "safe" territory.[52] With the exception of the Nazareth incident (which Luke clearly takes as a special case), Galilean opposition to Jesus is expressed most intensely by the Pharisaic deliberation regarding "what they might do to Jesus' (Luke 6:11).[53] This is in contrast with the deadly opposition expressed in the Synoptic parallels which depict Pharisees *in Galilee* plotting "how to destroy him."[54] Luke's Jesus does not experience

---

52. Luke distinguishes Galilean identity within broader Israelite identity (Luke 13:1–2; 22:59; 23:6). The disciples are categorized as Galileans before Pentecost both in social isolation (Acts 1:11) and in the context of other regional identities (Acts 2:7). Cf. Acts 5:37; 10:37. Josephus categorizes Galileans as an ἔθνος on two occasions (Josephus, *B.J.* 2.520; 4.105). Marquis (2007, 64) describes ongoing ambiguity in the relationship between Galilee and Jerusalem in the first century.

53. Vermes (1973, 57) argues Pharisaic opposition in Luke 6:11 was "mostly foreign and not local." Jesus encounters resistance in Luke 5:17–26, 29–39; 6:1–5, 6–11, but he never encounters the threat of deadly violence outside Judea (save for the exceptional case in Nazareth).

54. Mark 3:6 // Matt 12:14.

deadly opposition until he enters Judea and Jerusalem.⁵⁵ The relative safety of Galilee is highlighted by the emphatic turn toward Jerusalem in 9:51, which leads immediately to extreme anti-Samaritan ethnocentric polemic expressed by James and John promptly upon leaving their "home turf."⁵⁶ For Luke, "Galilean" is an in-group identity shared by Jesus and most other residents of Galilee. There is nothing in Luke 4 to suggest that Jesus' message is inherently offensive to members of the Galilean in-group.⁵⁷

4.5.3. *The Positive Reception of Jesus in Nazareth*

Jesus' reading of the composite passage from Isaiah is significant for Luke's portrait of Jesus for reasons that stretch beyond the compass of this study. I will mention two significant factors. First, Jesus identifies himself as a Spirit-anointed figure by claiming "The Spirit of the Lord is upon me" (Luke 4:18). We will see that, like John's Spirit-empowered inaugural appearance, Jesus' Spirit-anointed initial public appearance features a critique of an identity-based assumption. Second, the conflated Isaiah passage (Isa 61:1–2a; 58:6), perhaps an expression of Israel's Jubilee, suggests the conferral of unabashedly positive benefits, a factor that whets the appetite of Jesus' audience.⁵⁸ At stake in the response of the crowd and in Jesus' counter-response are questions regarding who, precisely, have access to the benefits conferred by Jesus. The interplay between identity and entitlement is clearly in play.

The crowd's response to Jesus' claim to have "fulfilled" the Isaianic quotation (4:21) is fully positive, a fact reflected by Luke's characteristic use of the verbs in question. The crowd gazes expectantly at Jesus: "the eyes of all in the synagogue were staring toward him" (4:20: ἦσας ἀτενίζοντες αὐτῷ), a phrase nearly identical to the disciples' post-Ascension "staring toward heaven" (Acts 1:10: ἀτενίζοντες ἦσαν).⁵⁹ ἀτενίζω

---

55. Luke 11:53–54 (in Judea); 19:47 (in Jerusalem); 20:19–20. Mark 3:6 sets murderous opposition to Jesus (from Pharisees and Herodians, the latter of which are likely from Galilee) in Galilee. Matt 12:14 omits the Pharisees, but places the same incident in Galilee prior to Jesus' entrance into Judea.

56. Luke 9:54.

57. Note as potential counter evidence the possibility of John the Baptizer's arrest as it might relate to the offense of his message. The Baptizer's arrest, however, is described by Luke as resulting from Herod's personal vendetta (Luke 3:19–20).

58. See Hultgren 2002, 164–65; Kyo-Seon Shin 1989; Strobel 1972 for the likely Jubilee theme. Cf. the use of Isa 61:1–2 in 11QMelch 2.7–16. Turner 1996, 266 suggests this is "New Exodus" imagery.

59. ἀτενίζω: Luke 22:56; Acts 3:4, 12; 6:15; 7:55; 10:4; 11:6; 13:9; 14:9; 23:1. Only Acts 13:9 carries a potentially negative sense, though the context suggests a gaze of perception, not a malicious glare.

expresses pensive wonder or the quest for perception. The crowd speaks well (ἐμαρτύρουν) of Jesus (4:22). Luke regularly uses μαρτυρέω to describe a community's positive reception of an individual based on that person's prior role within the community (Acts 6:3; 10:22; 16:2; 22:12).[60] Jesus' townsfolk speak positively of him based upon his persuasive words and, perhaps, based upon his prior role in Nazareth (entering the synagogue there was his "custom"—εἰωθα [4:16]). Finally, the crowd expresses amazement (θαυμάζω) about the words of grace that pour from Jesus' mouth. θαυμάζω is a close cognate of the *positive* reaction expressed by the crowd in Capernaum in Luke 4:36 (θάμβος).[61] "Words of grace" appear to be, for Luke, an idiom for the message of Jesus (cf. Acts 14:3). Thus far, this is not "Jesus' rejection in Nazareth" but rather the reception of a hometown boy made good.[62]

The catena of goodwill evident in 4:22 climaxes with the collectively asked question, "Is this not Joseph's son?" The question is not, as I will demonstrate below, a denigration of Jesus based upon the low honor status of his family.[63] Rather, the question celebrates the fact that Jesus is a member of their own subgroup because Nazareth is Jesus' πατρίς.[64] If this is correct, Jesus' harsh reaction to the initial crowd approval must be taken as his rejection of a social assumption (namely, an entitlement claim) based upon common Nazarene subgroup identity. To support this point I will first present data that demonstrate that Luke is not (as is the case with the Synoptic parallels) interested in Jesus' kinship-based honor status, but rather is concerned with dynamics arising from common village identity.

4.5.4. Nazareth as Jesus' πατρίς

Matthew and Mark make much less of this incident than Luke, and have a clear interest in Jesus' violation of his kinship-based honor status.[65] Readings that understand the Lukan treatment as an attack on Jesus

---

60. There are no negatively connotative deployments of μαρτυρέω in Luke–Acts (Luke 4:22; Acts 6:3; 10:22, 43; 13:22; 14:3; 15:8; 16:2; 22:5, 12; 23:11; 26:5).

61. Of the 18 appearances of θαυμάζω in Luke–Acts (Luke 1:21, 63; 2:18, 33; 4:22; 7:9; 8:25; 9:43; 11:14, 38; 20:26; 24:12, 41; Acts 2:7; 3:12; 4:13; 7:31; 13:41), three have possible negative connotations (Luke 1:63; 11:38; Acts 13:41), though the first two (at least) may connote surprise rather than animosity.

62. Talbert 1982, 56 appreciates that the pressure on Jesus is because he is a "hometown boy," yet he does not develop the social ramifications of his observation.

63. Contra Rohrbaugh 1995, 193–95.

64. For a similar position, see Porter 2006, 110.

65. Contra Fitzmyer 1981, 357, the proverbs do not have essentially the same force in Matthew and Mark as they do in Luke's unique rendering.

kinship-based honor are, I suggest, colored by the Synoptic parallels (Mark 6:1–6; Matt 13:54–58) more than by Luke's unique treatment. Luke's positioning of the pericope (the initial scene in Jesus' public ministry) and his extended treatment should be enough to alert us to the fact that Luke sees special significance in this event. A comparison with the Synoptic parallels underscores in three ways the fact that Luke does not think the crowd critiques Jesus for overstepping his kinship-based honor status. First, both Matthew and Mark emphatically situate Jesus within his kinship group by referring to his father, mother, sisters and brothers. Matthew especially suggests that Jesus' claims are incommensurate with his lineage ("Is this not the carpenter's son… Where then did this man get all this?" [Matt 13:55, 56]). Second, Jesus' response in Matthew and Mark indicates that honor (τίμη) is at stake (οὐκ ἔστιν προφήτης ἄτιμος… Mark 6:4; Matt 13:57), whereas "honor" is absent from Luke's account.[66] Third, the locus of the dishonor in Matthew and Mark is not only within the prophet's πατρίς, but also within his οἰκία (Mark 6:4; Matt 13:57) and among his συγγενής (Mark 6:4). Jesus' transgression of his honor status in Matthew and Mark causes great offense to the crowd (Mark 6:3; 13:57: σκανδαλίζω). Contrast this with Luke's presentation. Luke has no extended mention of Jesus' kinship group, only his father. Luke's Jesus does not sense that he is "dishonored" (ἄτιμος), but he is not "acceptable" (Luke 4:24: δεκτός). δεκτός appears in Luke 4:19 and is clearly *not* an honor word (cf. Acts 10:35!). Finally, Luke's Jesus is aware that the locus of his unacceptability is his πατρίς (Luke 4:24), not his οἰκία or his συγγενής. In short, Luke's portrayal of the Nazareth incident must be situated within Jesus' πατρίς and the local village identity arising from that affiliation, not within the confines of his family's honor status.[67] Luke emphasizes the significance of the πατρίς setting in other ways as well.

Luke introduces "Nazareth" in 4:16 with the relative clause οὗ ἦν τεθραμμένος: where he had been "reared," or more literally, "provided with food."[68] This is the only instance of τρέφω as a perfect participle

---

66. The parallel in John 4:43–44 is concerned with honor (τιμή), though the Johannine context and concerns are very different.

67. BDAG, 788 gives among possible definitions "a relatively restricted area as locale of one's immediate family and ancestry." Some English translations render the word "homeland," but this ignores both the contextual clues in 4:16 and the fact that Luke uses χώρα for something like "home-country" or "fatherland."

68. τρέφω occurs in passive voice only in Acts 12:20 and Rev 12:14 and indicates the dependence of the receiving party on the one making provision. See LSJ, τρέφω.

with passive voice in the New Testament.⁶⁹ Josephus uses the verb in this form, always with overtones of intimate familiarity.⁷⁰ Jesus was raised in Nazareth and these are, presumably, the people who know him best.⁷¹ In localized village settings, individuals are highly visible and pressure toward norm conformity is high.⁷² Moreover, rural settings tend to be more collectivistic than urban communities, a factor that leads to higher levels of group identity.⁷³

Jesus' familiarity in the village is underscored by Luke's attestation that it was customary for Jesus to attend the *Nazareth* synagogue, likely also implying that Jesus customarily read in the *Nazareth* synagogue:

Καὶ ἦλθεν εἰς Ναζαρά, οὗ ἦν τεθραμμένος, καὶ εἰσῆλθεν κατὰ τὸ εἰωθὸς αὐτῷ ἐν τῇ ἡμέρᾳ σαββάτων εἰς τὴν συναγωγὴν καὶ ἀνέστη ἀναγνῶναι.

When he came to Nazareth, where he had been brought up, he went to the synagogue on the Sabbath day, as was his custom. He stood up to read. (Luke 4:16)

While commentators usually assume that the clause κατὰ τὸ εἰωθὸς αὐτῷ refers to Jesus' custom simply to attend synagogue in whatever locale he found himself on the Sabbath (and indeed we can infer that fact as well), Luke's placement of the clause may indicate that Jesus regularly participated in the synagogue worship of his own village.⁷⁴ The synagogue itself should be understood as a primary locus of village life and identity.⁷⁵ Jesus is, as it were, a hometown boy made good who is now faced with the expectations commensurate with his village identity.

---

69. Paul uses ἀνατεθραμμένος when he presents Paul's attempt to establish common identity with Jerusalemites in Acts 22:3.

70. Josephus, *A.J.* 1.253; 10.226; 17.324; *C. Ap.* 1.141 (the latter work, especially, gives a sense of the familiarity one has in and with the place where they were "reared").

71. Jesus is known throughout Luke–Acts via his village identity: "Jesus of Nazareth" (Luke 4:34; 18:37; 24:19; Acts 2:22; 6:14; 10:38; 22:8; 26:9). In Acts 22:8 "Jesus of Nazareth" is Jesus' self-identification.

72. Cairns 1982, 282.

73. Colic-Peisker and Walker 2003, 356–57.

74. Nolland 1989, 195 suggests the "custom" was teaching in synagogues and not "his earlier practice in Nazareth, nor generally…his practice of attending synagogue." This would render 4:16 superfluous. We already know from 4:15 that Jesus was spending a lot of time in Galilean synagogues. We no longer need to be told that synagogue attendance was customary. Green 1997, 209 suggests reading the Scriptures in the synagogue was Jesus' "custom," but he does not locate this especially in Nazareth.

75. Levine 2005, 172: "The synagogue encapsulated Jewish communal life within its walls: the political and liturgical, the social and educational, the judicial and

4. Critiquing Defective Identities 89

Honor/shame readings of Luke 4:22 overlook the fact that in collectivistic societies success for one member of the group is a feather in the collective cap of the entire group.[76] This is evident in Israelite literature that ascribes great honor, in both life and in death, to local figures who have achieved success. This latter is evident in the customary desire to bury local heroes in their own πατρίς and so to honor them.[77] A similar phenomenon is evident in the honor ascribed to successful athletes in Greco-Roman contexts. Athletic victories were construed as a gift to the πατρίς and success "had a social importance that went well beyond the interest of the individuals concerned."[78] Honor for athletic success was accrued mainly by elites who had time and resources for training in the *gymnasion*, but low status local "heroes" were also honored.[79] An inscription from Asia Minor tells of L. Septimus Flavianus Flavillianus who won a wrestling title (in 212 C.E.) and received an honorary inscription from his πατρίς proclaiming that "the πατρίς honored [him] propitiously."[80] Contrary to readings of the Nazareth incident that assume that Jesus would be looked down upon because his lofty claims overstep his honor status, there is a sense of hometown pride in successful members of the πατρίς.

It appears that there were clear social expectations placed upon successful members of a πατρίς. Data from Josephus suggest it was normative for those who had achieved power or influence quickly to leverage their position to benefit their πατρίς:

---

spiritual." Josephus, *A.J.* 14.235, 256–61, describes the broad role of the synagogue for local community identity. Levine lists seven functions of the pre-70 synagogue: political deliberation (Josephus, *Vita* 271–98, 331); meeting place for subgroups within the community; professional guilds; worship; communal meals (*A.J.* 14.214–16; cf. *m. Zavim* 3.2); the place for the administration of justice—which in Judea was for the most part exercised on the local level (see Matt 10:17–18; 23:24; Mark 13:9; Luke 12:11; 21:12; Acts 22:19); perhaps hospitality for visitors—see the Theodotus inscription, though this might be unique to the Jerusalem pilgrimage. Most other evidence is post-70. See *y. Megillah* 3.1.73d; *y. Ketubbot* 13.35c; *b. Ketubbot* 105a—for the claim that there were 480 synagogues in pre-70 Jerusalem, each with two schools.

76. Chen et al. 1998, 1490–1502 demonstrate that the success of an individual in a collectivistic society increases in-group bias in the group. Triandis et al. 1990, 1007–8: "The self is defined as an appendage of the in-group in collectivist cultures and as a separate and distinct entity in individualist cultures." In a collectivist culture what happens to the individual happens to the in-group, for good or for ill.

77. E.g. 1 Macc 2:70; 9:19–21; 13:25–30.

78. Van Nijf 2001, 306.

79. Van Nijf 2001, 325.

80. *Supplementum Epigraphicum Graecum* xliv, 1194.

> When Antipater had made this speech, Caesar appointed Hyrcanus to be high priest… He also gave Hyrcanus permission to raise up the walls of his own city (πατρίς), upon his asking that favour of him, for they had been demolished by Pompey.[81]

> John's lack of money had hereto restrained him in his ambition after command and in his attempts to advance himself; but when he saw that Josephus was highly pleased with the activity of his temperament, he persuaded him, *in the first place*, to entrust him with the repairing of the walls of his native city (πατρίς) [Gischala].[82]

If Josephus is reflecting a cultural (and perhaps even distinctly Galilean!) assumption that successful individuals will first turn their benefaction to their πατρίς, then we have a clear expression of the possible assumptions behind the eager rhetorical question, "Is this not Joseph's son?" Jesus' fellow Nazarenes expect, by virtue of their common subgroup identity, that Jesus will extend them privileged access to the benefits he confers. This phenomenon has been regularly observed by SIT theorists and can, as I will now demonstrate, account for all the salient features of the pericope.

4.5.5. *Jesus' Awareness of Nazareth-specific Entitlement Claims*

To this point, Jesus has experienced only eager acceptance from his townsfolk. Jesus, however, appears to discern something unacceptable behind the adoring response of the Nazareth synagogue crowd. He is well-enough versed in the shared social script of his village that with confidence he can say,

> Doubtless (πάντως) you will say to me the parable, "Physician, heal yourself! That which we heard you did in Capernaum, do also here in your own hometown!"[83]

The introductory clause "Doubtless you will say" indicates that Jesus is well aware of the way a community could respond to a prominent village member who has the capability to bestow social benefits.[84] The enigmatic physician parable that follows reveals Jesus' interpretation of the assumptions of the crowd.

---

81. Josephus, *A.J.* 14.143–44.
82. Josephus, *B.J.* 2.590 (emphasis mine).
83. Luke 4:23.
84. "Doubtless" (πάντως) appears in Acts 21:22 and 28:4 to express a speaker's rhetorical certainty based upon local knowledge regarding social assumptions and probabilities.

Jesus makes a connection between the crowd's ability to locate him as "one of their own" (the son of Joseph) and their expectation that he will confer upon his own πατρίς the same kinds of beneficial deeds that he has done elsewhere.[85] This position is clarified by a proper understanding of the proverb, "Physician, heal yourself." The interpretation of this pithy saying is contested. Nolland has surveyed classical parallels, identifying a trajectory of development from Euripides (485–406 B.C.E.; "Doctor of others, himself full of sores") to the first century C.E. based upon the methodological premise that the best way to search for a parallel is not to look for verbal parallelism, but to search for common contexts and cousin-type phrases.[86] He concludes that the proverb is concerned with the irony of a sick physician; a physician who heals others but is himself unwell. Nolland paraphrases the proverb: "Who do you think you are to offer to us what you do not have for yourself?"[87] This interpretation may fit the Matthean and Markan parallels in which Jesus is rejected because of his low social status, but it does not reflect Luke's concern. Noorda counters Nolland by emphasizing the most closely contemporary and most closely parallel proverb, found in the *Discourse* of Dio Chrysostom (ca. 40–120 C.E.):[88]

> The function of the real philosopher is nothing else than to rule over human beings. But if a man, alleging he is not competent, is reluctant to administer his own city when it wishes him to do so and calls upon him, it is as if someone should refuse to treat his own body, though professing to be a physician, and yet should readily treat other men in return for money or honours, just as if his health were a smaller recompense than another kind...[89]

In this proverb the entire hometown is viewed as if it were the body of the physician himself, hence neglecting the πατρίς is akin to neglecting one's own body. It is unacceptable to treat others before or without treating your own πατρίς. This is precisely the thrust of Jesus' proverb:[90]

---

85. Contra Nolland 1989, 200, these words do not express "skepticism" about the reports from Capernaum, but eagerness to receive similar benefits.
86. Nolland 1979a. Euripides' proverb says ἄλλων ἰατρὸς αὐτὸς ἕλκεσιν βρύων. Nolland favors this proverb because it highlights the incongruity of a sick doctor.
87. Nolland 1989, 199.
88. Noorda 1982.
89. *Discourses* XLIX 13–14. Translation from Crosby 1946, *Loeb Classical Library*: Dio Chrysostom IV.
90. My reading differs from Nolland's individualistic suggestion that the crowd demands that Jesus should "look to his own needs!" (1989, 199, 202). Bock 1994, 416 similarly dismisses the collectivistic ramifications, suggesting it would give "a corporate force to the proverb that is unlikely," yet he gives no reason for

Physician,	heal *yourself*
ἰατρέ,	θεράπευσον σεαυτόν·
What we have heard you did at Capernaum	do in *your own* πατρίς
ὅσα ἠκούσαμεν γενόμενα εἰς τὴν Καφαρναοὺμ	ποίησον καὶ ἐν τῇ πατρίδι σου.

The σεαυτόν in v. 23 parallels πατρίδι and functions collectively. The second phrase functions epexegetically, clarifying the fact that doing good to your πατρίς is like doing good to your own body. In other words, Jesus interprets his townsfolk's words as something like, "Yes! You have done it in Capernaum and, because we are your people, you are bound to do it here as well!"[91] Jesus does not appear to think the crowd has, at this point, "rejected" him.[92]

Yet Jesus explicitly *rejects* the implicit assumptions of the crowd and the shared social script upon which they are based:

> Truly, I say to you that no prophet is acceptable (δεκτός) in his hometown (πατρίδι).[93]

The introductory formula ἀμὴν λέγω ὑμῖν is used characteristically by Luke to indicate teaching "considered to be of special importance" or conveying definitive clarification.[94] While the villagers might assume that their shared subgroup identity carries privileged access to the Isaianic benefits announced by Jesus, Jesus' "Truly, I say to you…" alerts us to the fact that their paradigm is about to be shifted. Moreover, despite interpretations that assume Jesus is unacceptable because he has made overzealous "honor claims" in his community or that they are "cutting him down to size," this parable has little explicitly to do with Jesus' honor.[95] It is rather that Jesus will not be "accepted" (δεκτός) because he is a

---

discounting the corporate force. A handful of interpreters in the past century have interpreted the σεαυτόν of 4:23 as referring to Jesus' hometown rather than to Jesus himself. See Zahn 1920, 240; Creed 1930, 687; Hill 1971, 169; Schürmann 1969, 236–37; Schneider 1977, 109; Hendrickson 1978, 257.

91. Cf. a similar reading by Hill 1971, 169.

92. I disagree with Johnson 1991, 82, who thinks that Capernaum here represents "Gentiles." The chief provocation is not the mission to non-Israelites (if this were true Jesus' message would ostensibly have been offensive in all of Galilee) but the refusal to privilege his own village. The pressure toward village-specific interests is highlighted in Luke 4:42–43 where Jesus resists the will of local village members who want to prevent him from leaving.

93. Luke 4:24.

94. O'Neill 1959, 1–9. Cf. Luke 4:24; 12:37; 18:17, 29; 21:32.

95. Malina and Rohrbaugh 2003, 243.

prophet.⁹⁶ But why are prophets unlikely to be accepted in a social setting where subgroups express resource entitlement based upon shared social identity?

4.5.6. *Prophets and the Out-group*

Jesus clarifies his perplexing "prophet" proverb with two accounts of prophetic intervention in the lives of non-Israelites. Two factors are in play here. First, Luke has a characteristic view of the unwillingness of prophets' own people to hear the prophetic word, regularly referring to the overwhelmingly negative response to prophets throughout Israelite history.⁹⁷ It may be the case that this is based upon the fact that prophets, by nature of their vocation, are not respecters of in-group identity. Israel's strongest prophetic critiques were often directed against the ethnic in-group. This is precisely what led to the death of the prophets. Luke, like Jesus, is painfully aware of this fact.⁹⁸

This first factor only takes us so far. What, precisely, leads to the rejection of the prophets in their hometowns according to Luke? Nolland rightly notes that it is *not* the case that rejection of Elijah and Elisha leads to prophetic ministration among other peoples. "Rejection is hardly prominent in these [Lukan] verses nor in their OT sources (1 Kings 17; 2 Kings 5)."⁹⁹ Elijah and Elisha do not encounter either the widow or Naaman because they have been rejected by Israel; they encounter these people because of divine sending (Elijah to the widow and Naaman to Elijah). Likewise, to this point in the pericope Jesus has not been rejected by his people. Instead, the Elijah and Elisha stories demonstrate that prophets are unbound by typical identity boundaries.¹⁰⁰ At God's impetus, Elijah and Elisha granted non-Israelites precisely the benefits to

---

96. Cf. Acts 10:35, which also reflects "acceptability" rather than "honor."

97. See Luke 6:23, 26; 11:47, 49, 50; 13:33, 34; 16:31; 24:25. Denova 1997, 132: "Typologically, the main characters in Luke–Acts are presented in the scriptural tradition of 'rejected prophet'."

98. Contra Kodell 1983, 16–18, it is difficult to imagine that the primary offense is initially the extension of the benefits of God to non-Israelites. Other intervening factors are in play. Denova 1997, 141 properly notes that it seems unlikely that Jesus would have had success in subsequent villages if the primary problem in Nazareth is only "Gentile triumphalism."

99. Nolland 1989, 201.

100. Nolland does not follow his observation to its obvious ends, noting instead that the problem is *unbelief* of the people of Israel (and by parallel, Nazareth). This misreads the eager anticipation of the people of Nazareth in Luke's telling. They are not "determined not to be drawn into Jesus' programme" (1989, 202), but instead express amazement and wonder.

94   *The Spirit and the "Other"*

which Israelites expected exclusive entitlement. Reading this interpretation back into the Nazareth pericope, this means that shared subgroup identity is *not* the basis of special claims of entitlement. Jesus presses home his subversion of the Nazarene assumption that privileged identity leads to privileged entitlement by implying that the benefits of God are available *beyond the primary category altogether*. The Elijah and Elisha stories indicate that, with regard to entitlement, ethnic identities are important yet not restrictive to the work of God that crosses group boundaries with impunity.[101] This emphatically does not mean that Israelites are rejected. Rather, Jesus' proclamation makes the circle of identities with access to God—the primary category—larger. It is for this reason, the unwillingness to privilege one's own people because of a commitment always to speak the word of God, that prophets are often unacceptable.

4.5.7. The Ramifications of Jesus' Rejection of the Social Script

Jesus' rejection of the social script of his πατρίς has swift and terrible consequences:

> And they were all filled with rage hearing these things *in the synagogue* (καὶ ἐπλήσθησαν πάντες θυμοῦ ἐν τῇ συναγωγῇ ἀκούοντες ταῦτα)… And they rose up and put him out of the city, and led him to the brow of the hill on which their city was built, that they might throw him down headlong.[102]

It is precisely "in the synagogue" (the dative clause is in the emphatic position at the head of the participial clause), the locus of village identity, that Jesus' words are so offensive. The murderous rage elicited by Jesus' subversion of identity norms nearly costs him his life and, more subtly, costs him his place in his own πατρίς. Though Luke has carefully placed Jesus in his own πατρίς and presents several πατρίς-specific concerns, Jesus' refusal to act in accord with the shared social script results in a subtle narratival shift from Nazareth as πατρίς to Nazareth as πόλις. In the crowd's rage Jesus is expelled from *the* πόλις (τῆς πόλεως) and nearly thrown off the cliff upon which is built *their* city (ἡ πόλις αὐτῶν).[103] By

---

101. Mathey 2000, 6 rightly observes that "Jesus proclaims that God's liberating power and solidarity is not exclusively meant for the benefit of the physical descendants of the patriarchs, of the people of the exodus and the great prophets."

102. Luke 4:28, 29.

103. Luke 4:29. Schweizer 1984, 86 overlooks the connection between in-group status and the presumption of privilege, leading him to claim that the shift from "hometown" in 4:23–24 to "homeland" in 4:27–29 is a "scribal Christian argument for the mission to the Gentiles."

virtue of his refusal to grant exceptional resources to his Nazareth in-group, Jesus is no longer an acceptable member of his πατρίς.

4.5.8. *Luke 4:14–30: Summary*
Attention to the proper layer of nested identity in Luke 4:14–30, Nazareth subgroup identity nested within broader Galilean and then Israelite identity, has helped us to locate the social assumptions that prompt Jesus' knowing response, "Doubtless you will say to me…" Jesus—who has been repeatedly placed under the influence of the Spirit (Luke 3:22; 4:1, 14, 18)—is reacting against claims to entitlement based upon the projection of Nazareth subgroup prototypicality. The resistance of Jesus' townsfolk is resistance to Jesus' refusal to privilege his subgroup while restricting the extension of benefits to the "other." This programmatic theme, unwillingness to use privileged identity only for self-benefit, is prominent throughout Luke.

4.6. *Conclusion*

In Luke 3–4 we see that individuals empowered by the Spirit have a transformed ability to look beyond the (privileged) identity of self or in-group and so to extend in-group benefits to all manner of "other." This is a fundamental human transformation. For John, this takes the form of prophetic exhortation leveled against those who would potentially claim privileged identity as an end in itself. Privileged identity is only rightly expressed when it bears a concern for the "other." For Jesus, the presence of the Spirit is linked with his personal resistance to the temptation to leverage his privileged "Son of God" identity solely for self-benefit. This posture stands in great relief against the entitlement claims of his πατρίς, claims based upon the projection of relative prototypicality and an inappropriate understanding of privileged identity. *Both John and Jesus, Luke's paradigmatically Spirit-empowered figures, begin their public ministries with critiques of defective expressions of privileged identity.*

While the Spirit largely disappears from Luke after ch. 4 (making brief appearances in Luke 10:21; 11:13 and 12:10, 12), the motifs awakened by Luke in these early chapters reverberate throughout the Gospel. Specifically, Jesus' life regularly reflects the allocentric impulse generated by the transformative work of the Spirit. Jesus teaches his disciples that privileged identity is demonstrated by placing others ahead of the self.[104] Jesus rebukes John for wanting to limit Jesus-centered ministry only to the

---

104. Luke 9:46–48.

disciples' in-group.[105] Jesus rebukes his disciples for an expression of ethnocentric hatred leveled at Samaritan "enemies."[106] Jesus teaches that much is expected from the one to whom much has been given.[107] Jesus reveals that the proper expression of his Messianic identity is to suffer on behalf of others.[108] For Luke, Jesus-like Spirit-formed allocentric identity is expressed through the turn away from singular focus on the self/group and the turn toward the "other."

Two things are clear from this reading of Luke 1–4. First, ethnic identity is not the identity that determines access to the benefits of God. Second, the influence of the Spirit upon individuals appears to bring a transformational openness to the "other"—an allocentric identity. What we see in the lives of individuals under the influence of the Spirit— namely, the Spirit-empowered ability to look beyond self and group (and hence to resist restrictive identity-based entitlement claims)—will become essential for the formation of the *type* of community described in Acts as the incubator of a new social identity capable of affirming, yet chastening and transcending, competing (especially ethnic) social identities.

---

105. Luke 9:49–50.
106. Luke 9:51–55.
107. Luke 12:32–35.
108. Luke 24:25–27.

Chapter 5

INITIATING A SCANDAL OF UNIVERSAL PARTICULARITY:
THE SPIRIT IN ACTS 1–2

The chain-link transition at the seam between Luke and Acts suggests that the concerns Luke develops in his Gospel—including the identity concerns—will serve as a reliable foundation for the relationship between the Spirit and identity that will be developed in Acts.[1] Indeed, the relationship between the Spirit and the creation of (allocentric) identity is taken up and clarified immediately in Acts. In his second volume, Luke presents the early community of Jesus-followers as a collective expression of the Spirit-formed allocentric identity exemplified by Jesus in the Gospel. It is participation in this community that incubates a superordinate social identity that affirms yet chastens and transcends ethnic identities *en route* to profound inter-ethnic reconciliation. As we will come to see, the Spirit is active at every level of the formation of this new trans-ethnic social identity.

This chapter will examine four facets of Luke's identity-forming program in Acts 1–2. First, I will discuss the social identities implicated in the text's programmatic statement, Acts 1:8, in order to identify the categorization of the disciples as *Galilean* Israelites commissioned to enact a Spirit-empowered mission across various (dangerous) social boundaries. Second, I will discuss the suggestive data in Luke's account of the selection of Matthias in order to demonstrate that, apart from the coming of the Spirit, Luke understands human identity processes to

---

1. Longenecker 2005, 166–67. Best 1984, 3; Dunn 1996; Marshall 1980, *inter alias* demonstrate the close relationship between Luke 24 and Acts 1. Borgman 2006, 31, 245, 253, 330 suggests Luke uses "signal words" in Acts that direct hearers back to concepts developed in the Gospel, thus moving the narrative forward without reintroducing significant themes. For the prologue, see Alexander 1993, but note the critique in Witherington 1998, 14–15; Moessner 1999. For comparable two-volume prologues, see Josephus, *Contra Apionem*; Diodorus Siculus, *Bibliotheca Historica*; Dioscorides Pedanius, *De materia medica* and Hippocrates, *De prisca medicina*.

function on a (now obsolete) criterion of social homogeneity. Third, turning to the Pentecost account, I will discuss the scandal of universal ethno-linguistic particularity implied by Luke's portrayal of what, in its context, should be considered a wholly "unnecessary" language miracle.[2] This gives the first real glimpse into the proper place of ethnic identity within a new Spirit-formed identity. Finally, I will examine Peter's unique use of Joel 3:1–5 LXX in his Pentecost speech in order to understand Luke's foundational conviction that the Spirit is the primary marker of human identity.

5.1. *The Spirit and Social Categories in Acts 1:1–11: Initiating an Allocentric Identity*

Acts 1:1–11 marks the third major introduction in Luke–Acts (with Luke 3:1–14 and 4:14–30) that draws attention to the relationship between the Spirit and social identities. The reading I will present in what follows will augment the typical geographical interpretation of Acts 1:8:[3]

> But you shall receive power when the Holy Spirit has come upon you; and you shall be my witnesses in Jerusalem and in all Judea and Samaria and to the end of the earth (ἕως ἐσχάτου τῆς γῆς).

Geographical interpretations of this text have led to an effort to define a precise referent for "end of the earth": predominantly Rome, but also Ethiopia, Spain or the boundaries of the land of Israel.[4] None of these suggestions is wholly satisfactory: the Gospel precedes Paul to Rome and renders his appearance there an anticlimactic climax; Spain is nowhere in view in the text; Ethiopia is reached by Acts 8 and then disappears; the idiosyncratic idea that the "end of the earth" refers to Israel's boundaries creates radical dissonance with Luke's emphasis on the spread of the gospel to non-Israelites. The major flaw in understanding Acts 1:8 only

---

2. Ethno-linguistic refers to a language of a particular ethnic group. Other ethnic groups (especially in Diaspora settings) often acquire these languages, but they are primarily identity markers for the group with which they are associated.

3. Wholly geographic approaches to Acts 1:8 are the norm. See Wall 2002, 43; Tannehill 1990, 17; Robinson and Wall 2006, 34; Van Unnik 1973; Fitzmyer 1998, 201; Dunn 1996, 11; Bruce 1951, 71; Conzelmann 1987, 7; Thornton 1978; Schwartz 1986; Ellis 1991; Hengel 1980; Johnson 1992.

4. Rome: Fitzmyer 1998, 201; Van Unnik 1973; Marshall 1980, 61 (Marshall sees Rome as the "completion of the first phase"); Dunn 1996, 11 (Dunn sees Rome as significant in the progression, but not "the goal itself"); Ethiopia: Cadbury 1955; Thornton 1978; Hengel 1980; Spain: Best 1984; Ellis 1991, 132; the boundaries of the land of Israel: Schwartz 1986.

5. Initiating a Scandal of Universal Particularity 99

geographically is the fact that the tensions created and resolved by the narrative do not arise when geographic boundaries are crossed. Narrative drama arises in the text when *social* (and particularly ethnic) boundaries are crossed. Luke's primary concern both in Acts 1:8 and in the text as a whole is with *people* as much, and likely more, than *places*. Place names such as Samaria, Judea and Galilee "are social products that reflect and configure ways of being in the world."[5] Geography, for Luke, is a signifier of a *primarily* ethnic referent.[6]

Because much of the narrative tension in Acts arises at social boundaries, it is essential to be clear on the social identities in view in this programmatic passage. In this section I will investigate Luke's understanding of the disciples' *Galilean* identity, an identity that distinguishes them from the other groups in Acts 1:8 and again in the Pentecost narrative. I will then demonstrate that Luke portrays the Spirit as the causative agent for a specific sort of *allocentric identity*.

5.1.1. *In-group Bias and a Truncated Expression of Israelite Identity*

In Acts 1:1–11, Jesus' disciples operate with two layers of social identity: Galilean and Israelite.[7] The disciples' Israelite identity is clearly expressed in response to Jesus' post-resurrection teaching concerning the kingdom of God and the coming of the Spirit: "Lord, will you at this time restore (ἀποκαθίστημι) the kingdom to Israel?"[8] Luke's use of ἀποκαθίστημι, commonly deployed by the LXX and Josephus to describe historic or hoped-for national restoration, makes it probable that Luke (who is aware of Roman domination in Judea) is depicting the disciples' hoped for national political liberation.[9] The question reflects a hope "fully in

---

5. Green 1998, 85 n. 5.
6. Brawley 1987, 32–33. Witherington 1998, 34–35 describes Greco-Roman "historiography κάτα γένος," exemplified by Ephorus, which describes events in relation to people groups rather than chronology. A people-centered hermeneutic does not obscure Luke's vision for the global reign of the exalted Jesus. It simply recognizes that Luke constantly invokes the Spirit as his text deals with *social* boundaries.
7. I will categorize Galilean identity as "regional" identity, though according to Barthian ethnic theory it could be legitimately called an ethnic identity. Pliny knows hundreds of local people groups who possessed what we would call ethnic identity (*Natural History* II.15.116; IV.10.33, 12.85; V.4.29–30).
8. Acts 1:6.
9. E.g. Exod 4:7; 14:27; Jer 15:19; 16:15; 23:8; 24:6; 50:19; Hos 11:11; 1 Esd 6:26; 2 Macc 11:25; Josephus, *A.J.* 11.2, 14, 58, 63, 88, 92, 144; 12.228; 13.261; 14.313. Peter uses ἀποκατάστασις with a broader scope in Acts 3:19–21. Cho 2005, 182 incorrectly claims nothing in the context suggests nationalistic implications.

continuity with the hope of Israel's prophets," but it also indicates the ready salience of Israelite group identity.[10] The assumption appears to be that "kingdom of God" (Acts 1:3) and "kingdom of Israel" (Acts 1:6) are co-terminus. We know from our discussion of SIT that groups are likely to ascribe access to desired outcomes only to themselves, and the disciples' question is another example of the phenomena noted in Luke 3:8 and 4:22. This (ultimately unsatisfactory) expression of the relationship between Israelite identity and resource allocation, even among followers of Jesus, provides a baseline against which Luke will develop a prominent motif: *the ongoing identity transformation of the in-group*. Neither the early community nor its individual members have immediate and full awareness of the proper expression of their identities, which can only be cultivated by the power of the Spirit. Luke appears to *expect* exclusivistic expressions of in-group bias apart from the Spirit.

5.1.2. The Salience of Nested Galilean Identity

When a person has multiple nested social identities, the identity of the out-group in view determines the salient social identity.[11] This, I suggest, is the case in Luke's sub-categorization of identities in Acts 1:1–11. Because Jesus' commission (Acts 1:8) includes both Israelites and non-Israelites, the most logical immediate level of social distinction (the mechanism through which group identity is maintained) is at the level of regional Israelite identity. While the disciples express fully Israelite ethnic identity in Acts 1:6, they cannot be categorized as Jerusalemites or (regionally) as Judeans.[12] It should not surprise that at this point Luke emphasizes the disciples' *Galilean* identity nested within their Israelite ethnic identity. Scholars sometimes puzzle over the apparent absence of Galilee in Jesus' commission, but evidence for the role of Galilean identity is close to hand:[13]

> Men of Galilee (ἄνδρες Γαλιλαῖοι), why do you stand looking into heaven? (Acts 1:11)

> Are not all these who are speaking Galileans (Γαλιλαῖοι)? (Acts 2:7)

---

10. Tiede 1986, 280; cf. Dunn 1996, 4.
11. Jenkins 1997, 85.
12. When I use the term "Judean" I am referring to residents of Judea proper, not all Ἰουδαῖοι.
13. Witherington 1998, 111 suggests Luke is unaware of the details of Galilean evangelization. Fitzmyer 1998, 206 says "Nothing should be made of the omission of 'Galilee' here; Luke is simply using a stock phrase in mentioning the two [Judea and Samaria]" (cf. Conzelmann 1987, 7). Pao 2003, 95 suggests that Acts 1:8 collapses Judea and Samaria (and Galilee?) into a "theo-political" unity.

The categorization of Jesus' disciples as "Galileans" at the beginning of Acts establishes that, for Luke, regional subgroup differentiation was a feature of Israelite ethnic identity. At the level of Galilean regional identity fellow Israelites could be categorized as "other."[14] The reality of the category "Galilean Israelite" may have been reinforced by distinct administrative structures, regional and class distinctions.[15] I have already discussed Josephus' awareness of distinct Galilean identity and Philo's evidence for dual identities in antiquity. Additionally, there is later Rabbinic evidence suggesting agonistic differentiation between Galilean and Judean identity, often marked by an air of Judean superiority.[16]

5.1.3. Luke's Gospel and Jesus' Commission: Encountering Perilous Identity Boundaries

Overt reference to Galilean identity indicates that each group implicated in the Acts 1:8 commission—Jerusalemites, Judeans, Samaritans and inhabitants of "the end of the earth"—possess distinct identities at least at a subgroup level and therefore constitute real social boundaries. Luke's Gospel provides the context for understanding that groups implicated in Jesus' commission could be "threatening others":

1. *"You will be my witnesses in Jerusalem…"* Subgroup identity differences are often amplified when subgroups have to work hard to achieve intragroup distinction from other subgroups who, by virtue of their participation in a common in-group, share similar identity characteristics.[17] This may be reflected in Luke's interest in Jerusalem (64 of the 77 New Testament references to "Jerusalem" appear in Luke–Acts). For Luke, Jerusalem is the center of Israelite ethnic identity and those who have positions of power in Jerusalem have a great stake in maintaining the prototypicality of

---

14. See Chapter 4 for Luke's emphasis on Galilee as a largely receptive "home base" for Jesus.

15. Reed 2000, 55; Vermes 1973, 43–44; Horsley 1996, 176–77. For Galilean identity, see Cromhout 2007, 209–35; Zangenberg, Attridge and Martin 2007.

16. Note *b. 'Erubin* 53b, which states: "The children of Judea who paid strict attention to the words of their masters and propounded many questions retained all they learned. The Galileans, however, who did not pay strict attention to the language of their masters, and did not question them, did not retain anything. The Judeans learned from one master, hence they remembered what they learned; but the Galileans had many teachers and in consequence they did not retain anything." Cf. *y. Shabbat* 15b; *b. Megillah* 24b. See Freyne 1987, 600; Vermes 1973, 42–57; Neubauer 1885, 51.

17. Grant 1993, 31 and Huddy and Virtanen 1995, 98 claim subgroup differentiation is strongest when there are objective status differences between subgroups.

their subgroup identity. This is a factor in the resistance to the (Galilean) Jesus movement both from high profile Jerusalemite leaders (Acts 4:1–21; 5:17–41) and from ordinary members of the Jerusalem subgroup (Acts 21:27–32; 22:22–23).[18] From a Jerusalem-centric viewpoint, Galilean identity was likely considered less prototypical than Jerusalemite identity.[19] Explicit intragroup conflict between Jerusalemites and Galileans appears in Josephus' account of Judean and Jerusalemite betrayal of Galilean interests by allowing fear of Roman intervention to take precedence over intra-Israelite loyalty in the wake of a Samaritan attack on Galileans ca. 50 C.E.[20] The group categorization described by Josephus indicates clear subgroup distinction between Galileans and Jerusalemites (especially Jerusalemite leaders). For followers of Jesus, just weeks after their leader was crucified at the hands of Judean and Roman leaders in Jerusalem, the call to Jerusalem was the call to cross a frightful boundary indeed.[21] This is reflected in Chrysostom's awareness that Jerusalem was the place in which the disciples were most "afraid."[22]

2. "...and in all Judea." Luke's differentiation between Galilean and Judean identity is most evident in Luke's decision to forestall accounts of mortal opposition to Jesus until Jesus has departed from Galilee and entered Judea.[23]

3. "...and Samaria." The commission to Samaria is an invitation to intergroup contact. Luke's interest in Samaritans is reflected in the parable of the merciful Samaritan (Luke 10:25–37) and the healing of the ten lepers (Luke 17:11–19), narratives whose rhetorical force assume significant social boundary issues between Israelites

---

18. In Acts 21, Israelites from Asia stir up the Jerusalem crowds, but they stir them up precisely by claiming that Paul has transgressed central markers of Israelite identity (the law and the Temple).

19. Alon 1967, 317 suggests Jerusalemites looked down on "rustic" Galileans; cf. the recognition of Peter's Galilean accent (Matt 26:73; cf. Luke 22:59).

20. Josephus, *B.J.* 2.232–37, esp. 237. Jerusalem leaders urge the people to "not bring the utmost dangers of destruction upon them, in order to avenge themselves upon one Galilean only."

21. Luke assigns culpability for Jesus' death to Jerusalem Israelites (Acts 2:36; 3:13–15), but not to Diaspora Israelites (see Acts 13:27–28). See Tannehill 1990, 28.

22. *Homilies on Acts of the Disciples* [NPNF 1.11.13]. Bauckham 2006, 183–201 suggests that Jerusalem was dangerous enough for Jesus' followers that the pre-Markan source of Mark 11, 14–16 (which he takes to have Jerusalem provenance) reflects a strategy "protective anonymity."

23. See Chapter 4 for Luke's differentiation between Galilee and Judea.

and Samaritans. This is supported by Josephus' multiple reports of Samaritan/Israelite (and even specifically Samaritan/Galilean) antipathy.[24] The social conflict that simmered just beneath the surface of Israelite–Samaritan relations is evident in possibly the ugliest passage in the Gospel tradition, James and John's request to destroy a Samaritan village with heavenly fire (Luke 9:51–56). It is no coincidence that this extreme expression of ethnocentrism is the disciples' first social interaction *outside the boundaries of Galilee* in Luke's Gospel.

4. "*…to the end of the earth.*" Two factors at this point require elaboration to support my argument that Acts 1:8 primarily concerns peoples and not places: (1) the phrase "end of the earth" at the very least implies the ἔθνη and (2) the ἔθνη, in Luke's view, constitute an often dangerous social boundary.[25]

The first point is clarified by the relationship between Luke 24:47–53 and Acts 1:1–11. Longenecker has demonstrated the thematic continuity rhetorically signified in the chain-link transition between these passages.[26] The parallels are clear: identification of disciples as μάρτυρες, allusion to "the promise of the Father" and commissions with common origin (Jerusalem) and broad scope. Johnson's view that Acts 1:1–11 is an "elaborate variant" of Luke 24:47–53 is warranted.[27] In this parallel structure, "end of the earth" in Acts 1:8 is set in tandem with "all the non-Israelites (ἔθνη)" in Luke 24:47. The passages both appear to draw on Isa 49:6 LXX, where "end of the earth" stands in poetic parallel with ἔθνη.[28] Paul's use of Isa 49:6 LXX to legitimate the broad ethnic scope of his mission (Acts 13:47) is further evidence of Luke's awareness that "end of the earth" implies the ἔθνη.

Luke describes intergroup tension in Israel's relationship with the ἔθνη that is bi-directional and pervasive:[29]

1. An Israelite mob is roused to a murderous fervor at the suggestion of the extension of in-group benefits to the ethnic "other" (Luke 4:24–26).

---

24. Josephus, *A.J.* 18.30; *B.J.* 2.232–37.
25. This augments the views of Wall 2002, 134 n. 324 who explicitly claims that "Jesus' prophecy in Acts 1:8 concerns the geography (not the biography) of mission."
26. Longenecker 2005, 166–67.
27. Johnson 1992, 28.
28. Haenchen 1971, 143 n. 9; Pesch 1986, 1:70; Moore 1998; Pao 2003, 91–96. See, e.g., Deut 28:49; Ps 134:6–7; Isa 8:9; 48:20; 49:6; 62:11; Jer 10:12; 16:19; 1 Macc 3:9.
29. See Chapter 2 for ἔθνη as an ethnic category.

2. Two Galilean Israelite disciples seek to annihilate a village of ethnic Samaritans (Luke 9:51).
3. Israelites refuse to share table fellowship with non-Israelites (Acts 11:1–3).
4. Romans defend their own ethnic *ethos* against ethnic pollution (Acts 16:19–23).
5. Ephesian townsfolk take vigilante action in defense of their ethnic customs and worship (Acts 19:23–41).

It is precisely this interethnic boundary that is most nettlesome in Luke's text and its navigation requires nothing less than the pneumatologically empowered development of a *new social identity*.

5.1.4. Identified by/Identifying with Jesus

The intergroup context envisioned in Acts 1:8 underscores the fact that Jesus' commission moves the disciples away from an identity centered primarily on their ethnic (sub-)group and toward a new identity centered on Jesus and empowered by the Spirit:

> So when they had come together, they asked him, "Lord, will you at this time restore the kingdom to Israel?" He said to them, "It is not for you to know times or seasons which the Father has fixed by his own authority. But you shall receive power when the Holy Spirit has come upon you; and you shall be my witnesses (ἔσεσθέ μου μάρτυρες) in Jerusalem and in all Judea and Samaria and to the end of the earth."[30]

Jesus' followers initially identify themselves via their ethnic identity (Israel), but Jesus expects his disciples to function not primarily as Israelites or Galileans in the fulfillment of their task; they are to function primarily as *witnesses of Jesus*—μου μάρτυρες. "Spirit of prophecy" advocates tend not fully to appreciate the possessive force of the μου in Acts 1:8. This leads to a one-sided emphasis on "witness" as an *activity to be undertaken* by the disciples that fundamentally requires verbal proclamation.[31] However, the fact that Jesus *identifies* the disciples as μάρτυρες rather than commanding them to engage in the activity of witness (μαρτυρέω) has important implications. μου μάρτυρες implies both witnesses *to* and witnesses *belonging to* Jesus.[32]

Two factors strongly support my suggestion that ἔσεσθέ μου μάρτυρες implies *identity* as well as activity:

---

30. Acts 1:6–8.
31. So Menzies 1991, 244; Cho 2005, 185.
32. Johnson 1992, 30 suggests μου μάρτυρες implies witness *to* Jesus and witnesses *belonging to* Jesus.

5. Initiating a Scandal of Universal Particularity

(1) Luke's only other use of εἰμι + μου + a noun in the genitive (cf. Acts 1:8) is εἶναι μου μαθητής (Luke 14:26, 27, 33):[33]

> If any one comes to me and does not hate his own father and mother and wife and children and brothers and sisters, yes, and even his own life, he cannot be my disciple (εἶναι μου μαθητής). Whoever does not bear his own cross and come after me, cannot be my disciple (εἶναι μου μαθητής)... Whoever of you does not renounce all that he has cannot be my disciple (εἶναι μου μαθητής).

"Be my disciple" implies both identity (in this context, membership within a group sharing a relationship to Jesus) and activity (discipleship).[34] As is the case with ἔσεσθέ μου μάρτυρες, identity and activity are inseparable and mutually constitutive.[35] The Jesus-centered identity μαθητής in Luke 14 transcends kinship identities just as the Jesus-centered identity μάρτυρες in Acts 1:8 transcends ethnic identities.

(2) Luke's use of Isa 49:6 in Acts 1:8 is part of a wider Lukan tendency to utilize Isa 40–55 for much of his imagery of "witness."[36] Deutero-Isaiah provides a rich context from which to understand the significance of a theocentric identity marked by both Spirit and "witness."[37] In Isa 44:1–8 LXX God promises to *place his Spirit* upon the seed and children of Jacob/Israel (44:3), causing them to spring up (44:4) and *identify themselves*:

> This one will say, "I am the Lord's," another one will call himself by the name of Jacob, and a different one will write "I am the Lord's because of the name of Israel." (Isa 44:5)

Subsequently, those who proclaim their God-centered identity are *witnesses* (μάρτυρες; Isa 44:8) of God's sovereignty. A similar link appears in Isa 43:4–13 LXX:[38]

> Everyone who is called by my name [*identity*], whom I created for my glory [*activity associated with identity*], whom I formed and made... You are my witnesses (ὑμεῖς ἐμοὶ μάρτυρες).[39]

---

33. Luke has 139 deployments of μου + a noun in the genitive.
34. Cf. the identity marker in 1 Cor 1:12: εἰμι Παύλου, ἐγὼ δὲ Ἀπολλῶ, etc.
35. The identity–activity relationship is put to the test in Jesus' temptation: "If you are the son of God..." See Chapter 4.
36. See Pao 2003, 70–110.
37. Bauckham 1998, 47 suggests Isa 40–55 was among the most important textual units for New Testament authors. For Luke and Isaiah, see Pao 2003; Koet 2005; 2008; Porter 2006; Mallen 2008.
38. Wright (2006, 66) claims "It is almost certain that Luke intends us to hear in this [Acts 1:8] an echo of...Isaiah 43.10–12."
39. Isa 43:7, 12.

In Deutero-Isaiah, "witness" implies both identity and activity.[40]

The relationship between ethnic identity and identity as a "witness" is significant here. Jesus' early followers are not told to engage the "other" primarily on the basis of their own ethnic identities, but as "witnesses" of/belonging to Jesus. "Witness" is the first of several categories (notably "slave"/"servant" and "disciple") that locate the identity of a person/group in relationship to Jesus. The activities implied by these identities will emerge as the norms of the Jesus-group, behaviors that faithfully express the prototypical characteristics of the group's identity.[41] "Witness" is an appropriate metaphor for an allocentric identity because it always involves "speaking and doing on behalf of, and in service to, something or someone beyond the self."[42] In Acts 1:8 the disciples' identity is reoriented around the person of Jesus and directed toward the "other."

The immediate ramification of this de-centered identity is the de-sacralization of ethnic identity, which is reinforced by the surprising outward trajectory of the commission. While Jerusalem remains a central point throughout the Acts narrative, Jesus suggests a centrifugal movement—*outward from Jerusalem, the ethnic heart of Israel, and toward the "other."*[43] "The Spirit drives outward and seeks to gather in, even in the midst of conflict and opposition."[44] This stands in contrast to centripetal expectations of the Old Testament, where the nations stream toward Israel.[45] If Jesus implicitly affirms (or at least does not deny) that the restoration of Israel is somehow at hand, the restoration in Acts 1:8 is restoration of Israel's identity as witness to the nations.[46]

---

40. "Servant" and "witness" express similar concepts in Isa 44:21; 45:4–6; 48:10–11; 49:1–6; 54:5; 55:4–5, a factor important for Peter's Pentecost speech.

41. Waldzus et al. 2003, 32. For group norms in collectivistic cultures, see Triandis 1990.

42. Weissenbeuhler 1992, 64. This witness-like turn toward the "other" will be evident in James' actions toward the ἔθνη in Acts 15.

43. Scott 2002, 57 notes "The geographical movement in Acts is centrifugal—away from Jerusalem," yet he does not develop the ethnic significance of this reorientation. Bauckham 1996, 480 notes this movement does not imply "corresponding centripetal movement" in which "the eschatological people of God must constantly look back."

44. Weissenbeuhler 1992, 64.

45. E.g. Isa 2:2–3; 60:18–20; Jer 3:17; Mic 4:1–2; Zech 8:22; 14:16; Tob 13:11; 14:6.

46. Wenk 2004, 241: "The contrast expressed by vv. 7–8 presents a change of emphasis from Israel's kingship to her task as servant bringing the light of God's salvation to the nations (cf. Isa 43.10–12; 49:6)."

Finally, it must be emphasized that the allocentric activity/identity "witness" is only available through the power of the Spirit.[47] The inseparable relationship between Spirit and "witness" will allow Luke to draw either explicitly on visible/audible Spirit manifestations (Acts 10:44-48; cf. Luke 3:22) or upon a manifestation of "witness" (Acts 9:27) in order to demonstrate a common identity that transcends social barriers.[48]

5.1.5. Acts 1:1-11: Summary

Acts 1:1-11, set within a context of entitlement expectations from ethnic Israelites (Acts 1:6), features a group of *Galileans* commissioned to exercise a new Jesus-centered identity toward all manner of "other." It is the Spirit that will enable them faithfully to express their new identity in these difficult social contexts. This passage continues Luke's penchant for connecting the Spirit and ethnic (or regional/local) identity in key introductory passages.[49] From this perspective, Acts 1:8 indeed serves as an organizational pattern for the book. Acts will describe, in order, interaction with Jerusalemites, (regional) Judean Israelites, Samaritans and finally the ἔθνη. A peoples-centered hermeneutic resolves the problem that arises when one attempts to locate a specific geographic referent for the "end of the earth."

5.2. Old Identity Paradigms Before Pentecost:
Choosing One Like Us

The selection of Matthias stands in jarring contrast to the outward press of the Acts 1:8 commission. While this episode is often taken as an example of the prayerful obedience of the church, I suggest that Luke subtly develops a parallel with an inappropriate expression of in-group identity from Luke 9:49-50.[50] If this is correct, Matthias' selection is

---

47. The use of ἐπέρχομαι in Acts 1:8 to describe the Spirit's coming is paralleled only by Luke 1:35, where the Spirit's role is clearly creative. Perhaps this anticipates the Spirit's "creation" of the new community.

48. This initiates a theme in Acts whereby both overt reference to the Spirit and reference to activities or dispositions elsewhere overtly connected to the Spirit can indicate the impact of the Spirit in an individual or group. This will be true especially of Barnabas (Acts 4:36-37; 9:27; 11:22-26) and James (Acts 15:13-21).

49. Cf. Luke 3:8-14; 4:16-30.

50. Bock 2007, 90; Johnson 1992, 39; Barrett 1994, 94. Hentschel 2007, 300 is characteristic: "Durch den positiven Ausgang der Rede wird einterseits die Autorität des Petrus als Schriftausleger und Gemeindeleiter bestätigt, andererseits wird die Rechtmässigkeit der Auswahl und Beauftragung des zwölften Apostels—und damit auch der zwölf Apostael insgesamt—durch Gott selbst beglaubigt."

an example of a (now defunct) paradigm of in-group homogeneity that exists apart from the Spirit and that bases entitlement claims on subgroup prototypicality.

Peter appears to ignore Jesus' command (Acts 1:4: παραγγέλω) simply to *wait* (Acts 1:4: περιμένω, cf. Luke 24:49) for the coming of the Spirit, possibly implying that Peter should implicitly be understood to act *without* the Spirit.[51] Correlated to this fact, Peter's criteria for a "witness" appear to be more socially exclusive than those of Jesus." According to Peter, Judas' replacement must be:

> One of the men who have accompanied us during all the time that the Lord Jesus went in and out among us, beginning from the baptism of John until the day when he was taken up from us—one of these men must become with us a witness (μάρτυς) to his resurrection.[52]

Jesus' criterion for witnesses includes a post-resurrection encounter with Jesus but *not* participation in Jesus' entire public ministry. Thus more people are eligible to be "witnesses" under Jesus' criterion than under Peter's:[53]

> And he said to them, "Thus it is written, that the Messiah is to suffer and to rise from the dead on the third day, and that repentance and forgiveness of sins is to be proclaimed in his name to all nations, beginning from Jerusalem. You are witnesses (μάρτυρες) of these things."[54]

The expansiveness of Jesus' commission is evident in the fact that Jesus gives his Lukan "witness-commission" to "the eleven gathered together *and* those who were with them" (Luke 24:33). The narrative flow of Luke 24 makes it highly plausible that Jesus designates as "witnesses" (Luke 24:48) "Mary Magdalene and Joanna and Mary the mother of James and the other women with them" (Luke 24:10). Yet these women do not appear in the Gospel until Luke 8:1–3, well after the selection of the

---

51. Roberts Gaventa 2004 notes the negative function of human initiative in Acts. Dunn 1996, 4 notes the strangeness of Peter's attempt to replace Judas. Conversely, it could be that the command to "wait" did not imply inactivity, but only the delay of active mission.

52. Acts 1:21–22.

53. In Acts "witness" only refers to those who have seen the risen Jesus. This extends to Paul by virtue of his experience on the Damascus road. See Acts 1:22; 2:32; 3:15; 4:33; 5:32; 10:39; 13:31; 22:18; 23:11; 26:16, 22. Fitzmyer 1998, 466 notes that more than twelve are "witnesses" in Acts because the criterion is simply a resurrection appearance. Luke will yet develop broader categories: servant, disciple and brother.

54. Luke 24:46–48.

apostles in Luke 6:13. Thus, the women have not been present from "the baptism of John" (Acts 1:22), yet they are witnesses. It is likely that there were others among the 120 who, like the women, had seen Jesus after the resurrection but had joined the movement after John's baptism. Yet for Peter, the criterion for the twelfth witness is social homogeneity; he/she must be an insider who is as much like the Eleven as possible.

Though it is difficult to say with certainty that Luke is unimpressed with Peter's action, a provocative parallel between Acts 1:21–22 and a defective expression of in-group membership in Luke 9:49–50 raises eyebrows. The following points suggest that Luke considers Matthias' selection to have been based upon a now-obsolete paradigm of social homogeneity:

1. Peter's criteria are suggestively similar to John's statement in Luke 9:49:

    > Master, we saw a man casting out demons in your name, and we forbade him, *because he does not follow with us.*

    For John the disciple, ability to participate in "apostolic" ministry (only the apostles had received authority over demons and disease in Luke 9:1) is contingent upon membership in the apostolic in-group. Jesus rebukes John, establishing sympathy with Jesus' mission as the sole criterion for ministry in Jesus' name:

    > But Jesus said to him, "Do not forbid him; for he that is not against you is for you."[55]

    In a manner similar to John, Peter hopes to choose a replacement for Judas from a pool of those who are *most similar* to the Eleven:

    > ...One of the men who have accompanied us during all the time that the Lord Jesus went in and out among us.[56]

2. John's expression of in-group bias comes just prior to the Jesus-group's departure from Galilee. Likewise, Peter's expression of in-group bias comes just before the Jesus-group's expansion beyond Galilean regional homogeneity. Hence, in both Luke and Acts the turn beyond "Galilee" is preceded by the (faulty) assumption that participation in Jesus' mission is determined by one's prototypicality relative to the apostolic in-group.

---

55. Luke 9:50.
56. Acts 1:21.

3. Departure from Galilee (Luke 9:51) and departure from Galilean homogeneity (Acts 2:1) are initiated with the phrase ἐν τῷ συμπληροῦσθαι τὴν ἡμέραν.[57] These are the only appearances of this construction in the New Testament or LXX.[58]
4. In Luke, following an expression of in-group bias, the turn from Galilee and the distinctive phrase ἐν τῷ συμπληροῦσθαι τὴν ἡμέραν, *non-apostles* participate in Jesus' mission at Jesus' behest. In Luke 10:1 Jesus sends out another (ἕτερος) seventy to do ministry in his name. Sandiyagu has demonstrated that Luke consistently uses ἕτερος to mean "another of a different kind" and ἄλλος to mean "another of the same kind."[59] In social contexts ἕτερος is a member of an out-group while ἄλλος refers to an in-group member.[60] Jesus' response to John's in-group bias (Luke 9:49) and the ethnocentric hatred expressed by John and James (Luke 9:54) is to send out 70 *of another kind*. In Acts 2:1–4 the Spirit empowers *all 120* (some of whom, like Mary and the women [cf. Acts 1:14], do not meet Peter's criteria for witness) to participate in the mission of Jesus as "witnesses" and to extend the benefits of Jesus to those that Acts 1:8 has categorized as "other"—in this case, non-Galileans.[61] The mission is accomplished by the Spirit's empowerment to speak in "other" (ἕτερος: Acts 2:4) languages. This decisive action of the Spirit is necessary *precisely when the disciples have to leave the social boundaries that mark their Galilean identity*.
5. Peter is one of the most dynamic characters in Acts and he experiences unmistakable transformation through the work of the Spirit. Peter is among the disciples who have difficulty discerning the implications of Jesus' teaching (Luke 9:44–45; 18:31–34). Peter experiences a Spirit-influenced change of heart regarding ministry in Samaria (Acts 8:1–25) and again in Cornelius' household (Acts 10:1–48). Peter is not alone; without the Spirit no human character in Luke (apart from Jesus), whether Israelite or non-Israelite, has impeccable behavior or understanding. Given the gradual metamorphosis of Peter's character, it would be unsurprising

---

57. Luke 9:51: "the days" = plural; Acts 2:1: "the day" = singular.
58. The parallel is noted by Tannehill 1990, 26, who suggests only that both constructions prepare for the fulfillment of prophecy (Luke 9:22, 31, 44; Acts 1:4–8).
59. Sandiyagu 2006, 108, 117.
60. ἕτερος: Luke 8:3; 10:1; Acts 15:35, passim. ἄλλος: Luke 7:19–20, 32; 9:8, 19; 20:16; Acts 15:2, passim.
61. Cf. Acts 2:8.

if Luke was here using Peter to demonstrate that the Spirit allows for a different method and criterion for determining who can participate in the mission of Jesus.[62]
6. Casting lots, the method of selection for Judas' replacement, was used in Luke's Gospel by *Roman soldiers* dividing Jesus' garment.[63]
7. Luke implies elsewhere that only Jesus or the Spirit have the authority to designate someone an "apostle."[64]

The parallel movements in Luke 9–10 and Acts 1–2 suggest that the selection of Matthias is an example of a now-obsolete criterion of social homogeneity.[65] The absence of overt critique by Luke indicates that this is perhaps the best that can be expected apart from the Spirit. Luke likely intends his description to function as an example of the difference in selection criteria pre- and post-Pentecost. After Pentecost the *Spirit* itself will be the chief criterion for the selection of commissioned agents of Jesus and regularly will commission *aprototypical* group members like Greek-speaking Israelites, former enemies of the church, and non-apostles to minister in the name of Jesus.[66]

5.3. *Pentecost and the Scandal of Universal (Ethno-linguistic) Particularity*

Pentecost stands in answer to Peter's criterion of social homogeneity and brings Galilean Jesus-followers into contact with other Israelite regional subgroups. In this section I will demonstrate that, at Pentecost, the Spirit preserves universal ethno-linguistic particularity in ways that stood in contrast with discernable first-century Israelite expectations. I will also discuss how Peter's distinct modification of Joel 3:1–5a LXX reveals a

---

62. Darr 1992, 53 notes that the appearance of the Scriptures does not ensure "narrative reliability." "The scriptures alone are not sufficient to legitimate anything: they too must be 'accredited' in each case by the Spirit, or by a figure who has the Spirit's sanction" (53). Here, Peter recognizes the role of the Spirit in the inspiration of Scripture, but Luke does not imply that Peter is an inspired interpreter of Scripture (at least at this point; cf. Acts 2:14–36).

63. Acts 1:26 = ἔδωκαν κλήρους; Luke 23:34 = ἔβαλον κλήρους. Cf. Zechariah's selection (Luke 1:9) = λαγχάνω; Judas' selection by Jesus in Acts 1:17= λαγχάνω.

64. See Luke 6:13; Acts 9:1–31; 13:2–4; 14:14.

65. Matthias' absence from the narrative highlights the questionable nature of his "Spirit-free" selection, as does the fact that, after the coming of the Spirit, there is no impulse to replace James (Acts 12:1–2).

66. See Acts 6:3; 13:2.

conviction concerning the inseparable connection between the Spirit and identity. This section will prepare Luke's hearers for the introduction of the early community, the social group that will become the incubator of the terminal social identity for its members.

5.3.1. *Subgroup Identities in the Pentecost Narrative*

The Pentecost account is littered with Israelite subgroup identities, each of which presumably bring a set of subgroup norms and project the prototypicality of their own identity within the larger ethnic in-group. We must reckon with Luke's emphasis on these distinct groups, beginning with a brief description of the identities formed by the social groups in view in Acts 2.

5.3.1.1. *Galilean Israelite Identity.* The initial group of Jesus-followers are identified by the crowd as "Galileans," implying both the salience of Galilean identity and differentiation between Galileans and the subgroup identities within the crowd (Acts 2:7; cf. 2:9–11). Evidence from the period indicates that Galileans had a distinctive accent of which Judeans made sport.[67] If Luke's hearers are aware of this point of subgroup differentiation, it would be especially relevant to emphasize Galilean identity in the midst of a linguistic miracle.

5.3.1.2. *Diaspora Israelite Subgroup Identity.* The list of regional identities in Acts 2:9–11 has generated much scholarly attention, especially concerning the provenance of the list and the appearance of Ἰουδαία in 2:9:[68]

> And at this sound the multitude came together, and they were bewildered, because each one heard them speaking in his own language. And they were amazed and wondered, saying, "Are not all these who are speaking Galileans? And how is it that we hear, each of us in his own native language? Parthians and Medes and Elamites and residents of Mesopotamia, *Judea* and Cappadocia, Pontus and Asia, Phrygia and Pamphylia, Egypt

---

67. Rabbinic sources lampoon Galilean accents due to their indistinct pronunciation of gutturals (see Neubauer 1885, 51; Vermes 1973, 42–57; b. ʿErubin 53; b. Megillah 24b). My emphasis on Galilean identity differs from suggestions that speculation about Galilean identity is "idle" (Fitzmyer 1998, 240; cf. Conzelmann 1987, 14). Dunn 1996, 27 is more sensitive, suggesting that the linguistic differentiation heightens the "antithesis between the small regional beginnings" and the "universal potential" of the call of Jesus.

68. Commentators have offered many readings for Ἰουδαίαν: Armenia (Tertullian, Augustine), Syria (Jerome), India (Chrysostom), Greater Syria (Hengel 2000), and variously Idumea, Ionia, Bithynia, Cilicia, Lydia and Adiabene.

and the parts of Libya belonging to Cyrene, and visitors from Rome, both
Jews and proselytes, Cretans and Arabians, we hear them telling in our
own tongues the mighty works of God."⁶⁹

While discussions of the list's provenance have led to widely divergent suggestions, the list is most intelligible in the context of other lists of Diaspora regions with large Israelite populations.⁷⁰ Attempts to explain Ἰουδαία in 2:9 have produced diverging results.⁷¹ Finally, some interpret the list as indicative of either the regathering of Israel or the anticipation of the spread of the gospel to non-Israelites.⁷²

Luke's list is broadly representative of Diaspora identities possessed by devout (εὐλαβεῖς) Israelites residing (κατοιλοῦντες) in Jerusalem (Acts 2:5).⁷³ Luke's characteristic use of κατοιλοῦντες implies if not permanent re-settlement in Jerusalem, at least some level of long term residency.⁷⁴ Luke thus identifies the whole crowd as ethnic Israelites (Ἰουδαῖοι: 2:5) and then lists their countries of origin, creating a scenario of nested local and regional identities (e.g. Cappadocian Israelites, Parthian Israelites, Judean Israelites, etc.). Taken this way, the presence in the list of Ἰουδαία is unproblematic.⁷⁵ Luke simply tells us that there are ethnic Israelites from Parthia, Libya and Egypt—and from Judea proper as well. Josephus demonstrates similar usage in a description of the crowds gathered for a

69. Acts 2:8–11.
70. See Philo, *Legat.* 281–82; *Flacc.* 45–46; Pseudo-Philo, *L.A.B.* 4.3–17; *Sib. Or.* 3.160–72, 205–9.
71. See the studies by Kilpatrick 1975; Bauckham 1995, 419, 425; 2001, 143; Scott 1993; 2002, 58–72; Hengel 2000.
72. The inclusion of non-Israelites is supported by Brinkman 1963. The regathering motif is advanced by Bauckham 1995; 2001; and Pao 2003, especially 130–31. Pao's suggestion that the Jerusalem crowd represents the in-gathered exiles must contend with the fact that if the people dwelling in Jerusalem have come of their own accord they have not been "regathered" by the work either of Jesus or of the Spirit.
73. Witherington 1998, 135 notes that εὐλαβεῖς is only used by Luke for ethnic Israelites, never God-fearers or proselytes.
74. So Johnson 1992, 43; Witherington 1998, 135. Bauckham 2001, 471–72 gives the alternate view. See Luke 11:26; 13:4; Acts 1:19, 20; 2:5, 9, 14; 4:16; 7:2, 4, 48; 9:22, 32, 35; 13:27; 17:24, 26; 19:10; 22:12. In each case, permanent or at least long-term residence is implied. Contrast this with Luke's use of καταμένω (Acts 1:13) for temporary residents. The main argument for the "pilgrim" view is the presence of κατοικοῦντες in Acts 2:9. We know with certainty, however, that there were many Diaspora Israelites returning to settle permanently in Jerusalem in the first century C.E.; cf. Acts 6:9. See Levine 2005, 45–80; Rahmani 1994, 17.
75. Bruce 1951, 85 notes that the "analogy of the accompanying place names is sufficient to explain the anarthrous *Ioudaian.*" Awareness of the realities of ethnicity in Luke's world removes the puzzlement surrounding Luke's inclusion of Ἰουδαία.

Pentecost festival, differentiating between those from Galilee, Idumea, Perea and Jericho (all of whom are ethnic Israelites) and people "actually from Judea" (ὁ γνήσιος ἐξ αὐτῆς 'Ιουδαίας λαός).[76] Because nested identities become salient based upon the out-group in view, the presence of other Israelite subgroups moves Galilean identity to the fore. The early stages of Acts 1:8 imply intra-Israelite interaction, and the Pentecost account gives us just that.

There is some textual and physical evidence that Diaspora identities remained salient for those who had returned to Jerusalem.[77] Luke, at least, envisions ongoing salience of Diaspora identities among re-settlers when describing Jerusalem synagogues oriented around Diaspora identities.[78] Rabbinic evidence points to a similar phenomenon.[79] We cannot know for certain whether the existence of homeland-specific synagogues would have created intra-Israelite tension, but the conflict among the Hebrew-speaking and Greek-speaking widows in Acts 6 suggests that Luke thought these types of identities did clash. For our purposes, the important point is that Luke is aware that the dually identified Israelites in Jerusalem were *not* Galileans. They were "other."[80]

5.3.1.3. The Spirit and the 120. The scene at Pentecost is marked by Israelite subgroup identities. Yet in this context of diverse identities, the *allocentric identity* best described as "witness" is activated by the coming of the Holy Spirit in fulfillment of Jesus' promises in Acts 1:5–8. The transformative effect of the Spirit on all those gathered is exemplified by the boldness of Peter who just weeks prior trembled before a lowly servant girl (Luke 23:54–62).[81] Peter representatively claims his witness

76. Josephus, *B.J.* 2.42–43. Translation by Esler 2003, 71–73.
77. Some Jerusalem ossuaries include the Diaspora homeland of the occupant (Rahmani 1994, 17).
78. Acts 6:9.
79. See Levine 2005, 21–44.
80. There is not space to discuss the relevance of the "proselytes" in Acts 2:11. Proselytes, though technically having fulfilled criteria for full social conversion to ethnic Israelite identity, continued to be viewed as less than prototypical. The distinction in the later material is not religious, but thoroughly ethnic and the restrictions leveled against proselytes were centered on marriage/procreation. See Exod 23:4; Lev 16:29; Num 9:14; Deut 1:16. For Qumran, see Pesher 2 Sam 7 (1–13); CD 14.4–6. For rabbinic evidence, see *b. Qiddushin* 75b; *b. Baba Qamma* 38b; *b. Hullin* 3b; *m. Qiddushin* 4.1; *m. Bikkurim*. For secondary literature, see Baumgarten 1982a; 1982b; Cohen 1999, 168; Fitzmyer 1998, 243; Johnson 1992, 44.
81. Luke is emphatic in 2:1–4 that the 120 were *all* together, the sound filled the *whole* house; tongues of fire rested upon *each* of them; they were *all* filled with the Spirit (Dunn 1996, 25; Menzies 1991, 208 n. 4; Wall 2002, 55).

identity in both word and deed, and the first impulse of the Spirit-empowered witnesses is *outward toward the crowd of "others."*[82]

5.3.2. Language and Identity at Pentecost
While Pentecost creates a wake that cuts through the entire text of Acts, I will confine myself to a discussion of two facets of the text that reveal Luke's distinct understanding of the relationship between the Spirit and identity: the role of the Spirit in the preservation of universal ethnolinguistic particularity and the role of Peter's modification of Joel 3:1–5a LXX in designating the Spirit as the primary marker of human identity.

The value of an approach to the text that is conscious of the social psychological realities of identity formation is especially evident in examining the Babel imagery in Acts 2, the clearest Old Testament allusion in the Pentecost account.[83] Babel and Pentecost share a concern with the way languages divide and unite by either solidifying existing identities or creating new identities. This same reality is present in many contemporary situations that reveal the enduring power of language difference to solidify competing group identities. Current conflicts between Tamil and Sinhalese speakers in Sri Lanka, the political impasse between French and Dutch speakers in Belgium and the ongoing political issues between French and English speakers in Quebec are evidence of the identity-shaping power of language and the tension manifest in language difference. The language miracle Luke describes at Pentecost thus involves a significant identity marker.

Commentators have interpreted Luke's presentation of the Pentecost miracle as myth, hearing miracle or speaking miracle, and if the latter, as diglossia, glossolalia or xenoglossy.[84] The fact that the Spirit falls on the

---

82. So Witherington 1998, 147; cf. Acts 2:32.

83. See *inter alias* Cyril of Jerusalem, *Catechetical Lecture* 17.16–17; Arator, *On the Acts of the Apostles* 29; Dunn 1996, 24; Bruce 1951, 86. But cf. Marshall 1980, 68; Wedderburn 1994; Witherington 1998, 131. For other Old Testament imagery in the Pentecost account, including a possible Sinai motif, see Philo, *Decal.* 33; *Spec. Leg.* 2.189; also *Jub.* 1:1, 5; 6:17–22; 14:20; 15:1, 4, 19; 22:1, 15; 29:7; CD 6.19; 8.21; 19.33; 20.12; 1QpHab 2.3. Especially tantalizing is the tradition attributed to R. Jochanan that at Sinai "each word which proceeded from the mouth of the Almighty divided into seventy tongues" (*b. Shabbat* 88b). For Pentecost as an echo of Sinai, see VanderKam 2002; Dunn 1996 (tentatively); Fitzmyer 1998; Turner 1996, 285–89; Wenk 2004, 246–51 and Johnson 1992. For dissenting views, see Menzies 1992 and Cho 2005.

84. Diglossia: Zerhusen 1995; xenolalia: Fitzmyer 1998, 236; Conzelmann 1987. Esler 1994, 37–51 thinks Luke was not familiar with glossolalia and interpreted the event as xenoglossy.

disciples suggests Luke understood the miracle to involve *their* speaking, and the confusion of the crowd (expressed with the verb συγχέω; cf. Gen 11:7–9) indicates that different languages were in play.[85] Luke clearly intends the reader to understand that extraordinary speech was made possible. The usual interpretation is that the Spirit at Pentecost overcame linguistic difference in order for the gospel to be heard.[86] But to the contrary, Luke expects that the Spirit actually *heightened* linguistic difference at Pentecost. It is this essential fact that underscores Luke's unique use of Babel imagery to highlight his understanding of the relationship between ethnic particularity and the gospel.

Luke describes a language miracle that was *unnecessary*.[87] Whether those present in the crowd had dwelled in Jerusalem for some time or were temporary pilgrims, the entire list of Diaspora identities falls into either Aramaic-speaking (eastern Diaspora) or Greek-speaking (western Diaspora) locales.[88] Increasing evidence of bilingualism in antiquity alerts us to the fact that communication among the crowd in Jerusalem would likely have been unproblematic.[89] It is unlikely that those hearing Luke's story would have expected the crowd to have been unable to communicate with one another, especially if many of these people had been dwelling (κατοικοῦντες) in Jerusalem for some time. Luke himself gives evidence of the intelligibility of both Greek and Hebrew/Aramaic in Jerusalem.[90] Schwartz contends that Hebrew, Aramaic and "biblical" Greek could all serve as markers of Israelite ethnic identity and could reasonably have been expected to serve as the *lingua franca* of the emerging group of Jesus-followers.[91] But Luke does not portray the Spirit as inspiring speech in Hebrew/Aramaic or Greek. The phrase "each in their own language in which they were born" (ἕκαστος τῇ ἰδίᾳ διαλέκτῳ ἡμῶν ἐν ᾗ ἐγεννήθημεν) refers to the languages of the hearers' places of origin—their Diaspora homelands.[92] This is emphasized again in Acts 2:11: "We hear them telling in our own tongues the mighty works of God."

---

85. Polhill 1992, 100.
86. E.g. Arrington 1988, 24.
87. Joel Green (2008, 198–213) develops a similar reading with regard to the language realities at Pentecost, though he does not investigate Second Temple eschatological expectations with regard to language.
88. Zerheusen 1995.
89. Wedderburn 1994, 49; Kee 1990, 44. Cf. John 12:21–22.
90. Acts 21:37, 40; 22:2. Cf. Bauckham 2006, 239.
91. Schwartz 1993, 45.
92. Hengel 2000, 166.

5. Initiating a Scandal of Universal Particularity

Luke suggests that the Spirit creates what can best be described not as a miracle of impossible communication made possible, but rather as *a miracle of universal particularity*. Rather than eliminating the cultural particularity marked by language, the Spirit explicitly *affirmed* ethnolinguistic diversity by allowing the crowd to hear Peter's address in the diverse languages of their respective births: ἤρχαντο λαλεῖν ἑτέραις γλώσσαις καθὼς τὸ πνεῦμα ἐδίδου ἀποφθέγγεσθαι αὐτοῖς (Acts 2:4).[93] This observation implies that something other than common language will serve as a primary identity marker for the emerging group of Jesus-followers. Moreover, because language is inseparable from wider cultural thought forms (indeed, Diaspora languages would largely have been constituted by and constitutive of *non-Israelite cultures* and the identities within which those cultures arose) it appears that common culture is also ruled out as a unifying factor in the early movement.

The particularity of the language miracle at Pentecost appears unexpected in Israelite tradition. Zephaniah 3:9 ("Yea, at that time I will change the speech of the peoples to a pure speech, that all of them may call on the name of the Lord and serve him with one accord") generated the idea that the day of the Lord would bring a return to the universal use of Hebrew, the presumed language of pre-Babel humankind. This tradition occurs in two pre-Lukan texts, 4Q464 and *Jubilees*. 4Q464 is reconstructed as follows:

line 5	] confused
line 6	]m to Abrah {r} am[94]
line 7	for ever, since he/it
line 8	r]ead the holy tongue
line 9	I will make] the people pure of speech[95]

Stone and Eshel read the fragment as a prediction of the reversal of Babel and universal return to Hebrew based upon Zeph 3:9. *Jubilees* 12:25–27 is more explicit, suggesting that Abraham was given angelic assistance in learning Hebrew, a language lost since the flood that gives privileged access to the books of the "fathers." The *Jubilees* passage underscores the role language plays in identity, in this case granting entrance to "a divinely selected group with access to esoteric knowledge inherited from the age before Babel."[96]

---

93. ἕτερος always means "another of a *different* kind" for Luke. See Sandiyagu 2006, 107.
94. 4Q464.5–9. Stone and Eshel 1992 are puzzled over the *resh* in the spelling of "Abraham."
95. Stone and Eshel 1993–94, 169–77.
96. Weitzman 1999, 41.

This tradition of anticipated ethno-linguistic homogeneity expands post-70, a period in which Hebrew "became a *commodity*, consciously manipulated by the leaders of the Jews to evoke the Jews' distinctness from their neighbors."[97] The effect of Paul's use of Hebrew/Aramaic in Acts 21:40 (cf. 26:14) gives evidence of Luke's awareness of this reality. Given the expectations of the Israelite ἔθνος, we might have expected the language miracle at Pentecost to be a *purification* of language and a return to Hebrew. It was, rather, an affirmation of the *pluralization* of language.

This has important ramifications for identity formation. Language is an essential marker of identity and contemporary research continues to demonstrate the role of language in both identity maintenance and intergroup conflict.[98] In the light of the potential for language to create a basis for group conflict (see Acts 6:1-6), it is striking that Luke's Spirit does not unite via unified language. Instead, the Spirit gives voice to the gospel in the lesser-known languages of Diaspora homelands. In Genesis, human speech, confused by God, divides. In Acts 2, human speech, facilitated and empowered by the Spirit, unites. Yet it unites in a way that *preserves* ethno-linguistic particularity.[99] Perhaps this should not be surprising, given the fact that Babel was not concerned chiefly with language, but with mutated human community. Pentecost, in its nuanced reversal of Babel, reveals that appropriate expressions of human community do not require linguistic homogeneity precisely because, by the work of the Holy Spirit, humans are being united not by cultural homogeneity but around the person of Jesus. The Spirit, therefore, not only creates common identity, but the Spirit also powerfully affirms the validity of ethno-linguistic particularity.

The celebration of linguistic diversity at Pentecost affirms particularity, but also subsumes it under a new identity. Never again are the first disciples collectively categorized as "Galileans." Regional origins remain important aspects of the identity of *individuals* in Acts, yet within the

---

97. Schwartz 1993, 4. See *y. Megillah* 71a; *Midrash Tanḥuma* 28; *Testament of Judah* 25.1-3. *Targum Pseudo-Jonathan* and *Targum Neophyti I* on Gen 11:1 insert "holy tongue" and "language of the sanctuary." *3 En.* 1:11-13 implies Hebrew is the angelic language. Cf. the possibility of "angelic language" as a status symbol in 1 Cor 12-14.

98. On language and identity, see Giles et al. 1977, 308. On the linguistic root of some inter-ethnic conflict, see Schiffman 1993.

99. Volf is alert to the importance of linguistic particularity at Pentecost, suggesting that "It would...be reductionist to understand...Pentecost simply as Babel in reverse" (1998, 268). Volf sees catholicity through many languages.

5. Initiating a Scandal of Universal Particularity 119

properly functioning in-group of believers Israelite subgroup identities are no longer *collectively* used to create subgroup barriers.[100]

5.4. Peter's Pentecost Discourse

While the Pentecost language miracle rules out both ethno-linguistic and regional identities as the unifying factors for the Jesus-movement, Peter's speech makes it clear that it is the *Spirit* who replaces these old identity markers as the new marker that definitively identifies those who are rightly related to God. The speech must be seen in a context of identity legitimation, with Peter acting as a representative of his group:[101]

> Peter, *standing with the eleven*, lifted up his voice and addressed them.[102]

Peter's identity legitimation is based upon several factors: (1) Peter claims that the Spirit is evidence both of God's in-breaking action and of the believers' identification with God through Jesus (2:17–19); (2) Peter makes claims about the identity of Jesus and the identity of his in-group in relation to Jesus (2:20–32) and (3) Peter claims that Jesus is the one who pours out the Spirit (2:33). I will discuss only the factors in the text relevant to Peter's defense of the group's identity—which he connects with the Spirit and with Spirit-empowered deeds.

Neither Peter's speech nor the crowd's response reveal a fundamental conflict between Israelite identity and the identity experienced by the Spirit-filled disciples.[103] Peter's progression of vocative nouns used to address the crowd demonstrates his continuing sense of Israelite identity: ἄνδρες Ἰουδαῖοι, ἄνδρες Ἰσραηλῖται and ἄνδρες ἀδελφοί.[104] The crowd's response in Acts 2:37 ("Brothers [ἀδελφοί], what should we do?") further underscores ethnic continuity.

Yet as Peter interprets the Spirit-manifestation to his ethnic kin, he makes an essential distinction concerning the relationship between

---

100. See Acts 4:36; 6:6; 13:1. It is hard not to envision Pentecost as an experience proleptically akin to Rev 7, where those gathered around the throne of God and the Lamb remain identifiable as people from "every nation, from all tribes and peoples and tongues."

101. Litwak 2005, 159 rightly notes that the use of "Joel 3 in Acts 2 provides an explanation of the events which have just occurred." In other words, Acts 2 legitimates the disciples' behavior by appeal to the Spirit, but does not implicitly restrict the Spirit only to the inspiration of prophetic speech.

102. Acts 2:14 (emphasis mine).

103. Peter's references to David (2:25, 29) demonstrate the movement's coherence with Israelite identity.

104. Acts 2:14, 22, 29. See Chapter 8 for detail on Luke's use of ἀδελφοι.

Israelite ethnic identity, the Spirit and identification with the God of Israel. The validity of ethnic identity, especially in relation to one's standing with God, is rendered secondary by Peter's deployment and "modification" of Joel 3:1–5a LXX.[105] There are five significant changes (marked by underlining in the following discussion) to Joel 3:1–5a LXX as well as three minor changes (italicised text).[106] Though all five major modifications are important in Luke's wider program, two in particular concern Luke's identity-forming program.[107]

5.4.1. Peter's "Modification" of Joel 3:1–5a LXX

(Joel 3:1//Acts 2:17)
καὶ ἔσται μετὰ ταῦτα [ἐν ταῖς ἐσχάταις ἡμέραις] [λέγεις ὁ θεός] καὶ ἐκχεῶ ἀπὸ τοῦ πνεύματός μου ἐπὶ πᾶσαν σάρκα, καὶ προφητεύσουσιν οἱ υἱοὶ ὑμῶν καὶ αἱ θυγατέρες ὑμῶν, *καὶ οἱ πρεσβύτεροι ὑμῶν ἐνύπνια ἐνυπνιασθήσονται, καὶ οἱ νεανίσκοι ὑμῶν ὁράσεις ὄψονται*· [transpose clauses]

(3:2//2:18)
καὶ [*γε*] ἐπὶ τοὺς δούλος [μου] καὶ ἐπὶ τὰς δουλάσ [μου] ἐν ταῖς ἡμέραις ἐκείναις ἐκχεῶ ἀπὸ τοῦ πνεύματός μου.

---

105. I enclose "modification" in quotes only to indicate that it is difficult to speak about New Testament "modification" of LXX texts since we are not privy to the Old Greek. In its context Joel 3:1–5 is a fulfillment of the Mosaic plea in Num 11 for assistance in managing the contentious life of the community. God responds by giving the Spirit to seventy elders of Israel (Num 11:17), thus establishing a close relationship between the Spirit and the welfare of the community. In Joel the Spirit is also poured out for the creation of a renewed community (Joel 2:21–27 LXX; see Wenk 2004, 254). This anticipates the link between Spirit-reception and community-formation in Acts 2. See Bock 1987, 163 for a detailed discussion of the text-critical issues in both the Joel passage and in Acts.

106. Minor alterations: (1) transposition of "young men" and "old men" in 3:1; (2) addition of γε in 3:2; (3) addition of ἄνω and κάτω in 3:3.

107. Briefly, concerning the other major alterations: ἐν ταῖς ἐσχάταις ἡμέραις in Isa 2:2 LXX marks the final exaltation of Zion that prompts the nations to stream toward Jerusalem. Cf. Jer 23:20; 30:24; 48:47; 49:39; Ezek 38:16; Hos 3:5; Mal 4:1. λέγει ὁ θεός in Acts 2:17 (cf. Joel 3:1 LXX) alerts the hearer that Peter is quoting divine speech contained in Joel's text (cf. Acts 7:6, 49; Rom 12:19; 1 Cor 14:21; 2 Cor 6:17). καὶ προφητεύσουσιν (omitted by D and Vg) re-emphasizes the Spirit-inspiration of the speakers (Fitzmyer 1998, 253). Menzies 1992, 221 (see also Cho 2005, 145) suggests this emphasizes that the Spirit is the "Spirit of prophecy." But in Acts 2 Peter is legitimating the identity of his group and its divine sanction by explaining both *this particular instance* and the eschatological moment that it portends with the Joel text. Peter is not limiting the Spirit only to the actions described in this passage from Joel.

(3:3//2:19)
καὶ δώσω τέρατα ἐν τῷ οὐρανῷ [ἄνω] καὶ [σημεῖα] ἐπὶ τῆς γῆς [κάτω], αἷμα καὶ πῦρ καὶ ἀτμίδα καπνοῦ·

(3:4//2:20)
ὁ ἥλιος μεταστραφήσεται εἰς σκότος καὶ ἡ σελήνη εἰς αἷμα πρὶν ἐλθεῖν ἡμέραν κυρίου τὴν μεγάλην καὶ ἐπιφανῆ.

(3:5a//2:21)
καὶ ἔσται πᾶς, ὃς ἂν ἐπικαλέσηται τὸ ὄνομα κυρίου, σωθήσεται.[108]

(1) Luke adds the possessive pronoun μου (2×) to the δοῦλοι and δοῦλαι in 2:18, thus no longer rendering Joel's male and female slaves as slaves in the socio-economic sense (as in the MT and LXX), but rather as *slaves belonging to God*.[109] This is similar to the reorientation of identity initiated by Jesus in Acts 1:8 (μου μάρτυρες) and, like Isaiah, sets both δοῦλος and μάρτυς as key metaphors for those properly related to God.[110] This modification establishes the Spirit as the *definitive identity marker* for those who rightly can be called the possession (μου) of God or Jesus.

The identity ramifications of this modification are significant. First, the modification legitimizes the identity of the disciples, marking them not as babblers/drunkards but as God's slaves. Second, Peter's in-group

---

108. Hull 1967, 63 notes that Joel likely means only Israelites in the "all" of Joel 3:5a, so perhaps Peter only has Israel in mind here. However, given the prophetic hope for the nations in some expressions of Israel's tradition, the eschatological freight with which Peter loads this passage makes it impossible to rule out the ἔθνη as included among the "all" of Joel 3:5a.

109. Menzies 1992, 219 (cf. Cho 2005, 144) suggests this demonstrates that the Spirit is a second blessing for those who are saved, but Peter shows no concern here for a systematic order of salvation, and Luke does not seem to bear a concern for a systematic order of salvation throughout the narrative. Others see this as part of Luke's "reversal" theme in which those who were previously "household slaves are transformed into 'my servants'" (Wall 2002, 64; cf. Witherington 1998, 142). This seems plausible. But we must also reckon with the fact that Peter is not concerned in this speech with a justice ethic. He is legitimating the activity and identity of his in-group. It should further be noted that the heavy emphasis on the proclamatory aspect of prophecy by scholars who emphasize the "Spirit of prophecy" model neglects the fact that prophecy is indicative of a certain *identity* marked by access to God (see 1 Sam 9:9). Moses, who is the paradigmatic prophet in Israelite tradition and central to Peter's presentation of Jesus (Acts 3:22–23; cf. Deut 18:18–19), is set apart because of his *relationship* with God: "And there has not arisen a prophet since in Israel like Moses, *whom the Lord knew face to face*" (Deut 34:10; cf. Num 12:6–8). The causal factor in making someone a prophet is not simply the action of prophecy, but a relationship with God that gives the prophet access to God.

110. "Servant" and "witness" express similar concepts in Isa 44:21; 45:4–6; 48:10–11; 49:1–6; 54:5; 55:4–5.

had assumed in Acts 1:6 that the benefits bestowed by God were limited to the ethnic in-group. Just as Jesus reoriented those expectations by defining the disciples in relationship to himself in Act 1:8 ("You will be my witnesses…"), so here Luke makes us aware that relationship to God will be marked now by the presence of the Spirit. This modification shifts a key identity boundary. Because social groups are formed by the boundaries established in relationship with other groups, shifting the boundary of the group to "relationship with God as identified by the Spirit" creates an entirely different dynamic for intergroup—and particularly interethnic—interaction. Subsequently, whenever social identity boundaries are in view in Acts, the appearance of the Spirit (on the basis of Peter's modification) identifies those who are rightly related to Jesus. This forms the basis for the recognition of a common social identity between those who were formerly "other." This will become increasingly important for Luke, but we must await his narration of the full force of this new reality.

(2) The final significant alteration of the Joel passage is the addition of σημεῖον in Acts 2:19 to render the passage "*wonders* (τέρατα) in the heavens above and *signs* (σημεῖα) in the earth below." The phrase "wonders and signs" (τέρατα καὶ σημεῖα) draws on an Old Testament tradition emphasizing God's use of the miraculous on behalf of his people.[111] Wenk argues that Old Testament wonders and signs are not only "attestation of a truth but the realization of salvation."[112] Luke follows this tradition, using the phrase to describe God's action that breaks into human affairs to bring deliverance, healing or salvation.[113] Peter's addition of σημεῖα in 2:19 creates an organic connection between (1) "wonders" in the Joel passage, (2) God's witness to Jesus through "wonders and signs" (Acts 2:22) and (3) the "wonders and signs" performed by the disciples (Acts 2:43).[114] Those who do "wonders and signs" are empowered by the Spirit and, thus, are δοῦλοι or δοῦλαι of God. This will serve as an auxiliary identity maker later in Acts. We will come to see that common identity can be established either by direct manifestation of the Spirit or by the performance of actions attributable to the Spirit.[115]

---

111. Exod 7:3; 11:9–10; Deut 4:34; 6:22; 7:19; 11:3; 26:8; 29:3; 34:11; Isa 8:18; Dan 4:34; 6:37.
112. Wenk 2004, 251.
113. Acts 2:19, 22, 43; 4:30; 5:12; 6:8; 7:36; 14:3; 15:12.
114. Wenk 2004, 250.
115. See especially Acts 9:26–31. This is true of "wonders and signs" and of "witness." This will be discussed further in regard to Barnabas and James later in Acts (see Chapters 6 and 8 below).

5.5. Conclusion

Working backward, we have seen in this section that Peter's modification of Joel 3:1–5 LXX establishes a paradigm whereby the Spirit, and not ethnic identity, marks all those who are rightly related to God through Jesus (either as "servants" or "witnesses"). This identity-marking role of the Spirit helps mitigate the difficulty in discerning a Lukan "order of salvation."[116] We will come to see that *the Spirit typically appears in the narrative precisely at the moment that human identity is in question*. Yet the work of the Spirit in both facilitating, marking and empowering this identity comes in a way that does not eliminate, but rather affirms (through an "unnecessary miracle"), the *particularity* of ethno-linguistic identities present at Pentecost. *This is an initial indication that ethnic identity, while it must be chastened, is not inherently incompatible with the emerging allocentric identity formed by the Spirit*. The extension of Spirit-empowered ministry to all 120 (Acts 2:1–4) and the affirmation of ethno-linguistic difference (Acts 2:5–11) stand in contrast to a final vestige of the Jesus-community's Spirit-less behavior, Peter's reliance upon in-group homogeneity in the effort to replace Judas. This is all set within the broader context of Jesus' commission to a group with Galilean identity to cross threatening social boundaries while operating with a Spirit-formed allocentric identity ("witness") whose trajectory is *outward toward the "other."*[117]

SIT has given us three interpretive advantages in this section. First, it underscores the reality that the presence of groups implies the presence of social boundaries. Second, it alerts us to the fact that Peter's criteria for Judas' replacement follow quite "normal" intragroup processes. Third, and most significantly, an understanding of nested identity is helpful to understand the layers of identity manifest in the linguistic miracle at Pentecost. The theory will provide additional heuristic benefit in sections to come.

The preaching at Pentecost affirms Jesus as the source of the Spirit (Acts 2:33), thus tightening the link between identification with Jesus and identification by the Spirit. Peter's message is met by Luke's ideal

---

116. Luke's order of salvation in Acts 2:38–39, while "normal" (Turner 1996, 384), is not "normative" (Witherington 1998, 154–55; contra Dunn 1996, 32). The connection between Spirit and identity will dissolve problems created by Luke's (seemingly) inconsistent chronologies.

117. Joel 3:5b LXX: "Because on the mountain of Zion and in Jerusalem it will be a remnant, says the Lord, and they will proclaim the good news, those whom the Lord summons." In Joel the Spirit creates a community of witness. The echo in Acts 2 is unmistakable.

response, "Brothers, what shall we do?," a response that itself indicates continuity ("*brothers*") with Israelite ethnic identity. Peter proclaims that those who repent and are baptized will "receive the gift of the Holy Spirit" (Acts 2:38). We now know that, according to Luke, those who receive this gift will undergo a transformation resulting in an allocentric identity. It is a new social group composed of these Spirit-transformed allocentrically oriented individuals that will form the incubator for a new social identity capable both of simultaneously loving the self/group and the "other" and surprisingly transcending intractable intergroup (and especially interethnic) identity barriers.

Chapter 6

CONSUMMATING A NEW IDENTITY:
THE COMMUNITY SUMMARIES
AND THE IDENTITY-FORMING POWER OF A GROUP

The Pentecost account, with its affirmation of universal ethno-linguistic particularity and emphasis on the Spirit as the definitive identity marker for the δοῦλοι of God, serves to destabilize the primacy of the regional and ethnic identities in view in Acts 1:1–11 and 2:1–11. Luke follows this destabilization of identity with his initial account of a new social group composed of Spirit-filled members. Bearing in mind Luke's understanding of the Spirit's allocentric influence upon individuals, the community described by Luke appears as both the *natural product* and *corporate expression* of an allocentric identity.[1] By Acts 5 this new social group will emerge as the incubator of a new *social* identity.

In this chapter I will discuss the following features of the community summaries in Luke's identity-forming project:[2]

1. Luke's use of narrative techniques and speech material to emphasize the primary importance of the community and its relationship to the Spirit;
2. Luke's portrayal of the community's collective relationship to the "other" as a subversion of typical identity-forming processes;
3. Luke's unique view of the relationship between the Spirit, possessions and the "other" (and, conversely, Satan, possessions and the "other") as it finds expression in the accounts of Ananias, Sapphira and Barnabas.

In broad brush strokes, the community summaries unveil Luke's definitive corporate expression of Spirit-formed allocentric identity as well as the definitive identification of the Spirit with the community.

---

1. Cf. Zechariah and Simeon (Luke 1–2); John (Luke 3); Jesus (Luke 4), Peter and the 120 (Acts 2).
2. "Community summaries" is shorthand for Acts 2:42–47 (Summary 1); 4:32–5:11 (Summary 2); 5:12–16 (Summary 3).

6.1. Understanding the Baseline Significance of the New Community

Luke's description of the new social group that comprises the early church is remarkable for the intensity of the self-ascription, the comprehensive nature of the communal life, the posture of the group toward the "other" and the relationship between the group and the Spirit. Contrary to interpreters who suggest that the community summaries only depict "the primordial beginning of the community,"[3] Luke's early establishment of the community forms a baseline assumption for the normative function of Jesus-following social groups.

Three factors in Acts 1–5 highlight Luke's emphasis on the community. First, Luke uses functional redundancy, especially in triplets, to highlight material of special importance.[4] This is as true with the community summaries as it is with the conversions of Saul and of Cornelius' household.[5] Introductions give essential information about characters and fix them in the "web of human relationships" in ways that endure throughout a narrative.[6] In just this way the triple-introduction of the community (2:42–47; 4:32–37; 5:12–16) grounds the communal norms in the mind of the hearer.[7]

Second, Luke places the community summaries in conspicuous proximity to the first three major Spirit-events in Acts.[8]

> And Peter said to them, "Repent, and be baptized every one of you in the name of Jesus Christ for the forgiveness of your sins; and *you shall receive the gift of the Holy Spirit*"… So those who received his word were baptized, and there were added that day about three thousand souls. And they devoted themselves to the apostles' teaching and fellowship, to the breaking of bread and the prayers. (Acts 2:38, 41–42)

---

3. Tannehill calls the summaries a "minor theme" (1990, 43). The failure to engage the summaries is a weakness of the studies of Borgman 2006, Pao 2003, Menzies 1992 and, to a lesser extent, Cho 2005.
4. Witherup 1992; 1993 identifies "functional redundancy" as a rhetorical strategy for Luke.
5. Saul: Acts 9:1–19; 22:3–16; 26:12–17; Cornelius: Acts 10:1–48; 11:1–18; 15:6–11.
6. Rowe 2006, 42–43. "Web of human relationships" is from Harvey 1965, 22.
7. Thompson 2006 analyzes the important role of the church throughout Acts.
8. Acts 2:1–41; 4:31; 5:1–11. The pattern endures less explicitly in 6:1–7. Despite protests from Cho and Menzies, the scholarly consensus continues closely to connect the Spirit and the community summaries. See Tannehill 1990, 44; Robinson and Wall 2006, 27; Turner 1996, 415; Johnson 1977, 184; Penney 1997, 90; Dunn 1970, 51.

And when they had prayed, the place in which they were gathered together was shaken; and *they were all filled with the Holy Spirit* and spoke the word of God with boldness. Now the company of those who believed were of one heart and soul, and no one said that any of the things which he possessed was his own, but they had everything in common. (Acts 4:31–32)

But Peter said, "Ananias, why has Satan filled your heart to lie *to the Holy Spirit* and to keep back part of the proceeds of the land?"... Now many signs and wonders were done among the people by the hands of the apostles. And they were all together in Solomon's Portico. (Acts 5:3, 12)

The first two summaries follow incidents that imply that *all the legitimate members of the group are influenced by the Spirit*. The third summary follows Luke's equation of a lie to the community with a lie to the Spirit, hence a definitive identification of the Spirit and the community (Acts 5:3).[9] Some proponents of the "Spirit of prophecy" model, following Gunkel's insistence that there is "not one syllable" in the summaries themselves attributing the life of the community to the work of the Spirit, are forced to read with a minimalist lens in order to avoid the natural progression from the appearances of the Spirit to the community summaries.[10]

Third, though often overlooked when discussing the summaries, Luke uses Peter's speech in Acts 3:12–26 to highlight the essential and life-giving connection between Jesus, the Spirit, the community and "salvation."[11] Peter's speech in Acts 3:12–26 addresses Israel's ignorance-based denial (ἀρνέομαι: 3:13, 14) of the Messiah and emphasizes the high stakes of membership in the new community.[12] Peter indicates that repentance and turning toward the "prophet like Moses" has several parallel effects:
1. "Times of refreshing" (3:19).
2. The return of Messiah and consequent "restoration of all things" (3:20–21).

---

9. While scholars often note the connection between lying to the community and lying to the Spirit (e.g. Bock 2007, 222; Fitzmyer 1998, 523) they do not note the significance for the group's *identity* in its broader narrative and social context.

10. Quote from Gunkel 1899, 10. Cf. Menzies 2000, 96–97. Cho 2005, 133 sees at best an indirect influence of the Spirit only through the communal response to Spirit-inspired prophetic speech.

11. Thompson 2006, 61–62, for example, calls Peter's speech an "explanation" of the miracle and a "call for repentance," but does not discuss the Spirit's role in either of those activities.

12. Peter's use of ἀρνέομαι evokes his own denial of Jesus (ἀπαρνέομαι: Luke 22:34, 61; ἀρνέομαι: Luke 22:57). The post-denial grace extended to Peter plausibly explains the gracious attitude Peter takes toward the Jerusalem crowd, Ananias and Sapphira, and even Simon the Samaritan.

3. Participation in the people (λαός; this is a logical obverse deduction from 3:23: "Every soul that does not listen to that prophet shall be destroyed from the people").
4. Blessing for all the families of the earth (3:25).[13]
5. Blessing for Israel manifest in a turn from "wickedness" (3:26).

The tightly woven connections that emerge from Peter's speech, set in its narrative context, are essential for understanding Luke's high view of the early community. The ultimate stake in response to Jesus is participation or non-participation in a people that exists within a larger teleological goal of ἀποκατάστασις πάντων (3:21).[14] Participation in this people is equated with καιροὶ ἀναψύξεως (3:20) and turning from πονηρία (3:26). If we align the logic of this speech with Peter's Pentecost speech (especially 2:38) we can see an interesting parallel between the community and the Spirit:

1. Proper response to Jesus results in the gift of the Spirit (Acts 2:38), salvation from this "corrupt generation" (2:40), "times of refreshing" (3:19), turning from wickedness (3:26), and *participation in a people* (3:23, by obverse).
2. Refusal to identify with Jesus results in no gift of the Spirit (2:38, by obverse) and *exclusion or destruction from the people* (3:23).

There is an implicit connection between the gift of the Spirit, the experience of times of refreshing and *participation in a people*. The link between community membership and "times of refreshing" is what Wenk calls in another context the "this-worldly dimension of salvation."[15] "Conversion," for Luke, is incomplete without full community incorporation in the immediate present.[16]

---

13. Here we see Luke's conviction that the Abrahamic covenant required that Israel's privileged identity before God was *for the sake of* the blessing of both Israel and "all the families of the earth." See Chapter 3 above for the significance of Abraham in Luke's project.

14. Cf. "restoration" in Acts 1:6.

15. Wenk 2004, 271.

16. Twelftree 2009, 45–51 makes a different argument, suggesting that community membership is not part of Luke's view of salvation, but is "a natural (perhaps expected or unavoidable) consequence or expression, even ongoing benefit of it" (49). It is difficult, given Luke's emphasis on community incorporation (2:42–47) as an immediate ramification of saving oneself from "this crooked generation" (Acts 2:40), to imagine that Luke sees membership in the people of God as distinct from and subsequent to "salvation." We will repeatedly see that participation in a people is a major component of salvation in Lukan perspective.

It is through this people gathered around Jesus, the prophet like Moses, that God will bless all the πατριαί of the earth (3:25). Luke's use of the Abrahamic covenant indicates his awareness that God's covenant with (ethnic) father Abraham was not for the creation of an ethnically exclusive people, but rather for the blessing of both Israel and "all the families of the earth."[17] Peter's use of "families (πατριαί) is closer to Gen 12:3 (φυλαί) than Gen 18:18; 22:18; 26:4, which use ἔθνη. Given the dramatic nature of Peter's new understanding of God's relationship to non-Israelites expressed at Cornelius' household conversion, it is quite plausible that Luke's Peter here retains (even if Luke himself has a fuller picture in view) an ethnically exclusive vision of God's work through Jesus in which the ἔθνη can only participate after undergoing full social conversion to Israelite ethnic identity. Yet what is emerging is the fact that the "people" within which one may or may not participate is not simply ethnic Israel, it is Luke's new community. The Barnabas, Ananias and Sapphira episode, discussed below, will give dramatic expression to Luke's high view of the new group as the Spirit-empowered community of life.

6.1.1. A Community of Intense Self-ascription

Having established the importance of the community in Luke's structure and the eschatological ministry of Israel's "prophet-like-Moses," we now turn toward the role of the community in the formation of social identity. Social identity cannot exist apart from a recognizable social group, which is constructed by the twin criteria of self-ascription and categorization by others.[18] The identity-forming power of groups is particularly potent in collectivistic cultures like those surrounding the ancient Mediterranean.[19] Moreover, research has demonstrated that highly relational groups in which members know one another and have regular and meaningful social interaction are more potent identity-forming entities than larger social categories.[20] In other words, in a collectivistic society, a relatively small and interconnected social group can have powerful effects upon the social identities of its members. This is precisely the sort of social entity Luke describes in the community summaries.

Evidence for self-ascription to the emerging community in Acts is pervasive and intense, a simple fact whose force is sometimes lost in the

---

17. Cf. Luke 1–3 for sustained reflection on Abraham and the Abrahamic covenant. See Esler 2006, 23–34 on Abraham and Israel's "ethnic" identity.
18. Turner 1982.
19. Brown 2000, 753; Brown and Aharpour 1999.
20. Rabbie and Horowitz 1988, 117–23.

quest for contextual parallels to the community in Acts.²¹ Consider the following features of the three summaries:
1. Commitment to teaching of the leaders (2:42; 4:33).
2. Commitment to intragroup relationships (2:42; 4:32; 5:12).
3. Commitment to common meals (2:42, 46).
4. Commitment to common worship (2:42, 46–47).
5. Commitment to care for needy members (2:45; 4:34–35).
6. Commitment to property sharing (2:44; 4:32, 34–35).

This level of self-ascription and intimacy in Luke's group has features usually only expected in kinship groups, which themselves are re-oriented in Luke's Gospel.²² It is well-known that kinship formed an important social category in first-century Palestine through which people could understand their relationship to their social world.²³ Kinship groups were characterized by "loyalty and trust, truth telling, homes open to all in the group, obligation to be certain that the needs of everyone in the group are met…and a sense of shared destiny."²⁴ The descriptions in Acts resonate strongly with this definition. They depict a community of loyal commitment (ἦσαν δὲ προσκαρτεροῦντες [2:41]; ἦν καρδία καὶ ψυχὴ μία [4:32]). The Ananias and Sapphira narrative demonstrates the centrality of truth-telling. The locus of the community's life revolves around both Temple and home, the latter of which is an innovation for social groups that are not based on kinship markers (2:46).²⁵ Physical needs are met by the group itself (2:45; 4:32b–35). The prayer of the believers in 4:24–30 is evidence of a sense of shared destiny. The element of the shared meal, coupled with communal provision for the needy, suggests

---

21. For potential parallels between the community summaries and groups within Luke's historical context, see the following: Essene/Qumran: Capper 1983; 1995; Greco-Roman friendship: Mitchell 1992; Greco-Roman utopian philosophies: Sterling 1994; kinship: Bartchy 1991; Greco-Roman associations: Harland 2003; Kloppenborg 1993; Kloppenborg and Wilson 1996. Jeremias 1966, 118–21 suggested the components formed a liturgical order for the community. Turner 1996, 413 is correct, the "total picture" and not the individual components is the key to the summaries.

22. Jesus critiques exclusivistic kinship structures in Luke (see Moxnes 2003, 142–57 [esp. 157]); Borgman 2006 suggests Luke subverts traditional "clan loyalty" and insists loyalty to Jesus trumped kinship affiliation (Luke 8:19–21; 14:26; 18:29–30; 21:12–17).

23. Kinship identities are essentially "micro-ethnicities." Networks of kinship groups that share a sense of "group-ness" form the basis of many ethnic groups.

24. Bartchy 1991, 313.

25. See Elliott 1991, though note that at least in Acts 2:42–47 there is not yet a sense of conflict between temple and household (*pace* Elliott 1991, 193–94).

that the summaries must be interpreted to describe more than just the "religious" or "moral" aspects of the early church.[26] All told, the intense self-ascription Luke describes points toward the group as an important source for members' social identities.

6.1.2. Identity Forged in the Midst of Conflict

The level of in-group identification evident in the summaries themselves is heightened by the fact that Luke places the summaries in contexts of social conflict, some of which is anticipated by the social boundary crossings implicated in Acts 1:8. Intergroup conflict, especially the perception of external threat directed toward the in-group, intensifies identification with the in-group in three related ways: it causes group members to develop a heightened sense of similarity to their own group (in-group homogeneity), it creates greater differentiation from out-groups (in-group bias) and it cultivates a stronger sense that out-groups have very little social differentiation (out-group homogeneity).[27] Stated simply, intergroup conflict tends to magnify the notions of "we" and "they."

Consider Luke's arrangement of material:
1. *Summary #1* (Acts 2:1–47). This summary is preceded by the initial out-pouring of the Spirit.
2. *Intergroup conflict #1* (Acts 4:1–22). Peter and John are accosted by the Jerusalemite authorities.
3. *Increased in-group solidarity* (Acts 4:23–30). The community prays, asking for the *intensification* of the expression of the group norm that elicited the intergroup conflict.
4. *Summary #2* (Acts 4:32–36). This summary is preceded by the second out-pouring of the Spirit and describes the community with greater relational intensity: "Now the company of those who believed were of one heart and soul" (Acts 4:31–36).

---

26. Esler 1987, 76 describes the shared meal as "an action expressing the warmest intimacy and respect." Luke's position is more comprehensive than that ascribed to him by both Wall 2002, 71–72 (who argues that the summaries describe a renewed "religious life") and Cho 2005, 130 (who argues that Luke is concerned simply with a description of normative "morality"). Scholars have broadly recognized that the particular category "religion" is difficult to isolate in the socially integrated ancient world. Moreover, such a category neglects the fact that the overtly cultic aspects of the summaries are integrated into a more comprehensive overall description. Similarly, the category "morality" disregards the integral relationship between identity and activity assumed by Acts. *Who* we are profoundly affects *how* we are, and both are affected by the Spirit.

27. Dietz-Uhler and Murrell 1998; Rothgerber 1997, 1209–10.

5. *Intragroup conflict #1* (Acts 5:1–11). Ananias and Sapphira betray the community from within. The community is identified closely with the Spirit and named ἐκκλησία.
6. *Summary #3* (Acts 5:12–16).
7. *Intergroup conflict #2* (Acts 5:17–42). Second confrontation with Jerusalemite authorities.
8. *Intragroup conflict #2* (Acts 6:1–6). Nested identities become (illegitimately) salient and cause intragroup division.
9. *"Summary" #4* (Acts 6:7). The group endures through conflict and continues to flourish.
10. *Intergroup conflict #3* (Acts 6:8–8:3). Stephen is martyred and the church is systematically persecuted. This results finally in the group expressing the identity and mission given to it by Jesus by crossing the ethnic boundaries between Israelite believers, the Samaritans and the ἔθνη.

Luke's description of the origins of the Jesus-community suggest that the identity of the community is forged in an atmosphere of intergroup and intragroup conflict. The intermingling of scenes featuring conflict featuring scenes depicting group life is a powerful identity-forming strategy by Luke. Those who oppose the group will now begin to form the "them" against which the Jesus-group's identity can be forged, yet the "them" will receive surprising treatment at the hands of the Jesus-group.[28]

6.1.3. Community and the Other: The Possibility of Out-group Love

The "other" comes into view in two ways in the community summaries. First, the early community is recognized as a viable social group by outsiders:

> None of the rest dared join them, but *the people held them in high honor.* And more than ever believers were added to the Lord, multitudes both of men and women.[29]

Categorization by outsiders is the second criterion (along with self-ascription) for the creation of a group capable of forming social identity, and this is a signal that Luke is aware of real intergroup contact between the Jesus group and out-groups in the context. A group that knows itself as "we," and is known by others as "they," is an entitative social group capable of forming social identity.[30]

---

28. See esp. Acts 9:1–31; 26:29.
29. Acts 5:13–14 (emphasis mine).
30. A group is "entitative" if it factors in the social operations of other groups in the context.

6. Consummating a New Identity   133

The presence of an in-group and out-groups provides grounds for the intergroup differentiation essential for the maintenance of positive social identity in the three-step identity-forming process of categorization, identification and differentiation. We have seen that this sort of intergroup differentiation is rarely benign but is usually associated with at least ambivalence, if not hostility, toward the (typically) negatively evaluated "other." The Jesus group, however, is described as simultaneously expressing intense in-group love and out-group concern. This is implied at a broad level by the metaphor "witness." Yet Luke makes it clearer in Acts 2:47:

> And day by day, attending the temple together and breaking bread in their homes, they partook of food with glad and generous hearts, praising God and *having favor toward all the people* (ἔχοντες χάριν πρὸς ὅλον τὸν λαόν).

While the final clause quoted above is often rendered "having favor with all the people" (RSV), Luke's other references conveying "having favor *with*" use either παρά or ἐνώπιον, not πρός.[31] Andersen's survey of Greco-Roman literature with χάρις πρός turns up six occurrences in Josephus and three in Philo, all of which refer to goodwill *toward* the object designated by πρός.[32] Further, πρός + accusative, according to Liddell and Scott (LSJ), indicates at least "intercourse or reciprocal action" when "with" is the preposition, thus indicating that if the sense is "favor with" the people, the favor is reciprocal.[33] Thompson further argues that the Jesus-followers are portrayed as *actors* in every other part of the summary, apart from the divine multiplication of the group in Acts 2:47.[34] This allows for parallelism in 2:47 between αἰνοῦντες τὸν θεόν and ἔχοντες χάριν πρὸς ὅλον τὸν λαόν. Both accusative nouns in the construction are the objects of their verbs. On balance, it is plausible that

---

31. Thompson 2006, 58 n. 131. See, e.g., Luke 1:30; 2:52; Acts 7:46.
32. Andersen 1988, 604–10. Josephus, *Vita* 252, 339; *A.J.* 6.86; 12.124; 14.146, 148; Philo, *Abr.* 118; *Conf.* 116; *Legat.* 296.
33. The traditional reading, "favor with all the people," still implies at least a reciprocal goodwill. Fitzmyer 1998, 273, who acknowledges the "favor toward" reading, argues it is "unlikely in the context," and points to a similar use of πρός in Rom 5:1; 1 Thess 1:8; 2 Cor 6:14; John 1:1. Barrett 1994, 171–72; Bruce 1951, 102; Dunn 1996, 36–37; Conzelmann 1987, 34; Johnson 1992, 59–60 make no mention of the issue. Bock 2007, 154 does not address the translation, but affirms that "having favor with all the people" suggests the community extends itself toward God and neighbor.
34. Thompson 2006, 57–58.

Luke intended to communicate that the group had an outward focus that extended goodwill "toward" all the people of Israel.[35]

If correct, this would be a significant conclusion. In the early stages of group identity formation, the community of Spirit-empowered individuals is able to express strong in-group bias without the typically correlate out-group antipathy. This, I suggest, is a corporate expression of allocentric identity in which in-group love and out-group love can go hand in hand. Such a posture remains a feature of the in-group throughout Acts as clear outsiders—even dangerous outsiders like the Philippian jailer (Acts 16:24–34) and King Agrippa (Acts 26:27–29)—are the object of concern from community members. While there is clear intergroup differentiation, it is not here expressed in a way that negatively impacts the "other." The openness to the "other" expressed by the early community stands in stark contrast to the intergroup behavior of the Jerusalem authorities (Acts 4:1–22; 5:17–42; 6:9–8:1) and non-Israelites later in Acts (Acts 17:5–9; 19:23–34), whose in-group bias leads to out-group antagonism. Seen through the lens of SIT, the simultaneous in-group love and out-group love expressed by the early group is a subversion of normal intergroup identity processes and is nothing less than a *different way of being human in community*. Yet this posture toward the "other" is difficult to maintain. In the following chapters, one of the primary roles of the Spirit, through both its identity-marking and identity-forming functions, will be to reshape continually the in-group's posture toward the "other," removing barriers to intergroup reconciliation.

The corporate life of the allocentric community has the internal effects discussed in the previous section as well as a dramatic external effect. Acts 2:47 concludes with "and the Lord added to their number day by day those who were being saved." The community description in 5:12 concludes with "more than ever believers were added to their number, multitudes of both men and women." The same pattern, though less explicitly, is evident in the "mini-summaries" of Acts 6:7 and 9:31. This leads us to an important conclusion: *properly reconciled intra-communal life (available only by the transformational identity-forming work of the Spirit) is itself an expression of witness*. Luke's emphasis on the life of the *community* as "witness" balances an either/or emphasis on the internal or external aspects of the community's life. Cho says "the outer life of witness evidently dominates the summaries: witness by works of power;

---

35. This position is also taken by Cheetham 1963; Gamba 1981 and is reflected in the Vulgate: "et habentes gratiam ad omnem plebem." The Syriac renders the preposition "before" (*qŭdām*).

witness by words of power."[36] Wall emphasizes the opposite facet, "While evangelism is certainly one effect of their life together, the primary purpose of their common life is to nurture Christian community."[37] I suggest that the distinction between the internal and external orientation of the group is unnecessary. Spirit-formed allocentric identity moves a person away from a self-center to a focus on the "other," both inside and outside one's own group. Luke presents an identity that extends toward the "other" in intragroup love and intergroup witness.

6.1.4. Summary

The community summaries describe group norms which, in their economic practice, fellowship, personal devotion and concern for the outgroup, are collective expressions of the allocentric identity characteristic of those influenced by the Spirit.[38] The identity-forming potential of a group like this is high, especially when set in the context of pervasive intra- and intergroup conflict, but it should be noted that Luke continues to see no radical disjunction between this new identity and Israelite ethnic identity. The summaries embrace the Temple (2:46; 5:12, 42) and Israelite praxis (especially daily prayer: 2:42; 3:1).[39] Peter uses language of ethnic self-identification even after the introduction of the new community (2:42–47), addressing the crowd as ἄνδρες Ἰσραηλῖται (3:12) and ἀδελφοί (3:17) and speaking of "the God of *our* fathers" (3:13; 5:30). Yet there are signs that ethnic identity continues to be chastened as a terminal identity. The quotation of Deut 18:16 in Acts 3:22 ("The Lord God will raise up for you a prophet from your brethren as he raised me up. You shall listen to him in whatever he tells you") assumes shared ethnic lineage, but is a part of Peter's warning that response to Jesus, *not ethnic affiliation*, is the criterion for membership in the new group. The social identity emerging from membership in the post-Pentecost community is not *de facto* at odds with Israelite ethnic identity, but the *inexorable trajectory of the Abrahamic covenant and Spirit-formed allocentric identity creates an unavoidable collision with the ethnic "other."*

---

36. Cho 2005, 128.
37. Wall 2002, 71. Wall later softens the distinction, suggesting that both internal and external activities (i.e. proclamation) "attract favorable attention from the people" (95).
38. In SIT, norms are behaviors prototypical to the in-group.
39. Dunn 1996, 36 notes continuity with Israelite identity expressed in the location of the first community in Jerusalem and, specifically, in the Temple. See Hamm 2003 for the importance of the twice-daily *Tamid* service in Luke–Acts.

6.2. The Spirit and the "Other," Satan and the Self: Barnabas, Ananias and Sapphira as Exemplars of Identity

Luke's interest in the use of possessions by the early community is unquestionable. Acts 4:32 in particular ("No one said that any of the things which he possessed was his own [ἴδιος], but they had everything in common") has generated great scholarly attention.[40] Parallel phenomena are useful, but a deep logic undergirds this passage that points toward Luke's understanding of the proper function of possessions within human community:[41]

> Now the company of those who believed were of one heart and soul, and no one said that any of the things which he possessed was his own (οὐδὲ εἷς τι τῶν ὑπαρχόντως αὐτῷ ἔλεγεν ἴδιον εἶναι), but they had everything in common... There was not a needy person among them, for as many as were possessors of lands or houses sold them, and brought the proceeds of what was sold and laid it at the apostles' feet; and distribution was made to each as any had need.[42]

The key to Luke's view of the relationship between Spirit, identity and possessions is found in his subtle yet consistent use of the adjective ἴδιος. Set in its socio-economic context, the claim οὐδὲ εἷς τι τῶν ὑπαρχόντως αὐτῷ ἔλεγεν ἴδιον εἶναι (4:32) stands in direct counterpoint to what was likely most common usage of ἴδιος in public space within the Roman Empire: honorary inscriptions. The phrase ἐκ τῶν ἰδίων occurs 1,766 times in the Packard Humanities Institute inscription database.[43] The phrase is extant in 75 inscriptions from Greater Syria and usually indicates that the object commemorated by the inscription was provided by a named donor.[44] The inscription functioned to ensure that the donor received the honor due from benefaction.[45] Contrary to this practice,

---

40. Johnson 1977; Seccombe 1983; Capper 1983; 1995; Gillmand 1991.
41. Four positions are noteworthy. Capper 1995 draws parallels with Essene/Qumran communities of goods. Mitchell 1992 sees a parallel and critique of the Greek philosophic friendship ideals. VanderKam 2002 sees a parallel with Israelite "ideal community" as expressed in national unity at Sinai. Bartchy 1991 argues for the historicity of the community of goods based on contextual precedents, while allowing the Acts community to be socially unique. See Kuecker 2009 for a more developed version of the following argument, focused more particularly on the relationship between identity, the Spirit or Satan and economic praxis.
42. Acts 4:32, 34–35.
43. http://epigraphy.packhum.org/inscriptions/ accessed 26 July 2010.
44. Theissen 1982, 148. See *CIJ* 548, 746.
45. See Winter 1988, 87–103 on public recognition for benefactors. Winter suggests some New Testament documents encourage public benefaction as a means

within the Acts community the placing of resources "at the feet of the apostles" separated the giver from benefaction claims.[46] Instead of affixing a donor's name to the good given ἐκ τῶν ἰδιῶν, the Acts community subverted reciprocity obligations by distributing goods through someone other than the giver. This is not because Luke is unaware of normal patron–client reciprocity or benefaction, for he elsewhere demonstrates his awareness of the demands of reciprocity (Luke 7:1–5; Acts 10:22; 12:12). The truly remarkable thing about the generosity of the early community is that it appears to have been giving *without* expected reciprocity.[47]

Reluctance to claim possessions as one's ἴδιος (4:32) is a practical expression of a social orientation expressed in Acts 4:23. There, after experiencing intergroup conflict, John and Peter return "to their own" (πρὸς τοὺς ἰδίους). Initially, ἴδιος in 4:23 creates differentiation between the new community and the Jerusalem leaders. The occurrence in quick succession of ἴδιος in 4:32 indicates that members of the community do not claim possessions as "their own," but they do claim that other community members are "their own."[48] This is an indication that the conceptualization or use of one's ἴδιος is a fundamental clue to one's orientation toward the community, the "other" and God.

This observation is borne out by the use of ἴδιος in Luke (6×) and Acts (17×) with two primary senses: (1) to describe personal possession (a mule as ἴδιος in relation to a Samaritan) or (2) to describe sequestered privacy (Jesus explains a parable to his disciples *in private* [ἴδιος]).[49] If something is ἴδιος in relation to a person or group, it cannot belong to someone else. An ἴδιος-designation is a boundary claim demarcating inclusion (for the owner[s]) and exclusion (for the non-owner[s]).

---

to secure approval of local authorities (e.g. Rom 13:3–4; 1 Pet 2:14–15). This would set Peter and Paul at odds with Luke on this issue.

46. *Pace* Johnson 1992, 91 who interprets this as submission to apostolic authority. Chrysostom (*Homilies on the Acts of the Apostles* 11 [NPNF 1.14.455]) was aware that apostolic distribution of goods eliminated the reciprocity ethic: "To them [the apostles] they left it to be the dispensers, and made them the owners that thenceforth all should be defrayed as from common, not from private, property. *This was also a help to them against vainglory*" (emphasis mine). For Greco-Roman reciprocity, see Moxnes 1991; Marshall 2009.

47. See Mitchell 1992, 266.

48. Johnson 1977, 193; 1992, 83 thinks ἴδιος in 4:23 refers only to the apostles, but there is no indication that the activities of 4:24–34 are restricted to a segment of the community. 4:31 states that they were *all* filled with the Spirit and leads directly into a summary of the life of the entire community, not just the apostles.

49. Luke 6:41, 44; 9:10; 10:23, 34; 18:28; Acts 1:7, 19, 25; 2:6, 8; 3:12; 4:23, 32; 13:36; 20:28; 21:6; 23:19; 24:23; 25:19; 28:30.

More specifically, stubborn retention of one's ἴδιος appears to be a significant barrier both to discipleship and human community.[50] For Peter, the fact that the disciples have relinquished any claim to hold something as ἴδιος is proof of whole-hearted identification with Jesus: ἰδοὺ ἡμεῖς ἀφέντες τὰ ἴδια ἠκολουθήσαμέν σοι.[51] Judas' decision to "go to his own place" (Acts 1:25: εἰς τὸν τόπον ἴδιον) led to his betrayal of, and self-imposed expulsion from, the community. The Spirit-enabled speech in Acts 2 allows Jerusalem residents to hear the wonders of God in their own language (Acts 2:8: τῇ ἰδίᾳ διαλέκτῳ; cf. 2:6). In an ironic way this prevents Galilean regional identity from being leveraged exclusivistically and orients the early community around the person of Jesus, not ethno-linguistic identity. Luke's definitive example of the proper use of one's ἴδιος is in Paul's speech in Miletus in Acts 20:28:

> Take heed to yourselves and to all the flock, of which the Holy Spirit has made you overseers, to care for the church of God which he obtained with his own blood (διὰ τοῦ αἵματος τοῦ ἰδίου).

Regardless of the syntactical object of the construction, the point is clear. The possessions and position of God—his ἴδιος—have not been leveraged only to God's advantage, but have been poured out *for the sake of the "other."* It is this expression of possession and position—of the things a person can claim as their ἴδιος—that marks the Acts community in 4:32-37.[52] Yet for Luke this is no mere human effort, the proper use of one's ἴδιος is dependent upon the Spirit and is definitively displayed by the exemplary figure Barnabas, and by the anti-exemplars Ananias and Sapphira.

6.2.1. *Barnabas: Exemplar of a New Identity*
As discussed in Chapter 2, exemplars are individuals who best embody the prototypical criteria of a social group.[53] Prototypical characteristics of the group are ascribed to the exemplar, and the characteristics of the exemplar are both desirable for and ascribed to the other members of the

---

50. Dunn 2008, 11, following Howard 1969, 336, recognizes the importance of ἴδιος in Romans for describing the danger that righteousness could become for some Israelites a righteousness "that is (exclusively) their own, theirs and not others." This, for Dunn, has devastating effects on the community and the rectification of this posture is central to Dunn's reading of Paul's gospel.
51. Luke 18:28.
52. Herodotus, *Histories* 4.18, 22 refers to the Scythians as an ἔθνος ἐὸν ἴδιον and an ἔθνος πολλὸν καὶ ἴδιον. This suggests that ethnic identity, when held tightly as ἴδιος, functions as a social boundary that can limit human community.
53. See Medin et al. 1984; Smith and Zarate 1992.

community.⁵⁴ Luke establishes Barnabas' exemplary status by portraying him as the embodiment of one of the primary group norms; Barnabas shares his possessions. As an exemplar, Barnabas represents the ideal expression of group identity.

Luke gives abundant identity-related information about Joseph Barnabas, who, not insignificantly, is the first newly introduced character in Acts who is neither an apostle nor a family member of Jesus.⁵⁵ He is a native of Cyprus and a Levite, thus a Cypriot Israelite with an important ethnic heritage.⁵⁶ His Cypriot identity indicates that Greek was likely the language of his birth, a tantalizing possibility given the linguistic tensions that arise in Acts 6. Luke's introduction tells hearers that Joseph Barnabas has several honorable nested social identities from which to draw.⁵⁷ Yet, after giving us this biographical information (which must not in any case be considered extraneous to Luke's purposes), Luke introduces Joseph with his new name—Barnabas.

Two factors must be kept in tension at this point: (1) nicknames were common among Israelites in the Greco-Roman world and (2) naming is extremely significant for the formation of identity. Bauckham's research on Israelite naming practices has demonstrated the prevalence of nicknames in ancient Judea.⁵⁸ There appears to have been a relatively small cohort of common names in use from 330 B.C.E. to 200 C.E. Extant data show that 15.6 percent of named males from the period possess one of the two most popular names, Simon or Joseph.⁵⁹ The large number of men with common names required strategies for differentiation, one of

---

54. Bodenhausen et al. 1995, 60. Turner 1982, 29: "Common category characteristics are inferred from the available exemplars of the category [social group], including oneself, and then automatically assigned, along with long-term criterial traits, to all members, again including oneself."

55. Joseph Barsabbas is named in Acts 1:23, but in the context of his consideration for apostleship. Dunn 1996, 59–60 notes that Barnabas is "an absolutely crucial figure in the early expansion of Christianity beyond Israel and out to the Gentiles."

56. Levites were not permitted to own property (Josh 14:4), but the restriction must have either fallen out of use or must not have been imposed in Barnabas' native Cyprus.

57. Saeed et al. 1999, 824–25 state, "Ethnic self-identification has usually been conceptualized in the literature as an option between two identities; in other words, an either/or phenomenon, tending not to accommodate the possibility of bi-cultural identification… This dichotomous model is simplistic. People may consider themselves to be members of two or more groups, in which case a single identity label would be insufficient." Cf. Burdsey 1999.

58. Bauckham 2006, 67–92. Cf. Ilan 2002.

59. Bauckham 2006, 71.

which was the adoption of a nickname.⁶⁰ At this level it is unsurprising that a Joseph (one of several in the early community, cf. Acts 1:23) would adopt a nickname.

The commonality of nicknames does not, however, preclude the importance of Luke's decision to introduce Barnabas by the name indicative of his identity as a member of the community. According to Philo, Old Testament name changes were often a reflection of the true identity or virtue of the re-named individual.⁶¹ Proselytes often changed their name to reflect their new "Israelite" identity, a phenomenon marked on ossuary inscriptions in Judea.⁶² New Roman citizens and freedmen received either the name of their former master or the benefactor through whom they received their citizenship and the *tria nomina* was a sign of Roman identity.⁶³ In short, new names locate people within a reconfigured social context. This is the case for Barnabas, whose name was given to him by the apostles for his identification *within the community of believers*.⁶⁴ Moreover, though interpreters express unanimous bewilderment at the lexical meaning of "Barnabas," the name as defined by Luke clearly marks Barnabas' function in the community.⁶⁵ At several key points in Acts Barnabas' encouragement serves the life of the community, often helping to abrogate social boundaries.⁶⁶ In other words, Barnabas' new name describes his allocentric identity within the context of his social group.⁶⁷ He is a Levite and a Cypriot, but primarily he is Barnabas, a member of the emerging Jesus group.

---

60. Bauckham 2006, 81. Cf. Joseph Barsabbas (Acts 1:23) and Simon Peter (Luke 6:14).

61. *Mut.* 70–71, 121.

62. Keener 1997, 64. See also Cohen 1999, 140–74.

63. Huskinson 2000, 131–32.

64. Similarly, Simon's nickname (Peter) reflects his role in the community, a fact made explicit in Matt 16:18. See Bauckham 2006, 103–4.

65. For the potential meanings of "Barnabas," see Barrett 1994, 259. Possibilities include "son of *a prophet* (Hebrew: נבא); "son of *comfort*" (Syriac: *br* + *nby'*); "son of *consolation*" (Hebrew: נחא). Bede finds an interesting connection between the Spirit as "Paraclete"/*paraclesis* (cf. John 14:16) and Barnabas' name (*Commentary on the Acts of the Apostles* 4.36b). I hold that, given Luke's treatment of the role of prophets in the community, "son of prophecy/exhortation" is preferable. See Kuecker 2009, 93–94 for a more extended argument focusing on the connection between changed names in general, and Barnabas' name in particular, for the designee's identity/role in a community.

66. Acts 9:27; 11:22; 13:2; 15:12; 37. In the last instance, Barnabas' encouraging nature causes sharp dispute with Paul. Johnson 1992, 87 attributes to Barnabas a "mediatorial" role in the community.

67. Wall 2002, 97 notes that names often change with "vocational changes."

What is indicated by Barnabas' new name is expressed by his voluntary handling of possessions.[68] His behaviour is a practical expression of the refusal to name any*thing* as one's ἴδιος. Barnabas sells a field and delivers the proceeds to the apostles for distribution with no hint of either reciprocity or complete divestiture.[69] Rather, Barnabas' goods are *unconditionally available* for the mitigation of poverty in the community.[70] Barnabas, a Spirit-filled member of the group (Acts 4:31; 11:24), uses possessions in a manner indicative of his disposition toward—or full identification with—the new group. He values his people as his ἴδιος but holds his possessions loosely and makes them available to others. This is one prominent expression of Spirit-influenced allocentric identity. Barnabas turns his whole self toward the community, embodies the community in his person and is a pattern to be imitated.[71]

6.2.2. Ananias and Sapphira: Intragroup Threat and the Community of the Spirit

If Barnabas exemplifies the emerging social identity formed by Luke's new group, Ananias and Sapphira are anti-exemplars, or villains.[72] Fitzmyer distills six approaches taken by modern scholars toward the difficult story of Ananias and Sapphira:[73]

1. An etiological reading based upon 1 Thess 4:13–17—divine judgment explains the death of Christians before the parousia.[74]
2. A Qumran reading comparing the couple's punishment with that of the Qumran initiate who deceives by concealing property.[75]
3. A typological interpretation based on Achan in Josh 7.[76]

---

68. On the voluntary nature of Barnabas' act, see Witherington 1998, 207–8; Marshall 1980, 84. This position differs from Capper 1995, 2009 who suggests "voluntary donation" but whose "virtuoso religion" model, tending toward a form of Qumran monasticism, leaves little room for voluntary choice beyond a certain point; see also Wall 2002, 73.
69. See 1QS 6.19–20 for a practice implying full divestiture.
70. Kollmann 2003, 12.
71. Barnabas' significance for early Christian identity is evident in other ancient writings: *Epistle of Barnabas*; *Gospel of Barnabas*; *Acts of Barnabas by John Mark*; *Acta Bartholomaei et Barnabae*; and *Laudatio Barnabae*. Tertullian attributed Hebrews to Barnabas (*De Pudicitia* 20). Öhler 2003 studies the "historical Barnabas."
72. Allen 1997, 124.
73. Fitzmyer 1998, 318–19. Fitzmyer thinks the narrative casts doubt on the historicity of Acts, but asserts this less emphatically than Conzelmann 1987, 37.
74. Barrett 1994, 263–64.
75. Capper 1983; 1995.
76. Johnson 1992; Cho 2005.

4. An institutional reading which interprets the episode as an excommunication from the church.⁷⁷
5. A history of salvation reading which views the incident as an obstacle to the Acts 1:8 commission.⁷⁸
6. An "original sin" reading that reads the episode as an example of sin at the beginning of the community's existence and hence a type of other accounts of sin at "beginnings" (e.g. Adam and Eve; sons of God [Gen 6]; the golden calf; David and Uriah).⁷⁹

While each of these approaches contains valuable insights, there is more to say regarding the connections between Spirit, identity and possessions, as well as the relationship between this couple and Barnabas.⁸⁰

Anti-exemplars—villains—have an important role in the formation of social identity, helping to establish boundaries for communities.⁸¹ The memories of villains help a society to define itself, largely by serving as models of behaviour to be avoided.⁸² For Luke, Ananias and Sapphira's attitude toward possessions emerges as a result of their decision to self-sequester into a sort of *anti-group*.⁸³ This is established in their introduction: "*Ananias, with his wife Sapphira*, sold a piece of property" and "*with his wife's knowledge* he kept back some of the proceeds."⁸⁴ Similarly, Peter asks Sapphira, "How is it that you have agreed *together* to tempt the Spirit of the Lord?"⁸⁵ The furtive actions of the couple imply the emergence of a subgroup that takes precedence over the group of believers. They are, as it were, counterfeit community members.⁸⁶ Unlike Barnabas,

77. Schille 1983, 151.
78. Brown 1969.
79. Marguerat 1993.
80. Marguerat's reading, where the sin of the couple is a retreat from the Edenic character of the community toward the individualism implicated in the "fall," is attractive because it understands that the identity of the community and community members is in play.
81. Fine 2001, 8.
82. Fine 2001, 11.
83. Seccombe 1983, 211 agrees that it is not as a "negative aspect of the sharing of goods" that the couple has importance, suggesting they function to illustrate the fear surrounding the community's holiness. These factors are important but subsequent to the role of Ananias and Sapphira in the narration of the community's identification with the Spirit.
84. Acts 5:1, 2.
85. Acts 5:9.
86. Bartchy 1991, 316: "By lying in order to achieve an honor they had not earned, Ananias and Sapphira not only dishonored and shamed themselves as patrons but also revealed themselves to be outsiders, non-kin."

they have retained possessions, but not community members, as their ἴδιος. Though the Spirit turns people toward community, Ananias and Sapphira have turned away.[87]

We must be emphatic that their misuse of possessions is not the *cause* but rather the *symptom* of a more fundamental disposition which reveals Luke's uniquely Spirit-focused understanding of identity, the "other" and possessions:[88]

> Ananias, why has *Satan filled your heart* to lie to the Holy Spirit?... How is it that *you have contrived this deed in your heart*? You have not lied to men but to God... How is it that you have agreed together to tempt the Spirit of the Lord?[89]

Ananias and Sapphira, in their deception, have (1) "lied to"/"falsified" (ψεύδομαι) the Holy Spirit (5:3), (2) lied to God (5:4) and (3) tempted the Spirit of the Lord (5:9).[90] It is best to take Peter's accusations not as differentiated infractions, but as a series set in parallel. Hence, the lies are the result both of Satan's filling of Ananias' heart (5:3) and of Ananias' and Sapphira's (5:9) own contrivance.

Ananias is not the first person in Luke's narrative to be "filled" by Satan. Judas, Luke's most infamous villain, was filled by Satan *before betraying the Jesus group* (Luke 22:3: "Then Satan entered Judas called Iscariot"). There are other parallels between Judas and Ananias and Sapphira, but most striking is the fact that in both narratives *the influence of Satan causes the creation of an anti-group through an act of self-sequestering which ultimately leads to community betrayal*.[91] This is emphasized by Peter in Acts 1:25, who notes that Judas self-sequestered by leaving the apostles to "go to his own (ἴδιος) place." The stories of these prominent villains give heightened attention to the relationship

---

87. The connection between the use of one's ἴδιος, the Spirit and the "other" appears in the *Epistle of Barnabas* (19:7–8) and the *Didache* (4:8–10). In the *Epistle of Barnabas*, one should share everything with his neighbor and not claim anything to be his ἴδιος because the Spirit comes without regard for "reputation." The *Didache* teaches its hearers to share with brothers and sisters in need and not claim that anything is your ἴδιος (4:8). The basis for this sharing is the common identity produced by the Spirit, who overcomes status distinctions (4:11).

88. Suggestions for the "sin" of the couple include misuse of possessions (Johnson 1977, 206; cf. 1992, 91), deception (Dunn 1996, 63) and "trifling" with the apostles (Barrett 1994, 262).

89. Acts 5:3, 4, 9 (emphasis mine).

90. The most proximate occurrence of "Lord" refers to Jesus (Acts 4:33).

91. Other parallels include the role of money and property (Ananias sells a field, Judas buys one).

between Satan and anti-groups, yet it is not only villains who are susceptible to satanic influence. Jesus warned Peter that Satan sought to "sift" him (Luke 22:31), but that Peter, afterward, should instead *strengthen his brothers* (Luke 22:32). For Luke, Satan seeks to turn humans away from the "other." Jesus himself (Luke 4:1–13) was tempted by Satan to turn inward and away from his true identity and mission. Satan, opposing the community of God, seeks to divide and isolate, while God, through his Spirit, seeks to unite and build up Jesus-centered community.[92]

The ramifications of the Satan/self and Spirit/other dynamic, expressed in Acts 4 and 5 by the way one handles possessions, are clarified by reading Ananias and Sapphira in light of Peter's speech in Acts 3. There we learned that improper response to Jesus leads to separation from the community and non-participation in the times of "refreshing" (Acts 3:19: ἀνάψυξις; verb = ἀναψύχω) given to those who repent and join the community. Ananias and Sapphira, filled by Satan, form an anti-group that tragically leads to their destruction from the people. Their destruction is described with the verbal opposite of ἀναψύχω (Acts 3:19), ἐκψύχω (Acts 5:5, 10).[93] For Luke, the community—inhabited by Spirit-filled people—is the *place of life*. This is true both temporally (based upon the immediate fate of the couple) and eschatologically (based upon the cosmic dualism evoked by the Spirit/God vs. Satan imagery).[94]

---

92. Longenecker 1999, 92–108 sees a similar relationship between spiritual influence, identity and behaviour in Galatians.

93. Acts 5:5, 10. The unmediated nature of Ananias and Sapphira's fate separates it from other "judgment miracles" in a way that elevates the necessity of community membership. A certain divine agency must be assumed in Acts 5:1–11, though Peter only announces (but does not invoke) punishment upon the couple and Luke does not narrate direct divine punishment. Contrast this with explicit judgment miracles in Acts 12:20–23 ("an angel of the Lord smote him [Herod]") and 13:9–11 ("The hand of the Lord is against you and you will be blind…"). Peter's words in Acts 5:1–11 are more "explanatory than condemnatory" (O'Toole 1995, 194) and, though they are often read as conveying stern rebuke or anger, they can as easily be read with a sense of disappointment, sadness or regret over something gone horribly wrong. This accords with Peter's frequent willingness to give second chances (e.g. Acts 3:17–26; 8:22) and is likely the result of his own rehabilitation back into the community (see the discussion of Peter's characterization in Bauckham 2006, 174–79). It is not Peter's decisive judgment (in fact, Peter gives Sapphira a chance to repent), but something that is apparently an inherent consequence of self-separation from the community.

94. Turner 1996, 406 suggests this cosmic dualism.

6.2.3. Forging an Identification Between the Spirit and the Community

Peter's initial question ("Why has Satan filled your heart to lie [ψεύδομαι] to the Holy Spirit?") can be taken in one of two ways, either of which highlight the identity of the community. ψεύδομαι + accusative object can mean "to lie to," but it can also mean "to falsify."[95] If "lie to" is the intended sense, Peter's question equates a lie to the community with a lie to the Spirit. If "falsify" is the intended sense (a judgment that can only tentatively be made) the implication is that by valuing possessions over people Ananias and Sapphira have "falsified" the work of the Spirit in the community. The deceit of Ananias and Sapphira stands in contrast to the allocentric identity of which the community is a collective expression, and thus has shone an unfavorable light upon (falsified) the Spirit's work. Hence, Peter notes that they are filled by Satan rather than the Spirit.[96] The dichotomy between Satan-influence and Spirit-influence gives us the definitive clue to the identity of the community. A lie to the community is a lie to the Spirit/God/Spirit of the Lord. The new community is *the community of the Spirit*, who comes to transform, to empower and to mark those who are identified with Jesus.

It is at this auspicious moment that Luke introduces the name ἐκκλησία for the Jesus group. For Israelites, the name evokes the LXX designation of the "Hebrews wandering in the desert, the assembly of returned exiles, or the cultic assembly of Israel."[97] In the broader Roman Empire, the name evokes Greco-Roman civic assemblies. Returning to the beginning of this section, we are reminded that social groups are defined by self-ascription and ascription by others.[98] The naming of the community after this first incident of intragroup conflict highlights the fact that the community, in Luke's view, has a definite social status. The reality of this new identity is evident in the response to the community from others in Jerusalem:[99]

> None of the rest dared join them, but the people held them in high honor. And more than ever believers were added to the Lord, multitudes both of men and women.[100]

---

95. Johnson 1992, 88. Parsons and Culy 2003, 86 note that when the context includes an actual lie, the emphasis could be "on the consequences or implications of lying."

96. Dunn 1996, 64.

97. Fitzmyer 1998, 325. Cf. Bruce 1952, 136.

98. Turner 1982, 15–16.

99. Johnson 1992, 95 thinks that only the apostles are intended in the final summary. To arrive at this, he must show that 4:23 implies only the apostles and not the broader community. I have demonstrated the difficulty of this position above.

100. Acts 5:13–14.

The conflation of fear over the prospect of violating the community and eagerness to be assimilated into the community is a reflection of the numinous awe elicited by the community itself and demonstrates a perception of something dangerously generative about this group.

6.2.4. Barnabas, Ananias and Sapphira: Summary

For Luke, a clear relationship exists between influence by the Spirit or by Satan, human identity as it impinges upon relationships with the "other," and the use of earthly goods. Possession of/by the Holy Spirit explicitly turns people away from the self and *outward* toward the broader community and the "other." The outcome of this allocentric identity is that people, and not possessions, become valued as one's "own" (ἴδιος). Spirit-influence thus leads to the unconditional availability of one's goods—expressed by the use of possessions freely for the "other," as is exemplified by Barnabas. In clear contrast, the influence of Satan turns people away from the broader community and the "other" and *inward* toward the self. The outcome of this egocentric identity is that possessions, and not people, become valued as one's "own" (ἴδιος). Satan-influence thus leads to the use of possessions solely for the self, as exemplified by Ananias and Sapphira. *Satan prompts a treacherous turn away from the community and leads to destruction* (ἐκψύχω: Acts 5:5, 10).[101] *The Spirit prompts a turn toward the community and leads to restored relationships and times of refreshing* (ἀναψύχω: Acts 3:19). The descriptions of Barnabas, Ananias and Sapphira serve powerfully to solidify the social identity commensurate with membership in the community. Their portrayal highlights Luke's conviction that the influence of the Spirit forms an allocentric identity that extends outward toward the "other," an identity often expressed by refusal to claim possessions as one's own.

6.3. Conclusion

Luke's community summaries present the gathering of Spirit-filled allocentric individuals into a social group with definite identity-forming capacity. The community features high self-ascription, has entitative status in the view of out-groups and is forged in an atmosphere of conflict. Each of these factors should be expected to heighten in-group bias and a correspondingly negative view of the "other," yet the community continues to express favor toward the "other" (Acts 2:47). SIT is helpful in demonstrating the ways in which this community stands in

---

101. Cf. Peter's rebuke of Simon the Samaritan's self-centered pneumatic interests in Acts 8:18–25 and Paul's rebuke of Elymas in Acts 13:8–11.

contrast to normal (often agonistic) intergroup identity-forming processes.[102] The community itself is a collective expression of the Spirit-formed allocentric identity we have traced through Luke–Acts. This identity, the importance of the community as the place of life and the proper use of possessions are all highlighted by Luke's treatment of Barnabas, Ananias and Sapphira, where influence either by Satan or the Spirit forges, alternatively, egocentric or allocentric identity. These identities are rife with ramifications for the use of possessions.

It is the reality of membership in this new group that, in Luke's presentation, begins to form a new social identity for its members. This will emerge as the primary way in which Jesus-followers know themselves in their context—it is their terminal social identity. Ananias and Sapphira demonstrate that whenever another (subgroup) identity takes precedence over the social identity formed by membership in the Jesus community, disaster strikes. The defective identity of Ananias and Sapphira anticipates the ethno-linguistic conflict in Acts 6:1–7 and the difficult social boundary crossings in Acts 8, 9, 10, 11 and 15. In these chapters the Spirit will unfailingly appear at just the moment human identity is in question and will mark the common identity of those who are divinely approved participants in the community of the Spirit.

---

102. The effective history of corporately expressed allocentric group identity appears to have endured as a hallmark of some sections of the Jesus movement. See Lucian of Samosata's *Passing of Peregrinus* 13 (ca. 125–180 C.E.) and Julian the Apostate's letter to the high priest of Galatia (362 C.E.).

Chapter 7

INCORPORATING THE "OTHER":
THE SPIRIT AND SUPERORDINATE IDENTITY
IN ACTS 6–9

The intergroup and intragroup encounters in Acts 6–9 serve as a testing ground, helping to determine the relationship between the social identity formed by participation in the Jesus group, old social identities and the "other." I will demonstrate that in this section the Spirit subverts normal (often exclusionary) identity processes in two ways. First, the Spirit *orchestrates* intergroup contact between the in-group and the "other." This is essential for maintaining the allocentric character of the community in the face of a willingness to settle into old exclusionary practices of intergroup behavior and identity formation. Second, the Spirit commandeers control of intergroup boundaries by serving as the primary *identity marker* for this new social identity. During critical intergroup encounters, the Spirit arrives at precisely the moment human identity is in question. The Spirit is thus involved in far more than "mission"; the Spirit is involved in the full *incorporation* of the "other" into the community. This regularly results in a dual identity transformation that requires both former out-group members *and in-group members* to reorient their own social identity to reflect changes in group composition.[1] For Luke, this sort of transformation is necessary for the creation of God's worldwide people, anticipated by the Abrahamic covenant and inaugurated through the bestowal of the Spirit by the ascended Lord Jesus.

7.1. *Acts 6:1–7: Subgroup Salience and Community Dysfunction*

By Acts 6, the community is clearly an entitative social group, functioning with its own authority figures (the Twelve instead of the Sanhedrin), meeting in home and Temple (Acts 5:42) and organizing a system of poverty relief. The latter is evidence for ongoing corporate expression of

---

1. Poole et al. 2004, 10.

Spirit-empowered allocentric identity.² It is thus unexpected when full-blown intragroup conflict erupts in this community of solidarity. The primary cause of the conflict is the rise to primacy of ethno-linguistic subgroup identities.³ As with Ananias and Sapphira (and as will continue throughout Acts), when subgroup identities become primary the community inevitably malfunctions.

The growth of the community (reported in 6:1; cf. Acts 2:41; 4:44) results in (1) a relatively large group that is (2) socio-economically and linguistically inclusive, both factors with ramifications for identity formation. SIT demonstrates that large groups with less personal relationships are less effective at fostering intragroup loyalty.⁴ Further, highly inclusive groups can prompt the reassertion of subgroup identity distinctions as an effort by group members to maintain positive identity.⁵ It is not implausible that the "Hebrews," as native speakers of the "language of Israel," understood themselves to be the prototypical subgroup in the community, thus locating Hellenist widows on the wrong side of a Hebrew entitlement claim.⁶ That this cleavage should come with regard to language is unsurprising. Language is a particularly important identity marker in situations similar to that described in Acts:

> Minorities who speak an international language of high status [Greek, in a Greco-Roman context] are advantaged compared to those who speak a language with less prestige value [e.g. Hebrew/Aramaic]. But within the boundaries of a certain territory—a commune, a country—the respective status of the languages used can be reversed.⁷

---

2. Seccombe 1978 argues against the view that pre-70 C.E. Jerusalem had a formal charity system (*contra* Jeremias 1969; Barrett 1994, 310; Dunn 1996, 81), suggesting evidence for a formal system is too late (*m. Ketubbot* 13.1-2; *m. Pesahim* 10.1; *m. Sheqalim* 5.6) or does not refer to general community charity (*m. Ketubbot* 13.1-2; *m. Sheqalim* 5.6). The only general distributions of charity were episodic crisis relief efforts (Herod's importation of grain for famine relief ca. 25 B.C.E. [Josephus, *A.J.* 15.299–316] and Queen Helena's disaster aid ca. 46 or 47 C.E. [*A.J.* 20.51–53]).

3. The current consensus is that the Hellenist–Hebrew distinction is linguistic, with context determining the broader ethnic implications (Witherington 1998, 242). For full discussions of the issue, see Bock 2007, 256–60; Esler 1987, 139–42; Witherington 1998, 240–47. For a refutation of the Baur hypothesis, see Hill 1992.

4. Rabbie and Horowitz 1988, 117–23. Koet 2008, 166 notes that the growth of the group is both the reason for the problem (6:1) and the result of the solution (6:7). It will become apparent that, for Luke, a small and sectarian group is not necessary for unity.

5. Hornsey and Hogg 1999, 543–50.

6. Cf. Luke 4:14–30. See Wenzel 2000; 2001; Weber et al. 2002; Wenzel et al. 2003; Waldzus et al. 2003; Waldzus et al. 2005. See Chapter 5 above for the ramifications of Hebrew/Aramaic for social status in first-century Palestine.

7. Giles et al. 1977, 312.

Diaspora Israelites gained advantage as fluent Greek-speakers. But the situation was the opposite in Jerusalem/Judea where Hebrew/Aramaic was the prototype. Hebrew/Aramaic-speaking widows were likely (though perhaps even subconsciously) favored by the Hebrew/Aramaic speaking leaders of the community based upon their common ethno-linguistic subgroup identity.[8] Thus, Acts 6:1–7 reflects an intragroup conflict of subgroup social identities, not an ideological or theological conflict. We already know from the Pentecost account that ethno-linguistic particularity is robustly affirmed by the Spirit—but not as a terminal identity. This passage is the first of several instances in which Luke will deploy the Spirit to chasten (otherwise valid) social identities that are improperly functioning as terminal identities.

Luke's narrative context makes it evident that he is not "papering over" a more vigorous dispute, but that this is a critical dysfunction within the community.[9] This incident, like that of Ananias and Sapphira, is a threat to the group's shared identity, to its public reputation for sharing goods and to the neediest members of the in-group.[10] Elsewhere in Luke–Acts, Luke stands within the broad biblical tradition that expresses particular concern for the plight of widows.[11] When it comes to the neglect of the Hellenist widows, "the church finds itself in an unholy alliance with unjust judges (Luke 18:1–8), hypocritical scribes (Luke 20:45–47), and an exploitative temple system (Luke 21:1–6)."[12] In the light of Acts 4:32–5:11, it is likely that the apostles themselves bore responsibility for the injustice—perhaps an unsurprising factor given the apostles' occasional tendency to have difficulty with various categories of "other."[13]

---

8. The imperfect tense of παραθεωρέω indicates achronic problem and the passive voice may indicate the powerlessness of the aprototypical Hellenists.

9. Many suggest Luke "papers over" a more serious intragroup conflict here (Conzelmann 1987, 44; Dunn 1996, 80, *inter alias*). Tannehill 1990, 81 suggests that Luke is only "exaggerating the ease with which they were solved."

10. Tannehill 1990, 80; Wall 2002, 114.

11. Luke 2:36–38; 4:25–27; 7:11–17; 18:1–8; 20:45–47; 21:1–4. Cf. Exod 22:21–24; Deut 10:17–19; 14:29; 24:17; 26:12; 1 Kgs 17:8–24; 2 Kgs 4:1–7; Isa 1:17, 23; 10:2; Jer 5:28 LXX; 7:6; 22:3; 49:11; Mal 3:5; Ezek 22:7; Pss 68:5; 93:6; 146:9.

12. Spencer 1994, 729.

13. Luke 9:48–50, 51–56; Acts 8:14–17; 9:26; 11:1–3. Spencer 1994, 729 notes that the Twelve show "disturbing traces of trivializing widows concerns." Fitzmyer 1998, 344; Wall 2002, 115 and, to a lesser extent, Johnson 1992, 105 assign culpability to the Twelve.

7.1.1. *The Spirit and the (Fractured) Life of the Community*

Luke's narrative presentation is elegantly simple and disappointingly brief.¹⁴ The Hellenists "complain" (6:1: γογγυσμός) against the Hebrews because of a malfunction of widow-care. The Twelve make a value judgment regarding time management, but then act decisively to delegate authority for redressing the grievance. There is no evidence that the apostles, once alerted to the issue, assumed that the service of the widows was of minor importance.¹⁵ To the contrary, the ministry of both the word and the table are called διακονία, thus ἀρεστός (6:2) is a "priority choice about observing the call of God versus a moral choice of right, wrong, and sin."¹⁶

The essential point is that Luke is not concerned with *how* the problem is addressed, or even *what* (in great detail) constituted the problem, but he is concerned with *who* is best equipped to manage the intragroup conflict.¹⁷ Luke showed himself capable of describing the mechanisms of intragroup poverty relief in Acts 4:32–37, but here Luke is concerned only with the selection criteria for the Seven—criteria that are strikingly *different* than the criterion of social homogeneity employed by Peter in Acts 1:21–22 (cf. Luke 9:49–50). In this case, the mediators of the intragroup conflict are to be "seven men of good repute (μαρτυρουμενός), full of the Spirit (πλήρεις πνεύματος) and of wisdom" (Acts 6:3).

---

14. Spencer 1994, 716 notes that interest has focused more on structural than pastoral concerns, especially with regard to hierarchy among community officials. See Koet 2005 for a history of research.

15. Some have downplayed the role of the Seven, calling waiting on tables "trivia" (Fitzmyer 1998, 344), a "humble task" (Penney 1997, 65 n. 11), one of the "lower tasks" in the community (Lienhard 1975, 232) or suggesting that Stephen's subsequent preaching is the "real" reason for Luke's narration of Spirit-influence in the 6:3 (Cho 2005, 132).

16. Bock 2007, 259; cf. Johnson 1992, 106. ἀρεστός (cf. Acts 12:3) appears to carry the sense of "pleasing" or "satisfactory" in Luke–Acts. καταλείπω (Acts 6:2) carries the sense of "leave behind" or "forsake," and is used by Luke to speak about leaving one place or item behind in favor of another (Luke 5:28; 10:40; 15:4; 20:31; Acts 18:19; 21:13; 24:27; 25:17). The Twelve recognized that they could not, given the size of the community, adequately perform both διακονίαι.

17. Acts 6:1–7 is problematic for the "Spirit of prophecy" paradigm. Cho 2005, 132 sidesteps the difficulty by claiming that being "full of the Spirit and wisdom Stephen was initially appointed as an inner server (human organization), and then becomes a powerful missionary as a witness (Spirit working) which is a more dominant feature than the former." This grossly misunderstands the high value that Luke places on "menial" tasks such as serving the marginalized (cf. Luke 4:18–20; 9:46–48; 22:24–27).

Luke characteristically uses μαρτυρέω as a passive participle to demonstrate that someone is "of good repute" within his or her community.[18] Those of "good repute" are clarified, epexegetically, to be those most clearly marked by the *Spirit* and wisdom. Cho is wrong to claim that the apostles' mandate is evidence that "*not all* the members of the community" have been "filled and used by the Spirit."[19] Luke's use of totalizing adjectives with regard to the Spirit has prepared us to expect that all who submit to Jesus' lordship are given the Spirit.[20] In the case of Acts 6:3, πλήρης + defining genitive indicates that Spirit-fullness is the "quality [that] clearly marks the person's life or comes to visible expression in his or her activity":[21]

> In Lukan terms, the criterion for judging whether it is appropriate to speak of someone as "full of the Spirit" is...whether the community of Christians *felt the impact of the Spirit* through that person's life and *saw the Spirit's graces and gifts regularly expressed* through him or her.[22]

The requirement that those chosen be marked by the Spirit results in seven designees, all native Greek speakers and even one proselyte, who were *aprototypical* relative to Hebrew/Aramaic-speaking Israelites, including the Twelve.[23]

Those suited to handle a crisis of identity in the community are those who are most marked by the Spirit. Luke has already demonstrated that the influence of the Spirit results in an expanded ethnic horizon and an allocentric turn toward the "other."[24] Likewise, the Spirit-filled Seven are capable of reaching across the ethno-linguistic subgroup boundary in a way similar to Barnabas (also πλήρης πνεύματος ἁγίου) in Antioch

---

18. Cornelius is "of good repute" because of his benefaction to the Israelite community (10:22). Ananias is "of good repute" in the eyes of his local community (22:12). Cf. Josephus, *A.J.* 12.150.

19. Cho 2005, 132 (emphasis original). Cho suggests that the point of the pericope is only to show spiritual distinctions in the community. He overlooks the social and cultural pressures evident in the text: "the conflict between the 'Hellenists' and 'Hebrews' in the church simply shows the different status of the spirituality of the members of the community."

20. Cf. multiple uses of "all" in Acts 2:4; 4:31; cf. 2:38.

21. Turner 1996, 167. Luke usually uses πίμπλημι for short-term episodic Spirit events and πλήρης/πληρόω for the gift of the Spirit received at conversion (Turner 1996, 167–69).

22. Turner 1996, 169 (emphasis original).

23. Israelites often had Greek names (Bauckham 2006, 67–92), but only Stephen and Philip were common Israelite names (Bock 2007, 261).

24. See Chapters 3 and 4.

(Acts 11:24). In Acts 6, the presence of the Spirit resists (in this case, "Hebrew") claims to entitlement based upon subgroup prototypicality, but instead shares the benefits of the group to the "other."

Acts 6:7 ("the number of disciples multiplied greatly in Jerusalem") indicates that the community was restored by the Spirit-filled Seven. Characteristic for Luke, based upon Acts 2:42–47 and 4:32–5:16, is the notion that proper community function inevitably results in group expansion.[25] Also characteristic is the emerging fact that Spirit-filled figures are best able to address group identity issues. The fact that "a great many of the priests were obedient to the faith" (Acts 6:7), especially given the likelihood that priests were high identifiers with the Israelite ἔθνος, highlights the fact that despite the community's developing distinctiveness, its identity was not *a priori* in conflict with Israelite ethnic identity.[26] Ethno-linguistic identity is chastened and shown to be inappropriate (and potentially destructive) as a terminal identity. Yet Pentecost demonstrated that, properly nested within the superordinate identity arising from membership in the Jesus group, ethno-linguistic identity is robustly affirmed by the Spirit.

7.2. Acts 8: Incorporating Those Who Identify Themselves With the God of Israel

Acts 8 narrates the incorporation of the Samaritans and the Ethiopian eunuch, both of whom occupy a liminal social category that can be conceptualized as those who desired to be joined to Israel's God, but, because of identity concerns, were not permitted. The intelligibility of the category arises from an understanding of the unique intergroup relations in view in Acts 8, as well as from an appreciation of Luke's allusions to Isa 56:3–7 LXX within these narratives. Both of the essential incorporative functions of the Spirit, *orchestration* and *identification*, are displayed in Luke 8 in order to bring the "other" into the group and thus to transform the social identities of both insiders and former outsiders.

---

25. Bock 2007, 261 suggests different groups "working together in a world… divided along ethnic lines" is a "powerful testimony."
26. The regular Qumran critique of the priesthood ("the last priests of Jerusalem…amass money and wealth by plundering the people" [1QpHab 9.4]) prompts fascinating speculation that potentially unscrupulous priests joined the community based upon the Spirit-empowered demonstration of economic self-sacrifice and concern for the "other."

7.2.1. *Luke's Socially Unique Samaritans*

The intergroup relationship between Samaritans and Israelites is unique from three perspectives: (1) historically, (2) within Luke's narrative presentation and (3) from an SIT perspective. Historically, from Israelite perspective, the Samaritans were syncretistic Assyrian re-settlers worshiping Israel's God only to escape deadly lion attacks.[27] Samaritans, however, viewed themselves as descendents of Jacob and defenders of Torah, while viewing Israelites as followers of Eli, a priest of defective lineage who established the Jerusalem cult as a rival to the legitimate national center in Shechem.[28] While there are reasons to doubt the accuracy of each of these conflicting accounts, the important point is that they are essentially *ethnic* in nature, both dealing with issues of physical descent.[29] This observation extends approaches to the Samaritan/Israelite question that are limited by only undertaking a comparison of "religions."[30] Samaritan and Israelite origin narratives reflect conflicting identities based upon contested claims to *the same ethnic social identity*: "true Israel."[31] This contested identity led to episodic violence that sometimes attracted Roman attention.[32]

The Samaritan–Israelite relationship is unique in Luke's Gospel as well. Because I have discussed Luke's special interest in Samaritans in Chapter 5 (Luke 9:51–56; 10:25–37; 17:11–19), I will here only note that

---

27. See 2 Kgs 17; Ezra 4:1–4. Josephus says that Samaritans claimed to be one with Israelites when politically expedient (*A.J.* 14.291), but that their origins were in exogamy (*A.J.* 11.302–24).

28. Purvis 1968, 88 n. 1.

29. Ethnic strife between Israelites and Samaritans existed well into the Rabbinic period. *Kutim* 6 teaches that Samaritans cannot marry into Israel because of "their bastards."

30. Pummer 1992, 42, for example, focuses on "samaritanischer Religion." Macchi 1994, 43; 1999, 241 suggests Samaritans are best conceptualized as another branch of the worship of YHWH. Thornton 1996, 130 calls the Samaritans a "religious community." Luke does not focus on the cultic distinctives (Gerizim vs. Zion; Samkutty 2006, 115), but on the group identities. Schur 1995, 289 properly understands the Samaritans as "a people, perhaps even a nation."

31. Cf. John 4:12.

32. See *Samaritan Chronicle* 34.648–58 (Stenhouse 1985). Samaritans rejected all Scriptures beyond their version of the Pentateuch and replaced "Jerusalem" with "Gerizim" in the Pentateuch (Hjelm 2000, 91). Josephus derogatorily referred to Samaritans as Cutheans (*A.J.* 9.288, 290; 10.184; 11.19–20, 88, 302; 13.256) or Shechemites (*A.J.* 11.342, 344, 347) and modified his Torah retelling with anti-Samaritan polemic (Thornton 1996). For episodes of violent conflict, see Josephus, *A.J.* 18.29–30; 20.118–36; cf. Sir 50:26; 2 Macc 6:2; Matt 10:5. See Samkutty 2006, 80–81 for Rabbinic depictions.

in Luke 17:18 Jesus calls the returning Samaritan leper a "foreigner," the only deployment of ἀλλογενής in the New Testament.[33] The word appears in the LXX in three characteristic contexts: (1) in the prohibition against non-Israelite spouses; (2) in juxtaposition to things that are holy or that have access to the holy (e.g. the ἀλλογενής cannot eat food sacrificed in Israelite worship); and (3) in texts that show that the ἀλλογενής is not permitted to walk through the Temple courts.[34] For Luke, the Samaritans are not quite ἔθνη, but they clearly are not Israelites—they are another form of "other."[35] The ambiguity provided by the term ἀλλογενής reflects a sentiment akin to *Kutim* 1, which simultaneously highlights Samaritan similarity and distinction. "The usages of the Samaritans are in part like those of the non-Israelites, in part like those of Israel, but mostly like Israel."

7.2.2. Social Similarity and Intergroup Conflict Intensity

The contested identity between Israelites and Samaritans leads to a unique intergroup relationship from an SIT perspective as well. Because intergroup distinctiveness is essential to positive identity and can only be maintained through intergroup differentiation, *intergroup similarity* can, under certain conditions, be experienced as a threat to in-group identity.[36] This is less the case for unimportant or trivial identities.[37] But for important (especially terminal) social identities, intergroup similarity can lead to an increased drive for group distinctiveness, especially for high identifiers under conditions of intergroup competition.[38] The drive for distinctiveness is heightened when there is overall pressure toward social assimilation and where groups have close proximity and regular interaction.[39]

---

33. ἀλλογενής was the boundary-marking term in the famous inscription from the Jerusalem Temple court of the non-Israelites: μηδένα ἀλλογεῆ εἰσπορεύεσθαι.

34. Gen 17:27; Exod 12:43; 29:33; 30:33; Lev 22:10, 12–13, 25; Num 1:51; 3:10, 38; 17:5; 18:4, 7; 1 Esd 8:66–67, 80, 89–90; 9:7, 9, 12, 17–18, 36; Judg 9:2; 1 Macc 3:36, 45; 10:12; Job 15:19; 19:15; Sir 45:13; *Pss. Sol.* 17:28; Joel 4:17; Obad 11; Zech 9:6; Mal 3:19; Isa 56:3, 6; 60:10; 61:5; Jer 28:51; 49:17; Ezek 44:7, 9; Dan 1:10.

35. Koet 2005, 184 notes that "Luke gives his readers the opportunity to interpret a passage from the Gospel with one from Acts," and I suggest that the phenomenon works the other direction as well. Hence, Luke's introduction to a Samaritan as a "foreigner" in Luke 17:18 sets the stage for our understanding of Samaritans when we reach Acts 8.

36. Jetten et al. 2004, 862.

37. Moghaddam and Stringer 1988, 112.

38. Moghaddam and Stringer 1988, 113; Jetten et al. 2001, 622.

39. Grant 1993, 43; Jetten et al. 2004, 846.

This proves to be a helpful frame for understanding the tension between Israelites and Samaritans, both of whom experienced identity threat from the assimilationist pressures of Hellenization, who had close geographical and social proximity and who made mutually exclusive claims to the *same identity*.[40] Such a fundamental clash of terminal identity narratives can be fertile soil for intractable intergroup conflict.[41] A parallel situation is evident in the contemporary Israeli–Palestinian conflict:

> Each national narrative is in a way based on a fundamental negation of the other's. For the Israelis, to accept the central piece of the Palestinian narrative that Palestine was indeed populated by indigenous people who were gradually and systematically dispossessed and replaced by newcomers means that the Jewish state was born in sin. Thus, the Israeli narrative denies this Palestinian account. For the Palestinians, to accept the central part of the Zionist narrative that the Jews are not to be seen as newcomers but a people returning to their own homeland—albeit after 2,000 years—means that Palestinians were aliens in their own land, a view that they by definition reject… Conflict and identity support each other in a mutual fortification process.[42]

This comment sheds valuable light on the nature of the Israelite–Samaritan relationship. The acknowledgment of the identity claim of the "other," for each group, results in the negation of the in-group's identity claim. From an etic perspective the socio-cultural differences between the groups appear insignificant, but from an emic perspective, "it is the perception of subjective differences rather than objective status that matters to groups."[43] Historically, for Samaritans and Israelites, these perceptions led to violent conflict that was episodic rather than chronic, but that (in Luke's view) simmered just below the surface of normal social intercourse (Luke 9:51–56).

7.2.3. *The Spirit and Social Tension in Acts 8:1–25: Dual Identity Transformation*

The distinctiveness of the Israelite–Samaritan intergroup relationship is paralleled by the Samaritans' apparently anomalous conversion experience in light of Peter's presumably normal order of salvation in Acts 2:38: repentance, baptism, Spirit reception, community incorporation—all in immediate succession. In Samaria, however, the Samaritans respond to Philip's message (8:5) and signs (σημεῖα: 8:6) with faith (πιστεύω: 8:12)

40. Hjelm 2000, 11.
41. Rouhana and Bar-Tal 1998, 763.
42. Rouhana and Bar-Tal 1998, 763, 767.
43. Dovidio et al. 1998, 110; cf. Hjelm 2000, 12.

and baptism (8:12), but they do not receive the Spirit (8:17) until (days?) later. Six basic approaches have been utilized to explain the "late" appearance of the Spirit:[44]

1. The text reflects a source-critical problem caused by Luke's conflation of several independent sources.[45] This "cut and paste" form-critical approach is outdated and not a serious consideration.
2. The Samaritans did not have adequate faith prior to the visit from Peter and John.[46] This requires believing the *exact opposite* of what Luke says in Acts 8:12–13. Dunn's suggestion that the dative construction with Philip as its object (ἐπίστευσαν τῷ Φιλίππῳ εὐαγγελιζομένῳ περὶ τῆς βασιλείας τοῦ θεοῦ καὶ ὀνόματος Ἰησοῦ Χριστοῦ) means "faith in Philip" is weakened when one notes similar constructions in Acts 13:12 and 16:14.[47] Likewise, Cornelius' household and the Samaritans both are said to have received the "word of God" (Acts 8:15; 11:1).
3. The Spirit-reception in Acts 8:17 is a second gift of charismatic empowerment.[48] Yet Luke appears emphatic that the Spirit had not yet fallen *at all*, thus Acts 8:17 is the initial manifestation of the Spirit.
4. Acts 8 describes a "Hellenistic-Pauline conversion-initiation pattern."[49] This depends on the Tübingen School's Hebrew–Hellenist, Peter–Paul dichotomy.
5. Acts 8 describes a relationship between Philip and Peter that is patterned after John and Jesus. The former initiate while the latter culminate.[50] But "culmination" is absent in other conversions, including Philip and the eunuch (Acts 8:26–40).
6. The Spirit is given in 8:17 specifically to empower mission.[51] But there is no evidence of any active mission by Samaritans.

More inviting is Wenk's suggestion that the Spirit becomes the "identity marker for a community that had *ipso facto* come to comprise both Jews and Samaritans."[52] Wenk's argument can be extended and strengthened

---

44. Discussion in Turner 1996, 361–73 and Wenk 2004, 291–94.
45. Bauernfeind 1939, 124–24; Dibelius 1971, 17.
46. Dunn 1970, 63–68 suggests Samaritan hope in the *Taheb* caused them confusion and that Samaritans were more interested in the signs and wonders. Dunn softens the certainty of these positions in 1993, 228; 1996.
47. For critique of Dunn, see Turner 1996, 362–67.
48. Beasley-Murray 1962, 118–19.
49. Quesnel 1985, passim; quotation is from Wenk 2004, 292.
50. Spencer 1992b, 211–41.
51. Menzies 1990, 248–60.
52. Wenk 2004, 294.

by attending to the powerful transformation that this new identity marker creates for the *apostles* who must themselves undergo identity transformation due to the incorporation of the Samaritans.[53]

I will demonstrate that Luke uses the Samaritan episode to underscore the identity-marking function of the Spirit, which prompts the apostles to recognize that they and the Samaritans share a common group and, hence, common social identity. I will suggest that Luke undergirds his treatment of Samaritan identity with a complex and powerful allusion to Isa 56:3a, 6–7 LXX in order to portray the Samaritans as a group that wished to attach itself to the God of Israel but that was historically forbidden. But now, Luke thinks, believing Samaritans are *identified* by the Spirit as δοῦλοι and δοῦλαι of God (cf. Acts 2:18).[54] This Spirit-identification results in the first of Luke's dual identity transformations.

7.2.4. Luke's Distinct Intergroup Focus in Acts 8:1–25

The text draws our focus to Samaritans *as a group* in several ways, thus alerting the hearer that this is an intergroup situation and that the Israelite–Samaritan intergroup relationship sits in the background. The anarthrous reading of the variant in 8:5 (Φίλιππος δὲ κατελθὼν εἰς [τὴν] πόλιν τῆς Σαμαρρείας), favorable for internal textual considerations, highlights the fact that the issue is not location, but a people group—the Samaritans.[55] Luke specifically refers to the Samaritans as an ἔθνος in 8:7.[56] The Samaritan response to the gospel message is given with the adjective ὁμοθυμαδόν, a word typically reserved for the single-minded devotion of the Jesus group.[57] Finally, Luke's hearers know the Samaritans as not just any ἔθνος, they are ἀλλογενής—and are named so by Jesus himself (Luke 17:18).

---

53. Wenk 2004, 274–308 describes this as reshaping of the church's "symbolic universe," which implies cognitive reconceptualization but not necessarily identity transformation.

54. For Luke's use of Isaiah, see Seccombe 1981; Pao 2003; Koet 2005; Porter 2006; Mallen 2008. While many see Isa 56:3–7 behind Acts 8:26–40, interpreters have not appreciated the full significance of the passage for Acts 8:4–25.

55. Barrett 1994, 401–3 discusses textual issues. τήν is likely a scribal insertion given for specificity. Internal considerations (the ambiguous "that city" in 8:8) favor the anarthrous reading. External evidence favors the article (P^{74}, ℵ, A, B, 69, 181, 460*, 1175, 1898).

56. Samaria, like Israel, can apparently be called ἔθνος, while not being included in the ἔθνη (cf. Acts 10:22). Cf. Sir 50:25–26. See Esler 2009 on ἔθνος vs. ἔθνη in Josephus, *Contra Apionem*.

57. Acts 1:14; 2:46; 4:24; 5:12; 8:6; 15:25. For unanimous consensus among non-believers, see Acts 7:57; 12:20; 18:12; 19:29.

7.2.5. The Delay (?) of the Spirit

The exegetical difficulty in the passage (most acute for those seeking a normative order of salvation, which Luke simply *does not present*) arises from the dissonance created by the apparently conflicting claims that the Samaritans

ἐπίστευσαν τῷ Φιλίππῳ εὐαγγελιζομένῳ περὶ τῆς βασιλείας τοῦ θεοῦ καὶ ὀνόματος Ἰησοῦ Χριστοῦ, ἐβαπτίζοντο ἄνδρες τε καὶ γυναῖκες.

They believed Philip, who was proclaiming the good news about the kingdom of God and the name of Jesus Christ, they were baptized, both men and women. (Acts 8:12)

but that the Holy Spirit

οὐδέπω γὰρ ἦν ἐπ' οὐδενὶ αὐτῶν ἐπιπεπτωκός...

For as yet the Spirit had not come upon any of them... (Acts 8:16)

All signs point to an authentic work in Samaria: signs and wonders are performed (cf. Acts 2:19); Samaritans experience joy, a Spirit-produced trait in Acts; they respond with one accord (ὁμοθυμαδόν), a trait of the community of the Spirit; the language of faith (ἐπίστευσαν) is similar to other "valid" conversions; they are baptized in Jesus' name (Acts 8:12, 16).[58] There is, apparently, no logical or theological reason the Samaritans should not have received the Spirit prior to the apostles' visit.

The news of Samaritan reception of the word of God, albeit without the Spirit, prompts an ambiguous visit from Peter and John. Because the apostles in Luke–Acts regularly have tended toward expressions of in-group bias that display reluctance to embrace the "other," one is inclined to suggest that the apostles' trip to Samaria was based upon their skepticism that this "other" had become "one of them." Examples of this apostolic reticence are plentiful: John's resistance to a non-apostle ministering in Jesus' name (Luke 9:49–50); James and John's anti-Samaritan bias (Luke 9:51–56); the reluctance of the Jerusalem disciples to incorporate Saul (Acts 9:26); Peter's reluctance to obey a heavenly vision (Acts 10:14); the Jerusalem disciples" reluctance to incorporate Cornelius, whose household, like the Samaritans, had received the "word of God" (Acts 11:1–3; cf. Acts 8:14); and the Jerusalem disciples' apparent skepticism concerning non-Israelite Jesus-followers in Antioch (Acts 11:22–24).

---

58. Joy: Luke 10:21; Acts 8:39; 13:52; 15:31; 16:14; cf. Rom 14:17; Gal 5:22. ὁμοθυμαδόν: Acts 1:14; 2:46; 4:24; 5:12; 8:6. The lone exception is 7:57, the collective rage of Stephen's attackers. Similar language of faith: Acts 13:12; 16:14. Baptism in Jesus' name: Acts 2:38; 10:48.

Luke demonstrates apostolic caution, if not outright reluctance, immediately to embrace non-Israelite Jesus-followers or various "threatening others." These incidents, Samaria included, are intelligible as expressions of in-group love that result in out-group ambivalence, if not antipathy. This leads us to a key point: *the identities that are challenged in Acts are not just out-group identities; the emerging identity of the Jesus group is challenged at many points, especially when various categories of "other" join the in-group.*

The "delay" of the coming of the Spirit functions to challenge the in-group identity of the apostles. The Spirit does not fall on the Samaritans until Peter and John arrive on the scene in Acts 8:17. Given Peter's modification of Joel 3:1–5a LXX at Pentecost, in which the addition of the double μου (Acts 2:18) made clear that the Spirit was the definitive identity marker for the servants/slaves of God, the Spirit's presence ratifies the Samaritans as members of Peter and John's group. This is Luke's first narrative demonstration that the Spirit *marks/identifies* former out-group members who now share a common identity with the Jesus group.[59] By identifying Samaritans as in-group members, the *Spirit* navigates the intergroup boundary in question.[60] This in itself is a departure from typical intergroup identity-formation processes. But this narrative is not only about Samaritan incorporation. Sometimes overlooked is the fact that the apostles' trip is less about apostolic verification, culmination or authorization, and more about apostolic *identity transformation*.[61] Whenever group composition changes, especially when a heretofore "other" is incorporated, social identity is transformed to reflect the newly constituted group. As Ely has suggested, "Demographic characteristics... help to shape the meaning people attach to their identity group memberships."[62]

The textual evidence for Peter and John's identity transformation is apparent in the matter-of-fact statement that they "returned to Jerusalem, preaching the gospel to many villages of Samaritans," an option evidently unthinkable on their way *to* Samaria.[63] This "dual identity

---

59. Seccombe 1997, 49 notes the Spirit is important for the acknowledgment of Samaritans as "fellow believers" but makes the apostles, not the Spirit, responsible for this recognition.

60. Squires 1998, 614 seems to attribute to the apostles what rightly belongs only to the Spirit in Acts: "Nothing in this section [Acts 8–12] takes place without being initiated or authorized by the community in Jerusalem."

61. Contra Schneider 1980, 492, the apostles are not the "Aufsichtsbehörde" nor are they the "unmittelbares Bindeglied zwischen Jesus und der Samariter gemeinde."

62. Ely 1994, 206–7.

63. Acts 8:25.

transformation" reflects the fact that the apostles now embrace the possibility that Samaritans can become a part of their in-group. An approach that appreciates the importance of a common identity for intergroup reconciliation and community formation can detect the fact that the Spirit, in Acts 8:4–25, came neither too soon nor too late, but at just the moment identity was in question. This new Spirit-marked identity bridges an ancient ethnic rivalry and brings together two competing identity narratives around the person of Jesus.[64]

7.2.6. Isaiah 56:3a, 6–7 as a Substructure for the Samaritan Incorporation
Luke's incorporative intention becomes more apparent when one examines the Isa 56:3–7 allusion lurking beneath Acts 8:4–40. The relevant Isaianic texts are Isa 56:3a, 6–7:

> Let not the foreigner (ἀλλογενής) who attaches himself to the Lord say, "Surely the Lord will separate me from his people (λαός)." And let not the eunuch say, "I am a dry tree"... And to the foreigners (ἀλλογενής) attaching themselves to the Lord to serve (δουλεύειν) him and to love the name of the Lord (τὸ ὄνομα κυρίου) to be to him male servants (δούλους) and female servants (δούλας)... I will bring them to my holy mountain and I will make them glad in my house of prayer... For my house will be called a house of prayer for all nations (ἔθνη).

The link between the passages is literary and historical. Historically, the Samaritans fit well the profile of "foreigners" who had attached themselves to the God of Israel, but whose attachment was not permitted. This is reflected (at an earlier date) in Ezra 4:1–4 and is likely evident to Luke's audience in the return of the Samaritan ἀλλογενής in Luke 17:11–19. The Samaritan in Luke 17 would almost certainly have been expected to be unwelcome before the priests at the Jerusalem Temple. Literarily, ἀλλογενής serves as a linking word that connects Samaritans with Isa 56:3a.[65] Initially, then, I question the majority interpretation that suggests

---

64. There is no space to discuss Simon's attempted manipulation of the Spirit for monetary gain, which stands in line with Luke's contrast between Satan, egocentrism and use of possessions, and the Spirit, allocentrism and use of possessions. Cf. Acts 4:36–5:11.

65. Litwak 2005 does not treat this passage in his extensive treatment of intertextuality in Luke–Acts. Pao 2003 applies Isa 56:3–5 only to the eunuch (Acts 8:26–40). The only interpreter to notice this connection between 8:1–25 and Isa 56 is Schneider 1980, 498, cited by Rusam 2003, 383, who hints ("vermuten") that the Samaritans and Eunuch together function "als Erfüllung der messianischen Verheißung für den ἀλλογενής und den εὐνοῦχος Jes 56.3–5 LXX." Schneider does not develop the allusion, nor does he connect the "Erfüllung" of Isa 56:3–7 to the Spirit or note the connection between this passage and Luke 17.

the Ethiopian eunuch fulfills both categories of Isa 56:3 (ἀλλογενής and εὐνοῦχος).[66] The plausibility of an Isa 56 intertext in general is high. Along with the regular conclusion that Acts 8:26–40 draws on Isa 56, Luke uses Isa 56:7 as Temple critique in Luke 19:46. Luke's use of Isa 53:7–8 in Acts 8:32–33 demonstrates he is working in Isaiah at this point and, as Seccombe has argued, "in approaching quotations from and allusions to Isaiah there is a presumption in favour of Luke's awareness of their context and wider meaning within Isaiah as a whole."[67]

The next two intertextual links, while intricate, solidify Luke's identity-forming agenda for this passage. First, the Samaritans are said to have ἐπίστευσαν τῷ Φιλίππῳ εὐαγγελιζομένῳ περὶ...τοῦ ὀνόματος Ἰησοῦ Χριστοῦ (Acts 8:12). This is the only time in Luke–Acts that anyone comes to "faith" in the "name" of Jesus Christ.[68] It evokes Isa 56:6, where the ἀλλογενής who attach themselves to God are said to ἀγαπᾶν τὸ ὄνομα κυρίου.[69] Those who love the "name of the Lord" in Isa 56 are subsequently identified as δοῦλοι and δοῦλαι of God. Thanks to the addition of the double μου in Acts 2:18, Luke's hearers know that when the Spirit falls upon Samaritans, they are deemed to be δοῦλοι and δοῦλαι of God. Isaiah 56:6 is the *only other instance* outside of Acts 2:18 in either the LXX or New Testament where people are identified as δοῦλοι and δοῦλαι of God.[70]

The intertextual logic for Luke runs as follows. Isaiah develops an eschatological scenario in which ἀλλογενής who have attached themselves to the Lord need not fear being "separated" from the people (Isa 56:3a); instead, if they love the "name (ὄνομα) of the Lord," they can become δοῦλοι and δοῦλαι of God and be welcomed to worship in the Temple, a "house of prayer for all nations" (Isa 56:6-7). In Acts 8, nested within the time of eschatological fulfillment signaled by Peter's use of Joel 3:1–5a LXX at Pentecost, the Samaritans—definitively ἀλλογενής (Luke 17:18)—believe the announcement about the "name (ὄνομα) of Jesus Christ" (Acts 8:12) receive the Spirit (Acts 8:17) and thus, by virtue of

---

66. Wenk 2006, 297; Tannehill 1990, 109; Robinson and Wall 2006, 118; Pao 2003, 142; Martin 1989, 109. Barrett 1994, 426 sees no Isa 56 background in Acts 8. Even Beale 2004, in his intertextual biblical theology of Temple, overlooks the significance of this passage for Samaritans.

67. Seccombe 1981, 259.

68. "In Jesus Christ" is normally a baptismal or a healing/exorcism formula (Acts 2:38; 3:6; 4:10; 10:48; 16:18).

69. Jesus is called κυρίου Ἰησοῦ in Acts 8:16. Associating the "Lord" of Isa 56:6 with Jesus would be an impressive Christological move by Luke.

70. Tandem occurrences of δοῦλοι and δοῦλαι, though not as genitive subjects of "God," appear in 1 Sam 8:16; 2 Chr 28:10; Joel 3:2; Isa 14:2.

Acts 2:18, are identified as δοῦλοι and δοῦλαι of God. It is hard not to wonder, given the plausible intertextual allusion to Isa 56 and the Temple critique by Stephen in Acts 7, whether Luke is presenting the new community as the eschatological Temple. Luke's use of Isa 56 in this section would explain why Luke (of all the evangelists!) stops short in his Gospel quotation of Isa 56:7, stating only that the Temple is a "house of prayer," but omitting "for all nations" (Luke 19:46; cf. Mark 11:17). Perhaps Luke forestalls his use of Isa 56:7 in order to give it narrative expression in Acts.[71]

As co-δοῦλοι with Israelite Jesus-followers, the Samaritan believers now exist as a part of one people—an essential factor in "salvation" according to Peter's Acts 3 speech. Luke is never satisfied to portray "salvation" as a status conferred. Instead, it always involves a people inaugurated and, subsequently, an identity consummated.

7.2.7. The Retention of Ethnic Particularity in Samaria

There are several ramifications in this pericope for the relationship between ethnicity and the Spirit. The Samaritans, to receive the Spirit, do not have to renounce either their Samaritan ethnic identity or (evidently) any of the markers of Samaritan identity that competed with Israelite identity markers. Given later rabbinic rhetoric, this is surprising.[72] It is foreigners *as foreigners* whom God will not separate from his people, but instead who will pray in the house of prayer *for all nations* (Isa 56:7). Yet this ethnic identity is chastened and can only function as a nested identity within the new superordinate identity formed by the Spirit. While these groups remain, at one level, composed of Israelites and Samaritans, the group functions properly when they relate as co-members of the community of the Spirit. The Spirit *marks* a new identity that destroys ethnic hegemonies and relegates ethnic identity always to a (wholly valid) penultimate level.

7.3. Acts 8:26–40: The Ethiopian Eunuch

Luke's treatment of the Ethiopian eunuch forms the second half of Luke's allusion to Isa 56:3–7 and the eunuch constitutes another member of the category "those who desired to attach themselves to the God of Israel, but

---

71. Dunn 1996, xv notes Luke's penchant for withholding Markan material from the Gospel in order to utilise the material in Acts, but he does not note this passage.

72. See, e.g., *Kutim* 28: "When shall we take them back? When they renounce Mount Gerizim, and confess Jerusalem and the resurrection of the dead. From this time forth he that robs a Samaritan shall be as he who robs an Israelite."

who were not permitted." While the man is an Ethiopian, Luke highlights his eunuch identity by designating him "eunuch" five times in twelve verses (8:27, 34, 36, 38, 39).[73] Because deviant labels ("eunuch") typically override conventional labels ("official," "Ethiopian"), his "eunuch" identity is clearly in view.[74] This passage allows Luke to demonstrate the second major incorporative function of the Spirit, the *orchestration* of intergroup contact. In this case, intergroup contact leads to the formation of a micro-community representative of the larger Jesus-following in-group.

The eunuch's identity caused him to be viewed as a grotesque "other," who, though politically influential, existed at the margins of both Israelite and Greco-Roman culture.[75] Eunuch identity was a formidable barrier to participation in the Israelite ἔθνος, a fact of which the eunuch was painfully aware after his visit to the Jerusalem Temple where his identity would have prevented him from full participation in Temple worship (see Deut 23:2 LXX; cf. Lev 21:17–21).[76] Some evidence suggests that, in the period, eunuchs were both castrated and partially or fully dismembered, thus rendering circumcision (and Israelite social conversion) impossible.[77]

7.3.1. *Spirit-orchestration of In-group Incorporation*

Philip's encounter with this "other" is a divinely orchestrated creation of a micro-community.[78] Philip is commanded by an angel to make a trip to an unlikely destination in 8:26.[79] Upon arrival and after noticing the eunuch, the *Spirit* speaks to Philip in 8:29 with a clear command:

---

73. He is only called an Ethiopian once (Acts 8:27). Thus Martin's focus solely on the eunuch's Ethiopian identity addresses a social boundary that is secondary in Luke's presentation (1989, 105–36).
74. Spencer 1992a, 156.
75. Parsons 1998, 108 n. 6. Lucian of Samosata, *The Eunuch* 6.11; Josephus, *A.J.* 4.290–91; Philo, *De specialibus legibus*; *t. Megillah* 2.7.
76. Parsons 2006, 123–42 studies ancient physiognomic methods of human description and connects conceptions of the eunuch's character to his physical deformity.
77. Witherington 1998, 296 n. 64. See Martin 1985 for a full treatment of eunuchs in the era.
78. Structurally, O'Toole 1983 modifies the analysis of Mínguez 1976 and sees "preaching about Jesus," baptism and the role of the Spirit as central to Luke's telling.
79. Strelan 2001 observes that revelations regarding the spread of the Gospel to non-Israelites frequently occur at noon: Acts 10:9; 22:6; 26:13; cf. John 4:6. μεσημβρίαν can mean either "noon" or "south."

Πρόσελθε καὶ κολλήθητι τῷ ἅρματι τούτῳ.[80]

Go and be joined to this chariot. (Acts 8:29, my translation)

This is the first instance of a highly significant aspect of Luke's presentation of the Spirit: *direct speech of the Spirit always directs the hearer toward non-Israelites* (Acts 8:29; 10:19; 11:12; 13:2).[81] This is a manifestation of the allocentric influence of the Spirit encountered in earlier sections. The Spirit commands Philip to "be joined/united to" (κολλάω) the eunuch's chariot. κολλάω is an important incorporation word, deployed by Luke at boundary-crossing moments and indicating the potential for the initiation of community and possible incorporation of out-group members.[82] In Acts 5:13 the numinous fear of the community prevents outsiders from daring to unite themselves (κολλάω) to the community. In Acts 9:29 Paul tries to unite himself (κολλάω) to the Jerusalem community. In Acts 10:28 Peter tells Cornelius that it is forbidden (ἀθέμιτος) for Israelites to unite themselves (κολλάω) to non-Israelites. In Acts 17:34 some members of the Aereopagus, believing, unite themselves (κολλάω) to Paul. The verb only appears in passive form—perhaps the divine passive—giving the sense that the "uniting to" is God's action exerted upon the person in question. P^{50} may give evidence that the early church recognized the importance of this boundary crossing word. The papyrus (ca. 4–5 C.E.) includes only Acts 8:26–32 and Acts 10:26–31. Both passages deal with conversion and baptism, but neither includes the climactic moments. They do, however, both share the verb κολλάω, perhaps indicating that early interpreters recognized the significance of Jesus-followers being united to (former) outsiders in these passages.[83]

The Spirit's command results in the formation of a micro-community between Philip and the eunuch, akin to the micro-(anti-)community formed by Ananias and Sapphira. Philip is "united to" the chariot (8:29),

---

80. The full force of the demonstrative pronoun is important and here, as elsewhere, gives emphasis to the particularity of the referent. Cf. Acts 10:36.

81. Hur 2001, 14 notices this pattern.

82. Luke 10:11 (dust that "clings" to feet) is an exception. See Luke 15:15; Acts 5:13; 8:29; 9:26; 10:28; 17:34. Cf. Matt 19:5; Rom 12:9; 1 Cor 6:17, 18; Rev 18:5. Its most frequent New Testament usage outside of Luke is to describe the intimate "cleaving" of marital or sexual union (Matt 19:5 [cf. 1 Esd 4:20; Sir 19:2]; 1 Cor 6:17, 18). More broadly in the LXX it can describe "clinging" to the testimonies of God (Ps 118:31), "cleaving" to the Lord (Deut 6:13; 10:20), God's "cleaving" to Israel and Judah (Jer 13:11) and the way that the scales of leviathan "cleave" to one another (Job 41:8).

83. Johnson 1992, 159–60.

he discusses the passage while "sitting with" the eunuch (8:31: παρεκάλεσέν τε τὸν Φίλιππον ἀναβάντα καθίσαι σὺν αὐτῷ) and emphatic repetition indicates that they go down into the baptismal waters together (8:38: κατέβησαν ἀμφότεροι εἰς τὸ ὕδωρ, ὅ τε Φίλιππος καὶ ὁ εὐνοῦχος).[84] The Spirit does not merely send Philip to the "other," it seeks to incorporate the "other" into the community of which Philip is a Spirit-filled exemplar (cf. Acts 6:3).

The pericope is driven by the eunuch's question regarding Isa 53:7–8b: "About whom, I pray thee, does the prophet say this, about himself or about someone else?" Luke then cites the text upon which the eunuch is ruminating:

> As a sheep led to slaughter
> and as a lamb before its shearer is silent,
> so he does not open his mouth.
> In humiliation his justice was taken away (αἴρω).
> Who will speak of his descendants (γενεάν)?
> For his life is being taken away (αἴρω) from the earth.[85]

It is not unusual for commentators to question why Luke does not include the sacrificial imagery of Isa 53 in this quotation.[86] Yet there is powerful—and overlooked—significance in Luke's emphatic declaration that Philip began his exposition *from this particular passage* (8:35: ἀρξάμενος ἀπὸ τῆς γραφῆς ταύτης).[87] In this very passage the eunuch identifies with Jesus.

Returning from Jerusalem, where the eunuch's identity prevented him from joining the people of God, the eunuch reads of another man who, like himself, cannot bear a family. The identification arises at Acts 8:33/ Isa 53:8: "Who can speak of his descendants?" The eunuch wants to know if the prophet—or someone else—shares his plight, the impossibility of familial generation.[88] This is, at least in part, the "humiliation" (Acts 8:33: ταπείνωσις) that both the eunuch and the Servant-figure share. Philip began *at this very passage* and εὐηγγελίσατο αὐτῷ τὸν Ἰησοῦν. The text allows for a connection between the family-less Isaianic servant and the

---

84. Spencer 1992a, 162 notes the community between the characters, but he does not develop its implications for the formation of common identity.

85. Luke uses αἴρω as a death metaphor in Luke 23:18–21; Acts 21:36; 22:22.

86. Barrett 1994, 429 thinks the "long journey" allowed for the entire fourth servant song to be discussed (Isa 52:13–53:12). Cf. Bruce 1989, 382; Marshall 1980, 164.

87. Again, note the full force of the demonstrative pronoun (cf. Acts 8:29; 10:36)

88. Cf. suggestions that this is an expression of "wonder" based on the innumerable disciples of Jesus. See, e.g., Barrett 1994, 431.

7. Incorporating the "Other" 167

family-less eunuch. If Isa 56:3–8 is in the background of this text, as most scholars assume, this observation is all the more certain.[89] The promise in Isa 56 is related to the ability of the eunuch to be a part of a household (family?):

> Let not the eunuch say, "I am a dry tree." This is what the Lord says to the eunuchs, as many as keep my Sabbaths and choose the things that I want and hold fast my covenant, I will give to them, in my house and within my walls, an esteemed place, better than sons and daughters; I will give them an everlasting name and it shall not fail.[90]

The Isaianic invitation to participation in the household of God reaches its climax with the prospect of participation in Temple worship (Isa 56:7)—a "house of prayer for all nations"—the very house that the eunuch was recently prohibited from entering. Just as Jesus' lack of "descendants" did not prevent God from giving him a new and large "family" (cf. Luke 8:21), the eunuch's lack of "descendants" will not prohibit him from being incorporated into a new and large "family."

7.3.2. Barrier Removal and Incorporation into the Community

The eunuch's final question indicates that, while previously he was prevented from joining the Israelite ἔθνος, there is now no reason that full incorporation into the Jesus group cannot happen:

> "Behold, water! What is to *forbid* (κωλύω) me from being baptized?"[91]

κωλύω gives the sense of "to stop or prevent against one's will," and for Luke regularly means forbidding access *to Jesus, to God* or the *benefits of God*.[92] It is a boundary word and is important in this section concerned with the incorporation of various "others" (esp. Acts 10:47; 11:17). Formerly, and painfully, it was identity as a eunuch that forbade the eunuch from participating in a community-entry ceremony.[93] But after Philip's exposition of the good news of Jesus, the eunuch recognizes that his eunuch identity is not his terminal identity and cannot bar him from the Jesus group. It is likely that Luke uses a play on words with κολλάω and κωλύω to frame the passage. Philip is *commanded by the Spirit* to be united (κολλάω, 8:29) to the eunuch because there is nothing that can

---

89. Porter 1988, 55 argues that Philip's exposition of Isaiah begins at the quoted passage and arrives climactically at Isa 56.
90. Isa 53:3b–5.
91. Acts 8:36 (emphasis mine).
92. Luke 6:29; 9:49, 50; 11:52; 18:16; 23:2; Acts 8:37; 10:47; 11:17; 16:6; 24:23; 27:6.
93. The prohibition is based upon Deut 23:2 LXX, a passage that bans eunuchs from the ἐκκλησία (!) of Israel.

forbid (κωλύω, 8:37) the eunuch his desire to enter the community. The eunuch, in his identification with Jesus, receives a *new superordinate identity* consummated by acceptance into the community of the Spirit (the ἐκκλησία) through baptism. Though the eunuch has no contact with a settled community of faith, he has clear micro-community with Philip—a Spirit-filled exemplar of the Jesus-group (Acts 6:3, 5)—and perhaps can anticipate his welcome from the Jerusalem believers next time around. The eunuch goes on his way rejoicing in the joy that is so characteristically Spirit-created for Luke, while the Spirit snatches Philip and thrusts him toward another category of "other" (Acts 8:39).

7.3.3. Summary

The incorporation of the eunuch highlights the Spirit's role in *orchestrating* intergroup contact and "fulfills" Isa 56:3b–5: the eunuch is no "dry tree," but, by virtue of his admission into the community represented by Philip, he becomes a member of a new group—even if from a distance. The eunuch now has a family. The Spirit overcomes the natural impulse to forbid (κωλύω) the incorporation of the "other" and instead joins (κολλάω) the "other" to the in-group. The eunuch, like the Samaritans, retains his old identities; but now those identities take on new and chastened significance thanks to the work of the Spirit. The eunuch can now know himself not primarily as "eunuch" but as a baptized (and Spirit-filled) member of the Jesus group.[94]

7.4. Acts 9: Spirit-orchestration and Identification for the Incorporation of an Enemy

Saul's encounter on the Damascus road is a striking example of the function of the Spirit in both the *orchestration* of intergroup contact and the *identification* of those who share a common social identity. Approaches to Saul's "conversion" evidence two main approaches: (1) discerning whether Saul experienced "conversion" or "commission" and (2) redaction-critical studies seeking either Luke's sources or Luke's redactional hand in the differences between the three tellings of the event.[95] Stendahl was the first to propose that Saul's conversion was no

---

94. Luke, as is frequently the case, is here *showing* rather than *telling* the full effect of the Spirit. The Western text makes explicit what Luke leaves implicit: "the Holy Spirit fell upon the eunuch, but the angel of the Lord snatched Philip away." See Fitzmyer 1998, 415.

95. See Hurtado 1993 for overview. Important works include DuPont 1970; Kim 1981; Roberts Gaventa 1986; Fredrickson 1986; Dunn 1987; Segal 1990. For redaction-critical treatments, see Hedrick 1981; Witherup 1992; Marguerat 2002.

conversion at all, but rather a commission similar to Old Testament prophetic commissions.[96] This position correctly appreciates that Saul never renounced his identity as a member of the elect Israelite ἔθνος, but does not do justice to Saul's changed behavior and group memberships.[97] Saul's experience is a social reorientation rooted in the fundamental transformation of his own identity.[98] I hope to keep both the "commissional" (allocentric) and "conversional" (identity-forming) aspects of Saul's experience in view through an approach in which the Spirit forms an allocentric ethos and fosters social identity through incorporation into the community. A close reading of the explicit and implicit functions of the Spirit, viewed through an intergroup lens and underscored by a comparative reading of Luke's repetitions of the Damascus incident (Acts 22:1–21; 26:4–23), highlights the fact that Luke's emphasis in Acts 9:1–31 is on the full incorporation of Saul into the Jesus-group via the identity-forming work of the Spirit upon *both* Saul and the Jesus-group.[99] This account is another double identity-transformation.

7.4.1. Social Identity and Intergroup Threat in Acts 9:1–31
Acts 9:1–31 should be read in the context of the group's response to external identity threat, a factor that increases in-group bias, minimizes intragroup difference and leads toward out-group antagonism and heightened group boundaries—especially among high in-group identifiers.[100] The threat introduced in the chapter heightens the barrier between Saul and the Jerusalem leaders and the μαθηταί. Both these groups are introduced in Acts 9:1 but are known from earlier in Luke's narrative. Saul is a persecutor (Acts 7:58; 8:3) in league with the unfavorably portrayed chief priests (Luke 3:2; 9:22; 19:47; 20:1, 19; 22:2, 4, 50, 52, 54, 66; 23:4, 10, 13; 24:20; Acts 4:6, 23; 5:17, 21, 24, 27; 7:1; 9:1, 14, 21).[101] This

96. Especially Isa 6; Jer 1:4–10. See Stendahl 1976, 89–91, who in part follows Munck 1959, 11–35. Cf. Roberts Gaventa 1986, 37–38, who claims that Saul underwent a "cognitive shift" based upon his new understanding of Jesus' identity.
97. Segal 1990, 11 notes the importance of Saul's change of communities, though he strangely calls Saul's new community a "gentile Christian community."
98. Marguerat 2002, 179–204 suggests that Saul's identity is transformed in this experience, though he does not clarify the manner of identity in view.
99. See Marguerat 2002, 185 n. 19 for Acts 9:1–30(31) as a single narrative unit. Taking Acts 9:1–31 solely as "commission for mission" is a key feature of "Spirit of prophecy" treatments. See *inter alias* Cho 2005, 150; Bruce 1951, 188–89; Roberts Gaventa 1986, 90–92; Menzies 1992, 260–63; Shelton 1991, 135; Huffman 1994, 168–75; Penney 1997, 97.
100. Dietz-Uhler and Murrell 1998, 33; Rothgerber 1997, 1207–10.
101. Hengel 1991, 81, 84 thinks that Saul felt the Jesus-followers were threatening the "traditional conception of Jewish theocracy" and leading the people "astray."

group is a tandem threat to the μαθηταί (Acts 9:14, 21) and has already engaged in deadly intergroup conflict with the Jesus-group (Acts 6:8–8:1, esp. 7:1; cf. Luke 22:2–6; Acts 5:17–18).[102] Luke here designates the community as μαθηταί, a name last used in the dispute between the Hebrew/Aramaic- and Greek-speaking widows (Acts 6:1, 2, 7) where it prepared hearers to recognize that the high priest assented to the death of a μαθητής (Acts 8:1). μαθηταί appears in 9:1 to describe the Jesus-followers as a group, in 9:10 to describe Ananias (who functions as a representative μαθητής), in 9:19 to describe the local Jesus-community in Damascus, in 9:25 in an odd usage to describe Saul's μαθηταί, and twice in 9:26 to describe the reluctance of the Jerusalem disciples to believe that Saul is a μαθητής.[103] The intergroup contact in the pericope is fully intra-Israelite and the narrative is intensely concerned with community incorporation. The question is: How can an enemy become a μαθητής? It is the work of the Spirit that brings Saul from the out-group to the in-group and that prompts the in-group to recognize Saul as "one of them."

7.4.2. Saul's Encounter with the Exalted Jesus

The place to begin the discussion is with the "unvarying kernel" repeated verbatim in Acts 9:4–5; 22:7–8; 26:14–15 (translation mine):[104]

Jesus:	Σαούλ Σαούλ, τί με διώκεις;[105]
	Saul, Saul, why are you persecuting me?
Saul:	τίς εἶ, κύριε;
	Who are you, Lord?
Jesus:	ἐγώ εἰμι Ἰησοῦς, ὃν σὺ διώκεις.[106]
	I am Jesus, whom you are persecuting.

These concerns are central to Israelite ethnic identity. Marshall 1980, 168 thinks the text implies intended murder of believers.

102. See 1 Macc 15:16–21; and Josephus, B.J. 1.474, A.J. 14.192–95 for the authority of extradition. Because Acts describes an intra-Israelite affair, it is likely that the chief priests were exercising their authority in the synagogues of the Diaspora and did not need authorization from Rome. For rabbinic discussions of "lynch laws," see m. Sanhedrin. Damascus had a large Diaspora population (B.J. 2.561; 7.368).

103. It is possible that αὐτοῦ in 9:25 is a corruption of αὐτόν, thus originally indicating not "disciples of Saul" but that the "disciples lowered him [Saul]" (Metzger 1975, 366; Haenchen 1959).

104. Marguerat 2002, 184.

105. The double naming of Saul provides an interesting parallel with Peter's double naming (Luke 22:31–32). There, as here, the plea by Jesus is that the double-named person work *for* and not against the Jesus-community. Koet 2008, 175 has noted that double naming can indicate the beginning of a call narrative (cf. Gen 22:11; Exod 3:4; Luke 10:41).

106. Acts 22:8 includes "Jesus *of Nazareth*."

The crucial question—"Who are you, lord?"—is a question of identity.[107] Much ink has been spilled trying to ascertain all that Jesus' self-revelation must have meant for Saul.[108] Saul's identity is transformed by at least two factors: (1) he discovers Jesus' true (and living) identity, and (2) Saul is transformed because *the exalted Jesus identifies himself with a particular group*—the very group Saul has been seeking to destroy. Saul is persecuting the μαθηταί, yet Jesus claims Saul is persecuting *him*. The double repetition of Jesus' identification as the persecuted one ("Why do you persecute me?"; "I am Jesus, whom you are persecuting") makes this unmistakable.[109] It was the combined force of Jesus' exalted status and Jesus' identification with Saul's enemies that shattered Saul's former identity. Saul's in-group was actively opposing God.[110] But God himself, through the exalted Jesus, was actively identifying with Saul's enemies.

7.4.3. The Role of the Spirit in the Incorporation of Saul
The Spirit is explicitly mentioned just once (9:17) in the account, but it implicitly pervades the narrative in order both to orchestrate intergroup contact and to identify Saul as a member of the Jesus group.[111] We learned in Acts 2:17 that visions (ὁράσεις) and dreams (ἐνύπνια) are the work of the Spirit. Ananias has a vision (ὅραμα) in which the Lord tells

---

107. Cf. the "identity" question of the eunuch in Acts 8:34. "Lord" should not here be taken with the full force of its LXX usage (contra Johnson 1992, 163). It is more, however, than the common "sir." Saul uses the word in response to a numinous vision—but the point of the question precludes that he already knows he is confronted by Jesus the exalted "Lord" (Witherington 1998, 317).
108. See, among others, DuPont 1970; Kim 1981; Dunn 1987.
109. Johnson 1992, 168: "Distinctive to Luke's account as well is the identification of the risen Lord with the community… Luke could scarcely have found a more effective way of establishing the living relationship and presence of the raised prophet with those who continued to live and speak and act with his prophetic spirit. And for Saul, if the living and powerful Lord identifies himself with this community, then joining this community is the sign of obedience to his presence." Cf. Luke 10:16; Matt 25:40, 45. See also 1 Sam 8:7 and perhaps Num 11:20 for God's identification with his representatives.
110. Cf. the equation between a lie to the community and a lie to God/Spirit in Acts 5:1–11.
111. Gill 1974, 547–48 demonstrates the near-perfect parallel between the two narrative settings (human hesitation, divine reassurance, fellowship, preaching, persecution, escape) in Damascus and Jerusalem, arguing the parallelism highlights solidarity in preaching and suffering (548). This may be true, but these should be situated within a more basic concern with the parallel emphasis on incorporation and identity formation.

him that Saul has had a vision (ὅραμα).[112] This is a common feature of this section of Acts; Acts 8:29; 9:10, 15; 10:19; 16:6–10 depict Spirit-inspired visions orchestrating intergroup encounters with sometimes threatening "others."[113] Wikenhauser has demonstrated that embedded visions (*Doppeltraume*) in Greco-Roman literature regularly indicate divine orchestration of events.[114]

Ananias, introduced as a μαθητής whose group is threatened by Saul, resists the direction of the vision out of fear.[115] Ananias' words express an identity under threat: "I have heard from many about this man, how much evil he has done to your saints in Jerusalem; and here he has authority from the chief priests to bind all who call upon your name" (Acts 9:13–14). This protest reveals both an identity shaped by community membership and the expected tightening of group boundaries as a result of identity threat.

The Lord, through the vision (presumably with some agency of the Spirit, based upon Acts 2:17), prevails upon Ananias, turns him in an allocentric direction and prompts one of the most poignant scenes in Acts.[116] Ananias, functioning as a representative μαθητής, goes to the enemy of his in-group, greets him as (ethnic?) "brother," lays his hands upon him, and prays that Saul will receive both his sight and the very Spirit that marks common identity as a δοῦλος of God.[117] Saul is cured

---

112. ὅρασις and ὅραμα are synonymous. Both are used to translate מראה, משא and חזיון. חזיון is translated ὅρασις in Joel 3:1 LXX, but is translated ὅραμα in Job 7:14 LXX (Michaelis 1967, 370–72). ὅρασις only appears in Acts 2:17; Rev 4:3; 9:17. Luke has eleven of the twelve New Testament occurrences of ὅραμα (Matt 17:9; Acts 7:31; 9:10, 12; 10:3, 17, 19; 11:5; 12:9; 16:9, 10; 18:9). Perhaps Luke wished to preserve the actual noun used in Joel 3:1 LXX (ὅρασις) in his Acts 2:17 quotation. All of Luke's modifications to Joel 3:1–5 LXX are additions or transpositions, not vocabulary alterations. Litwak 2005, 168 notices the connection between "visions" in 2:17 and "visions" in 9:10; 10:10–16, but he does not associate these visions explicitly with the Spirit.

113. So Wenk 2004, 289. Johnson 1992, 164 notes that visions are an important part of Spirit-inspiration for Luke.

114. Wikenhauser 1948, 100–11.

115. Robinson and Wall 2006, 136 argue instead that Ananias does not resist because of fear for his safety but because he makes "the 'hard rationalist's' case against the possibility of Saul's conversion—and by implication the full salvation of the gentiles." These options are not mutually exclusive, but it is hard to suggest that fear plays no part in Ananias' response.

116. Could it be that Ananias, whose group had suffered at the hands of Saul, now feels solidarity with the one who will also suffer for the name of Jesus (Acts 9:16)?

117. Bock 2007, 362 is correct to note that the laying on of hands serves to connect Saul to the new community, though he speeds ahead of the narrative in

of his blindness (Acts 9:18), filled with the Spirit, baptized and fed (the latter two presumably done by Ananias).[118] Though Luke does not explicitly narrate Saul's reception of the Spirit, it is unmistakably implicit. Jesus sent Ananias so that Saul might regain his sight and receive the Holy Spirit (Acts 9:17). Because the former happens immediately, we are undoubtedly to expect that the latter occurred immediately as well. The result of Saul's Spirit-filling and baptism is quick and complete incorporation into the Damascus community of believers. Saul remains with the μαθηταί in Damascus for many days, proclaiming the true identity of Jesus.[119] The wonder of the Damascus disciples, expressed in 9:21, makes the radical nature of Saul's identity transformation apparent:

> Is not this the man destroying (πορθέω) in Jerusalem those who are calling upon this name?[120]

The group boundary between the Damascus μαθηταί and Saul is overcome by the Spirit, who both orchestrates intergroup encounter and marks a common identity. For the Damascus disciples, the one who had set out to destroy the μαθηταί is now "one of us"—at least, that is, in Damascus.[121]

7.4.4. Apostolic Resistance to the Incorporation of Saul

The dynamic in Jerusalem is different for two likely reasons. First, no one in Jerusalem had witnessed the manifestation of the Spirit upon Saul, the usual signal of a common superordinate identity. Second, when faced

---

assuming that the appellation "brother" has at this point a "Christian" meaning. Though we cannot be certain, on balance it is likely that "brother" is a greeting of ethnic kinship here (with Dunn 1970, 74 and against Cho 2005, 149; Barrett 1994, 457; Bruce 1952, 202; Ervin 1984, 41–49; Shelton 1991, 131). Luke regularly depicts Jesus-following Israelites addressing fellow Israelites with the kinship-greeting "brother" (Acts 2:29; 3:17; 7:2; 13:26; 22:1; 23:1, 6; 28:17).

118. Heil 1999, 245: "Just as their sharing of food in meal hospitality 'in their houses' (2:46) was part of what united the newly baptized Jerusalem believers with all other believers (2:44), so the newly baptized Saul's taking of food in meal hospitality 'in the house of Judas' (9:11) is part of what unites him to the believing community at Damascus."

119. Intimate fellowship and gospel proclamation are two characteristics of the Jesus-following in-group (Acts 2:42; 4:33).

120. My translation.

121. Though I am not addressing it at length here, the sending of Saul to the ἔθνη is obviously of inestimable importance to Luke–Acts. It should be noted that all who are "elect" or "chosen" thus far in Acts are chosen for the sake of the "other" (Acts 1:8; 6:5; 9:15).

with external identity threat, those who highly identify with the in-group are the most prone to extreme in-group bias and out-group derogation.[122] In Jerusalem, the conflict is indisputably a conflict of identity:

> Καὶ πάντες [τοῖς μαθηταῖς] ἐφοβοῦντο αὐτὸν μὴ πιστεύοντες ἐστὶν μαθητής.
>
> And all [the disciples] were afraid of him, not believing he was a disciple.
> (Acts 9:29, my translation)

The μαθηταί cannot believe they share a common identity with Saul and evidently have no room for a (former) enemy in their conception of their identity. Much hangs in the balance here. Saul cannot be a full member of the community unless the Jerusalem community can reconceptualize their own group identity in such a way as to make room for this "other."[123] Something is necessary to convince the apostles that Saul is indeed "one of them."

Saul's own re-identification is made evident in his desire to "be joined to" (κολλάω) the Jerusalem disciples. Once more, Luke uses the important verb κολλάω (cf. Acts 5:13; 8:29; 10:28; 17:34), again in the divine passive, to highlight the work of God in forming this new group. To aid Saul's community incorporation, Luke reintroduces Barnabas (Acts 9:27)—the Spirit-filled exemplar of allocentric group identity last present in 4:36–38. It is Barnabas' Spirit-effected allocentric identity, I suggest, that moves him to reach across a social barrier to Saul.[124] Yet this is not done without good evidence of common identity:

> Barnabas took him, and brought him to the apostles, and declared to them how on the road he had seen the Lord, who spoke to him, and how at Damascus he had preached boldly in the name of Jesus.[125]

---

122. Rothgerber 1997, 1207.
123. Turner 1982, 27.
124. Scholars are sometimes surprised at the sudden reintroduction of Barnabas. Barrett 1994, 468 is representative: "Why he [Barnabas] should have acted as Paul's sponsor remains unknown." My approach explains the perceived anomaly: Barnabas is a Spirit-filled exemplar—just the person we would expect to navigate an intergroup identity dispute. Fitzmyer 1998, 438 (cf. Johnson 1992, 174) notes that "encouragement come[s] from the Holy Spirit, who makes Barnabas the mediator of it," but he does not note Luke's characteristic connection between the Spirit and one's posture toward the "other." Bock 2007, 370 suggests Barnabas' "stature and respect" could speak for Saul, but he makes no connection with the Spirit. Conzelmann 1987, 75 suggests Luke inferred Barnabas' role from later cooperation between Paul and Barnabas.
125. Acts 9:27.

Saul's preaching of the gospel to those who are now "other" is definitive evidence of the allocentric identity characteristically empowered by the Spirit.[126] But Barnabas, not Saul, must speak because Barnabas already shares a common identity with the Jerusalem μαθηταί.[127] Barnabas' testimony on Saul's behalf is simple: Saul has seen Jesus and spoken boldly in Jesus' name. Seeing Jesus and bearing witness are the two marks of a "witness of Jesus" (the very identity Jesus predicts will be empowered by the Spirit in Acts 1:8) according to Luke 24. While Saul's Spirit-reception was evident to the disciples in Damascus, neither Barnabas nor the Jerusalem disciples had eyewitness access. But so closely is "witness" connected to Spirit-formed identity that either the visible manifestation of the Spirit or the fruit of the Spirit—allocentric witness—can serve as evidence of a common identity.[128] This is enough for the Jerusalem community, and their own identity is transformed by virtue of Saul's incorporation. Saul, who once ravaged the church, entering (8:3: εἰσπορευόμενος) house after house *against them*, now joins the disciples, entering (9:28: εἰσπορευόμενος) and exiting *with them* and proclaiming the name of Jesus. Saul, the Damascus community and the Jerusalem community share a common identity in the Spirit-empowered community of witness.

7.4.5. Comparative Emphasis on Incorporation

A comparison of Luke's three repetitions of Saul's Damascus experience supports my argument that Acts 9:1–31 emphasizes Saul's incorporation into the community via a dual identity-transformation wrought by the orchestrating and identity-marking functions of the Spirit.[129] The varied narrative contexts of the repetitions cannot be overlooked: in Acts 9:1–31, the question is whether Saul can gain access to the Jesus group; in Acts 22:1–21 Saul defends his Israelite identity under duress at the

---

126. Dunn 1996, 126 suggests Saul's preaching is a recognizable identity marker for the movement. We can further ground preaching/witness in the work of the Spirit.

127. Barnabas is clearly the subject of εἶδεν in 9:27. See Fitzmyer 1998, 438.

128. A similar dynamic will appear in Acts 15 with regard to James, who (like Barnabas, whose actions in Acts 4 and 9 give evidence of the Spirit but who is not explicitly connected to the Spirit until Acts 11:24) will give ample evidence of the transformational power of the Spirit.

129. The recent studies that describe how narrative repetition emphasizes key motifs have tended to focus on the apparent discrepancies in the accounts rather than the shared material: "Who saw the light?," "Was there a sound?," and so on. See Hedrick 1981; Witherup 1992; Kurz 1993; Marguerat 2002, 179–204. For an overview, see Witherington 1998, 302–15.

Jerusalem Temple; in Acts 26:4–23 Saul makes a legal defense before an ethnically mixed crowd including Felix, Agrippa and Bernice. Scholars have noted the increasing prominence of Saul's commission to non-Israelites in the retellings of the story.[130] But a significant piece of counter evidence to those who connect the Spirit primarily or exclusively to empowerment for mission is the fact that as Saul becomes more and more explicit about his call to the non-Israelites, *the Spirit is altogether absent*.[131] While the close connection between the Spirit and boundary-crossing witness is already firmly established (Acts 1:8), I suggest that the overt presence of the Spirit in Acts 9:1–31 and its absence in the retellings highlights the Spirit's role in the formation of common identity. The Spirit is essential for Saul's incorporation into the community of believers.

All of the features essential for Saul's incorporation in Acts 9:1–31 are absent in Luke's two retellings of the event. Ananias, who represented the μαθηταί, prayed for Saul, witnessed his Spirit-reception, baptized him and ate with him becomes in Acts 22:12 simply "a devout man according to the law, well spoken of by all the Israelites in Damascus." This re-characterization of Ananias is a fitting modification for Saul's Jerusalem defense of his own ethnic identity. In Acts 22, Ananias heals Saul's blindness and gives Saul a commission to the nations, but he represents prototypical ethnic Israelites and the Jesus community. In Acts 26, Ananias disappears. Neither Acts 22 nor Acts 26 contain any mention of Barnabas' role in Saul's incorporation, any reference to fellowship with disciples in Damascus or Jerusalem or any mention of the Spirit-orchestrated intergroup encounter facilitated through the embedded vision (ὅραμα, cf. Acts 2:17) of Ananias. Most importantly, however, neither passage mentions the Spirit.[132] This is possibly because the retellings of Saul's transformation do not concern incorporation for the sake of common identity formation, but are focused instead upon Paul's mission to non-Israelites.

---

130. Dunn 1987, 255–56; Witherup 1992, 70.

131. Penney (1997) frames the Spirit as a "missions director." This is true but ultimately too restrictive as a dominant paradigm. Cf. the emphasis on empowerment for mission in Cho 2005 and Menzies 1991. I have yet to discover a single scholar who discusses the presence of the Spirit in Acts 9 vs. its absence in Acts 22 and 26, beyond those who suggest that the Spirit in Acts 9 is simply a Lukan addition but who do not comment on its *significance* (e.g. Hedrick 1981).

132. Hedrick 1981, 422 discounts the importance of the Spirit even in Acts 9:1–31: "The motif of receiving the holy spirit (9:17b) is probably a Lucan addition to a legendary miracle of Paul's healing."

My argument stands in even greater relief when viewed against Luke's retelling of the Cornelius incident. While the Spirit disappears from retellings of Saul's transformation when identity and incorporation are not in view, the Spirit remains a central feature in each telling of the Cornelius incident.[133] As we will see in the next chapter, this is because each retelling of the Cornelius incident concerns the navigation of identity barriers *en route* to Luke's demonstration that all who follow Jesus share a common identity.[134] When the context demands intergroup reconciliation, for Saul as for the ἔθνη from Cornelius' household, the Spirit is the agent that orchestrates intergroup contact, marks those rightly related to Jesus, and in so doing creates a community capable of incubating a new social identity.[135]

7.4.6. The Incorporation of the "Other": A Surprising Path to Peace

Luke concludes his treatment of the incorporation of Saul with a short summary:

> So the church throughout all Judea and Galilee and Samaria had peace and was built up; and walking in the fear of the Lord and in the comfort of the Holy Spirit it was multiplied.[136]

Just as 2:42–47, 5:12–16 and 6:1–7 ended with accounts of the successful growth of the community, so here also. When the community is faithful to its own identity the life of the community itself is witness to outsiders.

Three further points that implicate the Spirit, identity and group reconciliation bear mentioning here:

(1) ἐκκλησία appears in the singular in 9:31, a break with Luke's typical usage in which the word normally describes a localized community of believers.[137] This underscores the common identity shared by those

---

133. Acts 10:19, 38, 44, 45, 47; 11:12, 15, 16; 15:8, 28.
134. Acts 15:9; cf. 10:47; 11:17.
135. Marguerat 2002, 179–204 suggests Acts 9 is primarily about the reversal of Saul's identity and the role of ecclesial mediation in this reversal. Marguerat speaks of God's need to "convert his own church" (196), but he makes no connection with the Spirit. I extend Marguerat's argument by emphasizing the Spirit's role in Acts 9.
136. Acts 9:31.
137. See Barrett 1994, 473. Of the 23 occurrences of ἐκκλησία in Acts, four do not refer to the community of believers (Acts 7:38; 19:32, 39, 40). Acts 9:31 is the *only* time the word describes the community across a region. Twelftree 2009, 62 suggests that this is due not to a Lukan concern to present the unity of the one church across Judea, Galilee and Samaria, but instead to a copyist's error at the end of the first century. This seems to be an unnecessary explanation.

across greater Judea based upon their membership in the Jesus-following in-group.[138]

(2) Luke's description of Saul's initial response—that he was "led by the hand" and "he was without sight, and neither ate nor drank" (Acts 9:8, 9)—thrusts us back into the birth hymns in Luke 1. Mary rejoiced that God would "put down" the mighty and that he would fill the hungry with good things but send the rich away "empty" (Luke 1:52–53). Zechariah recognized that the coming of God's anointed servant would fulfill the covenant by granting that God's people, "being delivered from the hand of our enemies, might serve him without fear" (Luke 1:74). Saul, the enemy of the people of God, has been knocked low (Acts 9:4) and sent away empty ("hungry"; Acts 9:9) and the people have been delivered from their enemy.[139] It appears that God's people—the μαθηταί—will have the "peace" anticipated by Zechariah's claim that the Coming One would "guide our feet in the way of peace" (Luke 1:79). But "peace" comes not through the *destruction* of the enemy but through reconciliation and the incorporation of the enemy into *one's own group*.[140] This is a stunning subversion of typical intergroup processes and is revolutionary enough to repeat. *For the Spirit-empowered community of Jesus-followers, "peace" does not come by removing or destroying enemies but by welcoming enemies into the in-group. Divine victory comes through the transformation of humans and their groups, resulting in the creation of a common identity that allows enemies to become brothers and sisters.*

(3) Saul's retellings of his Damascus experience give us a critical window on the relationship between ethnic identity and the superordinate identity formed by membership in the community of the Spirit. Acts 22 makes it clear that Saul still fully identifies as an Israelite, though now he uses his varying nested identities strategically (as indicated by his deployment of Hebrew/Aramaic speech, Greek speech and Roman citizenship) in order to pursue his mission. He appears to be in a situation

---

138. This was hinted at in Acts 9:1–31 with the consistent use of the category "disciple" to refer to those in both Damascus and Jerusalem.

139. Conzelmann 1982, 73 says it well: "The appearance [of the exalted Jesus] serves first of all not to convert a sinner, but to put down the persecutor." Roberts Gaventa 2003, 147 treats Saul as an "overthrown enemy," but this should be extended in appreciation of its significance for the community's overall relationship to the "other." Cf. Roberts Gaventa 1985.

140. We should not miss the fact that Paul continues to describe himself as a prisoner to Christ, noting that he is "bound (δεδεμένος) by/to/in the Spirit" (Acts 20:22). The Spirit also tells Paul that the Israelites will bind (δήσας) him in Jerusalem (Acts 21:11). Binding (δέομαι) is precisely the activity this former enemy of the church was hoping to undertake in Damascus (Acts 9:2).

where he does not *lose* his ethnic identity (assimilation) or *abuse* his ethnic identity (ethnic hegemony), but he does *use* his ethnic identity to extend the gospel to "others" of many ethnic groups.[141] Saul's Israelite identity has been chastened—it is no longer his terminal identity, but it remains intact as a valid way, secondarily, of knowing himself in his social context. His willingness to render his Israelite identity secondary, however, brings murderous rage from those who do not identify themselves with the Jesus-group:

> Away with such a fellow from the earth! For he ought not to live.[142]

7.5. Conclusion

Much ground has been covered in Acts 6–9, and several salient points emerge. The ethno-linguistic conflict in Acts 6:1–7 is evidence that whenever identities other than identity drawn from membership in the Jesus group become salient, the community malfunctions and intragroup conflict occurs. Those best equipped to deal with such a crisis of identity are Spirit-filled members—those we can expect to have the ability to embrace the "other" through their Spirit-empowered allocentric posture. Yet even the Spirit-filled community needs constant identity transformation in order to accept the diverse group of "others" who now are joining their ranks. The incorporation of the "other" necessitates a "dual identity transformation" that challenges the in-group to transform its own group identity. The Spirit is central to this process and both orchestrates intergroup contact and marks those who share a common identity. The result is more than just "mission" to the "other"; it is full-fledged *incorporation* of the "other" into the community. It is, then, participation in this allocentric Jesus group that functions as the incubator for a new social identity capable of chastening and transcending ethnic identities, resisting ethnic hegemonies but affirming old identities at a penultimate level. The boundaries of this new identity are maintained by the Spirit and thus, rather than forming positive identity by denigrating the out-group, the group's identity is expressed rightly only when the group exists in an

---

141. Saul's use of a Hellenistic proverb (Acts 26:14: "It hurts you to kick against the goads") in his conversion story told in an ethnically mixed context and his famous quotation of Aratus' *Phainomena* in Acts 17:28 are examples of his "ethnic savvy."

142. Acts 22:22; cf. the rage directed toward Jesus after his refusal to privilege his village in-group in Luke 4:14–30. We should note that those who express the greatest resistance are arguably the stakeholders and high identifiers who benefit from current identity configurations and their concomitant power arrangements.

allocentric posture toward the "other." We are beginning to see that, for Luke, the goal of "witness" is a multi-layered reconciliation in which the "other" is brought into right relationship with Jesus and with the community. Tannehill, though writing with a different emphasis, summarizes nicely what my reading has revealed regarding the Spirit and the incorporation of the "other": "The church…has difficulty keeping up with such a God."[143]

---

143. Tannehill 1990, 117.

Chapter 8

TRANSCENDING ETHNICITY:
THE SPIRIT AND TRANS-ETHNIC IDENTITY IN ACTS 10–15

In Acts 10–15 Luke confronts the most intractable intergroup barrier in his context: ethnic identity. Here Luke will climactically press hearers toward a new social identity that affirms, but simultaneously chastens and transcends, ethnic identity. Many of Luke's identity-related themes rise to prominence in this section: Spirit-orchestration of intergroup encounters, Spirit-identification of those who are servants of God and the dual identity transformation created through incorporation of the "other" into the Jesus-community, to name but a few. My primary foci will include the extent of Luke's awareness of the interethnic issues in play, the role of the Spirit in circumnavigating interethnic barriers and Luke's awareness of the role of the Spirit in the formation of a new superordinate identity capable of reconciling various categories of ethnic "other."

8.1. *Interpreting Acts 10:1–11:18*

Scholars have offered the following readings for the function of the Cornelius episode:
1. an attempt to negotiate Israelite purity regulations and the on-going role of the Mosaic Law in the new community;[1]
2. the facilitation of table fellowship between Israelites and non-Israelites;[2]
3. the in-gathering of the nations as a result of God's eschatological restoration and cleansing of Israel;[3]
4. a transition from Temple and exclusivity toward household and inclusivity;[4]

1. Bauckham 1996; 2005.
2. Esler 1987, 93–109.
3. Turner 1996, 346.
4. Elliott 1991.

5. the Spirit's inspiration of speech and missionary activity;[5]
6. the Spirit's role in making a person a believer;[6]
7. the Spirit's indication that the "Gentiles" can be participants in salvation history;[7]
8. an expression of Luke's "universalism," the contemporary implications of which are often taken to be a hospitable pluralism.[8]

Indeed, Luke is concerned with the notions that "Gentiles" could participate in salvation history (a proposition widely affirmed in Israel's prophetic corpus), that non-Israelites could retain ethnic particularity and even that non-Israelites and Israelites could engage in fellowship with one another. But Luke's appreciation of these factors both stems from and, in practice, requires a clear reality: that all who identify with Jesus are incorporated into a group *sharing a common identity* that affirms yet transcends ethnic identity. The Spirit guarantees that those calling upon the name of Jesus form *one people*.[9] For Luke, this is the shape in which the Abrahamic promise (cf. Luke 1–2) comes to fruition, and it is the necessary corollary of the ascension—which identifies Jesus as the one Lord of all creation. It is the Spirit that brings diverse humans into this one new humanity, creating a unity that resists totalizing "sameness." In short, the formation of this one new people is the ultimate goal of Lukan pneumatology.

8.1.1. Resources from Social Identity Theory

SIT provides several theoretical resources that are useful for interpreting the intergroup dynamics and identity processes in Acts 10–15:

(1) The evaluative criteria upon which intergroup comparisons are made are fluid and change with respect to the target out-group in question. To maintain positive identity, groups base intergroup differentiation on criteria that give them comparative advantage. Luke reflects the fluidity of evaluative criteria by focusing on various aspects of the identity of the "other": linguistic distinctives (Acts 2:1–11; 6:1–7), eunuch (Acts 8:26–40), disciple/non-disciple (Acts 9:1–31) and in this section ἀδελφοί. Who can, or cannot, be identified as ἀδελφός reflects an ethnic boundary navigated in Acts 10–15.

---

5. Cho 2005, 150–54; Menzies 1991, 267.
6. Dunn 1970, 82.
7. Tannehill 1990, 144.
8. Bond 2002, 81; Stendahl 1977.
9. Contra Jervell 1972 who positions the Gentiles as an "associate" people of God.

(2) The maintenance of group boundaries is an *intra*group phenomenon superintended by the group itself. Common identity can only be achieved if the in-group assents to the incorporation of the "other."[10] The self-maintenance of in-group boundaries often becomes a locus at which group identity can be used as a weapon to exclude or oppress. Acts 10–15, however, describes a group that relinquishes the superintendence of their social boundary to the Holy Spirit. This is a unique feature of the Jesus group in Luke–Acts.

(3) SIT presents three primary strategies for intergroup reconciliation:

(a) The creation of cross-cutting evaluative criteria designed to destabilize social categories. For example, one could attempt to ease tension between Israelites and Romans by emphasizing the criterion "honor" in order to create social groups that incorporate members of each ethnic group. This strategy has proved unsuccessful in "real world" identity issues.[11]

(b) The creation of a superordinate identity that encompasses competing subgroup identities. This strategy has often led to chronic projection of subgroup prototypicality and a resulting inability to reach consensus regarding the prototypical attributes of the superordinate group.[12] We see something of this in the breakdown of community at a subgroup level in Acts 6:1–7.

(c) The creation of a superordinate identity with simultaneous retention of subgroup salience.[13] The superordinate identity "Rainbow People" in South Africa is an example of this strategy.[14] For this strategy to work, subgroup identities must remain valid but penultimate. I have suggested that Luke's narration of the Pentecost event and the incorporation of Samaritans and the eunuch in Acts 8 can be described in just this way. Sub-group identities are preserved in Luke's narrative, but not as terminal identities. This strategy has shown promise in "real world" conflict, though Hewstone contends that it may only be able to overcome powerful ethnic categorizations on a temporary basis.[15]

Ethnic identity is too often a bastion of intergroup conflict. Global history has demonstrated, and social research has corroborated, that ethnic intergroup bias is often intractable. This is heightened all the

---

10. Turner 1982, 22.
11. Brown 2000.
12. Mummenday and Wenzel 1999.
13. Dovidio et al. 1998; Gaertner et al. 1999; Brown 2000; Gonzalez and Brown 2000; Van Oudenhouven et al. 1996.
14. Tutu 1996; Gibson 2006.
15. Hewstone 1996, 351.

more when ethnic particularity is reinforced by religious particularity.[16] It is not overstatement, then, to claim that the boundary confronted in Acts 10, 11 and 15 is a serious social boundary. Luke's description of the Spirit's function at this boundary can be described as the creation of a superordinate category with the simultaneous retention of subgroup identities. One might even wonder if "witness" is a uniting collaborative goal.[17] Acts 10–15 reveals that the new primary social identity for Jesus-followers is an identity that transcends ethnicity. But it is equally clear that ethnic identity is a valid and valuable identity at a secondary level. To achieve this radical transformation of social identities Luke makes recourse again to the Spirit, aware that this delicate dance—intergroup reconciliation with the retention of subgroup (ethnic) salience—requires nothing less than the Spirit of God.

8.1.2. Luke's Use of "Ethnic Language"

Luke's use of "ethnic language" reveals the precision with which Luke handles inter-ethnic issues, especially in this section of Acts. Three ethnic categories are of concern in Acts 10–15: Ἰσραήλ, Ἰουδαῖος and ἀδελφοί.[18] Luke's usage of these identity-laden words describes the social context and forms raw material with which Luke will press for a new social identity. The changes in Luke's usage of these categories after the Cornelius episode in Acts 10 (changes solidified in Acts 15) are powerful reflections of the transformed social identities in view.

Ἰσραήλ and Ἰσραηλῖται are consummate insider terms, appearing twelve times in Luke and twenty times in Acts. Ἰσραήλ/Ἰσραηλῖται is only used in intra-Israelite dialogue, by the narrator (Luke 1:80; 2:25; Acts 5:21) or a divine messenger (Luke 1:16; Acts 9:15), but never by non-Israelites.[19] Acts 10:36 is the only time the word is spoken to a non-Israelite, but Cornelius was likely well-enough acquainted with intra-Israelite usage. Israel/Israelite is language of the ethnic in-group and (for Luke) language of ethnic privilege, even if in non-Israelite eyes "Israel" was a figment of the increasingly distant past.[20] Members of the Jesus group continued to identify both themselves and their hearers as

---

16. Wald 2005, 10.
17. Collaborative goals can reinforce newly shared identities (Brown 2000, 755).
18. See Elliott 2007 for New Testament usage.
19. Luke 1:16, 54, 68, 80; 2:25, 32, 34; 4:25, 27; 7:9; 22:30; 24:21; Acts 1:6; 2:22, 36; 3:12; 4:10, 27; 5:21, 31, 35; 7:23, 37, 42; 9:15 (God's speech); 10:36; 13:16, 17, 23, 24; 21:28; 28:20. This pattern conforms to the other Gospels (Matt 2:6, 20, 21; 8:10; 9:33; 10:6, 23; 15:24, 31; 19:28; 27:9, 42; Mark 12:29; 15:32; John 1:31, 47, 49; 3:10; 12:13).
20. See Luke 1–2.

Ἰσραηλῖται throughout Acts 1–14.[21] Remarkably, "Israel" is used only two times after Acts 15: once by Jerusalemites incensed over Paul's transgression of ethnic boundaries (Acts 21:28) and once in Paul's novel phrase "the hope of Israel" (Acts 28:20).[22]

Luke's usage of Ἰουδαῖος reveals a similar pattern. Ἰουδαῖος is categorical designation for "Israelites" used only by non-Israelites or by Israelites speaking to non-Israelites. The word appears five times in the Gospel: twice by the narrator (Luke 7:3; 23:51) and once each from Pilate (23:3), Roman soldiers (23:37) and on the *titulus* (23:38).[23] Ἰουδαῖος occurs 74 times in Acts and is the favorite category of the narrator (46 times) to describe the Israelite ἔθνος.[24] It is used six times by non-Israelites and 15 times by Israelites speaking to non-Israelites.[25] There are two possible exceptions to this pattern prior to Acts 15. Peter's address in Acts 2:14, ἄνδρες Ἰουδαῖοι καὶ οἱ κατοικοῦντες Ἰερουσαλὴμ πάντες, could be a geographic usage distinguishing regional Judeans (Ἰουδαῖοι) from Judea proper from those living in Jerusalem.[26] In Acts 12:11 Peter reflects internally about his deliverance from Herod and from all the plans τοῦ λαοῦ τῶν Ἰουδαίων. This is an exception to the rule, but we must at least account for the fact that Luke presents this event *after* Peter's transformative experience with Cornelius. Perhaps Luke deftly depicts Peter as anticipating the broader identity transformation that will

---

21. Acts 1:6; 2:22, 36; 3:12; 4:10, 27; 5:31; 7:23, 37, 42; 13:16, 17, 23, 24.

22. Paul's phrase "hope of Israel" (τῆς ἐλπίδος τοῦ Ἰσραήλ) occurs only here in the New Testament and nowhere in the LXX, Pseudepigrapha, Josephus, Philo or apostolic fathers. Cf. ὑπομονὴ Ἰσραήλ in Jer 14:8; 17:3 and Ezra 10:2 where ὑπομονή translates מקוה. In Acts, the phrase likely refers to the resurrection, which is the "hope" in Paul's speeches in Acts 23:6; 24:15; 26:6 (Haacker 1985, 437–51).

23. Cf. Ἰουδαῖος in the Synoptics. Narrator: Mark 7:3; Matt 28:15. Non-Israelites: Mark 15:2, 9, 12, 18, 26; Matt 2:2; 27:11; 29:37. John's unique usage cannot be treated here.

24. Narrator: Acts 2:5, 11; 9:22, 23; 11:19; 12:3; 13:5, 6, 43, 45, 50; 14:1, 2, 4, 5, 19; 16:3; 17:1, 5, 10, 13, 17; 18:2, 4, 5, 14, 19, 24, 28; 19:10, 13, 14, 17, 33, 34; 20:3; 21:27; 22:30; 23:12; 24:9, 27; 25:2, 7, 9, 15; 28:17.

25. Non-Israelites: Acts 10:22; 16:20; 18:12; 23:20, 27; 25:24. Israelites to non-Israelites: Acts 10:28, 39; 20:19, 21; 21:11 (at least an ethnically mixed group is implied in this text), 39; 24:5, 19; 25:8, 10; 26:2, 3, 4, 7, 21.

26. Cf. Josephus' ability to differentiate within a Pentecost crowd those who were "actually from Judea" from other regional identities of ethnic Ἰουδαῖοι (*B.J.* 2.43). A similar regional usage of Ἰουδαῖοι by Peter would thus differentiate those who had come from "Judea" (the Ἰουδαῖοι) for the festival from Diaspora Israelites who had resettled permanently (κατοικέω) in Jerusalem. Alternatively, perhaps Ἰουδαῖοι was used to refer to Diaspora Israelites, though I am not convinced this is Luke's usage.

grip the entire community after Acts 15.²⁷ Hence 69 of 74 occurrences of Ἰουδαῖος demonstrate no deviation from the pattern set forth in the Synoptics or Luke–Acts. The remaining five exceptions mark Luke's shift in usage after Acts 15 (Acts 21:20, 21; 22:3, 12; 28:19) and present Israelite *Jesus-followers* addressing other Israelites as Ἰουδαῖοι. This post-Acts 15 intra-Israelite usage never appears in the Synoptics. After Acts 15, those outside the Jesus group use Ἰουδαῖος when addressing non-Israelites, but *never when speaking to Israelites* (Acts 24:5; cf. 21:28). This indicates a significant shift in identity, the impact of which will be developed in this chapter.

The resulting image is striking: prior to Acts 15, Israelite Jesus-followers know themselves and their ethnic group as "Israel," an insider name connoting ethnic privilege before the Creator God. However, after Acts 15 Israelite Jesus-followers (even a character no less "conservative" or "Israelite" than James) abandon the category Ἰσραήλ and replace it with Ἰουδαῖοι, a category that, similar to the names of all other ancient ethnic groups, derives from the group's relationship to their territorial homeland Ἰουδαία.²⁸ It is difficult to know for certain what is happening here, though it would appear that Luke is convinced that Israelite identity is flowering into the covenantal purposes of God *for* and *through* Israel—namely, all the families of the earth are coming to be blessed. Israel is now functioning as a servant (cf. Luke 1:54), empowered by the Spirit to gather the nations through "witness" (cf. Isa 49:6). What will remain to be seen is whether this move will result in a two-tiered society of Israelites and the ἔθνη, or whether the fulfillment of Israel's servant vocation will result in God's one new humanity.

The remarkable nature of this apparent identity transformation is underscored by Luke's usage pattern for the ethnic insider term ἀδελφοί. Of its 23 occurrences in Luke's Gospel, the word is used to describe physical kin 21 times. In Luke 8:21 it describes Israelites in general and in Luke 22:32 it describes the disciples' in-group.²⁹ In Acts the word is used 54 times, either as an insider term for the Israelite ἔθνος or for the in-group of Jesus-followers.³⁰ The word functions primarily as an ethnic

---

27. Because this event took place in Jerusalem, Peter may have been using the geographic sense as well.

28. See Josephus, *C. Ap.* 1.179 and Esler 2009.

29. Luke 3:1, 19; 6:14, 41, 42; 8:19, 20, 21; 12:13; 14:12, 26; 15:27, 32; 16:28; 17:3; 18:29; 20:28 (3×), 29; 21:16; 22:32.

30. Acts 1:14, 15, 16; 2:29, 37; 3:17, 22; 6:3; 7:2, 13, 23, 25, 26, 37; 9:30; 10:23; 11:1, 12, 29; 12:2, 17; 13:15, 26, 38; 14:2; 15:1, 3, 7, 13, 22, 23, 32, 33, 36, 40; 16:2, 40; 17:6, 10, 14; 18:18, 27; 21:7, 17; 22:1, 5; 23:1, 5, 6; 28:14, 15, 17, 21.

descriptor for Israelites in the early sections of Acts.³¹ Yet in these early sections ἀδελφοί also can be used to describe the Jesus group as distinct from the larger ἔθνος (1:15, 16; 6:3; 9:30). Jesus' followers are able to identify in-group members as their "brothers" while simultaneously identifying all ethnic Israelites as "brothers."

Prior to Acts 15 *no non-Israelite is ever categorized as a "brother" of an Israelite.* Of the 96 deployments of ἀδελφοί in the Gospels, *no non-Israelites are ever included as "brothers" of Israelites.*³² In literature relevant to this period, the only instances I can discover in which non-Israelites are called ἀδελφοί by an Israelite are in Josephus' *Antiquitates judaicae* (12.225-28; 13:43-45, 163-70) and 1 Maccabees (12:1-23; cf. 1 Macc 14:16-23; 2 Macc 5:8-9), texts that describe the "brotherhood" between the Spartans and the Hasmonean dynasty. Yet these instances are severely qualified by their clear political expedience. Further, the generation-long delay in the Israelite response to the Spartans' overture indicates possible reluctance to assent to the relationship. Even so, the Spartan claim to "brotherhood" still rests on physical kinship—the "discovery" of common Abrahamic descent.³³ This strange exception serves to prove the rule that Israelites simply did not either call or conceptualize non-Israelites as "brothers."

8.1.3. *Ethnic Language and the Awareness of Ethnic Boundaries*
Luke's use of ἀδελφοί as the primary category name for the Jesus group in Acts 10-14 indicates that the in-group's identity is being defined against an ethnic "other."³⁴ Luke relies less heavily in this section upon the category μαθητής (a category more appropriate for differentiation within a group possessing common ethnic identity; cf. Acts 9:1-31) and relies more heavily upon the category ἀδελφοί to emphasize both the mutuality of the group and its ethnic homogeneity.³⁵ The use of ἀδελφοί is not the only clue that the ethnic boundary is primary in the Cornelius episode:

31. Acts 2:29, 37; 3:17, 22; 7:2, 23, 25, 26, 37.
32. Matt 1:2, 11; 4:18 (2×), 21 (2×); 5:22 (2×), 23, 24, 47; 7:3, 4, 5; 10:2 (2×), 21 (2×); 12:46, 47, 48, 49, 50; 13:55; 14:3; 17:1; 18:15 (2×), 21, 35; 19:29; 20:24; 22:24 (3×), 25 (3×); 23:8; 25:40; 28:10; Mark 1:16, 19; 3:17, 31, 32, 33, 34, 35; 5:37; 6:3, 17, 18; 10:29, 30; 12:19 (3×), 20; 13:12 (2×); For Luke, see n. 28. John 1:40, 41; 2:12; 6:8; 7:3, 5, 10; 11:2, 19, 21, 23, 32; 20:17; 21:23.
33. Katzoff 1985, 486-87.
34. In Acts 10-14 ἀδελφοί appears ten times (10:23; 11:1, 12, 29; 12:2, 17; 13:15, 26, 38; 14:2). Cf. the seven appearances of ἐκκλησία (11:22, 26; 12:1, 5; 13:1; 14:23, 27) and μαθητής (11:26, 29; 13:52; 14:20, 21, 22, 28).
35. Acts 15:4 may indicate that Samaritans were not categorized as a part of the ἔθνη even if they were a non-Israelite ἔθνος. See Chapter 7 above.

1. Cornelius is introduced as a Roman soldier (even if he practices acts of Israelite piety).[36]
2. Caesarea had an overwhelmingly non-Israelite population.[37]
3. Cornelius' envoys mark the contrast between Cornelius and the entire Judean ἔθνος (note the envoys' use of the out-group categorical ethnic designation "Judean" rather than the insider "Israelite" in 10:22).
4. The Spirit's command to Peter (10:19–20) and Peter's proclamation in Cornelius' household implicate ethnic issues (10:34–35).
5. Cornelius disappears from Luke's narrative repetitions, indicating that he is less interesting as an individual than as an exemplar of his category—the ἔθνη (Acts 11:1–18; 15:7–11).[38]

8.1.4. The Spirit at the Ethnic Boundary

The section in Acts most concerned with ethnic boundaries is also the section containing the densest cluster of Spirit-references. Acts 10:1–11:18 contains eight references to the Spirit, with Acts 10:44–47 and 11:12–16 each containing three references in a handful of verses. This is paralleled only by the prologue (three occurrences in eight verses: 1:2, 5, 8) and the incorporation of the Samaritans (four occurrences in five verses: 8:15, 17, 18, 19). As we have seen throughout, wherever identity is in question Luke makes recourse to the Spirit.[39] A close reading of Acts 10:1–11:18 and 15:1–31 will demonstrate that this section brings to a climax Luke's Spirit-fueled identity-forming project by describing the Spirit's work to incorporate the ethnic "other" through the orchestration of intergroup contact, to identify "others" who properly belong to the Jesus group and to reconcile competing identities via the formation of a new social group marked by allocentrism.

8.1.5. The Spirit and the Orchestration of Intergroup Encounter

The Spirit orchestrates the interethnic encounter between Cornelius and Peter through a series of visions (cf. Acts 2:17). Cornelius has an angelic

---

36. Acts 10:1–2. Bauckham 2005, 113 notes that Cornelius, like all non-Israelites and irrespective of his piety, was likely suspected of being idolatrous.
37. Bock 2007, 385. See Rowe 2005 for Caesarea's social significance.
38. Witherup 1993, 56, 62 notes Cornelius' absence but not its significance.
39. The density of Spirit references at identity boundaries stands in contrast to the surprising absence of Spirit references in the Pauline missionary speeches. There are *no references to the Spirit* in Paul's evangelistic speeches in Acts 13, 14, 16, 17 and 18, and there are *no references to the Spirit* in Paul's legal defense speeches in Acts 22, 23, 24, 25, 26 and 27. This is an obstacle for those who hold to a "Spirit of prophecy" model that restricts the Spirit's work to the inspiration of missionary speech.

8. Transcending Ethnicity

vision (ὅραμα) commanding him to send men to Joppa to ask after Peter (Acts 10:3). Peter, in the midst of noontime hunger pangs, receives a vision three times (ἔκστασις in 10:10), receives direct clarification from the Spirit concerning the ὅραμα (10:19) and reports his experience to the Jerusalem disciples (ἔκστασις and ὅραμα in 11:5). This is the second time Luke has used a double vision—a convention that asserts divine control over an encounter—in order to show the Spirit's orchestration of an intergroup encounter (cf. Acts 9:10–12).[40] Finally, the direct speech of the Spirit in Acts 10:19–20 (as in Acts 8:29) sends Peter to the ethnic "other":

> While Peter was pondering the vision (ὅραμα) the Spirit said to him, "Behold, three men are looking for you. Rise and go down, and accompany them without discriminating (διακρίνω); for I have sent them."

Ultimately, it is *Spirit-given* direction, not Peter's vision, that drives Peter to mix with non-Israelites.[41] The Spirit's orchestration of the interethnic encounter between Peter and Cornelius is evidence that boundary maintenance for the in-group is being commandeered by the Holy Spirit.[42]

Peter's initial vision *is* relevant for intergroup contact insofar as it deals with a prominent marker of Israelite ethnic identity. Peter sees all manner of clean and unclean animals, and hears the command:

> Rise, Peter! Kill (θύειν) and eat![43]

But Peter protests vehemently:[44]

> By no means (μηδαμῶς), Lord! For I have never eaten anything common or unclean.[45]

---

40. Wikenhauser 1948, 100–111. Achilles Tatius, *Clitophon and Leucippe* 4.1.4–8; Apuleius, *The Golden Ass* 11.6, 13, 22.

41. Esler 1987, 94.

42. The relentless work of the Spirit will be acknowledged overtly by James in the climactic pericope of this section: "It seemed good to the Holy Spirit and to us…" (Acts 15:28).

43. Acts 10:13. Bock 2007, 389; Barrett 1994, 507 and O'Toole 1996 have suggested that θύειν should be translated "sacrifice." Luke uses θύειν to mean "sacrifice" on several occasions (Luke 22:7; Acts 14:13, 18), but also for the non-cultic slaughter of animals before consumption (Luke 15:23, 27, 30). Fitzmyer 1998, 455 denies ritual or sacrificial meaning in Acts 10:13; 11:7.

44. Wall 1987, 80 helpfully names a "reluctance" motif in Acts 10 and Jonah. "The point is that Jonah's God is Peter's God and both have the prerogative to extend life to non-Israelites."

45. Acts 10:14. μηδαμῶς only appears in the New Testament here and in Peter's retelling in 11:8.

Yet the voice reasserts the meaning of the vision:

What God has cleansed you must not call common.[46]

The vision is puzzling and Luke expects his hearers to think as much, for he depicts Peter twice ruminating on its meaning (Acts 10:17, 19).[47] Initially, the vision indicates the freedom of God to declare all animals clean; Peter is to make no distinction between the animals.[48] But we must go further to recognize that food laws were one of Israel's most prominent markers of ethnic distinction vis-à-vis the ἔθνη.[49]

It is not, however, until the additional direction given to Peter by the Spirit in 10:19–20 that the interethnic boundary comes into view.[50] It may be the case that the Spirit's command to "make no distinction" between Israelites and non-Israelites (Acts 10:20) is not a clarification of Peter's initial vision, but rather that Peter's initial vision indicated the ability of God to destabilize one sort of (ritual) boundary in preparation for the Spirit's destabilization of another sort of (ethnic) boundary. While detailed arguments have been made concerning the nature of the "Jew"/"Gentile" boundary, especially as it relates to moral or ritual purity, Luke's primary concern is with the ethnic boundary.[51] My claim is supported by two facts. First, non-Israelites were not subject to ritual purity laws until the Tosefta and Talmud.[52] Second, there is no Levitical law prohibiting social intercourse or shared meals with non-Israelites, though, of course, intermarriage and participation in idol worship were forbidden.[53] Luke's emphasis on the ethnic nature of the boundary in view (manifest in his use of the category name ἀδελφοί) makes it quite plausible that ritual impurity is not the barrier to intergroup interaction, but rather the barrier is constituted by the identity of the ethnic "other." This is further augmented by two points. Returning both to SIT and

---

46. Acts 10:15.
47. Turner 1996, 379.
48. Bock 2007, 389.
49. Bauckham 2005, 94 notes the connection between Levitical food purity laws and Israel's distinct identity.
50. Elliott 1991, 103: "Concern for the purity of blood lines is replicated in a concern for the purity of food."
51. For purity distinctions, see Klawans 2006, 266–84; Bauckham 2005, 91–142. For impurity in the era, see Büchler 1928; Hoenig 1970, 63–75; Frymer-Kensky 1983, 399–414; Milgrom 1991, 37–38, 44–45; Chilton and Neusner 1991, 63–88.
52. Bauckham 2005, 92.
53. There appears to have existed a general fear that association with non-Israelites would inevitably lead to idolatry (Bauckham 2005, 97). Esler 1998, 93–116 discusses the danger of eating food associated with idols in a non-Israelite home.

Barthian ethnic theory, it must be noted that ethnic difference (or difference in traditional practices) is not the *a priori cause* of ethnic identity or ethnic differentiation. Rather, ethnic identity arises as a *result* of intergroup contact, and unique ethnic identity markers develop as a *result* of the distinction. With regard to Israelite purity laws, there is a bit of a chicken and egg argument. Does Israel's divinely ordained purity code create an impermeable boundary with the ethnic other, or does intergroup differentiation cause a certain reading of purity laws that reinforces the group boundary already present? The latter seems most likely, especially given the lack of Israelite statutory prohibitions for intergroup contact. Second, Peter does not claim that commiserating with non-Israelites was considered ἄνομος, but rather ἀθέμιτος ("forbidden," "disgusting") in Acts 10:28.[54] Danker states that ἀθέμιτος is primarily not what is forbidden by "ordinance" but by "violation of tradition."[55] This seems to be Luke's usage, especially when compared to his use of ἄνομος in Luke 22:37 clearly to indicate a legal transgression, not just an action that breaks the "canons of decency."[56] Regardless of the exact relationship between the purity issues in Peter's initial vision and Israelite–non-Israelite relationships, the ethnic boundary is subverted ultimately only by the Spirit's direct command in Acts 10:19–20.

The Spirit tells Peter not to discriminate (διακρίνειν) concerning Cornelius' envoys. διακρίνειν can mean "hesitate," "discriminate" or "make a distinction between them and us." This is evidence that Peter perceives an intergroup (ethnic) boundary.[57] Peter's extension of hospitality (ξενίζειν, in 10:23) to the non-Israelites from Cornelius demonstrates that, given the Spirit's instruction, Luke's Peter thinks a certain level of social intercourse is now possible that previously was unlikely.[58]

---

54. Turner 1996, 378, 387 is somewhat imprecise when he notes that Peter is accused of eating with "unclean" men in 11:2–3. Peter is actually accused of eating with "uncircumcised" men. The distinction is primarily ethnic, not ritual.

55. BDAG, 124.

56. BDAG, 124. ἄνομος is frequently is equated with sin (Matt 23:28; Rom 4:7; 6:19; 2 Cor 6:14; Titus 2:14; Heb 1:9; 10:17). Cf. 2 Macc 6:5, which may indicate that clarification is necessary if something is *legally* (vs. socially) ἀθέμιτος.

57. Bauckham 2005, 105; Johnson 1992, 185. Luke uses the word with the stronger meaning in Acts 11:2, 12; 15:9, texts that solidify the claim that διακρίνειν refers not to "hesitation" but to distinctions between peoples. The stronger meaning is appropriate in intergroup settings (cf. 1 Cor 4:7; 6:5; 11:31; Jas 2:4). The softer meaning ("hesitate") is appropriate in situations of trust or discernment (cf. Matt 16:3; 21:21; Rom 4:20; 14:23; Jas 1:6; Jude 1:22). Luke uses ἀναντιρρήτως for "hesitation" (Acts 10:29).

58. "Guestfriendship" is a common theme in Greco-Roman community foundation stories (Wilson 2001, 77–99).

Peter's revelatory proclamation in Cornelius' household indicates that his (Spirit-mandated) refusal to differentiate (διακρίνειν) is a reflection of God's unwillingness to draw distinctions based upon ethnic origin:

> In truth I am understanding (καταλαμβάνομαι) that God shows no partiality (οὐκ ἔστιν προσωπολήμπτης), but in any nation (ἔθνος) anyone who fears him and does righteousness is acceptable (δεκτός) to him.[59]

This text provides rich irony in the light of Jesus' claim that he is not δεκτός among the people most closely related to him (his πατρίς) because he is unwilling to restrict the benefits of his ministry to his townsfolk (Luke 4:24). Now Luke reveals that every ἔθνος can be δεκτός to God, should they properly submit to the God of Israel. The benefits of God transcend ethnic distinctions. This recognition, and the experience that illustrates this fact, only occur through the Spirit's comprehensive orchestration of this interethnic encounter.

8.1.6. *The Spirit as the Marker of a Superordinate Identity*

The orchestrating work of the Spirit is only half of what is necessary for the incorporation of the ἔθνη into the Jesus group and hence the creation of a common superordinate social identity among formerly ethnic "others." Acts 10–11 gives Luke's clearest evidence that the Spirit functions as the definitive identity marker for those who are rightly identified with Jesus. First, Peter's speech to Cornelius draws on Luke's intergroup "peace" motif to emphasize that one result of the reorientation of identity around Jesus is reconciliation with the ethnic "other" (Acts 10:36; cf. Luke 1:79 where the ἀνατολή from on high brings peace).[60] Second, Luke's presentation of the falling of the Spirit upon the ἔθνη definitively identifies the Spirit as the agent that overcomes the "us" vs. "them" distinction.

Peter's speech is a masterful recapitulation of Luke's Gospel, recounting Jesus' ministry from Galilee to the ascension.[61] Several themes re-emerge here:

---

59. Acts 10:33–34, my translation. There is no sense that by "the ones fearing him" (10:35: ὁ φοβούμενος αὐτόν) Luke intends only a category of "god fearers." Israelites are called "god fearers" (Luke 1:50: τοῖς φοβουμένοις αὐτόν), Jesus uses the language in a parable (Luke 18:2: τὸν θεὸν μὴ φοβούμενος) and non-Israelites who are clearly not technically "god fearers" come to faith in Jesus (see especially Acts 17:34).

60. Rowe 2005 describes the poignancy of the "peace" motif in an imperial context. See Rowe 2009 for a comprehensive reading of Luke–Acts in the Roman context.

61. Johnson 1992, 195. The suggestion that Cornelius was a "Christian" prior to Peter's coming (Wilckens 1963, 46–50; Arrington 1988, 114) is not sustainable given both Cornelius' "worship" of Peter (10:25–26) and Peter's speech in Acts 15:7.

1. Peter's speech begins with ethnic particularity: the message of Jesus was sent to the υἱοῖς 'Ισραήλ.
2. The speech names Jesus, emphatically, as Lord of all (Acts 10:36: οὗτός ἐστιν πάντων κύριος).[62] The notion that Jesus is Lord not just of Israel but of *all* is theologically foundational for the fact that all non-Israelites can submit to Jesus *as non-Israelites*.
3. The claim that Jesus is Lord of all opens an inclusio that emphatically names Jesus as judge of all (Acts 10:42: οὗτός ἐστιν ὁ ὡρισμένος ὑπὸ τοῦ θεοῦ κριτής ζώντων καὶ νεκρῶν).[63] This should be taken as a counterpoint to the Spirit's command in Acts 10:20 that Peter should not διακρίνω when his non-Israelite courtiers arrive in Joppa. Jesus alone is the ordained judge of people.
4. Jesus is depicted as the prototypical Spirit-inspired figure in the speech. Jesus' filling with the Spirit causes Jesus to "do benefaction" (εὐεργετέω) and healings in order to free people from the power of the devil (Acts 10:38). The use of εὐεργετέω is significant in a Greco-Roman context.[64] As in Luke's Gospel, Jesus is the exemplar of Spirit-enabled allocentric identity.
5. The latter point reveals again the Spirit–Satan dichotomy and its resulting effect upon a community. Spirit-filled Jesus thwarts the work of the devil just as Satan-filled characters (Judas, Ananias and Sapphira, Simeon, and Elymas) can destroy the Spirit's work in the Jesus group.

Peter's "aha!" moment in Acts 10:34–35 leads to the recognition that God is at work to incorporate the ἔθνη into the Jesus-group. In Acts 10:36, this leads Luke's Peter to organize the message under the rubric "peace through Jesus Christ." I would translate the verse as follows:

τὸν λόγον [ὃν] ἀπέστειλεν τοῖς υἱοῖς 'Ισραὴλ εὐαγγελιζόμενος εἰρήνην διὰ 'Ιησοῦ Χριστοῦ, οὗτός ἐστιν πάντων κύριος.[65]

---

62. Rowe 2005 discusses the force of the construction.
63. Witherington 1998, 358.
64. See Danker 1982; Bock 2007, 398 for benefaction in the Greco-Roman context. Jesus' allocentric benefaction is displayed in Luke 22:25–27.
65. Barrett 1994, 521 considers the verse nearly "untranslatable." If we retain ὃν (the majority and most difficult reading: P⁷⁴, ℵ, C, D, E, Ψ, *Byz*. Omitted in ℵ¹, A, B, 81) the relative pronoun is the direct object of οἴδατε in 10:37. This renders the phrase "the proclamation of good news of peace through Jesus Christ" and places it as the centerpiece of the message. My reading is with Fitzmyer 1998, 463 and Parsons and Culy 2003, 210, but against Witherington 1998, 356, who takes the statement as an apposition to the preceding clause, and Barrett 1994, 521–22, who suggests either dropping ὃν or assuming that "Luke, after writing his parenthesis (this Jesus is Lord

The word which he sent to the sons of Israel, proclaiming good news—
peace through Jesus Christ (this one is Lord of all). (my translation)

The message of "peace" through Jesus Christ is a result of the fact that Jesus is Lord of "all." This paradigmatic interethnic encounter is the only time in Acts that the apostolic kerygma is classified as a message of "peace." I have already demonstrated that other significant "peace" passages focus on the potential for real intergroup peace even with non-Israelites (esp. Luke 1:79; 2:14; Acts 9:31). The effect of narrative accumulation, building from Luke's earlier deployments of εἰρήνη, makes it highly likely that Acts 10:36 is another example of the surprising fact that peace with the enemies of Israel (in this case no less than a mid-ranking Roman military official) will come not through their destruction but through reconciliation and incorporation.[66]

Returning again to Acts 10:34–35, we can now see how the identity-marking function of the Spirit allows for the formation of a common identity that results in interethnic "peace" between Israelites and non-Israelites. καταλαμβάνω, for Luke, is closely connected to the discovery or comprehension of something that heretofore was unknown, a nuance consistent with Peter's ongoing identity-transformation in Acts.[67] προσωπολήμπτης and its verbal cognates appear in the New Testament consistently to indicate the fact that God treats each person according to their own relationship to him and not according to their social standing (Israelite/non-Israelite; master/slave, etc).[68] The word has its origins in a conflation of the LXX πρόσωπόν λαβεῖν and emerges as a key term for the impartiality of God that is also required of humans.[69] The point of Peter's declaration is clear: with God there is no bias on the basis of group identity.[70]

---

of All), forgot how the sentence was intended to run." Witherington's view would support my thesis because it would set God's refusal to make a distinction between peoples at the center of the gospel proclamation.

66. O'Toole 1996 suggests that "peace" here implies all the other nuances of "peace" throughout Luke–Acts. Thus, the word encapsulates the fullness of life described by the Hebrew *shalom*. O'Toole makes some reference to peace as the antithesis of "division" in Acts (p. 467), but he does not develop the intergroup implications of "peace."

67. See Acts 4:13; 25:25.

68. Rom 2:1; Eph 6:9; Col 3:25; Jas 2:1, 9. Cf. 1 Pet 1:17: ἀπροσωπολήμπτης.

69. See 2 Kgs 3:14; Lev 19:15; Deut 10:17; Ps 81:2 LXX; *Pss. Sol.* 2:18. For later usage, see *1 Clem* 1.3; *Epistle of Barnabas* 4.12; Polycarp, *Letter to the Philippians* 6.1. See the discussion in Johnson 1992, 191.

70. Interestingly, and further to this point, there are two things that God "remembers" (μιμνήσκομαι) in Luke–Acts: (1) the Abrahamic covenant in Luke 1:54,

What Peter recognizes cognitively in Acts 10:34–35 is depicted experientially—and definitively—in Acts 10:44–48. While Peter is still speaking the Spirit falls on the whole non-Israelite household of Cornelius. This obliterates ethnicity as a basis for intergroup comparison.[71] Here it becomes clear that Luke does not view "salvation" merely as a status conferred. Believers do not simply receive the status "saved"; they are incorporated into God's trans-ethnic people, a new social reality sharing a common identity. The language of the text highlights the fact that the Spirit is, in Luke's view, both source and evidence of that shared identity.[72] The following textual features highlight the identity formation of this one new people, the transformation (and retention) of subgroup identities and the role of the Spirit in these transformations:

1. The falling of the Spirit "even upon the non-Israelites" (καὶ ἐπὶ τὰ ἔθνη) amazes (ἐξίστημι) the "believers from the circumcision" (Acts 10:45). Apparently, even given Peter's new understanding that non-Israelites can be acceptable to God, nobody in Luke's narrative frame expected the Spirit to be given to non-Israelites *as non-Israelites*.[73]

2. The Spirit-manifestation is audible (and possibly visible). Every other visible/audible manifestation of the Spirit in Luke–Acts has served definitively to identify the person(s) in question (especially Luke 3:22; Acts 2:18; 8:17). The Spirit-manifestation marks

---

72 and (2) the almsgiving of a non-Israelite in Acts 10:31, a figure who is incorporated into the people of God *because of God's faithfulness to the Abrahamic covenant* (cf. Acts 3:25).

71. See Esler 1992, 136–42; Borgen 1994, 220–35 for tongues and social boundary crossing. Menzies 1991, 265, despite an absence of evidence for missionary proclamation, insists that this remains the "Spirit of prophecy" and that "we may presume that the prophetic band in Caesarea…by virtue of the pneumatic gift participated effectively in the missionary enterprise." Dunn 1970, 231–32 considers the Spirit to be the bearer of forgiveness here, based on a retroactive reading of a parallel between 11:17 and 11:18.

72. Menzies 1991, 265 is representative of the overwhelming number of scholars who recognize in this instance that the Spirit marks "Gentile" incorporation into the "community of salvation." Yet scholars do not regularly differentiate between common *status* as "saved" and common *identity* as a co-community member (cf. Acts 3:23). There is, indeed, a great practical difference. Cf. Cho 2005, 154.

73. Turner 1998, 346: "Their participation in the Spirit of prophecy shows that Cornelius' household has a part in the "Israel" the Messiah is cleansing/restoring by the Spirit." Turner is surely correct (though he does not grapple with the disappearance of the category "Israel" after Acts 15). I extend his position by examining what, precisely, happens to existing ethnic identities.

Cornelius and his family as δοῦλοι and δοῦλαι of God (cf. Acts 2:18) without requiring a social conversion to become a part of ethnic Israel.
3. Luke highlights the common identity shared by these ἔθνη and the Jesus group by using the verb ἐκχέω to describe the Spirit's falling in Acts 10:45, a word only used to describe the Spirit event at Pentecost (Acts 2, 17, 18, 33). The Spirit falls on non-Israelites in the *exact same manner* as it fell paradigmatically upon Israelite Jesus-followers in Acts 2.
4. Luke uses "us"/"them" language to describe the common experience of the Spirit in Acts 10:47. Non-Israelites can be baptized because "*these*" (τούτους) have received the Holy Spirit just like "*us*" (ἡμεῖς).
5. Peter's decision to baptize the members of Cornelius' household is the sign of their full incorporation into the Jesus group.
6. Peter remains with Cornelius for some days (Acts 10:48), an indication that Peter has also experienced identity transformation based upon the Spirit-attested fact that there is no distinction based upon ethnic identity.

Peter's identity transformation is underscored again by Luke's use of an inclusio framed by κωλύω/κολλάω in Acts 10:28 and 10:47 (cf. Acts 8:29, 36):

> You yourselves know how forbidden (ἀθέμιτος) it is for a Judean to unite with (κολλάω) or to visit any one of another nation (ἔθνος).[74]

> Is anyone able to forbid (κωλύω) water, that these who have received the Spirit just as we did should not be baptized?[75]

The Spirit overcomes Peter's identity-based reluctance to "be united to" (κολλάω) the ethnic "other" and Peter recognizes he cannot forbid (κωλύω) the Spirit-orchestrated incorporation of the "other" into full membership in Peter's own in-group. This full incorporation is effected by the surprising *pre-baptismal* arrival of the Spirit, and subsequently is marked by baptism and commensality (Acts 10:47–48). In SIT terms, what has occurred in the Cornelius episode is the creation of a superordinate social identity capable of transcending interethnic barriers.[76]

74. My translation.
75. My translation.
76. Turner 1996, 386 overlooks the community-forming role of the Spirit with regard to ethnic "others" when he suggests that the significance of the incorporation of "God-fearers" is that (1) they counterbalance "Jewish" rejection of the gospel and (2) they diminished the offense of the "law free" gospel because of their "Jewish"

By virtue of their incorporation into the Jesus group, both the ἔθνη of Cornelius' household and Peter's Israelite group experience identity transformation, now drawing their identity from their shared group membership. In the case of the characters from Acts 10, it is clear that this new identity is superordinate because it allows for expressions of intergroup behavior among diverse ethnic identities that were heretofore considered deviant (ἀθέμιτος; cf. 11:2-3) prior to the Spirit's work in incorporating non-Israelites into the group. This new identity transcends ethnic identity, yet ethnic particularity is not obliterated.

8.2. Criticism in Jerusalem: Evidence of an Intractable Boundary

The immediate reaction to Cornelius' incorporation indicates that the ethnic boundary is stubborn and reflects a prompt cultivation of Israelite subgroup distinctiveness in an effort to defend Israelite identity. The subgroup is categorized by Luke as "the believers from the circumcision" (Acts 10:45: οἱ ἐκ περιτομῆς τιστοί).[77] This is the second time (with the incident in Acts 6:1-7) that the incorporation of some category of "other" has led immediately to the reassertion of subgroup distinctiveness. The immediacy of this new subgroup identification is striking: in Acts 10:44 the Spirit falls on the ἔθνη, obliterating ethnic barriers, and in Acts 10:45 we are introduced for the first time to a subgroup identified as "circumcised," a category that arises again in Acts 11:2. From a social identity perspective, this reflects the fact that while the falling of the Spirit has created a common trans-ethnic identity, some Israelites clung to their ethnic identity as a means for creating intragroup differentiation between themselves and non-Israelite Jesus-followers. This should not be taken as an already-formed "conservative" Israelite subgroup existing among the larger community of Israelite Jesus-followers.[78] It is simply the new subgroup boundary with which Israelite Jesus-followers differentiate themselves *en toto* from non-Israelite Jesus-followers *en toto*.[79] This is expressed in Acts 11:3:

---

sympathies. This neglects Luke's boundary language and identity language, which points to the importance of this group not as God-fearing "Gentiles" but as ethnic non-Israelites. To this point, it would seem unlikely that all the "relatives and close friends" assembled by Cornelius would fit into the technical category "God-fearer."

77. Acts 10:45.
78. Johnson 1992, 197 thinks that "the circumcision" is already a distinct ideological group within the church.
79. So Bauckham 2005, 116-17.

Εἰσῆλθες πρὸς ἄνδρας ἀκροβυστίαν ἔχοντας καὶ συνέφαγες αὐτοῖς.

You went to uncircumcised me and ate with them! (my translation—though this follows the NAS)

The judgment (διακρίνω, Acts 11:2) against Peter for his transgression of ethnic boundaries is a statement of accusation (not a question, as in the RSV) and makes intergroup comparison on the basis of an identity marker (circumcision) that heretofore was irrelevant within the Jesus-community.[80] Peter responds with a defense speech that is a *tour de force* of common identity, but he does not call for a relinquishment of ethnic particularity:

1. The *Spirit* told Peter to go with the men from Joppa without discriminating (Acts 11:12: διακρίνω).[81]
2. The Spirit fell upon the non-Israelites as Peter was *beginning* to speak (Acts 11:15). The Spirit-interruption, which preceded any description of repentance, highlights the free action of God in accepting non-Israelites.
3. Peter uses "us"/"them" language to connect the experience of the ἔθνη to the paradigmatic experience at Pentecost, and thus demonstrates that the Spirit is the marker of a common identity: "The Holy Spirit fell on them (αὐτοὺς) just as (ὥσπερ) on us (ἡμᾶς) at the beginning" (Acts 11:15).
4. Peter recalls Jesus' teaching: "John baptized with water, but you (ὑμεῖς) will be baptized with the Holy Spirit" (Acts 11:16). The falling of the Spirit on the ἔθνη indicates that they are members *of the same group* implicated in Jesus' teaching to his (Galilean Israelite) disciples in Acts 1:5. The ἔθνη and the Israelite believers together constitute the plural "you" used by Jesus.
5. In Acts 11:17 Peter makes the logical assertion that faith in Jesus is marked by reception of the Spirit:
    a. "If then God gave the same gift to them (αὐτοῖς) as he gave to us (ἡμῖν) *when we believed in the Lord Jesus Christ*, who was I that I could withstand (κωλύω) God?"
    b. The reception of the Spirit marks the ἔθνη as servants of God (cf. Acts 2:18) and transcends the "us"/"them" ethnic distinction.

---

80. Ironically, the circumcised believers do to Peter (Acts 11:2) what the Spirit commanded Peter not to do on the basis of ethnic identity (Acts 10:20: διακρίνω).
81. Witherup 1993, 53 suggests the change of order—moving Peter's vision to the fore—highlights divine initiative.

6. Once again the Spirit overcomes human resistance (Acts 11:17: κωλύω), joining the "other" to Jesus and, by extension, to the Jesus group (cf. Acts 8:36; 10:47).

The Jerusalem brothers rejoice that God has given repentance unto life "even to the non-Israelites" (Acts 11:18: καὶ τοῖς ἔθνεσιν). Yet there is a significant gap between the accession of the Jerusalem brothers in 11:18 and the declaration of James in Acts 15:13–21.[82] It appears that Peter is convinced, through the Spirit's orchestration and identification, that there is no terminal identity differentiation between Israelites and non-Israelites who submit to Jesus. Yet the response of the Jerusalem believers ("God has given even to the non-Israelites repentance into life" [Acts 11:18]) implies *shared status*, but not *shared identity*.[83] This is highlighted by the apparent salience of ethnic subgroup identity (Acts 10:45; 11:3) and is a good example of social creativity—the attempt to maintain positive group identity by choosing alternative comparative criteria (here, circumcision vs. uncircumcision instead of Jesus-follower vs. non-Jesus-follower).[84] This is a common defense mechanism among social minorities who feel a sense of threatened identity.[85] In cases like these, minority groups elevate their distinctives or risk losing their group identity. The result of Israelite subgroup differentiation is that non-Israelites have been given repentance unto life, but they are not yet ἀδελφοί.

8.3. Acts 15: The Spirit and the Intragroup Expression of a New Identity

The projection of Israelite subgroup prototypicality (or, for Luke, any subgroup prototypicality) is a barrier to the development of common identity and, indeed, to the gospel. It arises again in Acts 15, the chapter Luke uses as the linchpin of his identity-forming project. In this section I

---

82. Wenk 2004, 301 is correct that the gift of the Spirit to non-Israelites testified to the membership of "Gentiles" in the people of God. He is wrong, I think, to call this entire body "restored Israel" without at least grappling with Luke's abandonment of the category "Israel" after Acts 15. Further, while he is correct that the gift of the Spirit to "Gentiles" "redefined the community at the same time," he has sped ahead of the text. Full incorporation via creation of a common superordinate identity does not occur until Acts 15.

83. This is noteworthy for those who think Acts 15 and Acts 11 involve the same decision. As we will see, Acts 11 does not establish common identity in the way Acts 15 does.

84. Dietz-Uhler and Murrell 1998, 25.

85. Tajfel 1981, 309–15.

will demonstrate that Luke's antithesis between divine and human intergroup boundary maintenance, especially as evident in the "unvarying kernel" extant in Luke's retellings of the Cornelius event, firmly establishes the role of the Spirit in the incorporation of non-Israelites *as non-Israelites* into the community of faith. Luke magnifies the boundary crossing work of the Spirit by presenting James as a *prototypical Israelite* and thus as the member of the early community who fully understands the relationship between the particularity of ethnic identity and the transethnic identity available through the Spirit. Finally, and climactically, I will demonstrate definitive evidence for the existence (at least in Luke's view) of a new, allocentric, Spirit-formed superordinate group identity that affirms yet chastens and transcends ethnic identity.

8.3.1. *Human Action vs. Divine Action at the Group Boundary*

In a typical social group, intergroup boundaries are maintained by group members themselves who act collectively in an evaluative process that aims positively to differentiate the in-group from the out-group. We see precisely this process in the activity of the "men from Judea" in Acts 15:1 who exert boundary control by teaching, "Unless you are circumcised according to the custom of Moses you cannot be saved." At stake here, viewed through Luke's inseparable relationship between community membership and "salvation" (cf. Acts 3:23), is "salvation" itself. The implicit claim of the "men from Judea" is that "salvation" (which has many features, primary among which is full membership and participation in the people of God) is only available to those who assimilate to the projected prototypicality of the ethnic Israelite subgroup.[86] Luke understands this to be a *human* impulse in its origin and execution, a fact made clear by the declaration of certain Jesus-following Pharisees in Acts 15:5:

> It is necessary (δεῖ) to circumcise them, and to charge them to keep the law of Moses.

The boundary-securing claim of the Pharisees implies an action *done by* ethnic insiders *to* ethnic outsiders and its emphatic nature is underscored by the use of δεῖ, a word normally used by Luke to indicate the divine plan.[87]

---

86. It is essential to note that some, but by no means all, ethnic Israelites held this position in Acts 15.

87. On Luke's use of δεῖ, see Cosgrove 1984, 168–90. Bock 2007, 496 thinks the use of δεῖ means this is perceived by the Pharisees to be a divine necessity.

Luke sets this attempted maintenance of the intergroup boundary in contrast with the divine maintenance of the boundary enacted by the Spirit.[88] The retelling of Cornelius' incorporation in Acts 15 is highly abbreviated, and Peter makes only five points:

1. *God* chose Peter to be the person through whom non-Israelites would hear the gospel and believe (Acts 15:7).
2. *God* has testified to the hearts of the non-Israelites by giving them the Spirit just as he had to the Israelites (Acts 15:8: ἡμῖν).
3. *God* has not made a distinction (διακρίνω) between *them* (αὐτῶν) and *us* (ἡμῶν), but has cleansed their hearts by faith (Acts 15:9).
4. We should not test (πειράζω) God by putting a yoke on the neck of the disciples (μαθητῶν) that the ethnic Israelites and their forbearers had been unable to bear (Acts 15:10).[89]
5. Through the grace of the Lord Jesus Christ *we* believe to be saved just as *they* (Acts 15:11).

Peter's testimony reflects the divine maintenance of community boundaries, especially through the work of the Spirit. *God does not discriminate* (διακρίνω) *on the basis of ethnic identity*. God is no mere tribal deity, but Lord of all peoples.[90] God chose Peter to go to the ἔθνη, God testified to the non-Israelites by giving them the Spirit and God did not make a distinction based upon ethnic identity.[91] The work of God is the discerning and cleansing of the human heart and subsequent navigation of the boundaries of the Jesus-following in-group. This is set in stark contrast to the boundary maintenance suggested by some Jesus-following Pharisees in Acts 15:5.

Spirit-maintenance of the intergroup boundary becomes even more evident when examining the "unvarying kernel" contained in Luke's triple telling of Cornelius' incorporation. The common thread that runs through this triplet is itself threefold:

88. Commentators largely overlook the contrast between human and divine maintenance of the group's boundary; see Fitzmyer 1998, 545–48; Bock 2007, 496. Marshall 1980, 248–50 notes God's initiative evident in Peter's speech, but does not contrast it with 15:5. So also Witherup 1993, 61; Conzelmann 1987, 116–17. Wall 2002, 207 notes that the issue has shifted from "soteriology to sociology," though, as we have seen, Luke does not seem to make this distinction but instead sees community incorporation (sociology) as one (essential) aspect of salvation.
89. It is possible that Peter's use of μαθητής is another indicator that Peter is convinced that the ethnic boundary is no longer operative within the people of God. Cf. the use of μαθητής and ἀδελφοί earlier in Acts 9–14 to indicate the type of intragroup boundary in view.
90. Lotz 1988, 201. Cf. Paul's concern in Rom 3:29–30.
91. Acts 15:8–10.

1. God's refusal to make a distinction based upon ethnic identity overwhelms the human tendency to form intergroup boundaries based upon ethnicity.[92]
2. The *Spirit* testifies to those whom God determines to be rightly related to him through the Lord Jesus.[93]
3. The group must not resist God by erecting barriers to the work of incorporation, reconciliation and identity-formation which God appears to be doing between non-Israelites and Israelites.[94]

This is combined with the striking fact that all mention of Cornelius as an individual drops from the retellings.[95] This functions to emphasize Cornelius' *social* identity as a non-Israelite and is unsurprising given they way Luke regularly uses individuals to represent their social group.[96] The clear point of the repetition of the Cornelius narrative in Acts 11:1-18 and 15:7-11 is that God himself placed no barrier between non-Israelites and participation in the people of God, and that resistance to this movement is nothing less than a struggle against God. In Peter's view, the Spirit has fully commandeered maintenance of the Jesus group's social boundary.[97] Thus the work of the Spirit explicitly resists ethnic hegemonies and exclusion based upon interethnic boundaries.

8.3.2. *James the Prototypical Israelite: The Universal Particularity of Spirit-formed Identity*

James' role in the meeting in Jerusalem is pivotal and it is his first explicit appearance in Acts (cf., implicitly, Acts 1:14). Both Acts and the broader

---

92. Acts 10:20, 27-28, 34-35; 11:12, 15:9. Dunn 1996, 200 goes so far as to say that Peter had been "forced by clear directive and approval from God to accept a Gentile."

93. Acts 10:44-47; 11:15-17; 15:8. Dunn 1996, 201 notes that the "Spirit is the central figure in this process of conversion-initiation." I agree, and press further to insist that the Spirit does not just "initiate" the non-Israelites, it *incorporates* them *en route* to the formation of a common identity. My distinction differs from that of Bock 2007, 500, who states that the gift of the Spirit "bore witness to their genuine response and God's acceptance of them." Proper response and divine acceptance are indicated already at Acts 11:18. Common identity, acknowledged for the first time in Acts 15, is yet one step further.

94. Acts 10:47; 11:17; 15:10.

95. Witherup 1993, 56 notes Cornelius' absence and suggests this highlights Peter's role and makes Cornelius a representative of the "Gentile world."

96. Cf. Ananias as representative of the Damascus disciples (Acts 9:10-20) and Philip as an exemplar of the early community (Acts 8:26-40).

97. Wenk 2004, 307 notes the church's submission to the Spirit's authority here. This acknowledgment can be extended by situating it in light of normal intragroup processes.

historical portrait of James indicate that he was held in high esteem by Israelites and non-Israelites. James was a "pillar of the church" (Gal 2:9). Eusebius suggests that James was the first "bishop" of the Jerusalem church.[98] Josephus reports that exemplary Israelites in Jerusalem honored James after his execution by Ananus (ca. 62 C.E.).[99] The *Gospel of Thomas* also takes a high view of James.[100] Though often depicted as a strong advocate of the Mosaic Law and "conservative Jewish Christianity," Luke presents James as a prototypical mix of ethnic particularity and the Spirit-empowered allocentrism characteristic of Luke's view of the Spirit.[101] This is evident in several nuanced hints regarding James' identity, his hermeneutical logic and his unwillingness to make Israelite ethnic markers the primary identity markers for the Jesus group.

James begins his speech with the address, ἄνδρες ἀδελφοί (Acts 15:13), and so indicates both the ethnic boundary in view and that James fully identifies as an ethnic Israelite.[102] James then alludes to the explanation by "Simeon" regarding God's decision to take a people for his name from the non-Israelites (Acts 15:14). Interpreters have wondered about Luke's reference to Simon/Simeon, with some suggesting that this refers to the conflation of two separate meetings with the second reflecting a decision involving Simeon of Niger (Acts 13:1) or, more idiosyncratically (though tantalizing in its implications), perhaps even Simeon from Luke 2:25.[103] But one need not look so far afield for a plausible reason for Luke's use of the Hebraicized version of "Simon." Bauckham has shown the widespread use of variant versions of names based upon differing linguistic contexts. Simon, the most commonly attested Hebrew name in the period, "was at one and the same time the Hebrew name Simeon and the Greek name Simon, with the latter treated virtually as the spelling in Greek letters of the Hebrew name."[104] Evidence in 1 Macc 2:3, 65 indicates that both "Simon" and "Simeon" can be used to refer to the same

---

98. *Ecclesiastical Histories* 2.23.4–7.
99. Josephus, *A.J.* 20.197–203.
100. *Gospel of Thomas* 12.
101. See Lockett 2008, who gives a more nuanced description of James' epistle, noting that James is not sectarian in a manner that calls for complete detachment from the surrounding culture. Lockett instead posits that purity is required for perfection, and requires a nuanced approach to cultural interactions. See also Harland 2003.
102. Luke is here still following a pattern in which ἀδελφοί can only refer to Israelites.
103. For Simeon of Niger, see Fitzmyer 1998, 552–53; for Simeon of Luke 2, see Reisner 1994, 263–78, a view shared by Chrysostom.
104. Bauckham 2006, 72.

person.¹⁰⁵ Luke is not conflating sources or events; he is describing James as a high-identifying ethnic Israelite. James alone, in all the Gospels and Acts, refers to his ethnic (and Jesus-following) brother Simon with the Hebraicized version of his name—Simeon—and thus reveals his own Galilean Aramaic-speaking background and identity.¹⁰⁶

The quick juxtaposition of James' address to his "brothers" in Acts 15:13 and his use of the Hebraicized "Simeon" in Acts 15:14 leads directly into the beginning of a hermeneutical logic which allows Luke to paint this prototypically Israelite leader of the community as one who deeply understands the relationship between Israel's privileged covenantal identity, the Spirit and ethnic particularity. This is evident in two ways. First, James interprets Peter's testimony as an indication that "*God visited* (ἐπισκέπτομαι) to take from the non-Israelites (ἔθνη) a people (λαός) for his name" (Acts 15:14). Seven of the eleven occurrences of ἐπισκέπτομαι in the New Testament occur in Luke.¹⁰⁷ While the word can mean "to select from" (Acts 6:3), Luke's most common usage is "to visit" (Luke 1:68, 78; 7:16). The sense "to visit" is most likely in Acts 15:14, not least because the word appears in this sense in 15:36. Moreover, whenever the subject of the verb is God/Jesus/an eschatological figure (Luke 1:68, 78; 7:16; Acts 15:14) the sense is always "to visit." The verb twice is used to describe God's visitation of his people in Zechariah's praise hymn (Luke 1:68, 78). In its initial appearance (1:68) it describes simply God's visitation of his people Israel. In its second appearance, the "visitation" (ἐπισκέπτομαι) of the ἀνατολή will

> give light to those who sit in darkness and in the shadow of death, to guide our feet into the way of peace.¹⁰⁸

I have argued, partly on the basis of this *Spirit-inspired* hymn of Zechariah, that "those who sit in darkness and the shadow of death" refers to non-Israelites, a feature that allows Luke to develop a theme of inter-ethnic peace with former enemies.¹⁰⁹ The language ascribed to James in Acts 15:14 is thus reminiscent of Luke's penchant for describing the in-breaking work of God as a "visitation" that includes non-Israelites and that can result in just the sort of *peace* implied by the creation of a singular λαός.

---

105. Bockmuehl 2005, 53–90.
106. Cf. 2 Pet 1:1.
107. Luke 1:68, 78; 7:16; Acts 6:3; 7:23; 15:14, 36.
108. Luke 1:79.
109. See discussion in Chapter 3.

Second, James includes for the first time non-Israelites as clear members of the formerly ethnically homogenous in-group called λαός. For Luke, prior to Acts 15:14 λαός in the singular *only refers to ethnic Israelites*.[110] After Acts 15:14, the usage of singular λαός becomes fluid, describing mainly non-believing Israelites but also used *to include non-Israelite believers* (Acts 18:10).[111] Bauckham is correct to note that James cannot conceive of the possibility of two peoples of God.[112] This prototypical Israelite's recognition that Israelites and non-Israelites compose the singular λαός of God is a major step on the way to the construction of a group identity that transcends ethnic identities.[113] This observation will have a hermeneutical payoff in ruling out one common suggestion regarding the prohibitions in the Jerusalem Decree.

James' use of Amos 9:11–12 LXX in Acts 15:16–18a further emphasizes his awareness that Israelites and non-Israelites share a common identity as the one people of God. While many passages describe the nations joining the people of God *as non-Israelites*, Amos 9:12 provides the only Old Testament instance in which non-Israelites (ἔθνη) are named as those over (or "upon") whom the name of God is called (πάντα τὰ ἔθνη ἐφ' οὓς ἐπικέκληται τὸ ὄνομά μου ἐπ' αὐτούς).[114] The phrase reflects an Old Testament tradition in which "the divine name is invoked over a thing (the temple, the ark, Jerusalem) or person(s) (e.g. Israel), indicating that a relationship of God's dominion and possession is established."[115] James thus declares that non-Israelites belong to God *as non-Israelites*.[116] Some

---

110. Singular λαός: Luke 1:10, 17, 21, 68, 77; 2:10, 32; 3:15, 18, 21; 6:17; 7:1, 16, 29; 8:47; 9:13; 18:43; 19:47, 48; 20:1, 6, 9, 19, 26, 45; 21:23, 38; 22:2, 66; 23:5, 13, 14, 35, 37; 24:19; Acts 2:47; 3:9, 11, 12, 23; 4:1, 2, 8, 10, 17, 21; 5:12, 13, 20, 25, 26, 34, 37; 6:8, 12; 7:17, 34; 10:2, 41, 42; 12:4, 11; 13:15, 17, 24, 31; 15:14; 18:10; 19:4; 21:28, 30, 36, 39, 40; 23:5; 26:17, 23; 28:17, 26, 27. Plural λαός: Luke 2:31; Acts 4:25, 27.

111. Acts 26:23 demonstrates that Paul can still work with these categories for unbelieving non-Israelites.

112. Bauckham 2005, 117.

113. DuPont 1985 rightly emphasizes that this is "one" people but he does not unpack the ramifications for ethnic identity.

114. Amos 9:12 LXX, Acts 15:17b. For other examples of non-Israelites coming to God as non-Israelites, see Ps 96:7–8; Isa 2:2–3; 25:6; 56:6–7; 66:23; Jer 3:17; Mic 4:1–2; Zech 14:16; *1 En.* 90:33.

115. Van de Sandt 1992, 89. For other uses, see 2 Sam 6:2; 1 Kgs 8:43; 2 Chr 7:14; Jer 14:9; Dan 9:19, and so on.

116. The reference to the "fallen tent of David" (Amos 9:11 LXX // Acts 15:16) has been interpreted as referring to the "people of Israel" (cf. Luke 1:69; Isa 7:2, 12; Jer 21:12; Zech 12:7–12), the Temple (cf. Neh 12:37) or the people of God as the eschatological Temple (Bauckham 1996).

commentators have suggested that the use of the LXX by such a "conservative" Israelite figure as James betrays the unhistorical nature of Luke's account, but this precisely misses the point.[117] The LXX provides the key alteration of the MT that makes the passage suitable for James' conclusion that non-Israelites as non-Israelites are equal members of the people of God. The MT version of Amos 9:12b reads:

> That they [the rebuilt tent of David from Amos 9:11] may possess (יִרְשׁ)
> the remnant of Edom and all the nations (גוים) over whom my name is
> called. (my translation)

Compare this with the LXX version of Amos 9:12b:

> ὅπως ἐκζητήσωσιν οἱ κατάλοιποι τῶν ἀνθρώπων καὶ πάντα τὰ ἔθνη,
> ἐφ' οὕς ἐπικέκληται τὸ ὄνομά μου ἐπ' αὐτούς.
>
> In order that they might seek me, the rest of the peoples and all the non-Israelites, upon whom my name has been called. (my translation)

In the MT reading, non-Israelites are incorporated but only after subjection to Israel. In the LXX reading, there is no sense of the ἔθνη being subservient to Israel or even to the ἔθνη living like Lev 17–18 aliens in the land of Israel. The point of James' use of Amos 9:11–12 LXX is that the key factor in the new work of God is the possession of a single people by God; they are one λαός, possessed by God who, as the world's one true Lord, has called his name over/upon them.[118] It is likely not coincidental, given the Spirit-based reasoning of James' decision, that the only other entity that comes upon/over non-Israelites in Acts is the Spirit itself:[119]

> καὶ ἐπὶ τὰ ἔθνη ἡ δωρεὰ τοῦ ἁγίου πνεύματος ἐκκέχυται.
>
> Even upon the non-Israelites the gift of the Holy Spirit has been poured out. (Acts 10:45, my translation)

---

117. Barrett 1998b, xxxvii–xxxviii.
118. Bauckham 1996, 170 suggests that the possible baptismal formula [τὸ] ὄνομα τὸ ἐπικληθέν ἐφ' ὑμᾶς in Jas 2:7 could be a secondary attestation of "incorporation of the Gentiles into the eschatological people of God with no requirements for admission other than baptism in the name of Jesus." The Epistle of *James* and Luke's *James* in Acts 15 produce the only two occurrences of this phrase in the New Testament. Cf. Sir 36:12; Bar 2:15, 26; 1 Macc 7:37; 1 Esd 4:63 for Second Temple occurrences of [τὸ] ὄνομα τὸ ἐπικληθέν ἐφ' ὑμᾶς which refer only to Israelites or Israelite institutions.
119. Darr 1992, 53 has alerted us to the fact that the Spirit inspires all authoritative interpretation in Luke–Acts. Levison 1999; 2009 sees inspired interpretation as one of the primary functions of the Spirit in Second Temple texts.

8. Transcending Ethnicity

καὶ πάντα τὰ ἔθνη ἐφ᾽ οὓς ἐπικέκληται τὸ ὄνομά μου ἐπ᾽ αὐτούς.

Even all the non-Israelites upon whom my name has been called. (Acts 15:17, my translation)

For Luke, the coming of the Spirit upon a person definitively identifies that person as God's possession (or "servant" [Acts 2:18], or "witness" [Acts 1:8]).

It is noteworthy that Luke has James cite the Greek rendering of Israel's prophets. Bauckham has demonstrated that Luke can rely on MT texts.[120] But I suggest that Luke uses James' recitation of the LXX to accommodate the members of the community who would have been included in a subservient sense were Luke to have given James Amos 9:12 MT as a text.[121] In Luke's portrayal, James is fully Israelite in his language, manner and custom, yet he understands that the privileged identity of Israel is for the sake of the nations.[122] Thus he uses a language aprototypical for the Israelite in-group to make a key point about a superordinate identity that can incorporate both Israelites and non-Israelites. James maintains his ethnic particularity, but his own ethnic identity is subjected to his identity formed by membership in the Jesus group.

8.3.3. The Jerusalem Decree: An Injunction Against the Trappings of Idolatry

James claims to give the definitively proper "judgment" (κρίνω cf. Luke's concern against ethnic διακρίνω) that the ἔθνη who are turning to God should not be troubled.[123] Proper interpretation of the Decree has ramifications for precisely which ethnic identity markers must be abandoned and which can be retained in this trans-ethnic group. Three basic positions exist regarding the significance of the Decree's prohibitions.[124] First, the Decree is a reflection of Noachide laws applicable to universal humanity. This is argued most thoroughly by Bockmuehl, who acknowledges Rabbinic genesis of the definitive Noachide tradition, but suggests the possibility that "proto"-Noachide laws undergirded the Decree.[125]

---

120. Bauckham 2001, 435–87.
121. See Chapter 4 for evidence that Hebrew/Aramaic was the anticipated language of restored Israel. Bauckham 1995, 415–80 shows that the MT version of Amos was known to the Jerusalem church. It follows that the decision to use the LXX was quite deliberate by James and/or Luke.
122. James' "pastoral" sensitivity to inter-ethnic issues is apparent again in Jerusalem in Acts 21:20–25.
123. Acts 15:19.
124. See Proctor 1996 for overview of positions.
125. Bockmuehl 2000, 164. Bockmuehl is followed in part by Taylor 2001, who suggests that James interpreted the command as Noachide, thus ensuring that there

Second, what is likely the majority view reads the Decree as dependent upon certain laws for resident aliens in Lev 17–18. This view is argued most forcefully by Bauckham and it allows James to uphold the Mosaic Law for Israelites and also—so far as they are implicated in the Law as "aliens"—for non-Israelites.[126]

Third, most convincing, in my view, are Wedderburn and Witherington, who argue (though from different angles) that Acts 15:20 is concerned with the avoidance of idolatry and the trappings of idol worship.[127]

I will briefly review the latter position and add several supporting arguments in its favor. The four prohibitions of the Decree are as follows:
1. ἀλισγημάτων τῶν εἰδώλοων (15:20) / εἰδωλοθύτον (15:29; 21:25).
2. πορνείαν (15:20, 29; 21:25).
3. πνικτός (15:20, 29; 21:25).
4. αἷμα (15:20, 29; 21:25).

Witherington argues that of the 125 references to εἰδωλοθύτον in the *TLG*, 123 are definitively Christian uses with the two exceptions (*4 Macc* 5:2; *Sib. Or.* 2:96) likely Christian interpolations.[128] He argues the word is a Christian neologism that functions as the negative counterpart to the Aramaic "corban" and is best translated as "idol stuff."[129] This gives the word a broader sense than the common translation "food devoted to idols" and incorporates all things associated with idol worship. The three items that follow are likewise associated with the trappings of idol worship. Wedderburn goes so far as to suggest that the first clause may serve as a heading to the list.[130] πορνεία is commonly associated with temple prostitution and differs from the common word for marital infidelity, μοιχεία.[131] αἷμα and πνικτός are both associated with pagan sacrifice, the latter of which may have either been a special method of cooking sacrificed meat seen as a "delicacy for demons" or a recognized sacrificial practice in which an animal was strangled in the presence of an idol so

---

was an enduring distinction and no commensality between Israelites and non-Israelites while Peter interpreted the command in accord with Lev 17–18 and the requirements for resident aliens, thus allowing for a level of intergroup commensality.

126. Bauckham 1996; 2005.
127. Wedderburn 1993; Witherington 1992; 1998, 460–67; 2001, 228–48. Cf. Pao 2003, 241.
128. Witherington 1998, 460–61.
129. Witherington 1998, 461. See *Didache* 6:2 for a similar use of εἰδωλοθύτον.
130. Wedderburn 1993, 378.
131. εἰδωλοθύτον and πορνεία are connected in Rev 2:14. Wis 14:12: "The idea of making idols was the beginning of πορνεία."

that the animal's "life" would animate the idol.¹³² Further, it is likely that the most common location in which people of average socio-economic status (that is, near subsistence level) would eat meat would have been festivals in pagan temples.¹³³ In essence then, this position reads the force of the Decree as "stay away from things associated with idol worship."¹³⁴

This is preferable to either the Noachide proposal or the Lev 17–18 proposal for a number of reasons:

1. Neither the Noachide lists nor Lev 17–18 can adequately account for the inclusion of πνικτός.¹³⁵
2. The sexual relations forbidden in Lev 17–18 concern sexual relations with people who are too closely related. πορνεία may not be a suitable category for these laws.
3. There is no coherent explanation for why these four alone, out of other "resident alien" laws, are singled out.¹³⁶
4. Imposition of the practical burden created by food laws upon non-Israelites (avoidance of blood and strangled things, according to Lev 17–18) violates James' own criterion not to "trouble" (παρενοχλεῖν) non-Israelites (Acts 15:19).
5. James' use of (singular) λαός to include Israelites and non-Israelites makes it difficult to imagine that he would then create the distinction required by the appropriation of Lev 17–18, which would maintain the primacy of ethnic Israel with non-Israelites existing only as "aliens in the midst."
6. Idolatry is a singularly non-Israelite problem in Luke–Acts, thus an injunction against idols fits well with Luke's portrayal of non-Israelites.¹³⁷

---

132. Wedderburn 1993, 383–89. For connections between blood and idolatry, see Minucius Felix 30.6; Tertullian, *Apologeticum* 9; Justin Martyr, *Dialogue with Trypho* 34.8. Klijn 1968, 308 shows that participation in sacrificial meals entailed public subjection to demons or false gods. For choking sacrifices, see Witherington 1998, 464; Ciraolo 1992, 240–54.

133. See Longenecker 2009 for economic measures of poverty in the Greco-Roman world.

134. McMillan 2001, 401 likely is correct that these are the minimum requirements for the church's distinction from culture. Note, however, that while he thinks it is distinction from a sex-saturated culture, I would suggest Luke views the cultural primarily as idol-saturated.

135. Callan 1993.

136. Callan 1993 lists 25 Levitical laws applicable to resident aliens.

137. See Acts 10:25–26; 14:11–18; 17:22–31; 19:22–35. Garrett 1989, 40 cites Luke's "horror at the prospect of misdirected worship" in conjunction with the first two of these passages.

7. Acts 10:34–35 makes the avoidance of idolatry the sole criterion for acceptability to God.
8. James' claim that non-Israelites have turned (ἐπιστρέφω) to God (and, presumably, away from idols) makes an anti-idolatry injunction fitting.[138]

For Luke, the Decree does not compel non-Israelites to take up certain Israelite identity markers, it compels them to abandon any of their own identity markers associated with idolatry or idolatrous practices.[139]

8.3.4. The Role of the Spirit in James' Logic

The four stipulations in the decree are introduced with the clause, "For it seemed good to the Holy Spirit and to us to lay upon you no greater burden than these necessary things" (Acts 15:28). Exactly what is intended by this agreement between the community and the Spirit is difficult to say. Some have suggested that the Spirit allows for complete freedom with regard to social issues.[140] McIntosh has suggested that the threefold witness provided by Peter, Barnabas and Paul, and James' citation of Amos entail the testimony of the Spirit.[141] Seitz suggests that the limit on the interpretive freedom of the community with regard to the interethnic issue is the Amos quotation; nothing contrary to the Scriptures can be the work of the Holy Spirit.[142] Some combination of the latter two views is the most coherent. The point, however, seems to be less *how* the church ultimately discerned its agreement with the Holy Spirit but rather *that* the church discerned its agreement with the Holy Spirit.[143] The following data demonstrate the pervasive impact of the Spirit in James' decision:

1. The language with which James renders the decision of the council, "It has seemed good to the Holy Spirit and to us" (Acts 15:28), is overwhelming proof that, for James, it is the Spirit that has wrought this new reality—the Israelite-plus-non-Israelite people of God—in fulfillment of the promises to David.

---

138. Acts 15:19.
139. This, of course, has enormous implications in both Luke's world and for contemporary Christians.
140. Johnson 1983, 82–99.
141. McIntosh 2002, 133.
142. Seitz 2001, 121–29.
143. My reading differs from Danker's suspicion (1983, 54) that benefaction from the Jerusalem church is an attempt to solidify a position of power by "bestowing their bounty on the Antiochenes by lifting all sanctions, except those specifically mentioned in Acts." I see rather a willingness to sacrifice ethnic primacy (and privilege) in submission to the work of the Spirit.

2. The data that James weighs in his decision overwhelmingly attribute the incorporation of non-Israelites *as non-Israelites* to the work of the Holy Spirit. Peter points to the coming of the Spirit to non-Israelites as non-Israelites (Acts 15:8–9). Paul and Barnabas testify to the signs and wonders done among the non-Israelites, a mark of the Spirit according to Peter's Pentecost speech (Acts 2:18) and a mark of the Spirit-empowered early community (Acts 2:42–47).
3. James' turn to the "other" for the sake of the full incorporation of non-Israelites *as non-Israelites* has, by this point in Luke–Acts, been demonstrated to be possible only through the work of the Spirit. We have traced this theme through the birth hymns, in the message of John the Baptizer, in the life of Jesus and in the early church. Time and again we have seen that the proper disposition toward the "other," marked often by the willingness to leverage privileged identity for the sake of the "other" (or, put another way, the ability simultaneously to love the in-group and the out-group), is a Spirit-created reality. In the portrayal of Barnabas, we have seen that Spirit-empowered actions, even without overt mention of the Spirit, can serve as evidence for the activity of the Spirit. Barnabas, for example, gives his goods to the poor in the community (Acts 4:36–37) and serves as a mediator helping to incorporate Saul into the (reluctant) community of believers in Jerusalem (Acts 9:27). Both of these actions have been marked by Luke as the work of the Spirit, and narratively Luke's hearers are primed to associate Barnabas' actions with the Spirit. The game is given away when, in Acts 11:24, Luke overtly tells us that Barnabas was "full of the Holy Spirit." So it is with James, whose willingness to extend the privileges of his Israelite ἔθνος to the ἔθνη is evidence of the transformational impact of the Spirit.[144] This is further highlighted by the fact that James does not suggest that either Israelites or non-Israelites need to abandon their ethnic particularity in order to participate in a "people for God's name" (Acts 15:14).

---

144. James' decision is not unlike the teaching in Jas 4:5–17, where James connects the Spirit of God to the right function of the community. Jas 4:5–17 is a precursor to James' insistence that, in a properly functioning community, the privileged should leverage their privilege for the sake of the poor (Jas 5:1–6). There are parallels between the epistles' exhortation of inclusiveness within the community and James' injunction in Acts 15. See Lockett 2008 for a nuanced reading of James that refutes the common position that James' "sectarian" stance demands complete detachment from the world.

4. Authoritative biblical interpretation in Luke–Acts is the fruit of the Spirit. This is paradigmatically true of Jesus in Luke 4:14–20. In Acts, Luke helps us to see that authoritative interpretation of Scripture is a post-Pentecost reality closely connected to the Spirit.[145] This is most evident in Acts 2:14–40 and 4:8–12. The need for divine assistance in the interpretation of Scripture hearkens back to Luke 24 where the proper interpretation of Scripture was found to be possible only through the (Spirit-empowered) teaching of Jesus (Luke 24:27, 32, 44–49; cf. Apollos in Acts 18:24).[146] It is a logical corollary that the Spirit—as the agent of the reign of the exalted Jesus (even named as the "Spirit of Jesus" in Acts 16:7)—would function to empower the authoritative interpretation of Scripture.[147]

These factors combine to demonstrate that, given Luke's narrative progression and presentation, the hearer should clearly appreciate the role of the Spirit in James' deciding. The Spirit, for Luke, has been the principal figure in the ongoing incorporation of all manner of "other." It is no longer surprising that Luke would here equate the Spirit with the decision *not* to require non-Israelites to sacrifice their ethnic "otherness" in order to join the Jesus-group.

8.3.5. *The Transformation of Identity After the Jerusalem Decision*
Nowhere is Luke's conviction that Israelite and non-Israelite believers share a common identity more evident than in his use of the heretofore ethnically exclusive group name ἀδελφοί to identify non-Israelites with Israelites. I demonstrated above that, for Luke, ἀδελφοί is used only as an intra-ethnic name among Israelites (both for believers and non-believers). Never once, prior to Acts 15, is a non-Israelite recognized as an ἀδελφός of an Israelite.[148] As in Acts 10–11, ἀδελφοί in Acts 15

---

145. Darr 1992, 53 has demonstrated the importance of the Spirit for authoritative interpretation of the Scriptures in Luke–Acts.
146. It is also relevant that in Luke 12:12 Jesus says that the Spirit will, in situations where testimony is needed, "teach you at that time what you should say." Jesus is here speaking of testimony before antagonistic judges, though perhaps this points more generally to the role of the Spirit in the cultivation of appropriate witness (cf. Acts 1:8; 5:32).
147. It should be noted, in general, that Luke sees a close connection between the prophetic word in the Scriptures and the Spirit (see Acts 28:25–27).
148. Acts 13:26, 38 may include proselytes as "brothers," but this is not obvious. Given the focus on ethnic Israel in Paul's speech in Antioch, it may well be that the narrowing focus on Israelite identity elicits Paul's use of "brothers" in these

highlights the ethnic boundary in view. ἀδελφοί appears in Acts 15:7, 13 and 22, each time referring to the ethnically exclusive group of Israelite Jesus-followers. The salient question is, "Now that non-Israelites are deemed to be the possession of God (cf. Acts 15:17), will they be viewed as ἀδελφοί of Israelites, or will ἀδελφοί (categorized on the basis of common ethnic identity) remain the primary intergroup boundary marker?"

But Luke begins a subtle reorientation of his usage in Acts 15:1:

> Some men came down from Judea and were teaching the brothers (ἀδελφοί), "Unless you are circumcised according to the custom of Moses, you cannot be saved."

And again in Acts 15:3:

> Being sent on their way by the church, they [Paul and Barnabas] passed through both Phoenicia and Samaria, reporting the conversion of the non-Israelites (ἔθνη), and they gave great joy to all the brothers (ἀδελφοί).

In Acts 15:3 ἀδελφοί cannot include those categorized as ἔθνη, for there is no reason that the ἔθνη would need to hear news that the ἔθνη had converted. Acts 15:1 is more ambiguous. When taken with the claim in Acts 15:24 that men from Jerusalem had troubled the ἔθνη, it is likely that Acts 15:1 implies that the ἔθνη are here counted as "brothers" of Israelites. This, however, is not clarified until Acts 15:24 and may have been less than clear upon an initial hearing of Acts 15:1.[149]

Luke, however, is not content to leave this issue ambiguous, and the salutation of the Jerusalem Decree brings the question of shared identity to climactic resolution:

> The brothers (ἀδελφοί), both the apostles and the elders, to the brothers from the non-Israelites (ἀδελφοῖς τοῖς ἐξ ἐθνῶν) in Antioch and Syria and Cilicia, greetings.[150]

We have here, in my estimation, the first unambiguous instance in the Gospel tradition or indeed in contemporary Israelite literature outside the New Testament (with the anomalous exception of the case of the Spartans described above) in which Israelites refer to non-Israelites as ἀδελφοί.[151]

---

instances. Either way, this is far from an unambiguous application of the word to non-Israelites *as non-Israelites*.

149. Pesch 1986, 75 thinks ἀδελφοί was "in der antiochenischen Diktion schon heissen," but not in Jerusalem.

150. Acts 15:23, my translation.

151. The construction "to the ἀδελφοί from (ἐκ) the ἔθνη" (Acts 15:23) cannot be taken to imply "the brothers taken out of the ἔθνη." Luke regularly uses ἐκ to denote the ongoing identity of figures in his narrative (e.g. Luke 1:5; 2:4).

Luke's use of ἀδελφοί after Acts 15:23 reflects a profound shift in the community's identity as it relates to ethnicity.[152] After Acts 15 ἀδελφοί appears in one of two ways: (1) to express ongoing ethnic solidarity with fellow Israelites or (2) to describe the Jesus group, irrespective of the ethnic identities of its members.[153] When Luke uses ἀδελφοί for the Jesus group after Acts 15:23 the category can include people of any ethnic identity. For example, in Acts 21:7, 17 and 22:22–23 Luke uses ἀδελφοί to describe (1) an undifferentiated community of Jesus-followers (21:7), (2) a group of Israelite Jesus-followers (21:17) and, in the same pericope, (3) to address non-believing Israelites (Acts 22:1, 5, 13). We see here that the trans-ethnic identity marked by the Spirit does not obliterate ethnic Israelite identity, as Israelite believers and non-believers can still know one another as ethnic "brothers." Yet this identity is subordinated to the identity formed by membership in the Jesus group—a group formed of "brothers" from many ἔθνη.[154] It is instructive that in the Acts 22 pericope, the transgression of ethnic boundaries resulting from the fact that Paul expresses the norms of his trans-ethnic identity at the expense of ethnic primacy, elicits murderous rage (Acts 21:27–31; 22:22–23). When the privileges of Israelite identity are shared with the ethnic "other," some non-believing Israelites defend their group identity by attempting to eliminate Paul.[155] It is apparent that Luke thinks that Spirit-empowered members of the Jesus group recognize the possibility of sharing with non-Israelites an identity as "brothers" without sacrificing ethnic particularity, while many outside the group do not, apparently, recognize this potential. Paul exhibits (in an exemplary manner) this ability to identify primarily as a "brother" of other Jesus-followers but also as an ethnic "brother" of Israelites in Acts 28:14, 15 and 17. It is fitting that Acts ends on this note—with Paul exhibiting both engagement and frustration with

---

152. Jervell 1998, 400, cited by Bock 2007, 512 n. 3, is the only interpreter I know who recognizes that this is the first use of "brothers" for non-Israelites, yet neither Jervell nor Bock develop the significance of this observation in historical context, in Luke's wider program or with reference to the Spirit.

153. For the use of "brother" to express intra-Israelite ethnic solidarity, see Acts 22:1, 5, 13; 23:1, 5, 6; 28:17, 21. For applications to undifferentiated groups of believers, see Acts 15:32, 33, 36, 40; 16:2, 40; 17:6, 10, 14; 18:27; 21:7, 17, 20; 28:14, 15.

154. The incorporation of non-Israelites into a group now collectively known as "brothers" calls for the radical redefinition of social identity for both in-group and former out-group members. This is just the sort of double identity transformation we have come to expect whenever the "other" is added to the community. For the impact of the addition of non-Israelites to the community, see Dollar 1993, 178–79; Haulotte 1970, 72.

155. Cf. Luke 4:14–30.

his ethnic brothers while now fully expressing the allocentric social identity formed by his participation in the Spirit-created group composed of all those in relationship with Jesus—a new kind of "brothers."

8.4. Conclusion

It is not difficult to document the pervasive activity of the Spirit in the *orchestration* of the intergroup encounter between Peter and Cornelius, nor is it difficult to see that the Spirit clearly *identifies* Cornelius as a member of the Jesus-group. What has not, to this point, been noticed is the fact that Luke presses these two Spirit-activities beyond the affirmation of a common *status* (e.g. member of the people of God, or "saved") and instead aims for the creation of a common *identity* (ἀδελφοί) through the work of the Spirit. This is evidence of the full incorporation of non-Israelites into the Jesus group, and it is only the appreciation of this full and common membership in the singular λαός that can allow for a common social identity to be recognized. According to Luke, therefore, membership in the community of believers—a social group composed of allocentrically oriented, Spirit-empowered individuals—cultivates a common superordinate identity that transcends ethnicity and allows for the supreme goal of "witness": multi-layered reconciliation that results in peace. In this sense, ethnicity is chastened as a terminal identity; it can no longer function hegemonically, nor can it be used as a criterion for exclusion. At the same time, ethnic identity is not obliterated. The Spirit defends subgroup particularity throughout the narrative, and even after Acts 15 Israelites can know themselves as the ethnic ἀδελφοί of other Israelites. Yet this ethnic identity can only function properly when it is subordinated to the Spirit-created and Spirit-marked identity cultivated by life in the Jesus group.

Chapter 9

CONCLUSION

Writing within living memory of the composition of Luke–Acts, Justin Martyr was able to proclaim:

> We who hated and killed one another and would not associate with people not of the same tribe because of customs, now after the coming of Christ live together and pray for our enemies and try to persuade those who unjustly hate us…so that they may share with us the good hope of receiving the same things from God, the master of all.[1]

Justin's declaration is a fitting encapsulation of Luke's identity-forming project. For Justin there was something wondrously unprecedented about the existence of a community of former enemies now united around Jesus and oriented toward the still-threatening "other." The possibility of just such a community is a vision that captivated Luke, who went beyond simply a description of such a community to describe *how*, precisely, this new trans-ethnic identity came into existence.

9.1. A Summary of Luke's Portrait of the Spirit, Social Identity and the "Other"

I have argued that, for Luke, the Holy Spirit is the central figure in the formation of a new social identity that affirms yet chastens and transcends ethnic identity. We have seen that the formation of this trans-ethnic social identity requires both a certain kind of person and a certain kind of group. The character and characteristics of these persons and this group are, for Luke, entirely Spirit-wrought realities.

The baseline for Luke's identity-forming project is a clear declaration that ethnic Israel enjoys a privileged identity by virtue of its position as God's elect people. This is immediately evident in the dense cluster of allusions to Gen 15–18 that combine to present Zechariah and Elizabeth

---

1. *1 Apology* 14.3.

as Abraham and Sarah-like exemplars of faithful Israelite identity (Luke 1:5–25). The birth hymns, with their focus on Israel's past covenantal history and anticipated future divine deliverance—especially set against the backdrop of Herodian client rule and Roman power (Luke 1:5; 2:1–2; 3:1–2)—further the notion that Israel's ethnic identity is uniquely privileged among other (seemingly higher status) ethnic groups. Luke celebrates Israel's identity and affirms robust intra-Israelite expressions of in-group love.[2] This Israelite privilege is in service of God's purpose for all humanity, the blessing of all the families of the earth as promised in Abrahamic covenant.

Yet Luke is keenly aware that in-group love focused too narrowly on Israel's, or for that matter, on any social group's, privileged identity is dangerously open to distortion.[3] Specifically, any expression of privileged identity that views in-group privilege as its own end is inherently defective. This is clarified during the initial public appearances of John and Jesus, Luke's Spirit-empowered figures *par excellence* (Luke 1:15; 3:22). John contrasts a defective expression of Israelite identity (Luke 3:8) with an exhortation not to use privileged identity to the detriment of the "other" (Luke 3:12–14) but instead to use privilege for the sake of the "other" (Luke 3:10–11). In Nazareth, Jesus resists his townsfolk's implicit entitlement claims founded upon the presumption that shared subgroup identity as members of Jesus' πατρίς afforded them uniquely privileged access to the benefits of his ministry. SIT indicates that shared identity and entitlement claims to group resources are mutually constitutive, but Luke resists this apparently normative impulse. For Luke, the restriction of entitlement to the in-group only is normative within his context but (in the light of the transforming power of the Spirit) is a decidedly defective way of expressing privileged identity. This old paradigm arises at various points in Luke and Acts and is consistently resisted by Luke (Luke 9:46–48, 49–50, 51–56; cf. Acts 1:5, 21–26; 6:1–7).

In contrast with this normative (and defective) expression of privileged ethnic identity, Luke is convinced that the transformative power of the Spirit creates a concern for the "other" expressed by the willingness to leverage privileged identity for the sake of the "other." This *allocentric identity*, defined in this study as the ability simultaneously to express

---

2. "In-group love" is the positive evaluation of the in-group and is drawn from Brewer's assertion that social identity is more about "in-group love" than "out-group hate," but that the evaluative nature of social identity ensures that in-group favoritism is "not benign" (Brewer 1999, 438).

3. Luke demonstrates this with regard to non-Israelite groups in Acts 16:19–21; 19:23–41.

in-group love and out-group love, is a defining characteristic for the kind of *person* capable of participation in a trans-ethnic social group. This Spirit-wrought transformation has intimately personal effects, as well as thoroughly social ramifications. Initially, for Luke, the influence of the Spirit upon individuals functions to broaden the "ethnic horizon" of those so affected. This is evident in the chiastic arrangement of Luke's birth hymns, which establish a relationship between the overt influence of the Spirit (for Zechariah and Simeon) and the extension of divine benefits to the ethnic "other." The motif is advanced in Luke's presentation of Jesus, whose life and teaching are the paradigmatic expression of a Spirit-empowered allocentric identity capable of extending in-group benefits beyond the self/group (Luke 4:1–13, 16–30; 12:32–35; 24:25–27). Jesus implies a causal link between the Spirit and his disciples' orientation toward the "other" in Acts 1:8, and throughout Acts those who are marked by the Spirit are those most capable of navigating identity conflicts that implicate the "other" (Acts 6:1–7; 11:24). For Luke, the relationship between the Spirit and a concern for the "other" stands in clear contrast with the alternative, which is a link between the influence of Satan and an egocentric identity often marked by an impulse to hoard personal resources (Acts 5:1–11; cf. Luke 4:1–13; 22:3, 31; Acts 1:15–26).

If the formation of trans-ethnic social identity requires Spirit-transformed allocentric individuals, it also requires a certain kind of *social group* capable of incorporating the "other." The early community (Acts 2:42–47; 4:32–38; 5:12–16) emerges as both the logical extension and the corporate expression of the Spirit-empowered allocentric identity evident in Luke's Gospel. Like all social groups, this group is an incubator of social identity for its members, and Luke's language reflects that the group is increasingly entitative in its context (Acts 2:47; 5:13; 6:7; 9:31). Unlike most social groups, the boundaries of the Jesus group are not primarily enforced through intragroup processes of intergroup differentiation. Instead, the Spirit maintains the group boundary and forms a specific type of community in two ways. First, the Spirit becomes the primary identity marker for those rightly related to God through Jesus. This is initially displayed at Jesus' baptism (Luke 3:22) but is expressed programmatically in Peter's modification of Joel 3:1–5a LXX (Acts 2:18) in which Luke establishes the fact that the Spirit is the definitive identity marker for all who are δοῦλοι and δοῦλαι of God. Luke draws on this at critical intergroup junctures in Acts—namely, wherever human identity is in question the Spirit appears to clarify identities and to identify who, precisely, is a participant in the people of the risen Lord Jesus (Acts 8:14–17; 10:44–47; cf. 11:15–18; 15:8–9). Second, the Spirit orchestrates intergroup encounters between (Israelite) members of the Jesus group and the (often ethnic) "other." This occurs through visions (cf. Acts 2:17) but also through the Spirit's direct speech (Acts 8:29; 9:10–17; 10:3–7, 10–16, 19–20; 13:2–4). Whenever the Spirit speaks in the narrative it commands Israelites to cross a significant boundary and extend the benefits of the Jesus group to the (usually ethnic) "other" (Acts 8:29; 10:19–20; 11:12; 13:2). The Spirit commandeers the boundaries of the Jesus group and fully incorporates the "other." The Spirit accomplishes this initially by orchestrating intergroup encounters and ultimately by marking common identity.

The result of the Spirit-guided incorporation of the "other" is consistently a "dual identity transformation" that reconfigures the identities of former non-believers as well as existing believers. Former out-group members reconfigure their social identity to reflect their membership in the Jesus group. Significantly, in-group members also are forced to reconfigure their own social identities to reflect the changing demographics of their group. The incorporation of the (sometimes threatening) "other" changes the in-group perspective on who, precisely, constitutes the "we" and the "they." The change in behavior elicited by these dual identity transformations is evident both in the changing usage of categorical language and changed behavior with regard to intergroup contact (Acts 8:25; 9:28–29; 10:48), though this is often not without reluctance (Acts 9:13–14, 26; 11:2–3; 15:1–5). Luke never shies away from the fact that the ethnic boundary regularly is intractable (see especially Luke 9:51–56). Indeed, Luke's text indicates that, apart from the Spirit, ethnic barriers are hopelessly intractable.

The ultimate result of the Spirit's work to gather allocentrically oriented individuals into a community composed of many categories of "other" is the formation of a new identity under the rubric ἀδελφοί (Acts 15:22). Luke's use of ethnic language both leading to and proceeding from Acts 15 highlights the fact that a profound shift of identity has taken place in accord with the work of the Spirit (Acts 15:28). The narrative admits no possibility of non-Israelites participating in the people of God in a manner analogous to the resident aliens of Leviticus, as a parallel but separate people. Likewise, there is no requirement for Israelite social conversion for non-Israelites. *For Luke, all who follow Jesus share a common identity marked by the Spirit.* The result of this new identity is intergroup peace, anticipated already in Luke 1:79 and 2:14 and narratively expressed through the incorporation of the "threatening other" (Acts 9:1–31; 10:36). The deliverance from enemies predicted in the birth hymns comes not through violent encounter but through reconciliation and incorporation. This is a profound and beautiful vision of other-centered identity.

The new social identity formed by participation in the Jesus group has important ramifications for ethnic identity. First, *ethnic identity must be submitted to the lordship of Jesus—not to do this would be unfaithful.* The practical effect of this posture is that identity as a Jesus follower must remain one's terminal identity. For Luke, there is no place for ethnic hegemonies or ethnocentrisms that use ethnic privilege to exclude, to oppress or to hoard resources (whether social or physical). Luke goes to great lengths to demonstrate that whenever subgroup identities (especially ethnic identities) become primary within the Jesus group, the group malfunctions (Acts 1:21–22 [subtly]; 5:1–11; 6:1–7; 11:1–2; 15:1–5). This leaves us with questions regarding the aspects of ethnic identities that remain acceptable for Jesus followers and the aspects that must be jettisoned. Luke gives us less help here, but he does not leave us helpless. The consistent call for those outside the Jesus group is simply to abandon idolatry and instead to worship the cosmic Lord. This is most evident in the anti-idol thrust of the Jerusalem Decree. Ostensibly, those aspects of ethnic identity not tainted by idol worship remain acceptable. This is a complicated matter in a context like Luke's where "religion" was embedded within political and kinship structures, thus allowing the taint of idolatry to spread to various quarters of society: games and festivals, the meat market, the public bath, and so on. How these ethnically embedded customs should be treated by Jesus followers would arise as a matter of some controversy. Yet it remains clear that ethnic identity can only exist as a penultimate layer of social identity.

Second, *ethnic identity must be retained—not to do this would be unfaithful.* Luke nowhere suggests that ethnic identity must be completely abandoned by those who choose to follow Jesus. To the contrary, Luke celebrates the diversity of ethnic identities within the Jesus movement. For Luke, the Spirit both navigates ethnic barriers, creating a community of peace, *and* resists a stultifying "sameness" in the Jesus-group. This bi-focal emphasis is evident in several crucial passages in Acts. This was expressed paradigmatically at Pentecost where, contrary to the discernable Israelite expectation of an eschatological return to the universal use of Hebrew, the Spirit radically *affirmed* ethno-linguistic particularity (Acts 2:4–11). Pentecost, for Luke, was not a miracle of impossible communication made possible, but a miracle that validated the Diaspora languages, cultures and identities of the Diaspora Israelites who had resettled in Jerusalem. Though we are forced in one way to argue from silence, given Luke's keen awareness of the ethnic issues at play in his text it is significant that Samaritans apparently do not need to abandon their ethnic distinctives in order to participate in the Jesus group. The Ethiopian eunuch (for whom full social conversion to the

9. Conclusion

Israelite ἔθνος may have been impossible) is welcome as both Ethiopian and eunuch. And, emphatically, the falling of the Spirit upon Cornelius' household comes without condition for ethnic assimilation. The greeting of the Jerusalem Decree made the nature of the relationship between membership in the Jesus group and ethnic identity clear: "To the ἀδελφοί from the ἔθνη." All who call on Jesus and are marked by the Spirit are ἀδελφοί, yet—significantly—they remain "brothers" from the ἔθνη. Membership in the Jesus group forms their terminal identity, yet they remain members of that group *as* ἔθνη. Paul becomes the exemplar of the appropriate ordering of identities within the Jesus movement later in Acts. *Paul never ceases to identify as an ethnic Israelite.* He identifies himself as an ethnic "brother" of other ethnic Israelites (Acts 22:1, 5; 23:1, 5, 6; 28:17), he refers to Israel's patriarchs as his "fathers" (Acts 26:6; 28:17) and he calls Israel his ἔθνος (Acts 24:17; 28:19). Yet his ethnic identity is now clearly nested within his new identity as a Jesus follower. The finest example of Paul's deployment of his nested identities is in his willingness to use, alternatively, Greek and Hebrew/ Aramaic in Acts 21:37-40 in order to gain an opening to proclaim the gospel. In short, Paul neither *abuses* (ethnocentrism) nor *loses* (assimilation) his ethnic identity, but he *uses* it to bear witness to the gospel of the exalted Lord— the orienting focus for the identity of all Jesus followers.

The transformation wrought by the Spirit in both persons and groups underscores the fact that, for Luke, the Spirit creates *a new way of being human in community*—especially as it relates to the "other." The Spirit molds followers of Jesus into Jesus' own allocentric image and forges an identity that transcends ethnicity, while refusing to eliminate all vestiges of "otherness." This, I suspect, is in large part Luke's narrative presentation of one aspect of the reality of New Creation. Apart from the Spirit, one's true identity can neither be adequately known nor faithfully expressed. Luke's description of this new way of being human contrasts quite distinctly with both the identity-forming processes described by SIT and the identity concerns expressed by other groups described in Luke–Acts. Luke's community—when keeping in step with the Spirit's influence—appears surprisingly able to love both the in-group and the out-group, a trait most evident in the community's willingness to extend the benefits of the in-group to the "other" through witness, hospitality and incorporation. But perhaps the most striking difference between Luke's community and most human social groups is that Luke portrays a community whose boundaries have been commandeered by the Holy Spirit, a figure who appears in the narrative as one determined to disregard social barriers in order to create a singular trans-ethnic people for God. This work of the Spirit is a necessary corollary of the now-ascended

Jesus' identity as the world's one true Lord. The unique features of the identity of the Jesus group are obvious when viewed against Luke's portrayals of other social groups in the text—both Israelite and non-Israelite groups—but also when examined in light of basic data from social groups across contemporary cultures.[4] The Spirit, for Luke, creates the possibility of loving the "other" and incorporating even the threatening "other" (while allowing the "other" to retain a large measure of ethnic particularity) in a way that simply does not occur very often in contemporary intergroup, and especially interethnic, situations.

It must be noted, however, that Luke does not produce a simple caricature of "universalistic Christianity" over against "particularistic Judaism."[5] Universalism, too often, can be taken to imply an absence of social boundaries. This is not only untrue of the Jesus movement; it is the case no social group can exist without boundaries. Thus to suggest that the Jesus movement does not imply a clearly defined "other" is misleading. The Jesus movement, as described by Luke, exhibits a "universal particularity," with its universal aspect defined by the cosmic lordship of the exalted Jesus. Jesus' lordship over all peoples is the prerequisite which allows all humans, regardless of class, ethnicity or gender, the opportunity to recognize, affirm and submit to Jesus' true identity. The Jesus community, marked by the Holy Spirit, is universally open to the "other," but acknowledgment of the lordship of Jesus remains a very real boundary in the group's conception of its social context. For Luke, one cannot be "in" until one has submitted to Jesus' cosmic lordship, full stop (e.g. Acts 10:36, 42). Luke's vision is more aptly described as a *Spirit-empowered "other-centered" particularity*. The particularity of the movement is marked by a resistance to "coercive sameness" through the affirmation of a broad array of subgroup identities but also through the unquestionable criterion of submission to Jesus' universal reign.[6] The "other-centeredness" of this Spirit-empowered group, at its best, does not denigrate the "other" but invites the "other" to join. This stands in contrast to some, but by no means all, Lukan descriptions of Israelite identity—as well as to some Lukan descriptions of non-Israelite identity.[7]

---

4. See the intragroup identity maintenance strategies exhibited by Jerusalem leaders (Acts 6:9–8:1; 9:1–2) and non-Israelites in Ephesus (Acts 19:24–29).

5. Several scholars have rightly expressed anxiety over dualistic reconstructions of ancient "Christianity" and "Judaism"; see Johnson 2006; Buell 2002; 2005; Barclay 1997; Dahl 1977.

6. "Coercive sameness" is a concern of Boyarin 1994, 233.

7. See the discussion of Second Temple literature in Chapter 2 for an example of the broad range of Israelite responses to the ethnic "other." For non-Israelite outgroup antagonism, see Acts 16:19–23; 19:24–29.

9. Conclusion

Having summarized the findings of this study, it can here finally be noted that approaches to the Spirit in Luke–Acts that conceptualize Luke as wed to a "Spirit of prophecy" motif culled from Second Temple Israel and the Old Testament are ultimately too restrictive. It cannot be doubted that Luke was heavily dependent on Old Testament materials, motifs and expectations at many points in his text—including a good deal of his Spirit material. The effort, however, to use a diachronic approach across texts, times and places to distill a "concept" or "conception" of the Spirit and then to reify the "concept" and use it heuristically for Luke–Acts creates a hermeneutical circle as well as the possibility that the aggregate "concept" intelligible within a conglomeration of particular textual witnesses was not held by any one real person. Further, these approaches have a tendency to admit little in the way of novelty with regard to Luke's treatment of the Spirit, a problematic feature when one considers the unexpected ways in which Luke concluded that the events surrounding Jesus "fulfilled" the Old Testament.[8] Old Testament texts, according to Luke, needed to be reinterpreted in light of Jesus' actual life, death and resurrection. This process filled old texts with new meaning.[9] Luke's narrative alternatively appropriated, reworked and, at times, moved beyond some apparently traditional Israelite expectations in order to describe "the things which have been accomplished among us" (Luke 1:1). It should not be surprising that Luke, reflecting on the early church's *experience* of the Holy Spirit, would redefine and broaden Old Testament and Second Temple expectations of the Spirit. Most importantly, however, "Spirit of prophecy" approaches—regardless of the content they ascribe to the concept—prove misleadingly restrictive in light of Luke's own presentation of the Spirit. Specifically, they do not account for the ostensible *goal* of the Spirit within the broader narrative, the social impact of Spirit-empowered characters, or the cumulative effect achieved when tracing the relationship between the Spirit, ethnicity and the "other." "Spirit of prophecy" approaches have many valuable insights, but they ultimately fall short of a fully orbed appreciation of Luke's view of the Spirit—a view that inseparably links the Spirit with human identity.

---

8. A crucified messiah, a resurrected messiah, an ascended messiah, a messiah who pours out the Spirit, the incorporation of the ἔθνη as ἔθνη, the gift of the Spirit to the ἔθνη, constitute just a few examples of the "unanticipated" features of Luke–Acts with respect to certain strands of Israelite tradition.

9. See, emphatically, Luke 24:27, 32, 44–49.

9.2. Social Identity Theory and a Different Way of Being Human in Community

This project reveals at least five significant ways in which SIT is useful for interpreting biblical texts. First, SIT helps interpreters to understand typical identity-forming processes within human groups. Increased scholarly interest in "identity" as an explanatory concept in biblical interpretation requires that we use our best resources to be precise in what interpreters *mean* when they invoke identity as a concept. SIT can help provide just such a level of precision. Understanding normative social processes provides a context against which Luke's depictions of the identity processes in the early Jesus movement often appear distinctive. Second, SIT reminds interpreters that even in overwhelmingly individualistic modern North Atlantic cultures, social groups are powerful identity-forming agents. This is amplified greatly in collectivistic societies such as the ancient Greco-Roman world.[10] In one way, SIT helps us to read as collectivists, aware that a group always stands behind an individual and that most social interactions have intergroup ramifications. This helps greatly to sensitize the interpreter to the effect of groups and group exemplars within the text. Third, SIT demonstrates the close connection between identity and resource allocation. This often overlooked phenomenon makes evident intragroup and intergroup tensions at multiple points in the text. This is especially useful for understanding the intragroup dynamics created through subgroup projection of relative prototypicality, as well as the entitlement claims that arise from such projection. Fourth, SIT sensitizes the interpreter to the stubborn nature of social boundaries between all groups, and perhaps especially between ethnic groups. The difficulty with which identity-based intergroup conflict is mitigated makes Luke's project shine for its uniqueness and the scope of the problems addressed. Finally, the use of SIT as an interpretive grid with which to read biblical texts forms a natural bridge across which ancient data can assume new relevance in modern intergroup contexts.

9.3. Possibilities for Future Comparative Work on Identity Within the Early Jesus Movement

This reading of Luke's treatment of the role of the Spirit in the formation of a superordinate social identity that affirms, yet chastens and transcends, ethnic identity raises interesting possibilities for further comparative work on identity in the early church. In light of the long history

---

10. Brown 2000, 753.

of research on the relationship between Lukan and Pauline conceptions of the Spirit, a fresh comparison with Paul's view of the Spirit seems a natural place to begin. A robust understanding of the relationship between the Spirit and identity in Luke–Acts grants the Spirit a much greater role in the lives of all Jesus followers than often is admitted by the strictest of the "Spirit of prophecy" proponents who regularly set Luke and Paul at opposite ends of a pneumatological spectrum.[11] While this is not the place for analysis, it is clear that for Paul (or, depending upon certain judgments regarding authorship, the Pauline school) the Spirit is a significant source of unity and identity within the early (multi-ethnic) church.[12] SIT would be a useful heuristic tool with which to compare and contrast Lukan and Pauline conceptions of the Spirit, ethnic identity and the "other." Likewise, Luke's view appears to bear some affinity with the catholic epistles, where the Spirit (and discerning the spirits), plays a central role in discerning accurately the identity of true and false teachers.[13]

A comparison of Luke's conception of the Spirit and identity and the positions expressed by early Christian apologists would also be of great interest. For many early apologists, the relationship between identity in Christ and ethnic identities formed a key pressure point with regard to the salience of ethnicity for those who had submitted to Jesus. Several recent treatments have analyzed the "ethnic reasoning" of the early apologists and have revealed that one common apologetic position was the categorization of the Jesus movement as an ethnic alternative to either "Jewish" or "Greek" ethnic identity.[14] This view, which seems to be at loggerheads with the Lukan view, expected that ethnic identities were obliterated by transferral into the Jesus group. This is blatantly evident in Aristides' *Apology* 2.2: "For it is clear that there are three kinds (γένη) of humans in this world: worshippers of so-called gods, Jews, and Christians." Likewise, Eusebius calls Jesus followers "a new ἔθνος called after his [Jesus'] own name."[15] Eusebius argues for a "rupturing of ethnic identities" which results in the ultimate unacceptability of Christians being "identified with any of the other nations."[16] Yet this position is markedly different from the *Epistle to Diognetus*, which claims that

---

11. This is most true for Gunkel, von Baer, Schweizer, Menzies and Cho.
12. E.g. Rom 8:14, 16; 14:17; 1 Cor 3:16; 6:19; 12:4, 7, 13; 2 Cor 1:22; Gal 4:16; Eph 1:13; 4:3–4; Phil 3:3; Titus 3:5; cf. Heb 6:4; 1 Pet 4:14; 1 John 3:24; 4:13.
13. See 2 Pet 1:16–2:22; 1 John 4; Jude 1:17–21.
14. Buell 2005; Johnson 2006.
15. *Demonstratio Evangelica* 3.6.
16. Johnson 2006, 200, 209–10.

Christians have a measure of ethnic continuity with their countrymen but ultimately have a higher level terminal identity to which they are faithful:

> For Christians are not distinguished from the rest of humanity by country, language, or custom. But while they live in both Greek and barbarian cities, as each one's lot was cast, and follow the local customs in dress and food and other aspects of life, at the same time they demonstrate the remarkable and admittedly unusual character of their own citizenship.[17]

It would be well worth enquiring into the identity-related pressures that caused ethnicity to be viewed with such variation in the early centuries of the Jesus movement.

Finally, fruitful comparisons could be made between Luke's vision of Spirit-formed trans-ethnic social identity and the other trans-ethnic identity on offer in Luke's context—Roman citizenship. Here I suspect that the chief difference will be in the view of the "other," especially given Luke's insistence that deliverance from the threatening other comes through the creation of a common identity that is initiated by a pneumatologically modulated encounter with Jesus, not by military domination.[18] Luke's view, on its surface, seems very different from the Roman metanarrative defined by the four virtues: *piety—war—victory—peace*.[19] It would be well worth investigating the way that these alternative visions of incorporation and the "other" shaped the identities of the ethnically diverse members of the Jesus movement and the Roman Empire.

9.4. Possibilities for Contemporary Application

It is deeply ironic that the rapid pace of globalization and the increased intergroup contact available on a worldwide scale due to modern technologies has led not to global homogenization, but to an entrenchment of ethnic identities and to increasing volatility at interethnic boundaries. SIT can explain the drive to assert identity distinctiveness in order to maintain positive differentiation from the "other" in the light of globalization's pressure toward assimilation. Yet while SIT can describe the reasons for heightened interethnic tension, it has proven exponentially more difficult to produce a strategy for the mitigation of ethnic

---

17. *Epistle to Diognetus* 5.1, 4.
18. See especially the incorporation of the former enemy Paul (Acts 9:1–31) and the Roman centurion Cornelius (Acts 10), and note Luke's distinct vision of the intergroup peace that is one result of the gospel (Luke 1:79; 2:14; Acts 10:36).
19. Crossan 2004, xi, 284; Galinsky 1996, 106–21.

intergroup conflict. More than ever it remains apparent that ethnic identity, and the interethnic social dynamics it creates, is one of the most pressing issues of our time. One can quickly produce a tragic litany of places and peoples ravaged by interethnic conflict, the ferocity of which has proved often to be nearly unimaginable and simply inhuman: Rwanda, the Balkans, Northern Ireland, South Africa, Sri Lanka, Darfur, and now recently Kenya and Kyrgyzstan—the list goes on. In addition to these widely publicized interethnic conflicts, ethnic tension simmers in plenty of other less publicized places: Moldova, Burundi, Georgia, Solomon Islands, New Guinea/Bougainville and Chiapas, Mexico. It is scarcely possible to reckon the lives lost, families destroyed, innocence stolen or memories seared by acts perpetuated in the name of ethnic identity. Perhaps most troubling is the unabated continuation of this trend despite increasingly intense attention given to ethnicity and ethnic conflict in the academy, by politicians and in the wider culture. A recent study has estimated that over 300 ethnic groups are currently either in protest or rebellion.[20] Over 30 intrastate wars are currently in progress, many spilling across national borders.[21] Tragically, both of these statistics are nearly double their level from just fifty years ago.[22]

These statistics, and the images from television news broadcasts that detail their reality, can seem so inconceivable that we can easily disassociate ourselves. But the conflict at the seam of competing ethnic identities is usually expressed in less violent though more pervasive ways. In the United States, as of 2007, families who categorize themselves as "Black" have a median annual household income of $40,143, while those who respond as "White" have a median income of $64,427 per household.[23] In Canada, the provincial government of Ontario has released a four-volume report detailing a more appropriate response to the protests of aboriginal peoples.[24] There also, the tension between French- and English-speaking Quebecers continues to simmer. In Germany, educational attainment for second-generation children of traditional migrant

20. Wimmer 2004, 2.
21. Centre for the Study of Civil War, International Peace Research Institute, Oslo, Norway. Data accessed 14 July 2010 at http://www.prio.no/sptrans/-193189583/Graph-conflictsbytype.pdf/.
22. For a comprehensive treatment of contemporary ethnic conflict, see Ganguly forthcoming.
23. U.S. Census Bureau data reflect income statistics from 2007. Accessed 14 July 2010 at http://www.census.gov/compendia/statab/2010/tables/10s0681.pdf/.
24. The Report of the Ipperwash Inquiry (released 31 May 2007) can be accessed via http://www.ipperwashinquiry.ca/report/.

workers lags far behind that of "native" Germans.²⁵ While these problems are symptoms of a complex nexus of societal factors, the clear distinctions between ethnic groups are telling.

Yet the problem moves even closer to home. Jokes are told in factory break rooms. Pulses and paces quicken on poorly lit roads when someone meets a passerby who is obviously an ethnic "other." Interethnic marriages still cause great angst in many quarters, not to mention the difficulties faced by the children of these marriages. People are frozen out of neighborhoods, social clubs and schools because they are not "one of us." Tragically, in the USA at least, the well-known claim that 11 AM on Sunday mornings is the most segregated hour in America seemingly remains irreversibly true.²⁶ One recent study has demonstrated that only 12 percent of American congregations report being even moderately diverse.²⁷ Supporting these data is meta-research on American religious life that has found the positive correlation between racism and religious affiliation to be so pervasive that researchers now identify the phenomenon as the "paradox of religious racism."²⁸

In the midst of a world scarred by interethnic antagonism, Luke's Spirit-centered vision stands as a challenge for contemporary Christian faith and practice. Luke–Acts confronts the church with the question, "Who are we?" There is no more basic—or important—question for discerning the appropriate posture toward the "other" on both an intra-church and intergroup level. The competing answers given to this question form the neuralgic points in ecumenical and missional issues. At an ecumenical (or intra-church) level, where ethnicity is less regularly in view, the issue often revolves around the place of denominational identities within a broader Jesus-centered identity. When it comes to interaction with Christians of differing doctrinal perspective, do we interact as Methodists and Roman Catholics, or primarily as Jesus followers? Properly understanding the primary nature of Jesus-centered identity reframes these conversations and locates the stakes of the conversation at an intragroup, not an intergroup level. This eases identity

---

25. Data can be accessed from the Institut für Arbeitsmarkt- und Berufsforschung via http://doku.iab.de/discussionpapers/2007/dp0407.pdf/.

26. 11:00 o'clock Sunday morning is the traditional hour for corporate, public Christian worship in the USA.

27. Schwadel 2009.

28. Hall, Matz and Wood 2010, 126–27. It is fascinating to note that the strongest link between religious identification and racism was among those who viewed religion as a means to the fulfillment of material or social needs. This resonates with Luke's descriptions of potentially problematic relationships between identity and resource allocation.

tensions and may create space for both more fruitful interaction and a more unified public face for Christianity. Moreover, Luke–Acts demonstrates that sub-group identities need not dissolve in order for deep peace to be experienced by church. In a world filled with competing identities, the ability of the church to exist as a community composed of former "enemies" and "others" would no doubt provide a compelling vision of the kingdom reign of the exalted Jesus.

With respect to Christian missions, the relationship between ethnicity and Christian identity moves to the fore. The broader Christian missionary movement is recovering from the ethnic imperialism that marked too many cross-cultural missionary endeavors in the previous two centuries. Questions remain, however, regarding the intersection between gospel and culture at points where one culturally specific expression of the gospel encounters the ethnic "other."[29] Here it seems clear that Luke would urge Jesus followers critically to examine the intersection between their Christian faith/praxis and its inherent cultural imbeddedness. Which aspects of sending or receiving ethnic identities must be jettisoned because of their resistance to Jesus' lordship? Which aspects must be allowed to flourish? How can Christians of divergent ethnic and cultural backgrounds help one another to cultivate the richness of their cultures and lovingly address one another's cultural blind spots?[30] These critical issues are of no little significance.

Both of these important factors are enveloped within a broader, and more profound, ramification of Luke's understanding of the Spirit, ethnic identity and the "other." Luke is utterly insistent that identity as a Jesus follower must remain the primary identity for all who follow Jesus. Christian identity, for Luke, is not first among equals; it is first—full stop. When it comes to one's sense of social identity in one's social context, Luke has no patience for the primacy of subgroup identities. One is never an Argentinean or a Democrat or a unionist first—one is a Jesus-follower first. All other social identities must be nested within one's identity as a member of the community of Jesus followers. Essential to recovering this fact is the reconceptualization of Christianity not as a "religious movement" or "belief system," but primarily as *participation in the people who belong to the Lord of the cosmos*. Not only have modern conceptions of "religion" (usually imagined as a system of beliefs and practices to which one voluntarily adheres) distorted readings of biblical texts, modern conceptions of "religion" inherently remove believers from the biblical notion that embeds all who affirm the lordship of Jesus within a *people*

---

29. This issue has been skillfully highlighted by Jenkins 2002; 2006.
30. Newbigin 1989 has suggested a model of mutual intercultural critique.

group that possesses its own ontological reality. Participation in this *people* serves as the incubator for a social identity that, by the power of the Spirit, can affirm yet transcend ethnic identities. The recovery of the ontological reality of the Jesus movement primarily as a *people* calls for a radical reconfigurations of social identity, perhaps in a manner akin to the identity transformations experienced by the Jesus group throughout Acts. The subjection of other social identities to one's identity as a Jesus follower is the necessary precondition for the manifestation of Luke's greatest contribution to the arena of human identity. Namely, Luke proclaims the Spirit-created possibility of a beautifully diverse community of peace that exists as an outpost of the eschatological new creation in the midst of a world marked by interethnic strife. The existence of such a community of former enemies who now share a common identity and who collectively are oriented toward the "other" may provide the world both a beacon of hope and a different way of being human in community. This Lukan vision allows for the fact that, when properly oriented, one need not *lose* (assimilation) or *abuse* (ethnocentrism) their subgroup (ethnic) identities. Instead, Jesus followers can *use* these identities—especially privileged identities—on behalf of the exalted Jesus and for the sake of the "other" in a multi-ethnic world. A possibility so great, however, requires nothing less than the transforming power of the Holy Spirit.

9.5. Conclusion

In the midst of pervasive interethnic tension, Luke was convinced that followers of Jesus had become something new and, as a result, now bore a new identity that transcended ethnicity, yet affirmed ethnic identity at a penultimate level. This new, Spirit-generated identity created the possibility of profound reconciliation between former enemies who heretofore had been divided by formerly incommensurate social identities. Luke's vision of this new community anticipates the vision of John of Patmos in Rev 7:9–10:

> After this I looked, and behold, a great multitude which no person could number, from every nation (ἔθνος), from all tribes and peoples and tongues, standing before the throne and before the Lamb, clothed in white robes, with palm branches in their hands, and crying out with a loud voice, "Salvation belongs to our God who sits upon the throne, and to the Lamb!"

In John's vision the heavenly throng possesses a common identity formed not by the denigration of the "other" but by the magnetic force of God's glory. Those sharing this identity are still recognizable on the basis of their ethnic identities; they have not become an amorphous, non-ethnic mass.[31] Centered upon the throne of God, these subgroup identities neither divide disparate groups nor form the pressure point for intergroup antagonism or violence. Rather, together they create a symphony of praise, the song of God's one redeemed people. The vision is John's, but it is shared by Luke. Within a world that has tasted the bitter fruit of interethnic hatred, this vision speaks of the hope that the people of God, through the power of the Spirit, can actualize the ontological reality of their shared identity—an identity that transcends intergroup antagonism and is formed within an allocentric community that lives in the way of peace and stretches outward toward the "other."

---

31. Neither Luke nor John give justification for Boyarin's fear that Christianity leads to a "coercive sameness" that eliminates "the rights of Jews, women and others to retain their difference" (1994, 233).

Bibliography

Abrams, Dominic, and Michael A. Hogg, eds. *Social Identity and Social Cognition*. Oxford: Blackwell.
Alexander, Loveday. 1993. *The Preface to Luke's Gospel: Literary Convention and Social Context in Luke 1.1-4 and Acts 1.1*. Society for New Testament Studies 78. Cambridge: Cambridge University Press.
———. 1999. Reading Luke-Acts from Back to Front. Pages 419-46 in Verheyden, ed., 1999.
Allen, O. Wesley. 1997. *The Death of Herod: The Narrative and Theological Function of Retribution in Luke-Acts*. Atlanta: Scholars Press.
Alon, Gedalyahu. 1967. *Studies in the History of Israel in the Days of the Second Temple and in the Mishna and Talmud Eras*. Tel-Aviv: Hakibbutz Hameuchad.
Andersen, T. David. 1988. The Meaning of Echontes Charin Pros in Acts 2.47. *New Testament Studies* 34:604-10.
Arrington, French L. 1988. *The Acts of the Apostles*. Peabody, Mass.: Hendrickson.
Ashburn-Nardo, Leslie, Corrine I. Voils and Margo J. Monteith. 2001. Implicit Associations As the Seeds of Intergroup Bias: How Easily Do They Take Root? *Journal of Personality and Social Psychology* 81, no. 5:789-99.
Baer, Hans von. 1926. *Der Heilige Geist in den Lukasschriften*. Stuttgart: Kohlhammer.
Bailey, Kenneth E. 1979. The Song of Mary: Vision of a New Exodus (Luke 1.46-55). *Theological Review* 2, no. 1:29-35.
Baldson, J. P. V. D. 1979. *Romans and Aliens*. London: Duckworth & Co.
Baltzer, Klaus. 1965. The Meaning of the Temple in Luke-Acts. *Harvard Theological Review* 58, no. 3:263-77.
Banks, M. 1996. *Anthropological Constructions of Ethnicity: An Introductory Guide*. London: Routledge.
Barclay, John M. G. 1996. "Neither Jew Nor Greek": Multiculturalism and the New Perspective on Paul. Pages 197-214 in *Ethnicity and the Bible*. Edited by Mark G. Brett. Leiden: Brill.
———. 1997. Universalism and Particularism: Twin Components of Both Judaism and Early Christianity. Pages 207-24 in Bockmuehl and Thompson, eds., 1997.
Barrett, C. K. 1994. *The Acts of the Apostles, Vol. 1 and 2*. International Critical Commentary. London: T&T Clark.
Bartchy, S. Scott. 1991. Community of Goods in Acts: Idealization Or Social Reality? Pages 309-18 in *The Future of Early Christianity: Essays in Honor of Helmut Koester*. Edited by Birger A. Pearson, A. Thomas Krabel, George W. E. Nickelsburg and Norman R. Petersen. Minneapolis: Fortress.
Barth, Fredrik, ed. 1967. *Ethnic Groups and Boundaries: The Social Organization of Culture Difference*. Boston: Little, Brown & Co.

Bartholomew, Craig G., and Robby Holt. 2005. Prayer in/and the Drama of Redemption in Luke: Prayer and Exegetical Performance. Pages 350–77 in *Reading Luke: Interpretation, Reflection, Formation*. Edited by Craig G. Bartholomew, Joel B. Green and Anthony C. Thistelton. Grand Rapids: Zondervan.

Bauckham, Richard. 1995. James and the Jerusalem Church. Pages 415–80 in Bauckham, ed., 1995.

———. 1996. James and the Gentiles (Acts 15.13–21). Pages 154–84 in *History, Literature and Society in the Book of Acts*. Edited by Ben Witherington III. Cambridge: Cambridge University Press.

———. 1998. *God Crucified: Monotheism and Christology in the New Testament*. Grand Rapids: Eerdmans.

———. 2001. The Restoration of Israel in Luke–Acts. Pages 435–87 in *Restoration: Old Testament, Jewish and Christian Perspectives*. Edited by James M. Scott. Leiden: Brill.

———. 2003. *Bible and Mission: Christian Witness in a Postmodern World*. Grand Rapids: Baker.

———. 2005. James, Peter, and the Gentiles. Pages 91–142 in *Missions of James, Peter, and Paul*. Edited by Bruce Chilton and Craig A. Evans. Leiden: Brill.

———. 2006. *Jesus and the Eyewitnesses: The Gospels as Eyewitness Testimony*. Grand Rapids: Eerdmans.

Bauckham, Richard, ed. 1995. *The Book of Acts in Its Palestinian Setting*. Grand Rapids: Eerdmans.

Bauernfeind, Otto. 1939. *Die Apostelgeschichte*. Leipzig: Deichert.

Baumgarten, Joseph. 1982a. The Exclusion of "Netinim" and Proselytes in 4q Florilegium. *Revue de Qumran* 80:87–96.

———. 1982b. Exclusions from the Temple: Proselytes and Agrippa I. *Journal of Jewish Studies* 33:215–25.

Beale, Gregory K. 2004. *The Temple and the Church's Mission: A Biblical Theology of the Dwelling Place of God*. Downers Grove, Ill.: InterVarsity.

Beasley-Murray, G. R. 1962. *Baptism in the New Testament*. London: Macmillan.

Best, Ernest. 1984. The Revelation to Evangelize the Gentiles. *Journal of Theological Studies* 35, no. 1:1–30.

Bettencourt, B. Ann, Nancy Dorr, Kelly Charlton and Deborah L. Hume. 2001. Status Differences and Ingroup Bias: A Meta-Analytic Examination of the Effects of Status Stability, Status Legitimacy, and Group Permeability. *Psychological Bulletin* 127, no. 4:520–42.

Bird, Michael. 2007. The Unity of Luke–Acts in Recent Discussion. *Journal for the Study of the New Testament* 29, no. 4:425–48.

Blenkinsopp, Joseph. 2006. *Opening the Sealed Book: Interpretations of the Book of Isaiah in Late Antiquity*. Grand Rapids: Eerdmans.

Bock, Darrell L. 1987. *Proclamation from Prophecy and Patter: Lukan Old Testament Christology*. Sheffield: JSOT.

———. 1994. *Luke: 1.1–9.50*. Baker Exegetical Commentary of the New Testament. Grand Rapids: Baker.

———. 1996. *Luke: 9.51–24.53*. Baker Exegetical Commentary of the New Testament. Grand Rapids: Baker.

———. 2007. *Acts*. Baker Exegetical Commentary of the New Testament. Grand Rapids: Baker Academic.

Bockmuehl, Markus. 2000. *Jewish Law in Gentile Churches: Halakhah and the Beginning of Christian Public Ethics*. Edinburgh: T. & T. Clark.

Bockmuehl, Markus, and Michael B. Thompson. *A Vision for the Church: Studies in Christian Ecclesiology*. Edinburgh: T. & T. Clark.

Bodenhausen, G. V., N. Schwarz, H. Bless and M. Wanke. 1995. Effects of Atypical Exemplars on Racial Beliefs: Enlightened Racism or Generalized Appraisals? *Journal of Experimental Social Psychology* 31:48–63.

Böhlemann, Peter. 1997. *Jesus und der Täfer: Schlüssel zur Theologie und Ethik des Lukas*. Cambridge: Cambridge University Press.

Bond, L. Susan. 2002. Acts 10.34–43. *Interpretation* 56, no. 1:80–83.

Bonnah, G. K. A. 2007. *The Holy Spirit: A Narrative Factor in the Acts of the Apostles*. Stuttgart: Katholisches Bibelwerk.

Borgen, Peder. 1994. Jesus of Nazareth, the Reception of the Spirit, and a Cross-national Community. Pages 220–35 in *Jesus of Nazareth: Lord and Christ: Essays on the Historical Jesus and New Testament Christology*. Edited by Max Turner and Joel B. Green. Grand Rapids: Eerdmans.

Borgman, Paul Carlton. 2006. *The Way According to Luke: Hearing the Whole Story of Luke–Acts*. Grand Rapids, Mich.: Eerdmans.

Bovon, Francois. 2002. *Luke 1: A Commentary on Luke 1–9.50. Hermeneia: A Critical and Historical Commentary on the Bible*. Edited by Helmut Koester. Minneapolis: Fortress.

———. 2006. *Luke the Theologian*. Waco, Tex.: Baylor University Press.

Boyarin. Daniel. 1994. *A Radical Jew: Paul and the Politics of Identity*. Contraversions: Critical Studies in Jewish Literature, Culture, and Society 1. Berkeley and Los Angeles: University of California Press.

Brawley, Robert L. 1987. *Luke–Acts and the Jews: Conflict, Apology, and Conciliation*. Society of Biblical Literature Monograph Series 33. Atlanta: Scholars Press.

———. 1999. Abrahamic Covenant Traditions and the Characterization of God in Luke–Acts. Pages 109–32 in Verheyden, ed., 1999.

Brewer, M. B. 1999. The Psychology of Prejudice: Ingroup Love or Outgroup Hate? *Journal of Social Issues* 55:429–44.

Brinkman, John Anthony. 1963. The Literary Background of the "Catalogue of the Nations" (Acts 2.9–11). *Catholic Biblical Quarterly* 25:418–27.

Brown, P. B. 1969. The Meaning and Function of Acts 5.1–11 in the Purpose of Luke–Acts. Ph.D. diss., Boston University.

Brown, Raymond. 1978. *The Birth of the Messiah: A Commentary on the Infancy Narratives in Matthew and Luke*. New York: Doubleday.

Brown, Rupert. 2000. Agenda 2000—Social Identity Theory: Past Achievements, Current Problems, and Future Challenges. *European Journal of Social Psychology* 30, no. 6:745–78.

Brown, Rupert, and S. Aharpour. 1999. Social Identity Theory and Group Diversity: An Analysis of Functions of Group Identification. Ph.D. diss., University of Kent.

Bruce, F. F. 1951. *The Acts of the Apostles: Greek Text with Introduction and Commentary*. London: Tyndale.

———. 1952. *The Acts of the Apostles*. Chicago: Intervarsity Christian Fellowship.

———. 1989. Philip and the Ethiopian. *Journal of Semitic Studies* 34, no. 2:377–86.

Brueggemann, Walter. 1982. *Genesis*. Atlanta: John Knox.

Büchler, Adolph. 1928. *Studies in Sin and Atonement in the Rabbinic Literature of the First Century*. London: Oxford University Press.
Büchsel, Friedrich. 1926. *Der Geist Gottes im Neuen Testament*. Gütersloh: Bertelsmann.
Buell, Denise Kimber. 2002. Race and Universalism in Early Christianity. *Journal of Early Christian Studies* 10, no. 4:429–68.
———. 2005. *Why This New Race: Ethnic Reasoning in Early Christianity*. New York: Columbia University Press.
Burdsey, Daniel. 2004. One of the Lads? Dual Ethnicity and Assimilated Ethnicities in the Careers of British Asian Professional Footballers. *Ethnic and Racial Studies* 27, no. 5:757–79.
Cadbury, Henry J. 1955. *The Book of Acts in History*. London: A. & C. Black.
Cairns, Ed. 1982. Intergroup Conflict in Northern Ireland. Pages 277–97 in Tajfel, ed., 1982.
———. 1994. *A Welling Up of Deep Unconscious Forces: Psychology and the Northern Ireland Conflict*. Coleraine: University of Ulster Press.
Callan, Terrance. 1993. The Background of the Apostolic Decree. *Catholic Biblical Quarterly* 55:284–97.
Capper, Brian J. 1983. The Interpretation of Acts 5.4. *Journal for the Study of the New Testament* 19:117–31.
———. 1995. The Palestinian Cultural Context of Earliest Christian Community of Goods. Pages 323–56 in Bauckham, ed., 1995.
———. 2009. Jesus, Virtuoso Religion, and the Community of Goods. Pages 60–80 in Longenecker and Liebengood, eds., 2009.
Carter, Warren. 1988. Zechariah and the Benedictus (Luke 1.68–79): Practicing What He Preaches. *Biblica* 69, no. 2:239–47.
Cheetham, F. P. 1963. Acts 2.47: Exontes Xarin Pros Olov Ton Laov. *Expository Times* 74:214–15.
Chen, Ya-Ru, Joel Brockner and Tal Katz. 1998. Toward an Explanation of Cultural Differences in In-Group Favoritism: The Role of Individual versus Collective Primacy. *Journal of Personality and Social Psychology* 75, no. 6:1490–502.
Cho. Youngmo. 2005. *Spirit and Kingdom in the Writings of Luke and Paul: An Attempt to Reconcile these Concepts*. Waynesboro, Ga.: Paternoster.
Christiansen, Ellen Juhl. 1995. *The Covenant in Judaism and Paul: A Study of Ritual Boundaries as Identity Markers*. London: Brill.
Ciraolo, L. J. 1992. The Warmth and Breath of Life: Animating Physical Object πάρεδροι in the Greek Magical Papyri. Pages 240–54 in *Society of Biblical Literature 1992 Seminar Papers*. Edited by Eugene H. Lovering, Jr. Atlanta: Scholars Press.
Cohen, Shaye J. D. 1999. *The Beginnings of Jewishness: Boundaries, Varieties, Uncertainties*. Berkeley: University of California Press.
Coleman, Simon, and Peter Collins. 2004. Introduction: Ambiguous Attachments: Religion, Identity and Nation. Pages 1–25 in Coleman and Collins, eds., 2004.
Coleman, Simon, and Peter Collins, eds. 2004. *Religion, Identity, and Change: Perspectives on Global Transformations*. Burlington, Vt.: Ashgate.
Colic-Peisker, Val, and Iain Walker. 2003. Human Capital, Acculturation and Social Identity: Bosnian Refugees in Australia. *Journal of Community and Applied Social Psychology* 13:337–60.
Collins, John J. 2005. The Judaism of the Book of Tobit. Pages 23–40 in Xeravits and Zsengeller, eds., 2005.

Conzelmann, Hans. 1960. *The Theology of St. Luke*. London: Faber & Faber.
———. 1961. *The Theology of St. Luke*. New York: Harper.
———. 1982. *The Theology of St. Luke*. London: SCM.
———. 1987. *Acts of the Apostles. Hermeneia: A Critical and Historical Commentary on the Bible*. Edited by Eldon J. Epp and Christopher R. Matthews. Philadelphia: Fortress.
Cosgrove, Charles. 1984. The Divine dei in Luke–Acts: Investigations into the Lukan Understanding of God's Providence. *Novum Testamentum* 26, no. 2:168–90.
Creed, J. M. 1930. *The Gospel According to St. Luke*. London: Macmillan.
Cromhout, Markus. 2007. *Jesus and Identity: Reconstructing Judean Ethnicity in Q*. Eugene, Ore.: Cascade.
Crossan, John Dominic, and Jonathan L. Reed. 2004. *In Search of Paul: How Jesus' Apostle Opposed Rome's Empire with God's Kingdom: A New Vision of Paul's Words and World*. New York: Harper San Francisco.
Dahl, Nils A. 1977. The One God of Jews and Gentiles (Romans 3.29–30). Pages 178–91 in *Studies in Paul: Theology for the Early Christian Mission*. Edited by Nils A. Dahl and Paul Donahue. Minneapolis: Augsburg.
———. 1980. The Story of Abraham in Luke–Acts. Pages 139–58 in *Studies in Luke–Acts*. Edited by Leander E. Keck and J. Louis Martyn. Philadelphia: Fortress.
Danker, Frederick W. 1982. *Benefactor: Epigraphic Study of a Graeco-Roman and New Testament Semantic Field*. St. Louis: Clayton Publishing House.
———. 1983. Reciprocity in the Ancient World and in Acts 15:23-29. Pages 49–58 in *Political Issues in Luke–Acts*. Edited by Richard J. Cassidy and Philip J. Scharper. Maryknoll, N.Y.: Orbis.
———. 1988. *Jesus and the New Age: A Commentary on St. Luke's Gospel*. Philadelphia: Fortress.
Darr, John A. 1992. *On Character Building: The Reader and the Rhetoric of Characterization in Luke–Acts*. Louisville, Ky.: Westminster John Knox.
Davila, James R. 2005. *The Provenance of the Pseudepigrapha: Jewish, Christian or Other?* Leiden: Brill.
Deaux, K., A. Reid, K. Mizrahi and K. Ethier. 1995. Parameters of Social Identity. *Journal of Personality and Social Psychology* 68, no. 2:280–91.
Dennison, Charles G. 1982. How Is Jesus the Son of God? Luke's Baptism Narrative and Christology. *Calvin Theological Journal* 17:6–25.
Denova, Rebecca I. 1997. *The Things Accomplished Among Us: Prophetic Tradition in the Structural Pattern of Luke–Acts*. Journal for the Study of the Old Testament: Supplement Series 141. Sheffield: Sheffield Academic.
deSilva, David A. 2002. *Introducing the Apocrypha: Message, Context and Significance*. Grand Rapids: Baker Academic.
Dibelius, Martin. 1971. *From Tradition to Gospel*. Cambridge: James Clarke.
Dietz-Uhler, Beth, and Audrey Murrell. 1998. Effects of Social Identity and Threat on Self-Esteem and Group Attributions. *Group Dynamics: Theory, Research, and Practice* 2, no. 1:24–35.
Dollar, Harold E. 1993. *A Biblical-Missiological Exploration of the Cross-Cultural Dimensions in Luke–Acts*. San Francisco: Mellen Research University Press.
Doran, Robert. 1981. *Temple Propaganda: The Purpose and Character of 2 Maccabees*. The Catholic Biblical Quarterly Monograph Series 12. Washington, D.C.: Catholic Biblical Association of America.

Dovidio, J. F., Samuel L. Gaertner and Ana Validzic. 1998. Intergroup Bias: Status, Differentiation, and a Common Ingroup Identity. *Journal of Personality and Social Psychology* 75, no. 1:109–20.

Duling, Dennis. 2005. Ethnicity, Ethnocentrism, and the Matthean Ethnos. *Biblical Theology Bulletin* 35:125–43.

Dunn, James D. G. 1970. *Baptism in the Holy Spirit: A Re-Examination of the New Testament Teaching on the Gift of the Spirit in Relation to Pentecostalism Today.* Studies in Biblical Theology, 2d series, 15. London: SCM.

———. 1987. "A Light to the Gentiles": The Significance of the Damascus Road Christophany for Paul. Pages 251–66 in *The Glory of Christ in the New Testament: Studies in Christology in Memory of George Bradford Caird.* Edited by L. D. Hurst and N. T. Wright. Oxford: Clarendon.

———. 1991. *The Partings of the Ways: Between Christianity and Judaism and Their Significance for the Character of Christianity.* London: SCM.

———. 1993. Baptism in the Spirit: A Response to Pentecostal Scholarship on Luke-Acts. *Journal of Pentecostal Theology* 3:3–27.

———. 1996. *The Acts of the Apostles, Epworth Commentaries.* Peterborough: Epworth.

———. 2008. *The New Perspective on Paul.* Rev. ed. Grand Rapids: Eerdmans.

DuPont, Jacques, O.S.B. 1970. The Conversion of Paul, and Its Influence on His Understanding of Salvation by Faith. Pages 176–94 in *Apostolic History and the Gospel: Biblical and Historical Essays Presented to F. F. Bruce.* Edited by W. Ward Gasque and Ralph P. Martin. Exeter: Paternoster.

———. 1979. *The Salvation of the Gentiles: Studies in the Acts of the Apostles.* Translated by John Keating, S.J. New York: Paulist.

———. 1985. Un people d'entre les nations (Actes 15.14). *New Testament Studies* 31:321–35.

Ego, Beate. 2005. The Book of Tobit and the Diaspora. Pages 41–54 in Xeravits and Zsengeller, eds., 2005.

Eliade, Mircea. 1954. *The Myth of the Eternal Return.* New York: Pantheon.

Elliott, John. 1991. Household and Meals vs. Temple Purity Replication Patterns in Luke-Acts. *Biblical Theology Bulletin* 21:102–8.

———. 1993. *Social-Scientific Criticism of the New Testament: An Introduction.* Minneapolis, Minn.: Augsburg Fortress.

———. 2007. Jesus the Israelite was Neither a "Jew" nor a "Christian": On Correcting Misleading Nomenclature. *Journal for the Study of the Historical Jesus* 5:119–54.

Ellis, Earle. 1974. *The Gospel of Luke.* Grand Rapids: Eerdmans.

———. 1991. "The End of the Earth" (Acts 1.8). *Bulletin for Biblical Research* 1:123–32.

Eltester, W. 1972. *Jesus in Nazareth.* Berlin: de Gruyter.

Ely, Robin J. 1994. The Effects of Organizational Demographics and Social Identity on Relationships among Professional Women. *Administrative Science Quarterly* 39, no. 2:203–38.

Endres, John C. 1987. *Biblical Interpretation in the Book of Jubilees.* The Catholic Biblical Quarterly Monograph Series 18. Washington, D.C.: Catholic Biblical Association of America.

Ervin, H. M. 1984. *Conversion-Initiation and the Baptism in the Holy Spirit: A Critique of James D. G. Dunn,* Baptism in the Holy Spirit. Peabody, Mass.: Hendrickson.

Esler, Philip. 1987. *Community and Gospel in Luke–Acts.* Cambridge: Cambridge University Press.

———. 1992. Glossolalia and the Admission of Gentiles into the Early Christian Community. *Biblical Theology Bulletin* 22, no 3:136–42.
———. 1994. *The First Christians and Their Worlds: Social-Scientific Approaches to New Testament Interpretation*. London: Routledge.
———. 1998. *Galatians*. London: Routledge.
———. 2000. Jesus and the Reduction of Intergroup Conflict: The Parable of the Good Samaritan in the Light of Social Identity Theory. *Biblical Interpretation: A Journal of Contemporary Approaches* 8, no. 4:325–57.
———. 2003. *Conflict and Identity in Romans: The Social Setting of Paul's Letter*. Minneapolis: Fortress.
———. 2006. Paul's Contestation of Israel's (Ethnic) Memory of Abraham in Galatians 3. *Biblical Theology Bulletin* 36, no. 1:23–34.
———. 2009. Judean Ethnic Identity in Josephus' "Contra Apionem." Pages 73–92 in *A Wandering Galilean: Essays in Honour of Sean Freyne*. Edited by Zuleika Rodgers, Margaret Daly-Denton and Anne Fitzpatrick McKinley. Leiden: Brill.
Farris, Stephen. 1985. *The Hymns of Luke's Infancy Narratives: Their Origin, Meaning, and Significance*. Sheffield: JSOT.
Fine, Gary Allen. 2001. *Difficult Reputations: Collective Memories of the Evil, Inept, and Controversial*. Chicago: University of Chicago Press.
Fishbane, Michael. 1985. *Biblical Interpretation in Ancient Israel*. Oxford: Clarendon.
Fitzmyer, Joseph A. 1981. *The Gospel According to Luke*. Vol. 1. Garden City, N.Y.: Doubleday.
———. 1998. *The Acts of the Apostles: A New Translation with Introduction and Commentary*. Anchor Bible 31. New York: Doubleday.
Fredricksen, Paula. 1986. Paul and Augustine. Conversion Narratives, Orthodox Traditions, and the Retrospective Self. *Journal of Theological Studies* 37:3–34.
Freyne, Sean. 1987. Galilee–Jerusalem Relations According to Josephus' "Life." *New Testament Studies* 33:600–609.
Frymer-Kensky, Tikva. 1983. Pollution, Purification and Purgation in Biblical Israel. Pages 399–414 in *The Word of the Lord Shall Go Forth: Essays in Honor of David Noel Freedman*. Edited by C. L. Myers and M. O'Connor. Winona Lake, Ind.: Eisenbrauns.
Fuller, Michael E. 2006. *The Restoration of Israel: Israel's Re-Gathering and the Fate of the Nations in Early Jewish Literature and Luke–Acts*. Berlin: de Gruyter.
Gaertner, S. L., J. F. Dovidio, M. C. Rust, J. A. Nier, B. S. Banker, C. M. Ward, G. R. Mottola and M. Houlette. 1999. Reducing Intergroup Bias: Elements of Intergroup Cooperation. *Journal of Personality and Social Psychology* 76:388–402.
Galinsky, Karl. 1996. *Augustan Culture*. Princeton, N.J.: Princeton University Press.
Gallo, Luis A. 1988. El Dios del Magnificat: Una Relectura Desde la Situación Latinoamericana. Pages 465–85 in *Virgo Fidelis: Miscellanea di Studi Mariani in Onone di don Domenico Bertetto, SDB*. Edited by Ferdinando Bergamelli and Mario Cimosa. Rome: Centro LiturgicoVincenziano-Edizioni Liturgiche.
Gamba, G. G. 1981. Significato letterale e portate dottrinale dell'inciso participiale di Atti 2.47b: *echontes charin pros holon ton laon*. *Salmanticensis* 43:45–70.
Ganguly, Rajat. Forthcoming. *A Dictionary of Ethnic Conflict*. Oxford: Routledge, Taylor & Francis.
Garret. Susan R. 1989. *The Demise of the Devil: Magic and the Demonic in Luke's Writings*. Minneapolis: Augsburg Fortress.

Gaventa, Beverly Roberts. 1985. The Overthrown Enemy: Luke's Portrait of Paul. *Society of Biblical Literature Seminar Papers* 24:439–49.

———. 1986. *From Darkness to Light: Aspects of Conversion in the New Testament.* Minneapolis: Fortress.

———. 2003. *The Acts of the Apostles.* Nashville: Abingdon.

———. 2004. Initiatives Divine and Human in the Lukan Story World. Pages 79–89 in Stanton, Longenecker and Barton, eds., 2004.

Geiger, Joseph. 2002. Language Culture and Identity in Ancient Palestine. Pages 233–46 in *Greek Romans and Roman Greeks*. Edited by Erik Ostenfeld. Aarhus: Aarhus University Press.

Gibson, James L. 2006. Do Strong Ingroup Identities Fuel Intolerance? Evidence from the South African Case. *Political Psychology* 27, no. 5:665–705.

Giles, H., R. Y. Bourhis and D. M. Taylor. 1977. Towards a Theory of Language in Ethnic Group Relations. Pages 307–48 in *Language, Ethnicity and Intergroup Relations*. European Monographs in Social Psychology 13. Edited by H. Giles. London: Academic.

Gill, David. 1974. Structure of Acts 9. *Biblica* 55, no. 4:546–48.

Gillmand, John. 1991. *Possessions and the Life of Faith: A Reading of Luke–Acts.* Collegeville, Minn.: Liturgical.

Goldingay, John, and David Payne. 2006. *Isaiah 40–55*, vol. 1. The International Critical Commentary. London: T&T Clark.

Gonzalez, R., and R. Brown. 2000. The Role of Categorization, Group Status and Group Size in Mediating Inter-Nation Attitudes in the European Union. Paper presented at the BPS Social Psychology Section Conference, September 2000.

Grant, Peter R. 1993. Reactions to Intergroup Similarity: Examination of the Similarity-Differentiation and Similarity-Attraction Hypotheses. *Canadian Journal of Behavioural Science* 25, no. 1:28–44.

Green, Joel B. 1997. *The Gospel of Luke*. The New International Commentary on the New Testament. Grand Rapids: Eerdmans.

———. 1998. "Salvation to the End of the Earth" (Acts 13.47): God as Saviour in the Acts of the Apostles. Pages 83–106 in Marshall and Peterson, eds., 1998.

———. 2008. "In Our Own Languages": Pentecost, Babel, and the Shaping of the Christian Community in Acts 2.1–13. Pages 198–213 in *The Word Leaps the Gap: Essays on Scripture and Theology in Honor of Richard B. Hays*. Edited by J. Ross Wagner, C. Kavin Rowe and A. Katherine Grieb. Grand Rapids: Eerdmans.

Gunkel, Hermann. 1899. *Die Wirkungen Des Heilige Geistes*. Göttingen: Vandenhoeck & Ruprecht.

———. 1979. *The Influence of the Holy Spirit: The Popular View of the Apostolic Age and the Teaching of the Apostle Paul: A Biblical-Theological Study*. Philadelphia: Fortress.

Haacker, Klaus. 1985. Das Bekenntnis des Paulus zur Hoffnung Israels nah der Apostelgeschichte des Lukas. *New Testament Studies* 31:437–51.

Haenchen, Ernst. 1971. *Acts of the Apostles*. Philadelphia: Westminster.

Hall, Deborah, David C. Malz and Wendy Wood. 2010. Why Don't We Practice What We Preach? A Meta-Analytic Review of Religious Racism. *Personality and Social Psychology Review* 14, no. 1:126–39.

Hall, Edith. 1989. *Inventing the Barbarian: Greek Self-Definition through Tragedy*. Oxford: Clarendon.

Hall, Jonathan M. 1997. *Ethnic Identity in Greek Antiquity*. Cambridge: Cambridge University Press.

Halpern-Amaru, Betsy. 1994. *Rewriting the Bible: Land and Covenant in Postbiblical Jewish Literature*. Valley Forge, Pa.: Trinity Press International.

Hamel, Edouard. 1979. Le Magnificat et le renversement des situations: Réflexion théologico-biblique. *Gregorianum* 60 no. 1:55–84.

Hamm, Dennis. 2003. The Tamid Service in Luke–Acts: The Cultic Background behind Luke's Theology of Public Worship (Luke 1.5–25; 18.9–14; 24.50–53; Acts 3.1; 10.3, 30). *Catholic Biblical Quarterly* 65, no. 3:215–31.

Hanson, K. C., and Douglas E. Oakman. 1998. *Palestine in the Time of Jesus: Social Structures and Social Conflicts*. Minneapolis: Augsburg Fortress.

Harland, Philip A. 2003. *Associations, Synagogues, and Congregations: Creating a Place in Ancient Mediterranean Society*. Minneapolis: Augsburg Fortress.

Harrison, Thomas, ed. 2002. *Greeks and Barbarians*. Edinburgh: Edinburgh University Press.

Harvey, W. J. 1965. *Character and the Novel*. Ithaca, N.Y.: Cornell University Press.

Hasitschka, Martin. 2002. Der Sohn Gottes—geliebt und gepruft: Zusammenhang von Taufe und Versuchung Jesu bei den Synoptikern. Pages 71–79 in *Forschungen zum Neuen Testament und seiner Umwelt: Festschrift fur Albert Fuchs*. Edited by Christopher Niemand. Frankfurt am Main: Lang.

Haulotte, E. 1970. Fondation d'une commuate de type universel: Actes 10.1–11.18. Etude critique sure la redaction, la "structure" et la "tradition" du recit. *Revue des sciences religieuses* 58:63–100.

Haya-Prats, Gonzalo. 1975. *L'esprit force de L'eglise*. Translated by J. Romero. Paris: Cerf.

Hays, J. Daniel. 2003. *From Every People and Nation: A Biblical Theology of Race*. Leicester: InterVarsity.

Hays, Richard. 1989. *Echoes of Scripture in the Letters of Paul*. New Haven: Yale University Press.

Hedrick, Charles W. 1981. Paul's Conversion: A Comparative Analysis of the Three Reports in Acts. *Journal of Biblical Literature* 100, no. 3:415–32.

Heike, Thomas. 2005. Endogamy in the Book of Tobit, Genesis, and Ezra–Nehemiah. Pages 103–20 in Xeravits and Zsengeller, eds., 2005.

Heil, John Paul. 1999. *The Meal Scenes in Luke–Acts: An Audience-Oriented Approach*. Atlanta: Society of Biblical Literature.

Hellerman, Joseph. 2003. Purity and Nationalism in Second Temple Literature: 1–2 Maccabees and Jubilees. *Journal of the Evangelical Theological Society* 46 no. 3:401–21.

Hendel, Ronald. 2005. *Remembering Abraham: Culture, Memory and History in the Hebrew Bible*. Oxford: Oxford University Press.

Hendrickson, W. 1978. *Exposition of the Gospel According to Luke*. Grand Rapids: Baker.

Hengel, Martin. 1980. *Acts and the History of Earliest Christianity*. Philadelphia: Fortress.

———. 1991. *The Pre-Christian Paul*. Philadelphia: Trinity Press International.

———. 2000. Ioudaia in the Geographical List of Acts 2.9–11 and Syria as "Greater Judea." *Bulletin for Biblical Research* 10, no. 2:161–80.

Hentschel, Anni. 2007. *Diakonia im Neuen Testament*. Tübingen: Mohr Siebeck.

Hewstone, M. 1996. Contact and Categorization: Social Psychological Interventions to Change Intergroup Relations. Pages 323–68 in *Foundations of Stereotypes and*

Stereotyping. Edited by N. Macrae, M. Hewstone and C. Stangor. New York: Guilford.
Hill, Craig C. 1992. *Hellenists and Hebrews: Reappraising Division within the Earliest Church.* Minneapolis: Fortress.
Hill, David. 1971. The Rejection at Nazareth. *Novum Testamentum* 13:161–80.
Hjelm, Ingrid. 2000. *The Samaritans and Early Judaism: A Literary Analysis.* Sheffield: Sheffield Academic.
Hoenig, Sydney B. 1970. Oil and Pagan Defilement. *The Jewish Quarterly Review* 61:63–75.
Hogg, Michael A., and Dominic Abrams. 1999. Social Identity and Social Cognition: Historical Background and Current Trends. Pages 1–25 in Abrams and Hogg, eds., 1999.
Hogg, Michael A., and Barbara A. Mullin. 1999. Joining Groups to Reduce Uncertainty: Subjective Uncertainty Reduction and Group Identification. Pages 249–79 in Abrams and Hogg, eds., 1999.
Hornsey, M., and M. Hogg. 1999. Subgroup Differentiation as a Response to an Overly Inclusive Group. *European Journal of Social Psychology* 29:543–50.
Horrell, David G., ed. 1999. *Social-Scientific Approaches to New Testament Interpretation.* Edinburgh: T. & T. Clark.
Horsley, Richard A. 1996. *Archaeology, History and Society in Galilee.* Valley Forge, Pa.: Trinity Press International.
Howard. G. E. 1969. Christ the End of the Law: The Meaning of Romans 10:4. *Journal of Biblical Literature* 88:331–37.
Huddy, L., and S. Virtanen. 1995. Subgroup Differentiation and Subgroup Bias among Latinos as a Function of Familiarity and Positive Distinction. *Journal of Personality and Social Psychology* 68, no. 1:97–108.
Huffman, D. S. 1994. *The Theology of the Acts of the Apostles: Lukan Compositional Markedness as a Guide to Interpreting Acts.* Ann Arbor: Bell & Howell.
Hughes, E. C. 1994. *On Work, Race and the Sociological Imagination.* Edited by L. A. Coser. Chicago: University of Chicago Press.
Hull, J. H. E. 1967. *The Holy Spirit in the Acts of the Apostles.* London: Lutterworth.
Hultgren, Stephen. 2002. *Narrative Elements within the Double Tradition: A Study of Their Place Within the Framework of the Gospel Narrative.* Berlin: de Gruyter.
Hur, Ju. 2001. *A Dynamic Reading of the Holy Spirit in Luke–Acts.* Sheffield: Sheffield Academic.
Hurtado, Larry W. 1993. Convert, Apostate or Apostle to the Nations: The "Conversion" of Paul in Recent Scholarship. *Studies in Religion/Sciences Religieuses* 22, no. 3:273–84.
Huskinson, Janet. 2000. *Experiencing Rome: Culture, Identity and Power in the Roman Empire.* New York: Routledge.
Hutchinson, John, and Anthony D. Smith, eds. 1996. *Ethnicity.* Oxford: Oxford University Press.
Ilan, Tal. 2002. *Lexicon of Jewish Names in Antiquity: Part I, Palestine 330 BCE–200 CE.* Tübingen: Mohr Siebeck.
Jenkins, Philip. 2002. *The Next Christendom: The Coming of Global Christianity.* Oxford: Oxford University Press.
———. 2006. *The New Faces of Christianity: Believing the Bible in the Global South.* Oxford: Oxford University Press.

Jenkins, Richard. 1997. *Rethinking Ethnicity: Arguments and Explorations*. London: Sage.
Jeremias, Joachim. 1958. *Jesus' Promise to the Nations*. London: SCM.
———. 1966. *The Eucharistic Words of Jesus*. New York: Scribner's.
———. 1969. *Jerusalem in the Time of Jesus: An Investigation into Economic & Social Conditions during the New Testament Period*. Trans. F. H. Cave and C. H. Cave. Minneapolis: Augsburg Fortress.
Jervell, Jacob. 1972. *Luke and the People of God: A New Look at Luke–Acts*. Minneapolis: Augsburg.
———. 1998. *Die Apostelgeschichte*. Göttingen: Vandenhoeck & Ruprecht.
Jetten, Jolanda, Tom Postmes and Russell Spears. 2004. Intergroup Distinctiveness and Differentiation: A Meta-Analytic Integration. *Journal of Personality and Social Psychology* 86, no. 6:862–79.
Jetten, Jolanda, Michael T. Schmitt, Nyla R. Branscombe and Blake M. McKimmie. 2005. Suppressing the Negative Effect of Devaluation on Group Identification: The Role of Intergroup Differentiation and Intragroup Respect. *Journal of Experimental Social Psychology* 41, no. 2:208–15.
Jetten, Jolanda, Russell Spears and Antony S. R. Manstead. 2001. Similarity as a Source of Differentiation: The Role of Group Identification. *European Journal of Social Psychology* 31:621–40.
Johnson, Aaron P. 2006. *Ethnicity and Argument in Eusebius' Praeparatio Evangelica*. Oxford: Oxford University Press.
Johnson, Luke Timothy. 1977. *The Literary Function of Possessions in Luke–Acts*. Society of Biblical Literature Dissertation Series 39. Missoula, Mont.: Scholars.
———. 1983. *Decision Making in the Church: A Biblical Model*. Philadelphia: Fortress.
———. 1991. *Luke*. Collegeville, Minn.: Liturgical.
———. 1992. *The Acts of the Apostles*. Collegeville, Minn.: Liturgical.
Jones, Sian, and Sarah Pearce, eds. 1998. *Jewish Local Patriotism and Self-Identification in the Graeco-Roman Period*. Sheffield: Sheffield Academic.
Katzoff, Ranon. 1985. Jonathan and Late Sparta. *The American Journal of Philology* 106 no. 4:485–89.
Kazmierski, Carl R. 1987. The Stones of Abraham: John the Baptist and the End of Torah (Matt 3.7–10 Par. Luke 3.7–9). *Biblica* 68, no. 1:22–40.
Keck, Leander E. 1971. The Spirit and the Dove. *New Testament Studies* 17:41–67.
Kee, Howard Clark. 1990. *Good News to the Ends of the Earth: The Theology of Acts*. London: SCM.
Keener, Craig S. 1997. *The Spirit in the Gospels and Acts: Divine Purity and Power*. Peabody, Mass.: Hendrickson.
———. 1999. *A Commentary on the Gospel of Matthew*. Grand Rapids: Eerdmans.
Kerr, Fergus. 2006. Rage Against Jesus. *Expository Times* 118, no. 3:139–40.
Kilpatrick, G. D. 1975. Jewish Background to Acts 2.9–11. *Journal of Jewish Studies* 66, no. 1:48–49.
Kim, H. S. 1993. *Die Geisttaufe des Messias: Eine kompositionsgeschichtliche Untersuchung zu einem Leitmotiv des lukanischen Doppelwerks*. Berlin: Lang.
Kim, Seyoon. 1981. *The Origin's of Paul's Gospel*. Grand Rapids: Eerdmans.
Klawans, Jonathan. 2006. Moral and Ritual Purity. Pages 266–84 in *The Historical Jesus in Context*. Edited by Amy-Jill Levine, Dale C. Allison Jr. and John Dominic Crossan. Princeton, N.J.: Princeton University Press.
Klein, Hans. 2006. *Das Lukas Evangelium*. Göttingen: Vandenhoeck & Ruprecht.

Klijn, A. F. J. 1968. The Pseudo-Clementines and the Apostolic Decree. *Novum Testamentum* 10, no. 4:305–12.

Kloppenborg, John S. 1993. Edwin Hatch, Churches and Collegia. Pages 212–38 in *Origins and Method: Towards a New Understanding of Judaism and Christianity*. Edited by Bradley H. McLean. Sheffield: Sheffield Academic.

Kloppenborg, John S., and S. G. Wilson, eds. 1996. *Voluntary Associations in the Graeco-Roman World*. London: Routledge.

Kodell, Jerome. 2003. Luke's Gospel in a Nutshell. *Biblical Bulletin of Theology* 11:16–18.

Koet, Bart J. 2005. Isaiah in Luke–Acts. Pages 79–100 in *Isaiah in the New Testament*. Edited by Steve Moyise and Maarten J. J. Menken. London: T&T Clark.

———. 2008. Luke 10.38–42 and Acts 6.1–7: A Lukan Diptych on ΔIAKONIA. Pages 163–85 in *Studies in the Greek Bible: Essays in Honor of Francis T. Gignac, S.J.* Edited by Jeremy Corley and Vincent Skemp. Washington, D.C.: Catholic Biblical Association of America.

Kollman, Bernd. 2003. *Joseph Barnabas: His Life and Legacy*. Collegeville, Minn.: Liturgical.

Kuecker, Aaron J. 2009. The Spirit and the "Other," Satan and the "Self": Economic Ethics as a Consequence of Identity Transformation in Luke–Acts. Pages 81–103 Longenecker and Liebengood, eds., 2009.

Kuhn, Thomas. 1970. *The Structure of Scientific Revolutions*. 2d ed. Chicago: University of Chicago Press.

Kurz, William S. 1993. *Reading Luke–Acts: Dynamics of Biblical Narrative*. Louisville, Ky.: Westminster John Knox.

Kyo-Seon Shin, Gabriel. 1989. *Die Ausrufung des endgülten Jubeljahres durch Jesus in Nazaret: Eine historisch-kritische Studie ze Lk 4.16–30*. Bern: Lang.

LaGrand, James. 1998. Luke's Portrait of Simeon: Aged Saint or Hesitant Terrorist? Pages 175–85 in *Common Life in the Early Church*. Edited by Julian V. Hill. Harrisburg, Pa.: Trinity Press International.

Lampe, G. W. H. 1951. *The Seal of the Spirit.* London: Longmans.

———. 1977. *God as Spirit: The Bampton Lectures, 1976.* Oxford: Clarendon.

Leisegang, Hans. 1919. *Der Heilige Geist: Das Wesen und Weden der Mystisch-Intuitiven Erkenntnis in der Philosophie und Religion der Griechen.* Berlin: Teubner.

———. 1922. *Pneuma Hagion: Der ursprung des Geistesbegriffs der synoptischen Evangelien aus der griechischen Mystik.* Leipzig: Hinrichs.

Levine, Amy-Jill. 1992. Diaspora as Metaphor: Bodies and Boundaries in the Book of Tobit. Pages 105–17 in *Diaspora Jews and Judaism: Essays in Honor of, and in Dialogue with, A. Thomas Kraabel.* Edited by J. A. Overman and R. S. MacLennan. Atlanta: Scholars.

Levine, Lee I. 2005. *The Ancient Synagogue: The First Thousand Years.* 2d ed. New Haven, Conn.: Yale University Press.

Levison, John R. 1997. *The Spirit in First Century Judaism.* Leiden: Brill.

———. 1999. *Of Two Minds: Ecstasy and Inspired Interpretation in the New Testament World.* North Richland Hills, Tex.: Bibal.

———. 2009. *Filled with the Spirit.* Grand Rapids: Eerdmans.

Lienhard, Joseph T. 1975. Acts 6.1–6: A Redactional View. *Catholic Biblical Quarterly* 37:228–36.

Lieu. Judith. 1997. *The Gospel of Luke.* Petersborough: Epworth.

Litwak, Kenneth Duncan. 2005 *Echoes of Scripture in Luke–Acts: Telling the History of God's People Intertextually.* London: T&T Clark.

Lockett, Darian. 2008. *Purity and Worldview in the Epistle of James.* London: T&T Clark.

Longenecker, Bruce W. 1991. *Eschatology and Covenant: A Comparison of 4 Ezra and Romans 1–11.* Sheffield: JSOT.

———. 1999. Until Christ is Formed in You: Suprahuman Forces and Moral Character in Galatians. *Catholic Biblical Quarterly* 61 no. 1:92–108.

———. 2005. *Rhetoric at the Boundaries: The Art and Theology of New Testament Chain Link Transitions.* Waco, Tex.: Baylor University Press.

———. 2009. Exposing the Economic Middle: A Revised Economy Scale for the Study of Early Urban Christianity. *Journal for the Study of the New Testament* 31, no. 3:243–78.

Longenecker, Bruce W., and Kelly D. Liebengood, eds. *Engaging Economics: New Testament Scenarios and Early Christian Reception.* Grand Rapids: Eerdmans.

Lotz, Denton. 1988. Peter's Wider Understanding of God's Will: Acts 10.34–48. *International Review of Mission* 77:201–7.

Luce. Kenneth Harry. 1933. *The Gospel According to St. Luke.* New York: Macmillan.

Macchi, J. D. 1999. *Les Samaritains: Histoire d'une légende. Israël et la province de Samarie.* Geneva: Labor et Fides.

Maddox, Robert. 1982. *The Purpose of Luke–Acts.* Edinburgh: T. & T. Clark.

Mainville, O. 1991. *L'esprit dans l'oeuvre de Luc.* Quebec: Fides.

Malina, Bruce J., and Richard L. Rohrbaugh. 2003. *Social-Science Commentary on the Synoptic Gospels.* Minneapolis: Augsburg Fortress.

Mallen, Peter. 2008. *The Reading and Transformation of Isaiah in Luke–Acts.* Library of New Testament Studies 367. London: T&T Clark.

Marguerat, Daniel. 1993. La mort d'Ananias et Saphira (Ac 5.1–11) dans la stratégie narrative de Luc. *New Testament Studies* 39, no 2:209–26.

―――. 2002. *The First Christian Historian: Writing the "Acts of the Apostles."* Translated by Ken McKinney, Gregory J. Laughery and Richard Bauckham. Cambridge: Cambridge University Press.
Marquis, Timothy Lukritz. 2007. Josephus's Use of 1 Maccabees 10.25–45 and the Term Ioudaios. Pages 55–67 in Zangenberg, Attridge and Martin, eds., 2007.
Marshall, I. Howard. 1978. *The Gospel of Luke: A Commentary on the Greek Text*. The New International Greek Testament Commentary. Exeter: Paternoster.
―――. 1980. *The Acts of the Apostles: An Introduction and Commentary*. Grand Rapids, Mich.: Eerdmans.
Marshall, I. Howard, and David Peterson, eds. 1998. *Witness to the Gospel: The Theology of Acts*. Grand Rapids: Eerdmans.
Marshall, Jonathan. 2009. *Jesus, Patrons, and Benefactors*. Tübingen: Mohr Siebeck.
Martin, Clarice J. 1985. *The Function of Acts 8.26–40 within the Narrative Structure of the Book of Acts*. Durham, Na.: Duke University Press.
―――. 1989. A Chamberlain's Journey and the Challenge of Interpretation for Liberation. *Semeia* 47:105–35.
Mathey, Jacques. 2000. Luke 4.16–30—the Spirit's Mission Manifesto—Jesus' Hermeneutics—and Luke's Editorial. *International Review of Mission* 89:3–11.
McIntosh, John. 2002. "For It Seemed Good to the Holy Spirit" Acts 15.28: How Did the Members of the Jerusalem Council Know This? *The Reformed Theological Review* 61, no. 3:131–47.
McLaren, James S. 2005. Jews and the Imperial Cult: From Augustus to Domitian. *Journal for the Study of the New Testament* 27, no. 3:257–78.
McMillan, David K. 2001. Acts 15.22–31. *Interpretation* 55, no. 4:420–22.
McVerry, Peter. 2003. Mary's Vision of Justice Outlined in the Magnificat. Pages 39–48 in *Windows on Social Spirituality*. Dublin: Columbia.
Medin, D. L., M. W. Altom and T. D. Murphy. 1984. Given Versus Induced Category Representations: Use of Prototype and Exemplar Information in Classification. *Journal of Experimental Psychology: Learning, Memory, and Cognition* 10:333–52.
Menzies, Robert P. 1991. *The Development of Early Christian Pneumatology with Special Reference to Luke-Acts*. Sheffield: Sheffield Academic.
Metzger, Bruce M. 1957. *An Introduction to the Apocrypha*. Oxford: Oxford University Press.
―――. 1975. *A Textual Commentary on the Greek New Testament*. London: United Bible Societies.
Mezzacasa, Florencio. 1988. El cantico de liberación de Maria: una reflexion catequética de Lk 1.46–56. *Cuadernos de Teología* 9 no. 2:133–50.
Milgrom, Jacob. 1991. *Leviticus 1–16: A New Translation with Introduction and Commentary*. New York: Doubleday.
Miller, Donald G. 1986. Luke 4.22–30. *Interpretation* 40, no. 1:53–58.
Miller, James E. 1993. The Birth of John the Baptist and the Gospel to the Gentiles. *Andrews University Seminary Studies* 31, no. 3:195–97.
Minguez, Dionisio. 1976. Hechos 8.25–40: Análisis estructural del relato. *Biblica* 57, no. 2:168–91.
Mitchell, Alan C. 1992. The Social Function of Friendship in Acts 2.44–47 and 4.32–37. *Journal of Biblical Literature* 111, no. 2:255–72.

Moessner, David P. 1999. *Jesus and the Heritage of Israel: Luke's Narrative Claim Upon Israel's Legacy*. Luke the Interpreter of Israel 1. Harrisburg, Pa.: Trinity Press International.

Moghaddam, Fathali M., and Peter Stringer. 1988. Out-Group Similarity and Intergroup Bias. *Journal of Social Psychology* 128:105-15.

Moore, Thomas S. 1997. "To the End of the Earth": The Geographical and Ethnic Universalism of Acts 1.8 in Light of Isaianic Influence on Luke. *Journal of the Evangelical Theological Society* 40, no. 3:389-99.

Moxnes, Halvor. 1991. Patron-Client Relations and the New Community in Luke-Acts. Pages 241-68 in *The Social World of Luke-Acts: Models for Interpretation*. Edited by Jerome H. Neyrey. Peabody, Mass.: Hendrickson.

———. 2003. *Putting Jesus in His Place: A Radical Vision of Household and Kingdom*. Louisville, Ky.: Westminster John Knox.

Mullen, B., R. Brown and C. Smith. 1992. Ingroup Bias as a Function of Salience, Relevance, and Status: An Integration. *European Journal of Social Psychology* 22:103-22.

Mummenday, A., and M. Wenzel. 1999. Social Discrimination and Tolerance in Intergroup Relations. *Personality and Social Psychology Review* 3:158-74.

Munck, J. 1959. *Paul and the Salvation of Mankind*. Atlanta: John Knox.

Neusner, Jacob, and Bruce Chilton. 1995. *Judaism in the New Testament: Practices and Beliefs*. London: Routledge.

Newbigin, Lesslie. 1989. *The Gospel in a Pluralist Society*. Grand Rapids: Eerdmans.

Neyrey, Jerome H. 1994. Josephus' VITA and the Encomium: A Native Model of the Personality. *Journal for the Study of Judaism in the Persian, Hellenistic and Roman Period* 25, no. 2:177-206.

Nolland, John. 1979a. Classical and Rabbinic Parallels to "Physician, Heal Yourself" (Lk. Iv.23). *Novum Testamentum* 21, no. 3:193-209.

———. 1979b. Impressed Unbelievers as Witnesses to Christ (4.22a). *Journal of Biblical Literature* 98, no. 2:219-29.

———. 1989. *Luke*. Word Biblical Commentary 35a, 35b, 35c. Dallas: Nelson.

Noorda. S. J. 1982. Cure Yourself, Doctor (Luke 4:23): Classical Parallells to an Alleged Saying of Jesus. Pages 459-67 in *Logia: Les Paroles de Jésus — The Sayings of Jesus. Mémorial Joseph Coppens*. Edited by Joël Delobel. Leuven: Leuven University Press.

Neubauer, A. 1885. The Dialects Spoken in Palestine in the Time of Christ. Pages 39-74 in *Studia Biblica: Essays in Biblical Archaeology and Criticism, and Kindred Subjects*. Oxford: Clarendon.

Öhler, Markus. 2003. *Barnabas: die historische Person und ihre Rezeption in der Apostelgeschichte*. Tübingen: Mohr Siebeck.

O'Day, Gail R. 1985. Singing Woman's Song: A Hermeneutic of Liberation. *Currents in Theology and Mission*, 12 no. 4:203-10.

O'Neill, J. C. 1959. The Six Amen Sayings in Luke. *Journal of Theological Studies* 10:1-9.

O'Toole, Robert F. 1983. Philip and the Ethiopian Eunuch. *Journal for the Study of the New Testament* 17:25-34.

———. 1995. "You Did Not Lie to Us (Human Beings) but to God" (Acts 5.4c). *Biblica* 76, no. 2:182-209.

———. 1996. Eirene, an Underlying Theme in Acts 10.34-43. *Biblica* 77, no. 4:461-76.

Pao, David W. 2002. *Acts and the Isaianic New Exodus, Biblical Studies Library*. Grand Rapids: Baker Academic.

Parsons, Mikeal C. 1998. Isaiah 53 in Acts 8: A Reply to Professor Morna Hooker. Pages 104–19 in *Jesus and the Suffering Servant*. Harrisburg, Pa.: Trinity Press International.

———. 2006. *Body and Character in Luke–Acts: The Subversion of Physiognomy in Early Christianity*. Grand Rapids: Baker Academic.

Parsons, Mikeal C., and Martin M. Culy. 2003. *Acts: A Handbook on the Greek Text*. Waco, Tex.: Baylor University Press.

Pearce, Sarah. 1998. Belonging and Not Belonging: Local Perspectives in Philo of Alexandria. Pages 79–105 in Jones and Pearce, eds., 1998.

Penney, John Michael. 1997. *The Missionary Emphasis of Lukan Pneumatology*. Sheffield: Sheffield Academic.

Pesch, Rudolf. 1986. *Die Apostelgeschichte*. Zurich: Benziger.

Pitkanen, Pekka. 2006. Family Life and Ethnicity in Early Israel and Tobit. Pages 104–17 in *Studies in the Book of Tobit: A Multidisciplinary Approach*. Edited by Mark Bredin. London: T&T Clark.

Polhill, John. 1992. *Acts*. Nashville: Broadman.

Poole, Marshall Scott, et al. 2004. Interdisciplinary Perspectives on Small Groups. *Small Group Research* 35, no. 3:3–16.

Porter, R. J. 1988. What Did Philip Say to the Eunuch? *Expository Times* 100:54–55.

Porter, Stanley E. 2006. Scripture Justifies Mission: The Use of the Old Testament in Luke–Acts. Pages 104–26 in *Hearing the Old Testament in the New Testament*. Edited by Stanley E. Porter. Grand Rapids: Eerdmans.

Proctor, John. 1996. Proselytes and Pressure Cookers: The Meaning and Application of Acts 15.20. *International Review of Mission* 85:469–83.

Pummer, R. 1992. Einführung in den Stand der Samaritanerforschung. Pages 1–66 in *Die Samaritaner*. Edited by F. Dexinger and R. Pummer. Darmstadt: Wissenschaftliche Buchgesellschaft.

Purvis, James D. 1986. *The Samaritan Pentateuch and the Origin of the Samaritan Sect*. Harvard Semitic Monographs 2. Cambridge, Mass.: Harvard University Press.

Quesnel, M. 1985. *Baptises dans l'Esprit*. Paris: Cerf.

Rabbie, J. M., and M. Horowitz. 1988. Categories versus Groups as Explanatory Concepts in Intergroup Relations. *European Journal of Social Psychology* 18:117–23.

Rad, Gerhard von. 1972. *Genesis, a Commentary*. London: SCM.

Radl, Walter. 1999. Die Beziehungen der Vorgeschichte zur Apostelgeschichte. Pages 297–312 in Verheyden, ed., 1999.

Rae, Murray A. 2005. *History and Hermeneutics*. New York: T&T Clark.

Rahmani, L. Y. 1994. *A Catalogue of Jewish Ossuaries*. Jerusalem: Israel Antiquities Authority and the Israel Academy of Sciences and Humanities.

Ravens, David. 1995. *Luke and the Restoration of Israel*. Journal for the Study of the New Testament Supplement Series 119. Sheffield: Sheffield Academic.

Reed, Jonathan L. 2000. *Archaeology and the Galilean Jesus: A Re-Examination of the Evidence*. Harrisburg, Pa.: Trinity Press International.

Reicke, B. 1978. Jesus, Simeon, and Anna (Luke 2.21–40). Pages 96–108 in *Saved by Hope*. Edited by James I. Cook. Grand Rapids: Eerdmans.

Reisner, R. 1994. James's Speech (Acts 15:13–21), Simeon's Hymn (Luke 2:29–32, and Luke's Sources. Pages 263–78 in *Jesus of Nazareth: Lord and Christ*. Edited by J. B. Green and M. Turner. Grand Rapids: Eerdmans.

Robertson, Bruce L. 1982. Luke 3.10–18. *Interpretation* 36:404–9.

Robinson, Anthony B., and Robert W. Wall. 2006. *Called to Be Church: The Book of Acts for a New Day*. Grand Rapids: Eerdmans.

Rothgerber, Hank. 1997. External Intergroup Threat as an Antecedent to Perceptions of Ingroup and Outgroup Homogeneity. *Journal of Personality and Social Psychology* 73, no. 6:1206–12.

Rouhana, N., and Daniel Bar-Tal. 1998. Psychological Dynamics of Intractable Ethnonational Conflicts: The Israeli–Palestinian Case. *American Psychologist* 53, no. 7:761–70.

Rowe, C. Kavin. 2005. Luke–Acts and the Imperial Cult: A Way through the Conundrum? *Journal for the Study of the New Testament* 27, no. 3:279–300.

———. 2006. *Early Narrative Christology: The Lord in the Gospel of Luke*. Berlin: de Gruyter.

———. 2009. *World Upside Down: Reading Acts in the Greco-Roman Age*. Oxford: Oxford University Press.

Ruether, Rosemary Radford. 1980. [Mary] She's a Sign of God's Liberating Power: "Liberation Mariology" Can Help Understand the Meaning and Role of the Church. *Other Side* 104:17–21.

Rusam, Dietrich. 2003. *Das Alte Testament bei Lukas*. Berlin: de Gruyter.

Saeed, A., N. Blain and D. Forbes. 1999. New Ethnic and National Questions in Scotland: Post-British Identities among Glasgow Pakistani Teenagers. *Ethnic and Racial Studies* 22, no. 5:821–44.

Sahlin, Harold. 1948. Die Früchte der Umkehr: Die Ethische Verkündigung Johannes des Taüfers nach Lukas 3.10–14. *Studia Theologica* 1:54–68.

Samkutty, V. J. 2006. *The Samaritan Mission in Acts*. London: T&T Clark.

Sanders, Jack T. 1987. *The Jews in Luke–Acts*. London: SCM.

Sandiyagu, Virginia R. 2006. "Heteros" and "Allos" in Luke. *Novum Testamentum* 48, no. 2:105–30.

Schiffman, H. F. 1995. Language Shift in the Tamil Communities of Malaysia and Singapore: the Paradox of Egalitarian Language Policy. *Southwest Journal of Linguistics, Special Issue on Language Loss and Public Policy* 1:151–65.

Schille, Gottfried. 1989. *Die Apostelgeschichte des Lukas*. Berlin: Evangelische Verlag.

Schils, Edward. 1957. Primordial, Personal, Sacred, and Civil Ties: Some Particular Observations on the Relationships of Sociological Research and Theory. *British Journal of Sociology* 8:130–45.

Schneider, Gerhard. 1977. *Das Evangelius Nach Lukas*, vol. 1. Wurzburg: Gutersloh.

Schur, N. 1995. Some Instances of the Impact of Samaritan Studies on the Historiography of the Holy Land. Pages 289–94 in *New Samaritan Studies of the Société d'Études Samaritaines III–IV: Essays in Honour of G. D. Sixdenie*. Edited by A. D. Crown and L. Davey. Sydney: Mandelbaum.

Schürmann, H. 1969. *Das Lukasevangelium*. (HTKNT III.) Erster Teil. Freiberg: Herder.

Schwadel, Philip. 2009. Neighbors in the Pews: Social Status Diversity in Religious Congregations. *Interdisciplinary Journal of Research on Religion* 5, no. 2:1–24.

Schwartz, Daniel R. 1986. The End of the "Ge" (Acts 1.8): Beginning or End of the Christian Vision? *Journal of Biblical Literature* 105, no. 4:669–76.

Schwartz, Seth. 1993. Language, Power and Identity in Ancient Palestine. *Past and Present* 148:3–47.

Schweizer, Eduard. 1956. 1984. *The Good News According to Luke*. London: SPCK.

Scott, James M. 1993. Luke's Geographical Horizon. Pages 483–544 in *The Book of Acts in Its Graeco-Roman Setting*. Edited by Bruce W. Winter and Andrew D. Clarke. Grand Rapids: Eerdmans.

———. 2002. *Geography in Early Judaism and Christianity*. Cambridge: Cambridge University Press.

Seccombe, David. 1978. Was There Organized Charity in Jerusalem before the Christians? *Journal of Theological Studies* 29, no. 1:140–43.

———. 1981. Luke and Isaiah. *New Testament Studies* 27:252–59.

———. 1983. *Possessions and the Poor in Luke–Acts*. Linz: Fuchs.

———. 1997. Luke's Vision for the Church. Pages 45–63 in Bockmuehl and Thompson, eds., 1997.

Segal, Alan F. 1990. *Paul the Convert*. New Haven: Yale University Press.

Seitz, Christopher R. 1991. *Figured Out: Typology and Providence in Christian Scripture*. Louisville, Ky.: Westminster John Knox.

Shaw, Brent D. 2000. Rebels and Outsiders. Pages 361–403 in *The Cambridge Ancient History*. Volume 11, *The High Empire, A.D. 70–192*. Edited by Alan K. Bowman, Peter Garnsey and Dominic Rathbone. Cambridge: Cambridge University Press.

Shelton, James B. 1991. *Mighty in Word and Deed: The Role of the Holy Spirit in Luke–Acts*. Peabody, Mass.: Hendrickson.

Shepherd, William H. 1994. *The Narrative Function of the Holy Spirit as a Character in Luke–Acts*. Society of Biblical Literature Dissertation Series 147. Atlanta: Scholars Press.

Slee, Michelle. 2003. *The Church in Antioch in the First Century C.E.: Communion and Conflict*. London: Sheffield Academic.

Smith, E. R., and M. A. Zarate. 1992. Exemplar-Based Model of Social Judgment. *Psychological Review* 99:3–21.

Snodgrass, Klyne. 1980. Streams of Tradition Emerging from Isaiah 40.1–5 and Their Adaptation in the New Testament. *Journal for the Study of the New Testament* 8:24–45.

Spencer, F. Scott. 1992a. The Ethiopian Eunuch and His Bible: A Social-Science Analysis. *Biblical Theology Bulletin* 22:155–65.

———. 1992b. *The Portrait of Philip in Acts: A Study of Roles and Relations*. Sheffield: JSOT.

———. 1994. Neglected Widows in Acts 6.1–7. *Catholic Biblical Quarterly* 56:715–33.

Squires, John T. 1998. The Function of Acts 8.4–12.25. *New Testament Studies* 44:608–17.

Stanley, Christopher. 1997. Ethnic Conflict in Greco-Roman Society. *Journal for the Study of the New Testament* 19:101–24.

Stanton, G. N., Bruce W. Longenecker and Stephen C. Barton, eds. *The Holy Spirit and Christian Origins: Essays in Honor of James D. G. Dunn*. Grand Rapids: Eerdmans.

Stendahl, Krister. 1976. *Paul among Jews and Gentiles and other Essays*. Philadelphia: Fortress.

———. 1977. It Took a Miracle to Launch the Mission to the Gentiles: The Cornelius Story (Acts 10.11–11.18). Pages 123–25 in *Faith in the Midst of Faiths*. Geneva: World Council of Churches.

Stenhouse, Paul, trans. 1985. *The Kitab Al-Tarikh of Abu'l Fath*. Sydney: Mandelbaum.

Sterling, Gregory E. 1994. "Athletes of Virtue": An Analysis of the Summaries in Acts (2.41–47; 4.32–35; 5.12–16). *Journal of Biblical Literature* 113, no. 4:679–96.

Stern, Mehahem. 1984. *Greek and Latin Authors on Jews and Judaism*. 3 vols. Jerusalem: Israel Academy of Science and Humanities.
Stone, M., and E. Eshel. 1992. An Exposition on the Patriarchs (4Q464) and Two Other Documents (4Q464a and 4Q464h). *Le Museon* 105:243-64.
―――. 1993-94. The Holy Language at the End of Days in Light of a Qumran Fragment. *Tarbiz* 62:169-77 [in Hebrew].
Strelan, Rick. 2001. The Running Prophet (Acts 8.30). *Novum Testamentum* 43, no. 1:31-38.
Strobel, August. 1972. Die Ausrufung des Jobeljahres in der Nazareth-predigt Jesus; zur apokalyptischen Tradition Lc 4.16-30. Pages 38-50 in Eltester, ed., 1972.
Stronstad, Roger. 1984. *The Charismatic Theology of St. Luke*. Peabody, Mass.: Hendrickson.
Tajfel, Henri. 1981. *Human Groups and Social Categories: Studies in Social Psychology*. Cambridge: Cambridge University Press.
Tajfel, Henri, ed. 1982. *Social Identity and Intergroup Relations*. European Studies in Social Psychology. Cambridge: Cambridge University Press.
Talbert, Charles. 1982. *Reading Luke: A Literary and Theology Commentary on the Third Gospel*. New York: Crossroad.
Tannehill, Robert C. 1972. The Mission of Jesus According to Luke 4.16-30. Pages 51-75 in Eltester, ed., 1972.
―――. 1986. *The Narrative Unity of Luke-Acts: A Literary Interpretation*, vol. 1. Philadelphia: Fortress.
―――. 1990. *The Narrative Unity of Luke-Acts: A Literary Interpretation*, vol. 2. Philadelphia: Fortress.
―――. 1996. *Luke*. Abingdon New Testament Commentaries. Nashville: Abingdon.
Taylor, Justin. 2001. The Jerusalem Decrees (Acts 15.20, 29 and 21.25) and the Incident at Antioch (Galatians 2.11-14). *New Testament Studies* 47, no. 3:372-80.
Taylor, Nicholas H. 1999. Luke-Acts and the Temple. Pages 709-21 in Verheyden, ed., 1999.
Theissen, Gerd. 1982. *The Social Setting of Early Christianity: Essays on Corinth*. Edinburgh: T. & T. Clark.
Thompson, Richard P. 2006. *Keeping the Church in Its Place: The Church as Narrative Character in Acts*. New York: T&T Clark.
Thornton, Timothy. 1978. To the End of the Earth: Acts 1.8. *The Expository Times* 89:374-75.
―――. 1996. Anti-Samaritan Exegesis Reflected in Josephus' Retelling of Deuteronomy, Joshua and Judges. *Journal of Theological Studies* 47, no. 1:125-30.
Tiede, David L. 1986. The Exaltation of Jesus and the Restoration of Israel in Acts 1. *Harvard Theological Review* 2:278-86.
Tonkin, Elisabeth, Maryon McDonald and Malcolm Chapman, eds. 1989. *History and Ethnicity*. ASA Monographs 27. London: Routledge.
Triandis, H. C. 1990. Cross-Cultural Studies of Individualism and Collectivism. Paper presented at the *Nebraska Symposium on Motivation 1989: Cross-cultural Perspectives*. Lincoln, Nebraska 1990.
―――. 1995. *Individualism and Collectivism*. Boulder, Colo.: Westview.
Triandis, H. C., C. McCusker and H. Hui. 1990. Multimethod Probes of Individualism and Collectivism. *Journal of Personality and Social Psychology* 59:1006-20.

Turner, J. C. 1982. Towards a Cognitive Redefinition of the Social Group. Pages 14–32 in Tajfel, ed., 1982.
———. 1996. Henri Tajfel: An Introduction. Pages 1–24 in *Social Groups and Identity: Developing the Legacy of Henri Tajfel*. Edited by W. Peter Robinson. Oxford: Butterworth-Heinemann.
———. 1999. Some Current Issues in Research on Social Identity and Self-categorization Theories. Pages 6–34 in *Social Identity: Context, Commitment, Content*. Edited by Naomi Ellemers and Russell Spears. Oxford: Blackwell.
Turner, Max. 1996. *Power from on High: The Spirit as Israel's Restoration and Witness in Luke–Acts*. Sheffield: Sheffield Academic.
———. 1998. The "Spirit of Prophecy" as the Power of Israel's Restoration and Witness. Pages 327–48 in Marshall and Petersen, eds., 1998.
Tutu, Desmond. 1999. *No Future without Forgiveness*. New York: Doubleday.
Twelftree, Graham H. 2009. *People of the Spirit: Exploring Luke's View of the Church*. Grand Rapids: Baker.
Tyson, Joseph B. 1992. *Images of Judaism in Luke–Acts*. Columbia, S.C.: University of South Carolina Press.
———. 1999. *Luke, Judaism and the Scholars: Critical Approaches to Luke–Acts*. Columbia, S.C.: University of South Carolina Press.
Tyson, Joseph B., ed. 1988. *Luke–Acts and the Jewish People: Eight Critical Perspectives*. Minneapolis: Augsburg.
Van de Sandt. Hubertus Waltherus Maria. 1992. An Explanation of Acts 15:6-21 in the Light of Deuteronomy 4:29-35 (LXX). *Journal for the Study of the New Testament* 46:73–97.
VanderKam, James C. 2002. Covenant and Pentecost. *Calvin Theological Journal* 37, no. 2:239–54.
Van Henten, J. W. 1997. *The Maccabean Martyrs as Saviours of the Jewish People: A Study of 2 & 4 Maccabees*. Leiden: Brill.
Van Nijf, Ono. 2001. Local Heroes: Athletics, Festivals and Elite Self-Fashioning in the Roman East. Pages 306–34 in *Being Greek under Rome*. Edited by Simon Goldhill. Cambridge: Cambridge University Press.
Van Oudenhouven, J. P., J. T. Groenewoud and M. Hewstone. 1996. Co-Operation, Ethnic Salience, and Generalization of Inter-Ethnic Attitudes. *European Journal of Social Psychology* 26:649–62.
Van Ruiten, J. T. A. G. M. 2000. *Primaeval History Interpreted: The Rewriting of Genesis 1–11 in the Book of Jubilees*. Leiden: Brill.
Van Unnik, W. C. 1973. *Sparsa Collecta: The Collected Essays of W. C. Van Unnik*. Leiden: Brill.
Verheyden, J., ed. 1999. *The Unity of Luke–Acts*. Leuven: Leuven University Press.
Verkuyten, M. 2005. Ethnic Group Identification and Group Evaluation among Minority and Majority Groups: Testing the Multiculturalism Hypothesis. *Journal of Personality and Social Psychology* 88, no. 1:121–38.
Vermes, Geza. 1973. *Jesus the Jew: A Historians Reading of the Gospels*. London: Collins.
Volf, Miroslav. 1998. *The Church as the Image of the Trinity*. Grand Rapids: Eerdmans.
Wald, Kenneth D., and Bryan D. Williams. 2005. The Diaspora Consciousness of Arab Americans: The Intersection of Social Identity and Global Politics. Working paper 22, Middlebury College, Rohatyn Center for International Affairs, available online: http://www.middlebury.edu/international/rcfia/ papers/PapersinSeries.

Waldzus, Sven, Amélie Mummendey and Michael Wenzel. 2005. When "Different" Means "Worse": In-Group Prototypicality in Changing Intergroup Contexts. *Journal of Experimental Social Psychology* 41:76–83.

Waldzus, Sven, Amélie Mummendey, Michael Wenzel and Ulrike Weber. 2003. Towards Tolerance: Representations of Superordinate Categories and Perceived Ingroup Prototypicality. *Journal of Experimental Social Psychology* 29:31–47.

Wall, Robert W. 1987. Peter, "Son" of Jonah: The Conversion of Cornelius in the Context of Canon. *Journal for the Study of the New Testament* 29:79–90.

———. 2002. The Acts of the Apostles. In *The New Interpreter's Bible*, vol. 10. Edited by Leander E. Keck. Nashville: Abingdon.

Wallman, Sandra. 1979. Introduction: The Scope for Ethnicity. Pages 1–17 in *Ethnicity at Work*. Edited by Sandra Wallman. London: Macmillan.

Walters, Patricia. 2009. *The Assumed Authorial Unity of Luke and Acts: A Reassessment of the Evidence*. Cambridge: Cambridge University Press.

Weber, Max. 1997. *Weber: Political Writings*. Edited by Peter Lassman and Ronald Speirs. Cambridge: Cambridge University Press.

Weber, Ulrike, Amélie Mummendey and Sven Waldzus. 2002. Perceived Legitimacy of Intergroup Status Differences: Its Prediction By Relative Ingroup Prototypicality. *European Journal of Social Psychology* 32:449–70.

Wedderburn, A. J. M. 1993. The "Apostolic Decree": Tradition and Redaction. *Novum Testamentum* 35:362–89.

———. 1994. Traditions and Redactions in Acts 2.1–13. *Journal for the Study of the New Testament* 55:27–54.

Weissenbeuhler, Wayne. 1992. Acts 1.1–11. *Interpretation* 46, no. 1:61–65.

Weitzman. Steve. Why Did the Qumran Community Write in Hebrew? *Journal for the American Oriental Society* 119, no. 1:35–45.

Wenk, Matthias. 2000. *Community-Forming Power: The Socio-Ethical Role of the Spirit in Luke–Acts*. Sheffield: Sheffield Academic.

Wenzel, Michael. 2000. Justice and Identity: The Significance of Inclusion for Perceptions of Entitlement and the Justice Motive. *Personality and Social Psychology Bulletin* 26:157–76.

———. 2001. A Social Categorization Approach to Distributive Justice: Social Identity as the Link between Relevance of Inputs and Need for Justice. *British Journal of Social Psychology* 40:315–35.

Wenzel, Michael, Amélie Mummendey, Ulrike Weber and Sven Waldzus. 2003. The Ingroup as Pars Pro Toto: Projection from the Ingroup Onto the Inclusive Category as a Precursor to Social Discrimination. *Personality and Social Psychology Bulletin* 29:461–73.

Westermann, Claus. 1975. *Genesis 12–50*. Darmstadt: Wissenschaftliche Buchgesellschaft.

Whyte, John. 1978. Interpretations of the Northern Ireland Problem: An Appraisal. *Economic and Social Review* 9 no. 4:257–82.

Wikenhauser, A. 1948. Doppeltraume. *Biblica* 29:100–111.

Wilckens, Ulrich. 1963. *Die Missionsreden der Apostelgeschichte*. Neukirchen–Vluyn: Neukirchener Verlag.

Williamson, H. G. M. 1985. *Ezra-Nehemiah*. Waco, Tex.: Word.

Williamson, Rick L. 2005. Singing: Luke's Songs as Melodies of the Marginalized. Pages 167–76 in *Vital Christianity: Spirituality, Justice, and Christian Practice*. Edited by David L. Weaver-Zercher and William Willimon. New York: T&T Clark.

Wilson, Stephen G. 1973. *The Gentiles and the Gentile Mission in Luke-Acts*. London: Cambridge University Press.

Wilson, Walter T. 2001. Urban Legends: Acts 10.1–11.18 and the Strategies of Greco-Roman Foundation Narratives. *Journal of Biblical Literature* 120, no. 1:77–99.

Wimmer. Andreas. 2004. Introduction: Facing Ethnic Conflicts. Pages 1–20 in *Facing Ethnic Conflicts: Toward a New Realism*. Edited by A. Wimmer, R. Goldstone, D. Horowitz, U. Joras, and C. Schetter. Lanham, Md.: Rowan & Littlefield.

Winter, Bruce W. 1988. The Public Honoring of Christian Benefactors: Romans 13.3–4 and 1 Peter 2.14–15. *Journal for the Study of the New Testament* 34:87–103.

Witherington III, Ben. 1992. Not So Idle Thoughts about Eidolothuton. *Tyndale Bulletin* 44 no. 2:237–54.

———. 1998. *The Acts of the Apostles: A Socio Rhetorical Commentary*. Grand Rapids: Eerdmans.

———. 2001. *New Testament History: A Narrative Account*. Grand Rapids: Baker Academic.

Witherup, Ronald D. 1992. Functional Redundancy in the Acts of the Apostles: A Case Study. *Journal for the Study of the New Testament* 48:67–87.

———. 1993. Cornelius Over and Over and Over Again: "Functional Redundancy" in the Acts of the Apostles. *Journal for the Study of the New Testament* 49:45–66.

Wright, C. J. H. 2006. *The Mission of God*. Leicester: Inter-Varsity Press.

Wright, Jacob L. 2004. *Rebuilding Identity: The Nehemiah-Memoir and Its Earliest Readers*. Berlin: de Gruyter.

Wright, N. T. 1996. *Jesus and the Victory of God*. Minneapolis: Fortress.

Xeravits, Geza G., and Jozsef Zsengeller, eds. *The Book of Tobit: Text, Tradition, Theology*. Leiden: Brill.

Zahn, T. 1920. *Das Evangelium des Lukas*. Wuppertal: R. Brockhaus.

Zangenberg, Jürgen, Harold W. Attridge and Dale B. Martin. eds. 2007. *Religion, Ethnicity, and Identity in Ancient Galilee: A Region in Transition*. Tübingen: Mohr Siebeck.

Zerhusen, Bob. 1995. An Overlooked Judean Diglossa in Acts 2. *Biblical Theology Bulletin* 25:118–30.

Zorrilla, C. Hugo. 1983. The Magnificat: Song of Justice. Pages 220–37 in *Conflict and Context: Hermeneutics in the Americas*. Edited by Mark Lau Branson and C. Rene Padilla. Grand Rapids: Eerdmans.

Indexes

Index of References

Hebrew Bible/Old Testament

Genesis
1–11	42
2:7	12
2:22	12
5:22	56
5:24	56
6	142
6:3	8
6:9	56
11:1	118
11:7–9	116
11:30	55
12:2	55
12:3	45, 54, 55, 129
14:1	55
15–18	55, 56, 216
15:1	55
15:2	54
15:5	55
15:6	55
15:13–14	55
15:18–21	55
17:1	55, 56
17:1 LXX	55
17:2–7	55
17:2	55
17:4–8	55
17:16	55
17:17	55
17:19	55
17:23	55
17:27	155
18:11–12	55
18:18	129
18:19	55
20:7	15
21:2	55
21:6	55
22:11	170
22:12	76
22:18	129
24:10	56
26:4	129
26:5	55
41:38	8

Exodus
3:4	170
4:7	99
4:22–23	76
4:22	76
7:3	122
11:9–10	122
12:6 LXX	57
12:43	155
14:27	99
22:21–24	150
23:4	114
29:33	155
30:33	155
31:3	8
33:11	15
35:31	8

Leviticus
4:3	56
16:29	114
17–18	206, 208, 209
19:15	194
21:17–21	164
22:10	155
22:12–13	155
22:25	155

Numbers
1:51	155
3:10	155
3:38	155
9:14	114
11	120
11:17	120
11:20	171
11:25	8
11:26	8
11:29	8
12:6–8	121
17:5	155
18:4	155
18:7	155
23:7	7
24:2	8
27:18	8

Deuteronomy
1:16	114
4:34	122
6:13	78, 165
6:16	78
6:22	122
7:1–4	44
7:19	122
8:3	78
10:17–19	150
10:17	194
10:20	165
11:3	122
14:1	76

Index of References

14:29	150	*2 Kings*		*Psalms*	
18:13	56	2:16	7	2 LXX	79
18:16	135	3:14	194	2:1	68
18:18–19	121	4:1–7	150	2:7	64, 76
23:2 LXX	164, 167	5	93	2:7 LXX	76
24:17	150	7:13 LXX	57	9:11–12	60
26:8	122	17	154	9:17–20	60
26:12	150			10:1–4	60
28:49	103	*1 Chronicles*		10:17–18	60
29:3	122	29:16 LXX	57	12:1–5	60
34:10	15, 121			13:3	66
34:11	122	*2 Chronicles*		18:25–29	60
		7:14	205	40:17	60
Joshua		28:10	162	55:14	56
7	141	31:18 LXX	57	68:5	150
14:4	139			70:5	60
		Ezra		72:2	60
Judges		1–6	44, 45	81:2 LXX	194
3:10	9	2:59–62	44	86:1	60
6:34	9	4:1–4	154, 161	93:6	150
9:2	155	4:1–3	45	96:7–8	205
11:29	9	4:2	45	104:29–30	12
13:2	54	4:3	45	106:10	63
13:25	9	7	44	106:10 LXX	63
14:6	7, 9	9–10	44	106:11	63
14:19	7	9:2	44	106:14	63
15:14	7, 9	10:2	185	109:22	60
				114:9	56
1 Samuel		*Nehemiah*		118:31	165
1:1–2	54	4:14	44	146:9	150
8:7	171	7:61–65	44	149:4	60
8:16	162	9:8	45		
9:9	121	10:30	44	*Isaiah*	
11:6	7, 9	12:37	205	1:17	150
		13	44	1:23	150
2 Samuel		13:30–31	45	2:2 LXX	120
6:2	205			2:2–3	106, 205
7	114	*Esther*		6	169
		3:12 LXX	56	7:2	205
1 Kings		8:13 LXX	56	7:12	205
4:25	46			8:9	103
8:43	205	*Job*		8:18	122
17	93	7:14 LXX	172	9:1	63, 64
17:8–24	150	15:19	155	9:2 LXX	63
18:12	7	19:15	155	9:6–7	63
				10:2	150

256 · Index of References

Isaiah (cont.)		49:8–9	64	15:19	99
11:1–9	12	49:9–10	63	16:15	99
11:1–4	9, 10	52:13–53:12	166	16:19	103
11:4	9	53	166	17:3	185
14:2	162	53:3–5	167	21:12	205
25:6	205	53:7–8	162, 166	22:3	150
32:15–20	9	53:8	166	23:8	99
36:16	46	54:5	106, 121	24:6	99
40–55	105	55:4–5	106, 121	28:51	155
40	72	56	161–63	31:33	6
40:3–5	72	56:3–8	167	49:11	150
40:6	72	56:3–7 LXX	153	49:17	155
41:3	67	56:3–7	158, 161, 163	50:19	99
41:8	76				
42	64	56:3–5 LXX	161	Ezekiel	
42:1–9	64	56:3–5	168	2:2	7
42:1	12, 64, 76	56:3	155, 158, 161, 162	3:12	7
42:4	64			3:14	7
42:5	64	56:6–7	158, 161, 162, 205	3:24	7
42:6	64, 76			8:3	7
42:6 LXX	64	56:6	155, 162	11:1	7
42:6–7	64	56:7	57, 162, 163, 167	11:5	7
42:7	63			11:24	7
42:9	64	58:6	15, 85	22:7	150
42:10	64	58:8	64	32:32 LXX	57
43:4–13 LXX	105	58:10	64	36:27	6
43:7	105	59:7–8	67	37:1	7
43:10–12	105, 106	60:1–3	63, 64	39:11 LXX	57
43:12	105	60:10	155	43:5	7
44:1–8 LXX	105	60:18–20	106	44:7	155
44:2	76	61:1–7	12	44:9	155
44:3 LXX	105	61:1–2	15, 85		
44:4 LXX	105	61:1	64	Daniel	
44:5 LXX	105	61:2	82	1:10	155
44:8 LXX	105	61:5	155	4:34	122
44:21	106, 121	62:11	103	6:37	122
45:4–6	106, 121	66:23	205	9:19	205
48:10–11	106, 121				
48:20	103	Jeremiah		Hosea	
49	15, 64	1:4–10	169	2:18	46
49:1–6	106, 121	3:17	106, 205	11:1	76
49:6	64, 65, 103, 106, 186	5:28 LXX	150	11:11	99
		7:6	150		
		10:12	103	Joel	
49:6 LXX	103	13:11	165	1:3–5 LXX	111
49:6–10 LXX	63	14:8	185	2:21–27 LXX	120
49:6–10	64	14:9	205	3	119

3:1–5 LXX	10, 13, 21, 23, 98, 115, 120, 123, 160, 162, 218	*1 Esdras*		*2 Maccabees*	
		4:20	165	1:27–29	47
		4:63	206	2:1–3	47
		6:26	99	4:11–17	46
		8:66–67	155	5:8–9	187
3:1 LXX	120, 172	8:80	155	6:5	191
3:2	162	8:89–90	155	6:25	154
3:2 LXX	120	9:6 LXX	57	7	47
3:3 LXX	120, 121	9:7	155	11:25	99
3:4 LXX	121	9:9	155	11:38	47
3:5 LXX	121, 123	9:12	155	12:40	47
4:17	155	9:17–18	155		
		9:36	155	*3 Maccabees*	
Amos		9:38 LXX	57	7:13 LXX	57
9:11 LXX	205	9:41 LXX	57		
9:11–12 LXX	205, 206	9:47 LXX	57	*4 Maccabees*	
9:12 LXX	205, 206			5:2	208
9:12 MT	206, 207	*Judith*			
		16:14	12	*Sirach*	
Obadiah				19:2	165
11	155	*1 Maccabees*		36:12	206
		1:41–2:1	38	39	12
Micah		1:41–64	46	39:1–6	7
4:1–2	106, 205	2:3	203	39:8	7
4:4	46	2:27	46	45:13	155
		2:45–46	46	50	56
Zephaniah		2:65	203	50:25–26	158
3:9	117	2:66–67	46	50:26	154
		2:70	89		
Zechariah		3:9	103	*Tobit*	
1:6	7	3:36	155	4:12	42
3:10	46	3:44–48	46	4:13	42
8:22	106	3:45	155	5:4–9	42
9:6	155	7:37	206	13:11	106
12:7–12	205	9:19–21	89	13:34	41
14:16	106, 205	9:63 LXX	57	14:5–8	41
		9:73	46	14:6	106
Malachi		10:12	155		
3:5	150	12:1–23	187	*Wisdom of Solomon*	
3:19	155	13:25–30	89	10:5	56
		13:41	46	14:12	208
APOCRYPHA/DEUTERO-CANONICAL WORKS		14:9	46	18:21	56
		14:12	46		
Baruch		14:16–23	187		
2:15	206	14:37	46		
5:7	72	15:16–21	170		

Index of References

PSEUDEPIGRAPHA		*Liber antiquitatum*		9:33	184
1 Enoch		*biblicarum*		10:2	187
26–27	56	4:3–17	113	10:5	154
49:2–3	12	27:9–10	12	10:6	184
49:3	7	32:14	12	10:17–18	89
62:2	7	36:2	12	10:21	187
90:33	205	*Psalms of Solomon*		10:23	184
		2:18	194	12:14	84, 85
2 Baruch		5:8–11	60	12:46	187
21:4	9, 12	17:28	155	12:47	187
23:5	9, 12	17:37	12	12:48	187
75:3-4	9	18:4	73	12:50	187
				13:54–58	87
3 Enoch		*Sibylline Oracles*		13:55	87, 187
1:11–13	118	2:96	208	13:56	87
		3:160–72	113	13:57	87
4 Ezra		3:205–9	113	14:3	187
6:39–41	9			15:24	184
6:39	12	*Testament of Judah*		15:31	184
13:38	44	25:1–3	118	16:3	191
13:41–42	43			16:18	140
13:46–47	43	*Testament of Moses*		17:1	187
14:21–22	12	10:3–4	72	17:9	172
14:22	9			18:15	187
		NEW TESTAMENT		18:21	187
Jubilees		*Matthew*		18:35	187
1:1	115	1:2	187	19:5	165
1:5	115	1:11	187	19:28	184
2	42	2:2	185	19:29	187
3	42	2:6	184	20:24	187
6:17–22	115	2:20	184	21:21	191
8:12	56	2:21	184	22:24	187
10:8–11	43	3:13–17	77	22:25	187
12:25–27	117	3:16	77	23:8	187
14:20	115	3:17	77	23:24	89
15:1	115	4:1	79	23:28	191
15:4	115	4:3	79	25:40	171, 187
15:19	115	4:6	79	25:45	171
15:27–28	42	8:10	184	26:73	102
22:1	115	4:18	187	27:9	184
22:15	115	4:21	187	27:11	185
22:16	43	5:22	187	27:42	184
29:7	115	5:23	187	28:10	187
		5:24	187	28:15	185
Letter of Aristeas		5:47	187	28:20	78
122	41	7:3	187	29:37	185
139	41	7:4	187		
142	41	7:5	187		

Index of References

Mark		1:5–25	217	1:68	56, 62,
1:9–11	77	1:5–6	53		184, 204,
1:10	77	1:5	51, 52, 55,		205
1:12	79		213, 217	1:69–71	54
1:16	187	1:6	55, 56	1:69	61, 205
1:19	187	1:7	55	1:71	61, 67
3:6	84, 85	1:9	111	1:72–73	22, 55
3:17	187	1:10	56, 205	1:72	61, 195
3:21	69	1:11	55	1:73	55, 61, 62
3:31	187	1:12	53	1:74	61, 62, 67,
3:32	187	1:13	55		178
3:33	187	1:15	55, 58, 73,	1:75	62
3:34	187		217	1:76–79	62
3:35	187	1:16–17	74, 75	1:77–79	62
5:37	187	1:16	58, 69, 184	1:77	56, 62, 205
6:1–6	81, 87	1:17	56, 59, 205	1:78–79	64
6:3	87, 187	1:18	55	1:78	62, 64, 204
6:4	87	1:21	56, 86, 205	1:79	62–66,
6:17	187	1:24	55		178, 192,
6:18	187	1:30	133		194, 204,
7:3	185	1:32–33	54, 59		219, 226
10:29	187	1:35	53, 58, 59,	1:80	184
10:30	187		61, 76, 107	2	68, 203
11:17	163	1:41–43	58	2:1–2	51, 52, 217
12:19	187	1:41–42	53	2:3	185
12:20	187	1:41	61	2:4	213
12:29	184	1:43	58	2:10–14	62, 68
13:9	89	1:46–55	66	2:10	68, 205
13:12	187	1:46–49	60	2:14	66, 68,
13:57	87	1:46	61		194, 219
15:2	185	1:50	60, 192	2:18	86, 121
15:9	185	1:51	60	2:25	70, 184,
15:12	185	1:52–53	178		203
15:18	185	1:52	60	2:26–27	68
15:26	185	1:53	60	2:29–32	66
15:32	184	1:54–55	22	2:29	66
		1:54	60, 184,	2:30–32	62
Luke			186, 194	2:31	205
1–4	51, 96	1:55	55, 60	2:32	56, 64, 65,
1–3	129	1:57	55		69, 184,
1–2	4, 20, 51,	1:58	55		205
	58, 59, 66,	1:59	55	2:33	86
	125, 182,	1:63	86	2:34–35	66, 69
	184	1:65–75	62	2:34	184
1	61	1:67	53, 62	2:36–38	150
1:1	223	1:68–79	66	2:38	66, 70
1:4	11	1:68–75	61, 62	2:49–51	70

Luke (cont.)		4:14–30	80, 81, 83,	6:41	137, 186
2:49	76		95, 98,	6:42	186
2:51	69		149, 179,	6:44	137
2:52	133		214	7:1–5	137
3–4	72, 95	4:14–20	212	7:1	205
3	125	4:14–15	81, 84	7:9	86, 184
3:1–14	98	4:14	79, 95	7:11–17	150
3:1–2	52, 72, 217	4:15	88	7:16	56, 204,
3:1	186	4:16–30	80, 81,		205
3:2	169		107, 218	7:19–20	110
3:4–6	72	4:16–18	8	7:28	70
3:6	72	4:16	86–88	7:29	205
3:8–14	107	4:18–20	151	7:32	110
3:8	73–76, 78,	4:18–19	8, 81	7:50	66
	80, 100,	4:18	64, 85, 95	8	153
	217	4:20	85	8:1–3	108
3:10–11	74, 217	4:21	85	8:3	110
3:10	73	4:22	81, 82, 86,	8:16	65
3:11	74		89, 100	8:19–21	130
3:12–14	74, 217	4:23–24	94	8:19	186
3:12	73	4:23	82, 90, 92	8:20	186
3:13	74	4:24–30	38	8:21	70, 167,
3:14	73, 74	4:24–26	103		186
3:15	205	4:24	87, 92, 192	8:25	86
3:16	75	4:25–27	150	8:47	205
3:18	205	4:25	184	8:48	66
3:19–20	85	4:27–29	94	9–10	111
3:19	186	4:27	184	9:1	109
3:21–22	76	4:28	94	9:8	110
3:21	77, 205	4:29	94	9:10	137
3:22	58, 64, 76,	4:31–44	84	9:13	205
	77, 79, 95,	4:34	88	9:19	110
	107, 195,	4:36	86	9:22	110, 169
	217, 218	4:42–43	92	9:31	82, 110
3:23–38	76	5–24	51	9:43	86
3:32–38	77	5:17–26	84	9:44–45	110
3:38	76	5:28	151	9:44	110
4	35, 85, 125	5:29–39	84	9:46–48	95, 151,
4:1–14	78	6:1–5	84		217
4:1–13	76, 144,	6:6–11	84	9:48–50	150
	218	6:11	84	9:49–50	96, 107,
4:1	8, 79, 95	6:13	109, 111		109, 151,
4:3–4	79	6:14	140, 186		159, 217
4:3	76, 79	6:17	205	9:49	109, 110,
4:9–12	79	6:23	11, 93		167
4:9	76, 79	6:26	11, 93	9:50	109, 167
		6:29	167		

9:51–56	38, 103, 150, 154, 156, 159, 217, 219	13:1–2	84	20:9	205
		13:4	113	20:16	110
		13:33	11, 93	20:19–20	85
		13:34	11, 93	20:19	169, 205
9:51–55	96	14	105	20:26	86, 205
9:51	85, 104, 110	14:12	186	20:28	186
		14:26	105, 130, 186	20:29	186
9:54	85, 110			20:31	151
10:1	110	14:27	105	20:45–47	150
10:5	66	14:32	66	20:45	205
10:6	66	14:33	105	21:1–6	150
10:11	165	15:4	151	21:1–4	150
10:16	171	15:15	165	21:7	214
10:21	95, 159	15:23	189	21:12–17	130
10:22	152	15:27	186, 189	21:12	89
10:23	137	15:30	189	21:16	186
10:25–37	102, 154	15:32	186	21:17	214
10:25–28	74	16:8	65	21:23	205
10:27	74	16:24	73	21:32	92
10:29–37	74	16:28	186	21:38	205
10:34	137	16:31	11, 93	22:2–6	170
10:40	151	17	161	22:2	169, 205
10:41	170	17:3	186	22:3–4	80
11:13	95	17:11–19	102, 154, 161	22:3	143, 218
11:14	86			22:4	169
11:21	66	17:18	155, 158, 162	22:7	189
11:26	113			22:12	152
11:27–28	70	18:1–8	150	22:24–27	151
11:33	65	18:2	192	22:25–27	193
11:34	65	18:16	167	22:30	184
11:35	65	18:17	92	22:31–32	80, 170
11:36	65	18:28	137, 138	22:31	144, 218
11:38	86	18:29–30	130	22:32	144, 186
11:47	11, 93	18:29	92, 186	22:34	127
11:49	11, 93	18:31–34	110	22:37	191
11:50	11, 93	18:37	88	22:50	169
11:52	167	18:43	205	22:52	169
11:53–54	85	19:38	66	22:54	169
12:3	65	19:42	66	22:56	65, 82, 85
12:10	95	19:46	57, 162, 163	22:57	127
12:11	89			22:59	84, 102
12:12	95, 212	19:47	85, 169, 205	22:61	127
12:13	186			22:65	82
12:32–35	96, 218	19:48	205	22:66	169, 205
12:37	92	20:1	56, 169, 205	23:2	56, 167
12:49–20	75			23:3	185
12:51	66	20:6	68, 205	23:4	169

262   *Index of References*

Luke (cont.)		4:12	154			188, 207,
23:5	205	4:43–44	87			212, 218
23:6	84	6:8	187	1:10		82, 85
23:10	169	7:3	187	1:11		100
23:13	56, 169,	7:5	187	1:13		113
	205	7:10	187	1:14		110, 158,
23:14	205	8:33–39	73			159, 186,
23:18–21	166	11:2	187			202
23:35	205	11:19	187	1:15–26		218
23:37	185, 205	11:21	187	1:15		186, 187
23:38	185	11:23	187	1:16		186, 187
23:51	185	11:32	187	1:17		111
23:54–62	114	12:13	184	1:19		113, 137
24	97, 108,	12:21–22	116	1:20		113
	175, 212	14:16	140	1:21–26		217
24:7	68	20:17	187	1:21–22		108, 109,
24:10	82, 108	21:23	187			151, 220
24:12	86			1:21		109
24:19	56, 88, 205	*Acts*		1:22		108, 109
24:20	169	1–14	185	1:23		139, 140
24:21	184	1–5	126	1:24–25		80
24:25–27	96, 218	1–2	21, 97, 111	1:25		137, 138,
24:25	11, 93	1	61, 97			143
24:27	7, 212, 223	1:1–11	98, 100,	1:26		111
24:32	212, 223		103, 107,	1:35		7
24:33	108		125	1:46		7
24:36	66	1:2	188	2		15, 112,
24:41	86	1:3	100			115, 118–
24:44–49	7, 212, 223	1:4–8	110			20, 123,
24:46–48	108	1:4	108			125, 138,
24:47–53	103	1:5–8	114			196
24:47	103	1:5	75, 188,	2:1–47		131
24:48	108		198, 217	2:1–41		126
24:49	108	1:6–8	104	2:1–11		125, 182
		1:6	99, 100,	2:1–4		77, 110,
John			107, 122,			123
1:1	133		128, 184,	2:1		110
1:29–34	77		185	2:4–11		220
1:31	184	1:7–8	106	2:4		110, 117,
1:32	77	1:7	137			152
1:40	187	1:8	64, 97–	2:5–11		123
1:41	187		101, 103–	2:5		113, 185
1:47	184		107, 110,	2:6		137, 138
1:49	184		122, 131,	2:7		84, 86,
2:12	187		142, 173,			100, 112
3:10	184		175, 176,	2:8–11		113
4:6	164					

2:8	110, 137, 138	2:42–47	19, 125, 126, 128, 130, 135, 153, 177, 211, 218	3:25	22, 54, 66, 75, 128, 129, 195
2:9–11	112			3:26	128
2:9	112, 113			4	175
2:11	114, 116, 185	2:42	130, 135, 173	4:1–22	131, 134
2:13	82	2:43	122	4:1–21	102
2:14–40	212	2:44	130, 173	4:1	205
2:14–36	111	2:45	130	4:2	205
2:14	113, 119, 185	2:46–47	130	4:6	169
2:17–19	119	2:46	130, 135, 158, 159, 173	4:8–12	212
2:17–18	15			4:8	205
2:17	120, 171, 172, 176, 188, 219	2:47	133, 134, 146, 205, 218	4:10	162, 184, 185, 205
				4:13	86, 194
				4:16	113
2:18	120, 158, 160, 162, 163, 195, 196, 198, 207, 211, 218	3	144, 163	4:17	205
		3:1	135	4:21	205
		3:4	82, 85	4:23–30	131
		3:6	162	4:23	137, 145, 169
		3:9	205	4:24–30	130
2:19	121, 122, 159	3:11	205	4:24	158, 159
		3:12–26	64, 127	4:25	68, 205
2:20–32	119	3:12	85, 86, 135, 137, 184, 185, 205	4:27	68, 69, 184, 185, 205
2:20	65, 121				
2:21	121				
2:22	88, 119, 122, 184, 185			4:30	122
		3:13–15	102	4:31–36	131
		3:13	127, 135	4:31–32	127
2:25	119	3:14	127	4:31	126, 137, 141, 152
2:29	119, 173, 186, 187	3:15	108		
		3:17–26	144	4:32–5:16	153
2:32	108, 115	3:17	135, 173, 186, 187	4:32–5:11	125, 150
2:33	119, 123			4:32–38	218
2:34–35	130	3:19–21	99	4:32–37	126, 138, 151
2:36	102, 184, 185	3:19	127, 128, 144, 146	4:32–36	131
2:37	119, 186, 187	3:20–21	127	4:32–35	130
		3:21	55	4:32	130, 136, 137
2:38–39	123	3:22–23	121		
2:38	124, 126, 128, 152, 159, 162	3:22	135, 186, 187	4:33	108, 130, 143, 173
		3:23	128, 195, 200, 205	4:34–35	136
2:40	8, 128			4:36–5:11	161
2:41–42	126			4:36–38	174
2:41	130, 149			4:36–37	107, 211

Acts (cont.)		6:1–7	9, 14, 19,	7:37	184–87
4:36	119		126, 147,	7:38	177
4:44	149		148, 150,	7:42	184, 185
5	125		177, 179,	7:46	133
5:1–11	80, 126,		182, 183,	7:48	113
	132, 144,		197, 217,	7:49	120
	171, 218,		218, 220	7:55	82, 85
	220	6:1–6	38, 132	7:57	158, 159
5:1	142	6:1	149, 151,	7:58	169
5:2	142		170	8–12	160
5:3	127, 143	6:2	151, 170	8	6, 16, 98,
5:4	143	6:3	14, 86,		147, 153,
5:5	144, 146		111, 151,		155, 157,
5:9	142, 143		152, 166,		162, 183
5:10	144, 146		168, 186,	8:1–25	10, 110,
5:12–16	125, 126,		187, 204		156, 158,
	132, 177,				161
	218	6:5	168, 173		
		6:6	119	8:1	170
5:12	122, 127,	6:7	132, 134,	8:3	169, 175
	130, 134,		149, 153,	8:4–25	158, 161
	135, 158,		170, 218	8:4–10	161
	159, 205	6:8–8:3	132	8:5	158
5:13–14	132, 145	6:8–8:1	170	8:6	158, 159
5:13	165, 174,	6:8	122, 205	8:7	158
	205, 218	6:9–8:1	134, 222	8:8	158
5:17–42	132, 134	6:9	113, 114	8:12–13	157
5:17–41	102	6:12	205	8:12	157, 159,
5:17–18	170	6:14	88		162
5:17	169	6:15	82, 85	8:14–17	150, 218
5:20	205	6:33	86	8:14	159
5:21	169, 184	7	7, 163	8:15	157, 188
5:24	169	7:1	169, 170	8:16	159, 162
5:25	205	7:2	73, 113,	8:17	77, 157,
5:26	205		173, 186,		160, 162,
5:27	169		187		188, 195
5:30	135	7:4	113	8:18–25	146
5:31	184, 185	7:6	120	8:18–24	80
5:32	108, 212	7:13	186	8:18	188
5:34	205	7:17	205	8:19	188
5:35	184	7:23	184–86,	8:22	144
5:37	84, 205		187, 204	8:25	160, 219
5:42	135, 148	7:25	186, 187	8:26–40	157, 158,
6–9	21, 148,	7:26	66, 186,		161–63,
	179		187		182, 202
6	35, 139,	7:31	86, 172	8:26–32	165
	148, 153	7:34	205	8:26	164
		7:36	122	8:27	164

8:29	164–67, 172, 174, 189, 196, 219	9:18	173	10:19	165, 172, 177, 189, 190
		9:19	170		
		9:21	82, 169, 170, 173	10:20	198, 202
8:30–35	7	9:22	113, 185	10:22	86, 137, 158, 185, 188
8:31	166	9:23	185		
8:32–33	162	9:25	170		
8:33	166	9:26–31	122	10:23	186, 187, 191
8:34	164, 171	9:26	150, 159, 170, 219		
8:36	164, 167, 196, 199			10:25–26	192, 209
		9:27	107, 140, 174, 175, 211	10:26–31	165
8:37	167, 168			10:27–28	202
8:38	164			10:28	165, 174, 185, 191, 196
8:39	159, 164, 168	9:28–29	219		
		9:28	175		
9–14	201	9:29	165, 174	10:29	191
9	147, 168, 175–77	9:30	186, 187	10:31	195
		9:31	66, 134, 177, 194, 218	10:33–34	192
9:1–31	19, 67, 111, 132, 169, 175, 176, 178, 182, 187, 219, 226			10:34–35	193–95, 202, 210
		9:32	113	10:35	87, 93, 192
		9:35	113	10:36	66, 165, 166, 184, 192, 193, 219, 222, 226
		10–15	181–84		
		10–14	187		
9:1–30	169	10–11	192, 212		
9:1–19	126	10	8, 39, 147, 184, 189, 226		
9:1–2	222			10:37	84, 193
9:1	169, 170			10:38	88, 177, 193
9:2	178	10:1–11:18	16, 181, 188		
9:3	65			10:39	108, 185
9:4–5	170	10:1–48	110, 126	10:42	193, 205, 206, 222
9:4	178	10:1–41	10		
9:8	178	10:1–2	188	10:43	86
9:9	178	10:3–7	219	10:44–48	107, 195
9:10–20	202	10:3	172, 189	10:44–47	188, 202, 218
9:10–17	219	10:4	85		
9:10–12	189	10:9	164	10:44–46	77
9:10	170, 172	10:10–16	172, 219	10:44	177
9:11	173	10:10	189	10:45	177, 195–97, 199
9:12	172	10:13	189		
9:13–14	172, 219	10:14	159, 189	10:47	167, 177, 196, 199, 202
9:14	169, 170	10:15	190		
9:15	172, 173, 184	10:17	172, 190		
		10:19–20	188–91, 219	10:48	159, 162, 196, 219
9:16	172				
9:17	171, 173, 176			11	147, 184, 199

Acts (cont.)		12:7	65	14:1	185		
11:1–18	38, 126, 188, 202	12:9	172	14:2	185, 186, 187		
		12:11	185, 205				
11:1–3	104, 150, 159	12:12	137	14:3	86, 122		
		12:15	82	14:4	185		
11:1–2	220	12:17	186, 187	14:5	185		
11:1	157, 186, 187	12:20–23	144	14:8–18	40		
		12:20	66, 87, 158	14:9	85		
11:2–3	191, 197, 219	13	16, 188	14:11–18	209		
		13:1	119, 187, 203	14:13	189		
11:2	191, 197, 198			14:14	111		
		13:2–4	111, 219	14:18	189		
11:3	197, 199	13:2	16, 111, 140, 165, 219	14:19	185		
11:5	172, 189			14:20	187		
11:6	82, 85			14:21	187		
11:7	189	13:4	16	14:22	187		
11:8	189	13:5	185	14:23	187		
11:12–16	188	13:6	185	14:27	187		
11:12	165, 177, 186, 187, 191, 198, 202, 219	13:8–11	146	14:28	187		
		13:9–11	144	15	18, 21, 48, 57, 68, 71, 106, 147, 175, 184–87, 195, 199, 201, 202, 206, 211, 212, 214, 215		
		13:9	16, 82, 85				
		13:12	157, 159				
11:15–18	218	13:15	186, 187, 205				
11:15–17	202						
11:15	177, 198	13:16	184, 185				
11:16	75, 177, 198	13:17	184, 185, 205				
11:17	167, 177, 195, 198, 199, 202	13:22	86				
		13:23	184, 185	15:1–31	10, 188		
		13:24	184, 185, 205	15:1–5	219, 220		
11:18	195, 199, 202			15:1–4	38		
		13:26	173, 186, 187, 212	15:1	186, 200, 213		
11:19	185						
11:22–26	107	13:27–28	102	15:2	110		
11:22–24	159	13:27	113	15:3	186, 213		
11:22	140, 187	13:31	108, 205	15:4	187		
11:24	141, 153, 175, 211, 218	13:36	137	15:5	200, 201		
		13:38	186, 187, 212	15:6–11	126		
				15:7–11	188, 202		
11:26	187	13:41	86	15:7	186, 192, 201, 213		
11:29	186, 187	13:43	185				
12:1–2	111	13:45	185	15:8–10	201		
12:1	187	13:47	64, 65, 103	15:8–9	211, 218		
12:2	186, 187	13:50	185	15:8	86, 177, 201, 202		
12:3	151, 185	13:52	16, 159, 187	15:9	177, 191, 201, 202		
12:4	205						
12:5	187	14	16, 188				

15:10	201, 202	16:20	185	19:21	16
15:11	201	16:24–34	134	19:22–35	209
15:12	122, 140	16:29	65	19:23–41	38, 48,
15:13–21	107, 199	16:36	66		104, 217
15:13	186, 203,	16:40	186, 214	19:23–34	134
	204, 213	17	16, 188,	19:24–35	83
15:14	203–205,		196	19:24–29	222
	211	17:1	185	19:29	158
15:16–18	54, 205	17:5–9	134	19:32	177
15:16	205	17:5	185	19:33	185
15:17	205, 207,	17:6	22, 186,	19:34	185
	213		214	19:39	177
15:19	207, 209,	17:10	185, 186,	19:40	177
	210		214	20:3	185
15:20	208	17:13	185	20:19	185
15:22	186, 213,	17:14	186, 214	20:21	185
	219	17:16–34	40	20:22	16, 178
15:23	186, 213,	17:17	185	20:23	16
	214	17:18	82	20:28	16, 137,
15:24	213	17:22–31	209		138
15:25	158	17:24	113	21	102
15:28	177, 189,	17:26	68, 113	21:4	16, 82
	210, 219	17:28	179	21:6	137
15:29	208	17:34	165, 174,	21:7	186, 214
15:31	159		192	21:11	16, 178,
15:32	186, 214	18	16, 188,		185
15:33	66, 186,		196	21:13	151
	214	18:2	185	21:17	186, 214
15:35	110	18:4	185	21:20–25	207
15:36	186, 204,	18:5	185	21:20	186, 214
	214	18:9	172	21:21	186
15:40	186, 214	18:10	205	21:22	90
16	13, 16, 188	18:12	158, 185	21:25	208
16:2	86, 186,	18:14	185	21:27–32	102
	214	18:18	186	21:27–31	214
16:3	185	18:19	151, 185	21:27	185
16:6–10	172	18:24	185, 212	21:28	184–86,
16:6	16, 167	18:27	186, 214		205
16:7	16, 212	18:28	185	21:30	205
16:9	172	19:2	16	21:36	166, 205
16:10	172	19:4	205	21:37–40	221
16:14	157, 159	19:6	16, 77	21:37	116
16:18	162	19:10	113, 185	21:39	83, 185,
16:19–24	38, 48	19:13	185		205
16:19–23	104, 222	19:14	185	21:40	116, 118,
16:19–21	217	19:17	185		205

268   *Index of References*

Acts (cont.)		24:19	185	28:17	173, 185,
22	16, 176,	24:23	137, 167		186, 205,
	178, 188,	24:27	151, 185		214, 221
	214	25	16, 188	28:19	39, 186,
22:1–21	169, 175	25:2	185		214
22:1	173, 186,	25:8	185	28:20	184, 185
	214, 221	25:9	185	28:21	186, 214
22:2	116	25:10	185	28:25–27	212
22:3–16	126	25:15	185	28:26	205
22:3	88, 186	25:17	151	28:27	205
22:5	86, 186,	25:19	137	28:28	72
	214, 221	25:20	82	28:30	137
22:6	65, 164,	25:24	185	33	196
	214	25:25	194	37	140
22:7–8	170	26	16, 176,		
22:8	88, 170		188	*Romans*	
22:9	65	26:2	185	2:1	194
22:11	65	26:3	185	3:29–30	201
22:12	86, 113,	26:4–23	169, 176	4:1	73
	176, 186	26:4	39, 185	4:7	191
22:13	214	26:5	86	4:20	191
22:17–23	38	26:6–7	57	5:1	133
22:18	108	26:6	185, 221	6:19	191
22:19	89	26:7	185	8:14	225
22:22–23	102, 214	26:9	88	8:16	225
22:22	166, 179	26:12–17	126	12:9	165
22:30	185	26:13	65, 164	12:19	120
23	16, 188	26:14–15	170	13:3–4	137
23:1	85, 173,	26:14	118, 179	14:17	159, 225
	186, 221	26:16–18	65	14:23	191
23:5	186, 205,	26:16	108		
	221	26:17	205	*1 Corinthians*	
23:6	173, 185,	26:18	65	1:12	105
	221	26:21	185	3:16	225
23:11	86, 108	26:22–23	65	4:7	191
23:12	185	26:22	108	6:5	191
23:19	137	26:23	65, 205	6:17	165
23:20	185	26:27–29	134	6:18	165
23:27	185	26:29	132	6:19	225
				11:31	191
24	16, 188	27	16, 188	12–14	118
24:2	39, 66	27:6	167	12:4	225
24:5	185, 186	27:20	65	12:7	225
24:9	185	28:4	82, 90	12:13	225
24:10	39	28:6	82	14:21	120
24:15	185	28:14	186, 214		
24:17	39, 221	28:15	186, 214		

2 Corinthians		4:5–17	211	1QS	
1:22	225	5:1–6	211	3:7b–8a	12
6:14	133, 191			6:19–20	141
6:17	120	1 Peter		8:12–16	43
		1:17	194	8:14–15	72
Galatians		2:14–15	137	9:19–20	72
2:9	203	4:14	225		
4:16	225			1QpHab	
5:22	159	2 Peter		2:3	115
		1:1	204	9:4	153
Ephesians		1:16–2:22	225		
1:13	225			4Q464	
4:3–4	225	1 John		5–9	117
6:9	194	3:24	225		
		4	225	CD	
Philippians		4:13	225	6:19	115
2:15	56			8:21	115
3:3	225	Jude		14:4–6	114
3:6	56	1:17–21	225	19:33	115
		1:22	191	20:12	115
Colossians					
3:25	194	Revelation		TALMUD, MISHNAH AND	
		2:14	208	RELATED LITERATURE	
1 Thessalonians		4:3	172	Mishnah	
1:8	133	7	119	Ketubbot	
2:10	56	7:9–10	230	13:1–2	149
3:13	56	9:17	172		
4:13–17	141	12:14	87	Pesahim	
5:23	56	18:5	165	10:1	149
Titus		NEW TESTAMENT		Qiddushin	
1:12	28	PSEUDEPIGRAPHA		4:1	114
2:14	191	Epistle of Barnabas			
3:5	225	4.12	194	Sheqalim	
		19.7–8	143	5:6	149
Hebrews					
1:9	191	Gospel of Thomas		Zavim	
6:4	225	12	203	3:2	89
10:17	191				
		QUMRAN		Babylonian Talmud	
James		11QMelch		Baba Qamma	
1:6	191	2:7–16	85	38b	114
2:1	194				
2:4	191	1QH		'Erubin	
2:7	206	6:13–14	12	53	112
2:9	194	20:11–13	12	53b	101

Hullin		*De gigantibus*		12.225–28	187	
3b	114	19–55	12	12.228	99	
				13.43–45	187	
Ketubbot		*De mutatione nominum*		13.163–70	187	
105a	89	121	140	13.256	154	
		70–71	140	13.261	99	
Megillah				14.143–44	90	
24b	101, 112	*De plantatione*		14.146	133	
		18–26	12	14.148	133	
Qiddushin				14.192–95	170	
75b	114	*De somniis*		14.214–16	89	
		2.252	12	14.235	89	
Shabbat				14.256–61	89	
88b	115	*De specialibus legibus*		14.291	154	
		2.189	115	14.313	99	
Jerusalem Talmud				15.267–76	52	
Ketubbot		*Legatio ad Gaium*		15.267	52	
13:35	89	296	133	15.298	52	
				15.299–316	149	
Megillah		JOSEPHUS		15.363–64	52	
3:1:73d	89	*Antiquitates judaicae*		17.255	52	
71a	118	1.253	88	17.324	88	
		3.123	56	18.29–30	154	
Shabbat		3.180–87	56	18.30	103	
15b	101	4.290–91	164	20.51–53	149	
		6.86	133	20.118–36	154	
Tosefta Talmud		9.288	154	20.197–203	203	
Megillah		9.290	154			
2:7	164	10.184	154	*Contra Apionem*		
		10.226	88	1.141	88	
Sotah		11.2	99			
13:2	7	11.14	99	*Vita*		
		11.144	99	252	133	
PHILO		11.19–20	154	271–98	89	
De Abrahamo		11.302–24	154	331	89	
118	133	11.302	154	339	133	
		11.342	154			
De confusione linguarum		11.344	154	*Bellum judaicum*		
116	133	11.347	154	1.403	52	
		11.58	99	1.404	52	
De decalogo		11.63	99	1.414	52	
33	115	11.88	99, 154	1.474	170	
		11.92	99	2.42–43	114	
In Flaccum		12.124	133	2.43	185	
45–46	113	12.138–44	38	2.44	52	
45b–46a	29	12.150	152	2.232–37	102, 103	

2.237	102	4.11	143	Minicius Felix	
2.520	84	6.2	208	30.6	209
2.590	90				
4.105	84	Dio Chrysostom		Pliny	
		Discourses		*Natural History*	
GREEK/ROMAN/		XLIX 13–14	91	II.15.116	38, 99
CLASSICAL AND EARLY				IV.10–33	99
CHRISTIAN SOURCES		Diogenes Laertius		IV.10.33	99
1 Clement		*Life of Plato*		IV.12.85	99
1.3	194	3.1–2	77	V.4.29–30	38, 99

Achilles Tatius
Clitophon and Leucippe
4.1.4–8   189

Epistle to Diognetus
5.1   226
5.4   226

Plutarch
Parallel Lives
2.1   77

Apuleius
The Golden Ass
11.6   189
11.13   189
11.22   189

Eusebius
Demonstratio Evangelica
3.6   225

Polycarp
Letter to the Philippians
6.1   194

Ecclesiastical Histories
2.23.4–7   203

Tacitus
Geography
5.4.153–59   38

Arator
On the Acts of the Apostles
29   115

Herodotus
Histories
4.18   138
4.22   138

Tertullian
Apologeticum
9   209

Astrid
Apology
2.2   225

Homer
Aeneid
I.278–79   42

De Pudicitia
20   141

Bede
Commentary on the Acts of the Apostles
4.36b   140

Iliad
65   28

RABBINIC WORKS
Ecclesiastes Rabbah
12:7:1   7

Chrysostom
Homilies on the Acts of the Apostles
1.11.13   102
11   137

Justin Martyr
1 Apology
14.3   216

Kutim
6   154
28   163

Dialogue with Trypho
34.8   209

Lamentations Rabbah
12   7

Cyril of Jerusalem
Catechetical Lecture
17.16–17   115

Lucian of Samasota
The Eunuch
6.11   164

Leviticus Rabbah
1:1   72
1:14   72

Didache
4.8–10   143
4.8   143

Passing of Peregrinus
13   147

Numbers Rabbah
15:10   7

Pesiqta Rabbati
29/30A   72
29/30B   72
30   72
33   72

Tanḥuma
8   118

SAMARITAN SOURCES
Samaritan Chronicle
34.648–58   154

INDEX OF AUTHORS

Abrams, D. 26, 28
Aharpour, S. 129
Alexander, L. 18, 97
Allen, O. W. 141
Alon, G. 102
Altom, M. W. 29, 138
Andersen, T. D. 133
Arrington, F. L. 116, 192
Ashburn-Nardo, L. 30
Attridge, H. W. 101

Baer, H. von 4, 5
Bailey, K. E. 60
Baldson, J. P. V. D. 48
Baltzer, K. 56
Banker, B. S. 33, 183
Banks, M. 37
Bar-Tal, D. 156
Barclay, J. M. G. 25, 222
Barrett, C. K. 107, 133, 140, 141, 143, 158, 162, 166, 173, 174, 177, 189, 193, 206
Bartchy, C. K. 130, 142
Barth, F. 36, 37
Bartholomew, C.G. 57
Bauckham, R. 47, 70, 102, 105, 106, 113, 116, 139, 140, 144, 152, 181, 188, 190, 191, 197, 205–8
Bauernfeind, O. 157
Baumgarten, J. 114
Beale, G. K. 162
Beasley-Murray, G. R. 157
Best, E. 97, 98
Bettencourt, B. A. 30, 31, 49
Bird, M. 22
Blain, N. 29, 139
Blenkinsopp, J. 44
Bless, H. 29, 139
Bock, D. L. 54–56, 58–60, 63, 66, 72, 75, 76, 79, 81, 107, 120, 127, 133, 149, 151–53, 172, 174, 188–90, 193, 200–202, 214
Bockmuehl, M. 204, 207
Bodenhausen, G. V. 29, 139
Böhlemann, P. 73

Bond, L. S. 182
Bonnah, G. K. A. 11, 12
Borgen, P. 195
Borgman, P. C. 67, 97, 126, 130
Bourhis, R. Y. 118, 149
Bovon, F. 4, 6, 74, 75
Boyarin, D. 222, 231
Branscombe, N. R. 155
Brawley, R. L. 2, 56, 61, 99
Brewer, M. B. 29, 30, 32, 217
Brinkman, J. A. 113
Brockner, J. 89
Brown, P. B. 142
Brown, R. 26, 27, 28, 32, 33, 49, 50, 68, 69, 129, 183, 184, 224
Bruce, F. F. 98, 113, 115, 133, 145, 166, 169, 173
Brueggemann, W. 55
Büchler, A. 190
Büchsel, F. 4, 75
Buell, D. K. 25, 222, 225
Burdsey, D. 29, 139

Cadbury, H. J. 98
Cairns, E. 29, 33, 38, 50, 88
Callan, T. 209
Capper, B. J. 130, 136, 141
Carter, W. 56
Chapman, M. 39
Charlton, K. 30, 31, 49
Cheetham, F. P. 134
Chen, Y.-R. 89
Chilton, B. 190
Cho, Y. 8, 9, 59, 61, 68, 69, 75, 81, 99, 104, 120, 121, 126, 127, 131, 135, 141, 151, 152, 169, 173, 176, 182, 195
Christiansen, E. J. 42, 43
Ciraolo, L. J. 209
Cohen, S. J. D. 52, 77, 114, 140
Coleman, S. 35
Colic-Peisker, V. 88
Collins, J. J. 42
Collins, P. 35

Conzelmann, H. 4, 6, 98, 100, 112, 115, 133, 150, 174, 178, 201
Cosgrove, C. 200
Creed, J. M. 92
Cromhout, M. 101
Crossan, J. D. 226
Culy, M. M. 145, 193

Dahl, N. A. 25, 54, 55, 222
Danker, F. W. 54, 56, 63, 78, 82, 193, 210
Darr, J. A. 11, 111, 206, 212
Davila, J. R. 41, 43
Deaux, K. 29
Dennison, C. G. 75, 77
Denova, R. I. 93
deSilva, D. A. 41, 43, 46, 47
Dibelius, M. 157
Dietz-Uhler, B. 131, 169, 199
Dollar, H. E. 214
Doran, R. 46
Dorr, N. 30, 31, 49
Dovidio, J. F. 31, 33, 156, 183
DuPont, J. 68, 168, 171, 205
Duling, D. 26
Dunn, J. D. G. 5, 6, 25, 46, 59, 75, 81, 97, 98, 100, 108, 112, 114, 115, 123, 126, 133, 135, 138, 139, 143, 145, 149, 150, 157, 163, 168, 171, 173, 175, 176, 182, 195, 202

Ego, B. 42
Eliade, M. 56
Elliott, J. 25, 39, 130, 181, 184, 190
Ellis, E. 81, 98
Ely, R. J. 160
Endres, J. C. 43
Ervin, H. M. 173
Eshel, E. 117
Esler, P. 2, 14, 22, 25, 26, 38, 39, 41, 44, 49, 55, 74, 83, 114, 115, 129, 131, 149, 158, 181, 186, 189, 190, 195
Ethier, K. 29

Farris, S. 59–63, 69
Fine, G. A. 142
Fishbane, M. 54
Fitzmyer, J. A. 54, 57, 58, 63, 66, 68, 69, 73, 77–79, 81, 86, 98, 100, 108, 112, 114, 115, 120, 127, 133, 141, 145, 150, 151, 168, 174, 175, 189, 193, 201, 203
Forbes, D. 29, 139

Fredricksen, P. 168
Freyne, S. 101
Frymer-Kensky, T. 190
Fuller, M. E. 43

Gaertner, S. L. 31, 33, 156, 183
Galinsky, K. 226
Gallo, L. A. 59
Gamba, G. G. 134
Ganguly, R. 227
Garrett, S. R. 209
Gaventa, B. R. 19, 108, 168, 169, 178
Geiger, J. 83
Gibson, J. L. 33, 52, 183
Giles, H. 118, 149
Gill, D. 171
Gillmand, J. 136
Goldingay, J. 64
Gonzalez, R. 33, 183
Grant, P. R. 52, 101, 155
Green, J. B. 53, 55–57, 63, 66, 78, 81, 83, 88, 99, 116
Groenewoud, J. T. 33, 183
Gunkel, H. 3, 127

Haacker, K. 185
Haenchen, E. 103, 170
Hall, D. 228
Hall, E. 48
Hall, J. M. 48
Halpern-Amaru, B. 42
Hamel, E. 59
Hamm, D. 57, 135
Hanson, K. C. 77
Harland, P. A. 130, 203
Harrison, T. 48
Harvey, W. J. 52
Hasitschka, M. 76
Haulotte, E. 214
Haya-Prats, G. 5
Hays, J. D. 2
Hays, R. 55
Hedrick, C. W. 168, 175, 176
Heike, T. 42, 44
Heil, J. P. 173
Hellerman, J. 42
Hendel, J. 54, 77
Hendrickson, W. 92
Hengel, M. 98, 112, 113, 116, 169
Hentschel, A. 107

Hewstone, M. 33, 38, 183
Hill, C. C. 149
Hill, D. 82, 92
Hjelm, I. 154, 156
Hoenig, S. B. 190
Hogg, M. A. 26, 28, 149
Holt, R. 57
Hornsey, M. 149
Horowitz, M. 129, 149
Horrell, D. G. 25
Horsley, R. A. 101
Houlette, M. 33, 183
Howard, G. E. 138
Huddy, L. 28, 101
Huffman, D. S. 169
Hughes, E. C. 36
Hui, H. 89
Hull, J. H. E. 121
Hultgren, S. 85
Hume, D. L. 30, 31, 49
Hur, J. 11, 16, 165
Hurtado, L. W. 168
Huskinson, J. 140
Hutchinson, J. 37, 39, 51, 53

Ilan, T. 47, 139

Jenkins, P. 229
Jenkins, R. 29, 36, 37, 39, 83, 100
Jeremias, J. 82, 130, 149
Jervell, J. 182, 214
Jetten, J. 32, 155
Johnson, A. P. 37, , 222, 225
Johnson, L. T. 58, 63, 78, 79, 92, 98, 103, 104, 107, 113, 114, 126, 133, 136, 137, 140, 141, 143, 145, 150, 151, 165, 171, 172, 174, 191, 192, 194, 197, 210
Jones, S. 29

Katz, T. 89
Katzoff, R. 187
Kazmierski, C. R. 74
Keck, L. E. 77
Kee, H. C. 116
Keener, C. S. 78, 140
Kerr, F. 81, 83
Kilpatrick, G. D. 113
Kim, H. S. 5
Kim, S. 168, 171
Klawans, J. 190

Klein, H. 62, 75, 77, 78
Klijn, A. F. J. 209
Kloppenborg, J. S. 130
Kodell, J. 93
Koet, B. J. 64, 105, 149, 151, 155, 158, 170
Kollman, B. 141
Kuecker, A. J. 34, 136
Kuhn, T. 16
Kurz, W. S. 175
Kyo-Seon Shin, G. 85

LaGrand, J. 66, 68
Lampe, G. W. H. 5
Leisegang, H. 4
Levine, A.-J. 42
Levine, L. I. 88, 113, 114
Levison, J. R. 11–15, 16, 206
Lienhard, J. T. 151
Lieu, J. 63, 66, 77
Litwak, K. D. 119, 161
Lockett, D. 203, 211
Longenecker, B. W. 44, 97, 103, 144, 209
Lotz, D. 201
Luce, K. H. 82

Macchi, J. D. 154
Maddox, R. 22
Mainville, O. 5
Malina, B. J. 53, 81, 92
Mallen, P. 105, 158
Manstead, A. S. R. 155
Marguerat, D. 142, 168–70, 175, 177
Marquis, T. L. 84
Marshall, I. H. 72, 74, 79, 82, 97, 98, 115, 141, 166, 170, 201
Marshall, J. 137
Martin, D. B. 101
Martin, C. J. 162, 164
Mathey, J. 94
Matz, D. C. 228
McCusker, C. 89
McDonald, M. 39
McIntosh, J. 210
McKimmie, B. M. 155
McLaren, J. S. 52
McMillan, D. K. 209
McVerry, P. 59
Medin, D. L. 29, 138

Menzies, R. P. 4-8, 61, 68, 69, 75, 81, 104, 114, 120, 121, 126, 127, 157, 169, 176, 182, 195
Metzger, B. M. 46, 68, 170
Mezzacasa, F. 59
Michaelis, W. 172
Milgrom, J. 190
Miller, D. G. 76
Miller, J. E. 62
Minguez, D. 164
Mitchell, A. C. 130, 136, 137
Mizrahi, K. 29
Moessner, D. P. 97
Moghaddam, F. M. 155
Monteith, M. 30
Moore, T. S. 103
Mottola, G. R. 33, 183
Moxnes, H. 130, 137
Mullen, B. 33
Mullin, B. A. 28
Mummenday, A. 33, 34, 149, 183
Munck, J. 169
Murphy, T. D. 29, 138
Murrell, A. 131, 169, 199

Neubauer, A. 101, 112
Neusner, J. 190
Newbigin, L. 229
Neyrey, J. H. 53
Nier, J. A. 33, 183
Nolland, J. 51, 54, 56, 58, 63, 64, 75-77, 81, 82, 88, 91, 93
Noorda, S. J. 91

O'Day, G. R. 59
O'Neill, J. C. 92
O'Toole, R. F. 144, 164, 189, 194
Oakman, D. E. 77
Öhler, M. 141

Pao, D. W. 103, 105, 113, 126, 158, 161, 162, 208
Parsons, M. C. 2, 145, 164, 193
Payne, D. 64
Pearce, S. 29
Penney, J. M. 126, 151, 169, 176
Pesch, R. 103, 213
Pitkanen, P. 42
Polhill, J. 116
Poole, M. S. 148

Porter, R. J. 167
Porter, S. E. 81, 86, 105, 158
Proctor, J. 207
Postmes, T. 155
Pummer, R. 154
Purvis, J. D. 154

Quesnel, M. 157

Rabbie, J. M. 129, 149
Rad, G. von 56
Radl, W. 69
Rae, M. A. 16
Rahmani, L. Y. 113, 114
Ravens, D. 51, 53, 67
Reed, J. L. 101
Reicke, B. 69
Reid, A. 29
Reisner, R. 203
Robertson, B. L. 74
Robinson, A. B. 98, 126, 162, 172
Rohrbaugh, R. L. 53, 81, 86, 92
Rothgerber, H. 28, 131, 169, 174
Rouhana, N. 156
Rowe, C. K. 52, 54, 58, 126, 188, 192, 193
Ruether, R. R. 59
Rusam, D. 161
Rust, M. C. 33, 183

Saeed, A. 29, 139
Sahlin, H. 73
Samkutty, V. J. 154
Sanders, J. T. 2
Sandiyagu, V. R. 110
Schiffman, H. F. 118
Schille, G. 142
Schils, G. 36
Schmitt, M. T. 32
Schneider, G. 63, 92, 160, 161
Schur, N. 154
Schürmann, H. 81, 92
Schwadel, P. 228
Schwartz, D. R. 98
Schwartz, S. 116, 118
Schwarz, N. 29, 139
Schweizer, E. 5, 56, 66, 73
Scott, J. M. 106, 113
Seccombe, D. 136, 142, 149, 158, 160, 162
Segal, A. F. 168, 169
Seitz, C. R. 210

Index of Authors

Shaw, B. D. 38, 48
Shelton, J. B. 5, 169, 173
Shepherd, W. H. 11, 61
Slee, M. 2
Smith, A. D. 37, 39, 51, 53, 138
Smith, C. 33
Smith, E. R. 29, 138
Snodgrass, K. 72
Spears, R. 155
Spencer, F. S. 150, 151, 157, 164, 166
Squires, J. T. 160
Stanley, C. 39, 40
Stendahl, K. 169, 182
Stenhouse, P. 154
Sterling, G. E. 130
Stern, M. 48
Stone, M. 117
Strelan, R. 164
Stringer, P. 155
Strobel, A. 85
Stronstad, R. 5

Tajfel, H. 26-28, 31, 32, 155, 199
Talbert, C. 63, 86
Tannehill, R. C. 61, 80, 83, 98, 102, 110, 126, 162, 180, 182
Taylor, D. M. 118, 149
Taylor, J. 207
Taylor, N. H. 56
Theissen, G. 136
Thompson, R. P. 15, 18, 126, 127, 133
Thornton, P. J. 98, 154
Tiede, D. L. 100
Tonkin, E. 39
Triandis, H. C. 32, 89, 106
Turner, J. C. 26-28, 30, 49, 129, 139, 145, 174, 183
Turner, M. 2-5, 7-10, 15, 26, 58, 59, 61, 68, 69, 81, 85, 123, 126, 130, 144, 152, 157, 181, 190, 191, 195, 196
Tutu, D. 33, 183
Twelftree, G. H. 17, 128, 177
Tyson, J. B. 2

Validzic, A. 31, 33, 156, 183
Van de Sandt, H. W. M. 205
VanderKam, J. C. 115, 136
Van Henten, J. W. 50
Van Nijf, O. 89
Van Oudenhouven, J. P. 33, 183

Van Ruiten, J. T. A. G. M. 42
Van Unnik, W. C. 98
Verkuyten, M. 52
Vermes, G. 84, 101, 112
Virtanen, S. 28, 101
Voils, C. I. 30
Volf, M. 118

Wald, K. D. 33, 184
Waldzus, S. 34, 35, 49, 106, 149
Walker, I. 88
Wall, R. W. 98, 103, 114, 121, 126, 131, 135, 140, 141, 150, 162, 172, 189
Wallman, S. 37
Walters, P. 22
Wanke, M. 29, 139
Ward, C. M. 33, 183
Weber, M. 36
Weber, U. 34, 149
Wedderburn, A. J. M. 115, 116, 208, 209
Weissenbeuhler, W. 106
Weitzman, S. 117
Wenk, M. 3, 5, 7, 10, 17, 68, 69, 78, 81, 106, 120, 122, 128, 157, 158, 162, 172, 199, 202
Wenzel, M. 33, 34, 49, 59, 149, 183
Westermann, C. 55
Whyte, J. 38
Wikenhauser, A. 172, 189
Wilckens, U. 192
Williamson, H. G. M. 44, 45
Williamson, R. L. 59
Wilson, S. G. 2, 130
Wilson, W. T. 191
Wimmer, A. 227
Winter, B. W. 136
Witherington III, B. 8, 42, 97, 99, 100, 113, 115, 121, 123, 141, 149, 164, 171, 175, 193, 208, 209
Witherup, R. D. 126, 168, 175, 176, 188, 198, 201, 202
Wood, W. 228
Wright, C. J. H. 105
Wright, J. L. 45
Wright, N. T. 59, 78

Zahn, T. 92
Zangenberg, J. 101
Zarate, M. A. 29, 138
Zerhusen, B. 116
Zorrilla, C. H. 59